D0267106

Corporate Crime

Gary Slapper and Steve Tombs

with a Foreword by
Michael Mansfield QC

LONGMAN

Pearson Education Limited
Edinburgh Gate,
Harlow,
Essex CM20 2JE,
United Kingdom
and Associated Companies throughout the world

© Pearson Education Limited 1999

The right of Gary Slapper and Steve Tombs to be identified
as the authors of this Work has been asserted by them in
accordance with the Copyright, Designs and Patents Act 1988.

All rights reserved; no part of this publication may be
reproduced, stored in a retrieval system, or transmitted
in any form or by any means, electronic, mechanical,
photocopying, recording, or otherwise without either the
prior written permission of the Publishers or a licence
permitting restricted copying in the United Kingdom
issued by the Copyright Licensing Agency Ltd,
90 Tottenham Court Road, London W1P 9HE.

First published 1999

ISBN 0-582-29980-2 PPR

Visit our world wide web site at http://www.awl-he.com

British Library Cataloguing-in Publication Data

A catalogue record for this book is available from the British Library

Set by 3 in 10/12 New Baskerville

Printed in Great Britain by Henry Ling Limited, at the Dorset Press, Dorchester, DT1 1HD

Contents

Series Editor's Preface

Our society appears to be increasingly preoccupied with crime and with criminal justice. Despite increasing affluence in the post-war period, crime has continued to rise – often at an alarming rate. Moreover, the pace of general social change at the end of the twentieth century is extraordinary, leaving many feeling insecure. High rates of crime, high levels of fear of crime, and no simple solutions in sight, have helped to keep criminal justice high on the political agenda.

Partly reflecting this state of affairs, the study of crime and criminal justice is burgeoning. There are now a large number of well-established postgraduate courses, new ones starting all the time, and undergraduate criminology and criminal justice degrees are also now appearing regularly. Though increasing numbers of individual textbooks are being written and published, the breadth of criminology makes the subject difficult to encompass in a satisfactory manner within a single text.

The aim of this series as a whole is to provide a broad and thorough introduction to criminology. Each book covers a particular area of the subject, takes the reader through the key debates, considers both policy and politics and, where appropriate, also looks to likely future developments in the area. The aim is that each text should be theoretically-informed, accessibly written, attractively produced, competitively priced, with a full guide to further reading for students wishing to pursue the subject further. Whilst each book in the series is designed to be read as an introduction to one particular area, the Longman Criminology Series has also been designed with overall coherence in mind.

This, the fourth book in the series, examines the very important but often under-discussed area of corporate crime. It takes the reader through the thorny issues of definition (what is corporate crime?), provides a guide to the key debates over how such crime is to be understood, examines the costs and consequences of corporate crime, and considers how it might be better regulated. The authors argue, convincingly, that the costs associated with corporate crime – the economic and the physical costs – far outweigh those associated with more traditional forms of crime and, moreover, that the impact of such crime impacts disproportionately on the poor and vulnerable.

It seems that no matter how often criminologists note that disproportionate attention is paid to crimes of the 'powerless', it remains the case that the crimes of the 'powerful' remain largely hidden from view. The authors of this book conclude with a note of sadness that the record of academics in the study of corporate crime is not especially impressive to date. Gary Slapper and Steve Tombs describe this book as a piece of 'partisan scholarship' and their work represents an authoritative challenge to the silence that surrounds so much corporate crime. As such it deserves to be read by all students of criminology and criminal justice.

Tim Newburn
February 1999

Foreword

There are many assumptions made about corporate crime and, as Gary Slapper and Steve Tombs prove in this book, there are several definitions, various standpoints and considerable argument over what constitutes corporate crime, both past and present. However, it would appear that from the layperson's point of view there is still a general belief that it is 'victimless crime'.

On a daily basis, crime depicted as murder, assault, or violent robbery fills the newspapers and our television screens and each produces readily defined 'victims'. Trials for these crimes, as and when they come to court, can focus on the concrete, visible misdemeanours of individuals, and reports can be distilled down to seemingly easy to grasp issues – did they or didn't they do it, were they or weren't they there, for example.

Corporate crime however, as is shown in this book, can not only prove harder to detect, but harder too to prove. As the authors demonstrate, this is because it can not only be a crime devised and perpetrated by the lone individual within the corporate structure, but also a problem inherent in, and perpetuated by, the whole corporate structure itself.

International corporations – and, indeed, corporate bosses – wield seemingly ever-increasing power. The supranational nature of corporations coupled with modern technological and communication advances place them in an unparalleled position to affect all our lives. No one can, in reality, be free from their influence for we all now have an investment in corporations in some shape or form – we are employed by them, we drive the cars they build, we eat the food they produce and, over the last few years, we have also been encouraged to invest our savings in their shares. It could well be argued then that we are all potential victims of corporate crime, and that this status could equally apply to governments and national economies as well as to individuals.

Yet as the authors point out in their text there appears to be little public debate about the nature of corporations and corporate criminality. Few cases grab the public imagination, or the headlines. However, one of the few that in recent times can make this claim is, perhaps, the 'McLibel' case, in which two young people took on the mighty McDonald's Corporation. They did not take it on, in my view, for personal gain – they had nothing, would gain nothing and, indeed, were liable to lose everything. It was neither a question of personal aggrandisement, nor a matter of profit for them. They however withstood the legal assault upon them by McDonald's where many others had not. In similar circumstances, the media and newspapers had backed down and apologised, but Helen Steel and Dave Morris did not.

The pamphlets that they had been circulating made claims about the effects of fast food production on, amongst other things, the rain forests in South America, the nature of the Corporation's workforce, factory farming, hygiene, health and nutrition. Few cases perhaps could be said to embrace more important issues. They are, after all, current and important issues for all of us, and they are both political issues – with a small 'p' – and also essential environmental issues.

Helen Steel and Dave Morris conducted their own case and the whole proceedings went on for *five years* making it the longest trial in British history. Yet they did it without Legal Aid and without a jury. No jury, it was thought, would understand the many complicated points of scientific interest involved and only a judge was deemed able to deal with the whole.

Irrespective of the Judgement, which, when it came, was somewhat of a split decision – six of one and half a dozen of the other – in my view, the proper adjudication of issues of such public importance is by the public's representatives. That is to say, through a jury sitting in a court. Public debate can only be sparked by public involvement. The removal of a jury from the McLibel case, and the consideration currently being given by government to the removal of juries from fraud cases for the same reasons, will only further curb this essential debate.

It is the authors' stated intention that this book should stimulate, provoke, surprise and encourage as well as raise issues that, in their view, demand further consideration by everyone. It is my hope and belief that it will do all these things and encourage us all to question the nature and scope of all corporate activities – be they legal, illegal, morally defensible or morally dubious. Furthermore, that it will prompt us to examine and reassess the regulatory systems currently in place that govern the actions of corporations, and to fight the marginalisation of public involvement in the justice process when alleged corporate illegality, in whatever form, is brought to trial.

Michael Mansfield QC

Acknowledgements

While this is a joint work, it is clearly the product of a division of labour, and our respective contributions owe their own respective debts.

Gary would like to express his gratitude to the following people for their help, support and inspiration in the writing of this book: Suzanne, Hannah, Emily, and Charlotte, Doreen and Ivor Slapper; Julie and David Whight; Marilyn Lannigan for her excellent contribution as a research assistant; Hugh McLaughlan; Professor David Asch at The Open University for supporting the project; the OUBS Research Committee; Elaine Genders at University College, London; and Professor Robert Reiner at the London School of Economics.

The chapters for which Steve has taken primary responsibility here owe a great deal to others, and to two people in particular. Chapters 1 and 8 draw heavily upon material developed with Frank Pearce; Chapter 5 has benefited enormously from working with Dave Whyte. Both Frank and Dave will also see echoes of their advice and insight in (the better parts) of Chapters 3 and 4. His work, and life, would be a great deal poorer without either of them. Warm thanks also go to Joe Sim, Pete Gill, Pam Davies, Charles Woolfson, and to cj361 students. Responsibility for any weaknesses in his contribution to this text remains his alone. It is dedicated to Pamela and to Patrick. In Peace, Love and Struggle.

We are very grateful for the encouragement and friendly professional advice of Brian Willan at Addison Wesley Longman and the thoughtful assistance of Professor Tim Newburn at the University of London. We are also very thankful to Deborah Bennett for her copy-editing, and to Louise Harley, our in-house editor.

Gary Slapper
Steve Tombs

Chapter 1

Introduction

Introduction

It is hardly surprising, perhaps even highly predictable, that the first chapter of this text should be devoted to a consideration of definitional issues relating to the concept of corporate crime. Yet this is not due to some academic convention, nor even simply for the sake of clarity. Rather, definitional issues are crucial in the context of a discussion of corporate crime. Here, 'the problem of definition cannot just be put aside in order to get on with more interesting matters because it determines the findings of any investigation' (Nelken 1994a: 363). Definitional questions raise substantive issues regarding extent, causation, and regulation; they problematise the nature, and boundaries, of academic criminology; more generally, they raise issues regarding the legitimate nature of academic work.

We begin with the work of Edwin Sutherland, and in particular address some definitional issues through reference to the now classic debate between Edwin Sutherland and Paul Tappan. We begin with Sutherland's contribution not out of some generalised respect for a 'founding father'. Indeed, in many respects his general criminological project was deeply flawed, while his particular efforts to redirect the energies of academic criminology were, in the immediate term at least, a failure. But Sutherland's contribution is important for the questions it raises, not least because these seem to us to be at the heart of many contemporary discourses regarding the nature, or legitimacy, of any academic enterprise focusing around what he called 'white-collar crime'. Certainly when we turn to the Sutherland–Tappan dispute, not only did each of these thinkers set out clearly what is at stake in particular, if ideal-typical, definitions of corporate crime, but they also raised questions which endure in contemporary studies of, and disagreements around, the phenomenon which is marked by the label corporate crime. And so we pay close attention to that debate here.

Finally, none of this is to imply that Sutherland was the first social scientist to raise the issue of 'white-collar crime'. As David Friedrichs has (rightly) noted, in both Europe and North America there have been long traditions within which it has been recognised that 'the powerful and the privileged commit "crimes", loosely defined, as a consequence of the character of the economic system, and their special status within it' (1992: 6). In Europe, this work can be traced through the work of Proudhon (1840), the Fourierists, and Marx and Engels. Significantly, at the beginning of this century, the criminologist Bonger, pointed out that the normal workings of the capitalist economic system and its motivating ideologies tends to generate crime amongst the bourgeoisie. Uncontrolled economic fluctuations means that businessmen facing bankruptcy often resort to swindling or fraud. A society which enjoins morality on such narrow self-interested bases as 'Honesty is the best policy' and which generally upholds the principle of 'Each man for himself' does not encourage its respectable members to accept misfortune. In a society where the ostentatious display of wealth is encouraged and where the wealthy ignore the social costs of accumulation there is a relative indifference to the illegality of methods of profit maximisation like the adulteration of food. There will not be the same indifference to the perhaps less morally reprehensible practice of manipulating stock prices and issuing worthless shares. These are classed as crimes because

> They are harmful to the regular progress of capitalism and consequently are threatened with penalties. The punishment of the adulteration of food stuffs, on the contrary, is a consequence of the opposition of the consumers to one of the harmful effects of the system.
>
> (Bonger 1905 and 1969: 142)

Bonger raises a significant point here, and we will consider this distinction between different types of corporate illegalities in Chapter 4, and indeed throughout this text.

While Europe has a long tradition of radical and critical social theory, the United States has a much richer tradition in terms of *explicit* treatment of corporate crime; it is hardly unrelated that, as we shall see, North America remains the key site for empirical and theoretical work around corporate crime. Here, the origins of a popular concern with corporate crime can be located within the populist movement – which it has been said had a profound influence on the young Sutherland in rural Nebraska (Geis 1992: 32) – the decline of which was in one sense marked by the passing of the Sherman Anti-Trust Act which condemned conspiracies in restraint of trade. Subsequently, the muckraking tradition still continued to expose the dangers, injustice and chicanery so prevalent in the emerging corporate capitalist industrial order. One of the movements with which muckraking was articulated was progressivism, concerned not with the elimination of capitalism, but in the taming of evident excesses of individual capitalists. It was within this progressivist tradition that the sociologist Edward A. Ross, in 1907, identified the 'criminaloid':

> [T]he director who speculates in the securities of his corporation, the director who lends his depositors' money to himself under divers corporate aliases, the railroad official who grants a secret rebate for his private graft, the builder who hires walking delegates to harass his rivals with causeless strikes, the labour leader who instigates a strike in order to be paid for calling it off, the publisher who bribes his textbooks into the schools.
>
> (1907 reprinted in Geis and Meier 1977: 27)

There was little further written on this issue in American sociology until 1935 when, six years after the Great Crash and one year after the Nye committee's investigation of the role played by Bankers and Armaments manufacturers in America's involvement in World War I, Albert Morris, developed an extensive listing of 'criminals of the upperworld' which included those engaging in financial fraud, fraudulent jingoistic propaganda and violations of international law (Geis 1967: 34–9). In the same period of time the revelations about the degree of concentration of wealth and the Brandeisian attack on monopoly provided the context for the development of Edwin Sutherland's concept of 'white-collar crime'.

What is crime, who is the criminal? The Sutherland–Tappan debate

In a series of papers, articles and a book published between 1940 and 1949 Sutherland developed the concept of 'white-collar crime' – 'a crime committed by a person of respectability and high social status in the course of his occupation' (1983: 7). He thus challenged the stereotypical view of the criminal as typically lower class since 'powerful business and professional men' also routinely commit crimes. Criminal acts are not restricted to those dealt with in criminal courts. Other agencies such as juvenile courts may deal with 'violations of the criminal law' and some offences can be dealt with by either criminal courts or civil courts. Some individual white-collar offenders avoid criminal prosecution because of the class bias of the courts – although businessmen could often be charged as accessories to such crimes as bribery, unlike politicians they usually escape prosecution – but more generally they are aided by 'the power of their class to influence the implementation and administration of the law'. Thus the crimes of the upper and lower classes 'differ principally in the implementation of the criminal laws that apply to them' (1940: 35–7). Given that 'upper class' criminals often operate undetected, that if detected they may not be prosecuted, and that if prosecuted they may not be convicted, Sutherland argued that the criminally convicted are far from the closest approximation to the population of violators.

In his 1945 article 'Is "White-Collar Crime" Crime?' Sutherland drew upon Jerome Hall to produce a more encompassing and abstract definition of crime. Crime requires the 'legal description of an act as socially injurious and legal provision of a penalty for the act' (1945: 132). Notice that while Sutherland holds on to the law in his definition of crime, he extends relevant bodies of law beyond the criminal law. He recognised that many laws which are enforced by administrative bodies through the civil courts also regulate actions which cause injuries to specific individuals or which undermine social institutions and they also routinely impose punitive sanctions. Moreover, *contra* the view that such acts are merely 'technical violations and involve no moral culpability' in fact they are 'distributed along a continuum in which the *male in se* are at one extreme and the *mala prohibita* at the other' (*ibid.*: 139). The content of laws and such legal distinctions are themselves social products (Sutherland 1945).

In other words, Sutherland argues that crimes are illegalities which are contingently differentiated from other illegalities by virtue of the specific administrative procedures to which they are subject. The corollary of this is that 'successful' criminalisation of the illegalities of the powerful would pre-empt them from arguing that their illegalities are merely 'regulatory offences', merely *male prohibita*. And there are persuasive arguments that it *matters* both practically and ideologically whether something is defined as a crime or a civil offence: that is, to be subject to one rather than another set of procedures has important differential effects. It is in such a context that David Nelken has recently reminded us that 'the topic of white-collar crime illustrates the possibility of divergence between legal, social and political definitions of criminality – but in so doing it reminds us of the artificiality of all definitions of crime' (1994a: 366). This, he notes, was exactly what 'the labelling perspective tried to force criminologists to face' (*ibid.*). If Durkheim has been credited with an early focus upon the significance of societal reaction in defining crime (Sumner 1994: 16, 21), then Sutherland was following in this Durkheimian tradition.

Indeed, on this latter point it is important to note that Sutherland's arguments regarding the nature and significance of 'white-collar' crime were part of a much broader theoretical project organised around the explanatory concept of 'differential association'. Through this concept, Sutherland sought, albeit ultimately highly imperfectly, to provide an explanation for lower-class and upper-class crime; we shall discuss this attempt at a general theory of crime in Chapter 6.

Sutherland's definition of 'white-collar crime' has a number of significant theoretical and empirical implications. On the basis of such an inclusive definition, one would find: *first*, that the common image of typical crimes and typical criminality was inaccurate, crime is widespread throughout society; *second*, that a reductionist criminology which explained criminal behaviour in terms of the pathology of lower class

individuals or their families was inadequate whereas differential association theory was adequate; *third*, that the scope of criminology needed to
be widened to take account of a wider range of conduct and the political
processes that defined it as criminal or not; and, *fourth*, that one must
explain, and guard against *both*, the predatory crimes of the poor and
the abuses of their power by the wealthy; that one did not do so was due to
the latter's manipulation of public consciousness by the media with the
collusion of the courts.

In his article 'Who is the Criminal?', Paul Tappan developed a
systematic criticism of Sutherland's work. Tappan began his critique of
Sutherland's sociological definition of corporate crime by first providing
'rigorous' (legalistic) definitions of crime and the criminal:

> Crime is an intentional act in violation of the criminal law (statutory and case
> law) committed without defence or excuse, and penalised by the state as a
> felony or misdemeanour. In studying the offender there can be no
> presumption that arrested, arraigned, indicted, or prosecuted persons are
> criminals unless they also be held guilty beyond a reasonable doubt of a
> particular offence.
>
> (1947: 100)

Notice here Tappan's emphasis upon intention, upon the criminal law,
and upon successful prosecution following due process. In Tappan's view,
it is illegitimate of Sutherland to describe people as criminal when they
have not been successfully prosecuted for a crime and, moreover, he
illegitimately extends the concept of crime to cover acts that do not
violate the criminal law.

> In light of these definitions the normative issue is pointed. Who should be
> considered the white-collar criminal? Is it the merchant who, out of greed,
> business acumen, or competitive motivations, breaches a trust with his
> consumer by 'puffing his wares' beyond their merits, by pricing them beyond
> their value, or by ordinary advertising? Is it he who breaks trust with his
> employees in order to keep wages down, refusing to permit labour
> organisation or to bargain collectively, and who is found guilty by a labour
> relations board of an unfair labour practice? May it be the white-collar worker
> who breaches trust with his employers by inefficient performance at work, by
> sympathetic strike or secondary boycott? Or is it the merchandiser who
> violates ethics by undercutting the prices of his fellow merchants? In general
> these acts do not violate the criminal law? *All are within the framework of normal
> business practice.*
>
> (1947: 99, emphasis added)

Tappan is making at least three substantial points here which remain of
enormous significance.

First, he is arguing that once one extends the label 'crime' beyond
those who have been formally and successfully processed as criminals, one
enters the sphere of normative reasoning, or moralising. Previewing what
was to become a fierce, long-running, and contemporary, dispute, Tappan notes that while such an extended definition may serve as a term of

'propaganda', 'For purposes of empirical research or objective description, what is it?' (1947: 99). In other words, Tappan is aware that to shift from a focus upon unequivocally defined criminal laws is a shift along a continuum which extends to social harms at the other extreme. Once one vacates the terrain of the criminal law, strictly defined, who then is to make judgements about what constitutes crime-as-social harm, not least in morally pluralistic societies?

Second, Tappan is arguing that those offences typically committed by business people are inherently different from criminal offences; and this view, that there are qualitative differences between criminal offences on the one hand and regulatory offences on the other, is one which is still widely held, and we shall consider this in greater detail throughout this text.

Third, also a point of consistent interest throughout this text, and intimately related to the previous point, is Tappan's claim that many of the actions and omissions that Sutherland's definition would define as criminal are in fact 'within the framework of normal business practice'.

While these claims will be considered in detail, it is worth emphasising at this point, however, that Sutherland was well aware that certain kinds of actions were viewed not as 'real crimes' but as normal business practice and, as such, did not attract popular moral opprobrium. Yet he (rightly) refused to accept that this mitigated the harm they caused:

> The law is pressing in one direction and other forces are pressing in the opposite direction. In business, the 'rules of the game' conflict with the legal rules. A businessman who wants to obey the law is driven by his competitors to adopt their methods. This is well illustrated by the persistence of commercial bribery in spite of the strenuous efforts of business organisations to eliminate it.
>
> (Sutherland 1940: 38)

Nevertheless, Tappan was correct to criticise the looseness with which the category of criminal is sometimes extended to those who, if they were subject to the due process of the law, would not be found guilty beyond reasonable doubt of any offence. But this point does not logically entail the subsequent conclusion that there are no acts which whilst currently unknown would not lead to a successful prosecution if the relevant facts were known. In other words, he is wrong to imply that it makes no sense to discuss undiscovered murders, or more generally, the 'dark figure of crime'.

Further, Tappan imputes a degree of clarity to the law and to legal processes which lacks empirical support. Thus the law is by no means consistent about what differentiates a crime from other offences nor what constitutes due process. Sutherland had anticipated that his claim that many civil offences were really crimes would

> be questioned on the grounds that the rules of evidence used in reaching these decisions are not the same as those used in decisions regarding other

crimes, especially that some of the agencies which rendered the decisions did not require proof of criminal intent and did not presume the accused to be innocent. These rules of criminal intent and presumption of innocence, however, are not required in all prosecutions under the regular penal code and the number of exceptions is increasing. In many states a person may be committed to prison without protection of one or both of these rules on charges of statutory rape, bigamy, adultery, passing bad checks, selling mortgaged property, defrauding a hotel keeper, and other offences ... On the one side, many of the defendants in usual criminal cases, being in relative poverty, do not get good defence and consequently secure little benefit from these rules; on the other hand, the commissions come close to observing these rules of proof and evidence although they are not required to do so.

(Sutherland 1945: 195–6)

Sutherland therefore raises questions regarding how, and, indeed whether, 'due process' is actually achieved in the application of criminal law, questions which Tappan fails to address.

Sutherland also raised the crucial issue of how the relative power of different social groups affected what became criminalised and when.

Embezzlement is usually theft from an employer by an employee, and the employee is less capable of manipulating social and legal forces in his own interest than is the employer. As might have been expected, the laws regarding embezzlement were formulated long before laws for the protection of investors and consumers.

(1940: 36)

Sutherland is also aware that the 'meaning' of law is not closed nor simply to be read off from the avowed intentions of legislators. Thus he notes how the Sherman antitrust legislation, while 'enacted primarily because of fear of the corporations', was mostly used as the basis for criminal prosecutions against trades unions in its first thirty or so years (1983: 57).

Further, he demonstrated the contingent nature of the distinction between criminal and other offences by tracing the genealogy of the laws regulating competition (antitrust), false advertising, labour relations, and infringements of patents, copyrights, and trademarks. Each

has a logical basis in the common law and is an adaptation of common law to modern social organisation. False advertising is related to common-law fraud, and infringement to larceny. The National Labour Relations Board Law, as an attempt to prevent coercion, is related to the common-law prohibition of restrictions on freedom in the form of assault, false imprisonment and extortion. For at least two centuries prior to the enactment of the modern anti-trust laws, the common law was moving against restraint of trade, monopoly and unfair competition.

(1945: 133)

Thus there are good reasons for suspecting that the differential application of law, the development of different legal categories, and

distinct enforcement modus operandi for 'street' and corporate offenders are not rooted in any intrinsic differences in the offences *per se.*

Finally, Sutherland is quite clear that the differential interpretation and
enforcement of law against white-collar crime is partially based upon the
fact that legislators, judges and administrators within the criminal justice
system are either subject to the material and ideological influence of
business-people, or share common ideological and/or cultural world-
views (1945: 137–8). Concomitantly, when what Sutherland calls the
'status' of business-people declines, they become prone to the more
rigorous enforcement of laws designed to regulate their anti-social
conduct (*ibid.*).

Beyond the concept of white-collar crime

We have indicated that many aspects of the dispute between Sutherland
and Tappan have endured and remain pertinent for defining and
understanding white-collar crime. In our view, Tappan's criticisms of
Sutherland's claims regarding white-collar crime raise a number of
problems with this term as it was first developed. Most problematically,
Sutherland's usage of the terms seeks to cover a quite heterogeneous
range of actions, with different kinds of offenders, offences and victims:
the *victims* vary – workers, consumers, other businesses, one's own
business, a business's shareholders, and so forth; the *consequences* of the
illegality vary – they may be trivial or may have significant economic
effects, and/or damage life and limb; the *modus operandi* varies – an
illegality may be undertaken alone, or in concert; the *goal* of the illegality
varies – it may be primarily for personal gain or in the interest of an
organisation; and the *capacity to avoid detection and responsibility* varies as do
the consequences of detection.

Thus while there is much to be commended in Sutherland's sociological enterprise, enormous problems with his definitional arguments
remain. As Nelken has noted, if Sutherland 'merited a Nobel prize ... for
pioneering this field of study, he certainly did not deserve it for the clarity
or serviceableness of his definition' (1994a: 361).

These aspects of the looseness of Sutherland's definition, exposed by
Tappan, have led to intense debate regarding the most appropriate
definition of white-collar crime, and numerous attempts to delineate a
clear field of inquiry. Amongst the most well-known efforts in the sphere
have been attempts to define a field of enquiry in terms of business crime
(Clarke 1990), commercial crime (Snider 1992), corporate crime
(Braithwaite 1984; Clinard and Yeager 1980; Pearce and Snider 1995),
crimes of capital (Michalowski 1985), crimes of the powerful (Pearce
1976), crimes at the top (Douglas and Johnson 1978), crimes of the suites
(Timmer and Eitzen 1991), economic crime (Edelhertz 1970), elite

deviance (Simon and Eitzen 1986), occupational crime (Green 1990), organisational deviance (Ermann and Lundman 1982; Punch 1996; Vaughan 1983) or white-collar crime (Croall 1992; Geis and Stotland 1980; Nelken 1994). Now, of course, amongst this apparent heterogeneity of approaches and definitions it is perfectly possible to define some significant commonalties and types of particular approaches to the study of 'white-collar crime'. A recent attempt to impose some order upon this conceptual effort has been sketched out by Friedrichs, who distinguishes between groups of researchers in terms of their belief/agnosticism in the possibility of one definition; he then examines particular aspects of the nature and substance of their respective enterprises (Friedrichs 1992: 7–12).

One of the points clearly conveyed by Friedrichs, and others (see, for example, Green 1990; Croall 1992; Snider 1993; and Nelken 1994), is that these definitional disputes are not merely – or perhaps even – semantic. These disputes are intimately related to how 'white-collar' crime is to be represented, measured, explained, prevented, regulated, sanctioned, and so on. Further, these disputes also entail disagreements about values, politics, theory, epistemology and methodology, even if these issues are not made explicit, and even if they cannot be dismissed in these terms.

Certainly, there are important issues at stake in these disputes. But given that Friedrichs sums up the intensity of these debates by reference to 'the war of the white-collar criminologists' (1992: 8), it remains somewhat intriguing why contemporary criminologists are so divided over the issues at hand. There are some reasons which may go some way towards explaining the intensity of these disputes. We shall state these briefly; many are pursued in greater detail throughout the rest of the text.

First, it seems to us that many of these issues remain unresolved simply because they remain relatively peripheral for much of what passes for criminology. Thus it remains the case that white-collar crime remains relatively under-developed as an area of academic enquiry, certainly in theoretical terms (Coleman 1987; Cressey 1989), with much 'white-collar crime' work based upon, and often restricted to, empirical case-study. Thus such disputes may be partially an effect of disciplinary immaturity. It is commonplace to note the theoretical under-development of the area of inquiry marked broadly by white-collar crime. While there is undoubtedly now an impressive body of work within this sub-discipline, the study of white-collar crime remains relatively marginal within criminology and criminal justice studies. In what is best understood as a self-perpetuating cycle of omission and ignorance, most standard texts on criminology pay little or no attention to it; most theoretical criminology does not attempt to explain it; most undergraduate courses in criminology or criminal justice marginalise it. Certainly if one of the aims of Sutherland was to redirect the energies of academic criminology, then his efforts can largely be judged as a failure. Moreover, this failure is particularly marked in the context of the UK, from which we write and work, and upon which this text is largely focused. While there is a significant body of work, and academic attention, devoted to corporate crime in North America, academics in the UK remain relatively backward in addressing such issues. And it is hardly unrelated that the various branches of criminal justice systems operating in the UK have not addressed various forms of corporate crimes with the same degree of scrutiny as has been the case in the US.

Second, these disputes bear upon differing conceptions of the (putative) scientificity of academic criminology in particular and academic social science in general. As a discipline criminology has struggled constantly, alongside but also perhaps in competition with many other social sciences, to assert its scientificity. From the development of the *scuola positiva* onwards, until relatively recently, criminology was dominated by various forms of positivism. This dominance creates problems of legitimacy for various manifestations of inclusive definitions of corporate crime – that is, those that go beyond the criminal law or formal legal processes. For in the very process of moving from the more tangible, then one immediately opens oneself up to charges of moralising, crusading, politicking, and so on. Thus charges of moralising, or moral entrepreneurship, are frequently levelled at those operating on the basis of inclusive definitions (Levi 1994; Nelken 1994; Shapiro 1983). Either implicit, or explicit, in such charges is the claim that 'moral outrage may be good politics but bad science' (Meier 1986, cited in Friedrichs 1992: 9). This charge has been levelled at sociologists in particular (Hirschi and Gottfredson 1987), and precisely echoes one of the concerns raised by Tappan regarding Sutherland's enterprise.

Third, one of the reasons for the dominance of positivism across criminology for the greatest part of its history has been that in both individual and social/sociological manifestations it has largely operated within the domain assumption of a consensual social order (Young 1981). Such an assumption is particularly attractive to those minority class interests which systematically benefit from the structured inequalities upon which capitalist societies are *actually* founded. The maintenance of assumptions of consensus are hardly likely to be furthered by criminologists who attempt to bring within the ambit of criminological discourses the activities of the most powerful individual and corporate actors. On this basis, it is reasonable to suggest that if academic work into corporate criminality is to be conducted, and established as a legitimate area of criminological concern, then it must do so in the face of hostile and particularly powerful interests. These interests may predominate within academic institutions (hiring, promotion, and so on), within academic publishing outlets, amongst those who hold the purse strings of funding, across various popular media outlets, and so on. To make these points is not necessarily to imply any form of conscious manipulation nor conspiracy; rather, it is certainly to assert that there predominate particular versions of what forms of criminology are acceptable, feasible, utilisable, even of general interest, and so on. Some of these points are considered at greater length in Chapter 4.

Fourthly, and related to the last point, is the issue of what policy effects academic study into corporate crime can and does have. If in the past 30 years there has undoubtedly developed something closer to a theoretical pluralism within academic criminology, the emergence of law and order politics in both North America and Western Europe as each side of the Atlantic has experienced (albeit highly differing forms of) crises of hegemony has entailed the explicit politicisation of criminology as it has tied itself into, and been tied into, policy-making processes. This imbrication of criminologies within crime, law and order agendas, which have themselves been a crucial element of what has been called the 'Great Moving Right Show' (Hall 1983), may have served to narrow the range of legitimate reforms that criminologists might legitimately propose, and this has particular effects for a sub-discipline which, if it is to make policy proposals, is likely to make such proposals of a particularly radical, and/ or controversial, nature. Again we address this issue in relation to Britain in Chapter 4. Certainly Braithwaite has argued that 'white-collar crime research marks a rare case of sociological scholarship having a substantial impact on public policy' (1995: 116). However, the emergence of laws and agencies designed to regulate white-collar and corporate conduct are neither necessarily evidence of academic influence, nor indicative of any necessary progressive effects: aspects of post war political economy in developed capitalist states are a more useful general guide to the emergence and actual enforcement of regulations (Snider 1991). We address the latter issue Chapter 5 in relation to the recent emergence of political concern in serious fraud in Britain, while questions of regulatory reform are taken up at greater length in Chapters 8 and 9.

Finally, perhaps most significantly, and in a sense drawing together many of the particular points made above, is that these definitional disputes around corporate crime are very much an index of disputes about what constitutes the legitimate subject matter of criminology *per se*, or even whether criminology is a viable academic discipline. This is a recurring theme of the text.

As we have indicated, Sutherland's general project amounts to a sociological critique of legal categories and processes, and of a discipline which restricts itself to a focus upon these. Relevant to the substance of the dispute between Sutherland and Tappan is precisely that the former was a sociologist, the latter describing himself as a 'lawyer-sociologist' (Tappan 1947: 96; Geiss and Goff 1983: xxix). Part of this dispute, then, is clearly a disciplinary one:

> Sutherland's operationalising of the new concept also came under attack from
> lawyers. Sutherland was content to consider illegal behaviour as white collar
> crime if it were punishable, even if not punished, and if the potential
> offenders for infringements were civil rather than provided for in a criminal
> code. Tappan led a tradition insisting on proof beyond reasonable doubt in a

> criminal court before anything could be called a crime. Sutherland's counter is today accepted by most sociologists – that to do this would be to sacrifice science to a class-based administration of criminal justice ... Sutherland was right in principle, but in practice he and his disciples often counted actions that were not violations of law (eg. recalls of hazardous consumer products) as instances of white-collar crimes.
>
> (Braithwaite 1995: 118)

In writing this text we, too, are clear about the need to avoid limiting our field of enquiry to what Braithwaite terms here 'a class-based administration of criminal justice'. Thus, integral to any consideration of particular aspects of law – such as the question of what constitutes 'white-collar crime' – is the need for an understanding of the coverage and omissions of legal categories, the presences and absences within legal discourse, the social constructions of these categories and discourses, their underpinning of, treatment within and development through criminal justice systems, the ways in which particular laws are enforced (or not enforced), interpreted, challenged, and so on. In other words, as a criminologist, Sutherland's line of argument opens up the need for a transcendence of criminology – the questions that he raises cannot be resolved within that particular discipline.

One direction that this might take us is into the sociology of law, the focus of which is a focus upon both those 'factors which determine how rules are interpreted in particular contexts', and 'the content of the rules themselves' (Cotterrell 1984: 45). Relatedly, criminology might be transcended by the emerging disciplinary area of socio-legal studies (see Thomas, ed. 1997).

Indeed, both Marxists and feminists have claimed that a Marxist or feminist criminology is neither feasible nor desirable. It is of particular interest that one contribution to the Marxist literature on the impossibility of a Marxist criminology is based partly upon a discussion of the work of Sutherland. Pat O'Malley has argued that, while Sutherland's work was responsible for generating a number of difficulties within bourgeois criminology – notably concerning the definition of crime – his work aimed at the creation of a unified theory of criminality. Thus with respect to his 'most troublesome work on white-collar crime, he was still concerned to integrate this into the same general process as other criminal behaviour, namely differential association' (1987: 24, Footnote 7).

Thus while Sutherland remained committed to criminology, there is a real sense in which a development of his arguments entails a transcendence of the boundaries of criminology (Nelken 1994a: 366). For criminology is a discipline which is organised around a unifying concept, namely crime. Moreover, within legal discourse, crime bears a consistent relationship to a wide array of other theoretical concepts and assumptions – for example, that crime is a violation of rights and duties of some community, that the state acts on behalf of the interests and 'social consciousness' of this unitary community, and that the state represents an injured (collective) party in a criminal case and inflicts punishment on behalf of society. Within this theoretical context, 'criminology as a unified science makes sense' (O'Malley 1987: 9), but at the same time renders a Marxist criminology a contradictory enterprise:

> What theoretical or political unity could be formed under the banner of 'Marxist criminology' if some criminal actions represent forms of popular struggle (eg illegal strike action and picketing, resisting legal prohibitions of demonstration and on free speech), while others represent complex effects of brutalisation among the working class, which harm fellow working people ('mugging') and still others represent the less complex effects of pressures for profitability which lead corporations to endanger the lives of employees. Moreover, many such actions which are highly injurious to working people – such as the exposure of workers and their families to health-endangering pollution   may not appear as criminal at all, but are classified under some other legal category.
>
> (O'Malley 1987: 12–13; see also Hirst 1972; Pearce 1976; Jones 1982)

From a feminist perspective, Carol Smart has also argued that criminology is a 'doubtful project' (1995: 13), and that rather than working within a discourse which claims 'to be the study of criminal acts', we should 'be deconstructing the meaning of crime, not concretising it' (*ibid.*: 14).

While the rejection of criminology as a viable critical discipline by both feminists and Marxists differ in their detailed substance, they each have significant analogies with Sutherland's critique of the organisation of a discipline around the criminal law. And as with Sutherland's argument, when placed in the context of a consideration of white-collar crime, these arguments have particular force.

However, notwithstanding the fact that such critiques of criminology are well-made, they seem to us to entail a reification of criminology *as is*, when one of the tasks of the legitimate tasks of 'white-collar' criminologists can be to reshape the nature and boundaries of the discipline. After all, if we modify Pat Carlen's arguments, made in the context of a stringent critique of feminist rejections of criminology (a rejection which, ultimately, she endorses), it is perfectly possible for any form of critical social science to recognise the ideological power of the empirical referent without one's radical enterprise being subverted by it:

> there is no reason why they [radical theorists] should not both take seriously, that is recognise) and deny the empirical referent's material and ideological effects ... the very task of theory is to engage in a struggle for power over the 'meaning of things'.
>
> (Carlen 1992: 54, 62)

Our approach to the study of white-collar crime in this text is one that accepts the poverty of dominant criminological discourses, but argues that these are a site of struggle. Thus we seek throughout this text to examine the extent to which white-collar crime can be treated adequately with reference to criminological theorising and conceptualisation, thereby testing limits of this discourse.

From white-collar to corporate crime

Within the research traditions that have followed Sutherland's initial characterisation of white-collar crime, we can witness precisely such a struggle over the meaning of concepts. But as we have indicated earlier, it is possible to group broad types of work which have followed on from his early characterisation of this phenomenon, each of which has clarified and developed a particular aspect of the phenomenon which he loosely identified.

Amongst these clarifications, perhaps the most significant has been that which distinguishes between occupational and organisational crimes. This distinction between organisational and occupational crimes was present, but remained in a highly confused state, in Sutherland's work. Donald Cressey has noted that while Sutherland defined white-collar crime in terms of persons, he then went on to study corporations (1989). Indeed, for Cressey, not only did Sutherland's work constantly vacillate between a focus upon crimes of business people and corporate crimes (so conflating the two), but in his consideration of the latter he anthropomorphised the corporation (*ibid.*: 41), that is, he 'unthinkingly attributed human capabilities to these corporations' (Friedrichs 1992: 18–19).

Of course, there is a sense in which this is understandable, since corporations require human actors to function, even if they are not reducible to such human agency. Indeed, those actions and omissions upon which we focus in this text do centre around human agency, but, without previewing in too much detail here our later discussion of the causes of corporate crime (Chapters 6 and 7), what is crucial for us is the structural context and consequences of such agency. Our own view is that the term white-collar crime should be restricted to the study of crimes by the individually rich or powerful which are committed in the furtherance of their own interests, often against corporations or organisations with, for or within which they are working. These occur when individuals or groups of individuals make illegal use of their occupational position for personal advantage and victimise consumers or their own organisation, for example, either directly through theft or indirectly by damaging its reputation. Organisational illegalities, on the other hand, are individual or collective illegalities that are perceived as helping to achieve, or are congruent with, the organisational goals set by the dominant coalition within an organisation. The utility of this definition – one developed by Sherman (1982) and Ellis (1988) – is that it allows one to focus on organisational features.

We are concerned, then, with crimes by formal, legitimate organisations, rather than 'white-collar crime'. The latter term places too much emphasis upon the social characteristics of individual offenders; it leads to ultimately inadequate attempts to characterise certain forms of criminality in terms of respectability, status, trust, and so on; moreover, as we have noted (following Tappan), it subsumes within one category what are a heterogeneous group of phenomena. Indeed, despite the fact that the term white-collar crime was coined by Sutherland, and was defined explicitly in relation to people (that is, 'businessmen'), it is clear that what he actually studied empirically were corporations (Friedrichs 1992: 18–19). Indeed, a further clarification is required here. For our concern is not with legitimate organisations *per se*, but with the predominant form of economic organisation, namely the limited liability corporation. It is within these particular organisational forms, the genesis and legal status of which will be considered in Chapter 2, that the vast majority of people in modern Western economies now work; it is these organisations that provide the vast range of goods and services to the citizens of these polities (Pearce and Tombs 1998: 106). Indeed, given the massive privatisation programmes which have occurred across the world in the past two decades (*ibid.*: 14), the significance of the corporate form has assumed even greater empirical (and, for us as academics, theoretical) proportions.

We should note, however, that the distinction between occupational and organisational crimes can be overdrawn and may take attention away from the possible relationship between occupational crime and certain organisational features. For one thing, we should recognise that in many organisational crimes, advantages may accrue to both individuals and organisations (Wheeler and Rothman 1982: 1405). Somewhat differently, we also need to recognise that there are many occasions where an organisational form produces a relatively unsupervised individual, who is therefore able to engage in occupational crime; this may be a means of encouraging the same or other individuals to engage in organisational crime. Individuals may also be told to achieve particular profit targets which, in the circumstances, could only be achieved by breaking the law. By non-supervision, corporate executives may practise what has been labelled 'wilful blindness' or 'concerted ignorance' (Wilson 1979; Braithwaite 1984, 1989; Pearce and Tombs 1989, 1993).

Further, inter-organisational structures may have similar effects – it has been argued that many large automakers force those who hold distribution franchises to sell cars at an uneconomic price therefore the latter often can only make a 'normal' profit by illegally overcharging for maintenance and repairs (Farberman 1975). Similarly, individual police misconduct is likely to flourish under conditions of general corruption – or indifference to the rule of law – sanctioned by relatively superior officers (Ellis 1988; Knapp Commission 1973). In these cases one is describing *criminogenic organisations* which produce *both* occupational *and* organisational crime. This means that to understand corporate and organisational offending we may often need to move outside of the confines of discrete organisational entities. Again, here, we see how questions of definition are inevitably questions about how we theorise and understand the phenomenon at issue; we will return to these considerations explicitly in Chapters 6 and 7.

Corporate crime

It remains for us in this introductory chapter to provide a definition of white-collar crime around which this book is constructed. If there is no one accepted definition of this term – and the above indicates that there clearly is not – then the minimal obligation upon scholars is to define how they intend to use it and, crucially, what purpose that particular definition is intended to serve (Friedrichs 1992).

Our understanding of corporate crime – and one which will form a definitional reference point throughout this text – is based upon definitions already proposed by Kramer, Box, Schrager and Short, and Clinard and Yeager. Kramer's comments on the concept of corporate crime are a useful starting point:

> By the concept of 'corporate crime', then, we wish to focus attention on criminal acts (of omission or commission) which are the result of deliberate decision making (or culpable negligence) of those who occupy structural positions within the organization as corporate executives or managers. These decisions are organizationally based – made in accordance with the normative goals (primarily corporate profit), standard operating procedures, and cultural norms of the organization – and are intended to benefit the corporation itself.
>
> (1984: 18)

While this definition has enormous merit, it remains overly restrictive to the extent that many laws, enforced by administrative bodies through the civil courts, also regulate actions which cause injuries to specific individuals or which undermine social institutions. They also routinely impose punitive sanctions. Indeed, following Sutherland, the content of laws and the nature of legal distinctions such as those between crimes, torts and administrative sanctions, between acts *mala in se* and *mala prohibita*, are conventional, time-bound social products without an intrinsic substantive meaning that transcends their social or historical contexts; what acts or omissions constitute crime must be understood in terms of contingency (Lacey 1995). Thus, we extend Kramer's definition: first, to encompass 'any act committed by corporations that is punished by the state, regardless of whether it is punished under administrative, civil or criminal law' (Clinard and Yeager 1980: 16; see also Schrager and Short 1977; Box 1983); and, second, so that, in line with our earlier discussion, it includes acts that are subject to tortious litigation whatever the formal status of the litigant.

Through references to negligence and the use of the phrase 'omission or commission', Kramer's definition avoids the trap of arguing that for corporate crime to exist there must be *actus reus* (a prohibited act) and *mens rea* (a guilty mind). Given the organisational locus or origins of corporate crime, to emphasise either an illegal *act* or an *intention* is often inappropriate, for two reasons. First, each term is anthropomorphic and individualising, and by definition is problematic in its application to a corporate entity which is more than, or different to, the sum of individual human actors. Second, intention in particular implies a relatively unproblematic link between an act or omission and its consequence – yet this simplistic causal sequencing leads to an obscuring of the construction and maintenance of a situation or context which, as a consequence, is fertile ground for violations. Any focus upon corporate crimes requires us to examine these in terms of their *organisational production*.

On the former point, it has been argued that 'most corporate crimes cannot be explained by the perverse personalities of their perpetrators' (Braithwaite 1984: 2), and this claim calls into question the proclivity within individualistic liberal or bourgeois cultures to locate the source of evil deeds in evil people (*ibid.*; see also Schrager and Short 1977: 410; Snider 1993a: 61). Corporate crime can be produced by an organisation's structure, its culture, its unquestioned assumptions, its very *modus operandi*, and so on. Thus its understanding requires a shift from a humanist to a structural problematic.

These points concerning the organisational nature of corporate crime are not made to absolve individuals of any responsibility. They simply involve a recognition that organisations are the sites of complex relationships, invested with power and authority, between individuals and wider groups, between these groups themselves, between these groups and something called the 'organisation', and between the organisation and its various operating environments, key actors within the latter being other organisations. Some of this complexity is highlighted by Box:

> the pursuit of organisational goals is deeply implicated in the cause(s) of corporate crime. But it is important to realise that these goals are not the manifestation of personal motives cast adrift from organisational moorings, neither are they disembodied acts committed in some metaphysical sense by corporations. Rather, organisational goals are what they are perceived to be by officials who have been socialised into the organisational 'way of life' and who strive in a highly co-ordinate fashion to bring about collectively their realisation.
>
> (1983: 21)

To speak of organisational goals, as does Box, or of the normative goals of an organisation, as we have done through Kramer's definition of corporate crime, should not be read as implying that there necessarily exists any simply identified set of goals within any particular organisation.

Of course, to refer to organisational goals is important; for example, such a reference begins to separate corporate crime from occupational crime; it may provide a central element in theorising the origins and nature of corporate crime (see Chapter 7). However, the reference to the furthering or pursuit of organisational goals can be problematic, since it is often read as if it conjures up images of perfect rationality on the part of corporations – that is, it implies that corporations have unequivocal sets of goals, are aware of these, that these are consistent, and that they are strategically developed and operationalised. Questions raised by the issue of corporate rationality are addressed in Chapter 8, and at length elsewhere (see Pearce and Tombs 1998). It is simply worth noting at this point that whether or not corporations are rational actors, they certainly represent themselves as such (Keane 1995).

The definition of corporate crime used in this text is, then, an explicitly inclusive one. That is, throughout this text we discuss *as crimes* many acts and omissions which have not been subject to any formal judicial process; thus these are phenomena which have not been interrogated as, let alone proven to be, violations of the criminal, or indeed any other form of, law. To fail to do otherwise would, for us, lead us into the study of what Braithwaite called class-based administration of criminal justice, thereby obscuring precisely the most useful insights of Sutherland regarding the class-biased development law and its differential implementation.

However, we seek to retain law as a reference point and, in doing so, we must be clear that this law is capitalism's law. This does create tensions, but we believe that these are manageable, while such an approach is legitimate on several grounds.

First, we have one highly pragmatic rationale for this approach: we assess the acts and omissions of companies and organisations simply because, in a morally pluralistic society, law remains the most generally accepted standard by which 'right' and 'wrong' are judged.

Second, we discuss under the rubric of crime in this text acts and omissions that have not been processed successfully through any criminal justice system; that is, where no legal verdict has been reached, let alone a guilty verdict in a criminal court. We seek to do so through the use of publicly available evidence which is examined both sociologically and through reference to existent legal categories; and we attempt to do so with sufficient rigour that our judgements are open to contestation. That is, our general aim is to bring to bear academic rigour to issues that have not raised or settled within formal legal fora. To refrain from such analyses would mean that some of the most egregious corporate acts and omissions remained free of critical scrutiny through reference to the law, in many cases (as we shall see) merely because the exercise or existence of corporate power (as particular effects of class power), conflicts of interest within and between national states, or indeed technical inadequacies in state and national state legal systems had prevented the details of a case from receiving a public airing.

Third, we reject the claim that to engage in such form of argument is to engage in mere moralising. On the one hand, we are clear that we discuss within the rubric of crimes phenomena for which there exists evidence pointing to some form of legal infraction; we are not discussing (our particular version of) social harms. On the other hand, because we accept that distinctions between types of law is both non-necessary and in many ways motivated, through retaining a reference to existent legal categories we avoid the frequent charge of mere moralising, or moral entrepreneurship (Levi 1994; Nelken 1994; Shapiro 1983). Thus it has been claimed that 'moral outrage may be good politics but bad science' (Meier 1986, cited in Friedrichs 1992: 9; see also Hirschi and Gottfredson 1987, who level this charge at sociologists in particular). Yet as Michalowski and Kramer have rightly noted, using the law to define the boundaries of any criminological enterprise is itself 'suffused with moral choice' (1987: 45).

In other words, whilst drawing our definitional boundary, we are clear that this is in itself a value-laden exercise. Within our definition of corporate crime we encompass acts and omissions which existent bodies of law proscribe and/or require, albeit through different forms of law or within different national jurisdictions; beyond that definition lie social harms, a wide range of acts and omissions that law does not encompass, even though we might wish that this were otherwise (see Gordon and Pantazis 1997). This is not to deride academic work which focuses upon the latter forms of activity, since both moral critique and arguments with respect to social harm and human rights are crucial aspects of academic and popular critique and struggle (Kramer 1989). But in our view they are less appropriate for a text that seeks to deal with corporate crime. Indeed, through maintaining reference to existing legal categories, this text allows us to make what ultimately is a significant political point – that *despite the fact that we are discussing bourgeois legal categories, capitalist corporations by and large do not and cannot routinely adhere to them.*

Aims and outline of the book

The aims of this book are fourfold.

First, we aim to map the different types of corporate offences, both in their contemporary and historical forms, tasks which seem to us of particular importance given the relative absence of such phenomena from dominant crime, law and order agendas. We address issues specifically related to this aim in Chapters 2, 3 and 4. In Chapter 2, we chart the emergence of corporate crime through a brief historical overview of the legal creation of the corporation and successive legal attempts to create boundaries around the nature of its legitimate activities. In Chapters 3 and 4, we attempt to map the forms, scale and consequences of corporate crimes. More specifically, in Chapter 3, we present material which has sought to measure the extent of corporate crime, drawing upon quantitative and qualitative work. In the following Chapter (4), we present and review existing estimates on the relative costs of corporate and street crimes. Chapter 5 then examines the mechanisms and processes through which corporate crime, now established through previous chapters as a pressing social issue, remains relatively absent from dominant crime, law and order agendas. These first four chapters, then, devote a great deal of time and attention to rendering corporate crimes visible, and it is of interest to us that so much effort must be expended in this task for readers who are well-versed in many criminological concerns.

The *second* key aim of this text, addressed most explicitly in Chapters 6 and 7, is an attempt to account for the existence of corporate crime; this is partly an empirical, but largely a theoretical task. Specifically, in Chapter 6, we address efforts to explain corporate crime which draw upon, or develop, modes of theorising and explanation developed within the disciplinary confines of criminology itself, and which have largely been developed to account for so-called traditional crime. Chapter 7 draws upon, but largely transcends, criminological theory, through assessing explanations of corporate crime which locate its genesis and nature in some aspect of dominant political economy.

Third, we examine the ways in which the state treats and responds to corporate crimes. Thus, in Chapter 8, we critically examine existent literature on the regulation of corporations, while in Chapter 9 we examine current forms of, and proposals for reform in, the ways in which corporate offenders, both individuals and the corporate entity, are and might be subject to punishment.

While each of the three aims, or themes, set out here are dealt with explicitly in particular chapters, their intimately inter-related nature means that their consideration is pervasive. This is particularly the case with the *fourth* general theme of this text: in a brief concluding chapter, we assess the extent to which corporate crime is a phenomenon which either is, or can be, treated within the confines of the discipline of criminology, but this is a theme which runs throughout the text, and indeed has been a major consideration of this chapter, not least through our treatment of the Sutherland–Tappan debate. To pose the question of whether the study of corporate crime through some form of corporate criminology is either desirable or possible is, in many respects, the most pervasive theme of the book. This text therefore stands as a work which is situated within, but which also explores the limits of, criminology.

In addition to stating what the text aims to do, we should immediately absolve ourselves from several potential obligations, by stating what the text is *not* intended to be. In contrast to the dominant (but not only) trend within contributions to the topic of corporate crime, this text is not organised around, although it makes consistent reference to, empirical case studies. So, it is not a book of case studies. To the extent that we examine case studies in particular, but have an explicit focus in general, then we seek to draw upon British experiences. However, as will also become clear, while the reason for such a focus is the relative dearth of British (as opposed to North American) work on corporate crime, this same absence makes it impossible to focus entirely upon this geographical context. So, it is not a book which seeks to provide a balanced representation of work from the US. Further, a text such as this can only be indicative rather than in any way comprehensive of the range of works conducted of relevance to the theme of corporate crime. Indeed, our treatment of this topic also reflects our own substantive interests and expertise in safety and health crimes; and such a focus can be further justified by the facts that such crimes have enormous social, physical and economic costs, and are almost invisible when compared even with some forms of corporate crimes (see Chapters 4 and 5). So we draw in particular upon examples from this area, which means that this is not a text which treats corporate crime homogeneously, nor is it a text which devotes equal amount of space and consideration to all forms of corporate crime.

Taking these points together, we intend that the text is at once descriptive and discursive: that is, while we seek to introduce readers to, and develop understanding of, a field of enquiry, we also hope to challenge, subject to critique and ultimately contribute to that field of enquiry. Finally, while this is clearly a text written by academics, with the relative privilege as well as constraints thereby entailed, we hope that this is more than simply an academic text: for us, this is also an attempt to engage on both practical (policy-making) and political levels.

Chapter 2

The emergence of corporate crime

'Corporation – an ingenious device for obtaining individual profit without individual responsibility.'

(A. Bierce, *The Devil's Dictionary*, 1958)

Introduction

There are about 1 060 000 companies in the UK (Department of Trade and Industry, 1997), and many thousands of public organisations. As we shall see in the next two chapters, there is a good deal of evidence that the activities of these companies result in a substantial number of legal wrongs, with enormous economic, physical and social costs.

This chapter, traces, albeit in necessarily broad sweep only, the way the institution of the company originated socially, economically and in law, and looks at the way the law was shaped in a way which was notably favourable to companies. Legal doctrines evolved which meant that it was very difficult to find companies guilty of serious crimes because the ordinary criminal law required defendants to have guilty minds before they could be convicted.

In its incipient form, in the twelfth century, criminal law was focused exclusively on individual wrongdoers. It was not until the middle of the nineteenth century that the malfeasance of corporations was within its scope. The extent of corporate criminal liability has been extended both by parliament and the courts. In this chapter we examine the development of the corporation in its social and historical settings and then trace the evolution of its legal liabilities.

Corporate offending only arose historically with the emergence of such social institutions, although some nascent forms of business crime can be identified in biblical times. Geis and Edelhertz (1973: 990, cited in Croall 1992: 6) suggest that Christ's driving of the money lenders from the temple was an early response of moral outrage 'against business cheating and indecency'.

The early law

In societies characterised as primitive, sanctions tended to be collective (Durkheim 1984 (1893); Garland 1990). The breaking of a taboo was sanctioned, in many societies, to appease the supernatural, and punishment was by and for the whole group. Even individual disputes produced a collective response (Plucknett 1956: 410–16). By contrast, feudal sanctions were individualistic (Radzinowicz 1948). While the emergent criminal justice system was becoming more formalised, other major socio-economic changes were taking place. Late feudal Europe saw the development of shipping, at the heart of the trading economy, begin to flourish. The vessels built for exploration and trade became larger, faster and more profitable. They also became much more expensive to finance. The prevalence of piratical attacks made the dangers of the sea even greater. Merchants were pressured to pool their resources and investments and collective ventures gradually became more common. The earliest joint stock companies can be traced to these circumstances (Hadden 1977: 13; Gower 1992: 21).

During the period when mercantile capitalism was growing from the old feudal order, there was a transfer of power from the aristocracy to the boroughs and counties where important decisions affecting trade were being taken. The Crown could tax the authorities and grant or withhold business privileges. It extended its control over the towns and boroughs and their mercantile interests by using the Royal Charter, an official grant which conferred a distinct legal status and existence. From even earlier, since the twelfth century, the Crown had sought to limit blood feuds by usurping the process of prosecution (Baker 1971: 252–7).

It was during the late medieval period that the concept of legal personality really began to be elaborated. Much of this theory derived from the Roman Law principle of *societas*, an association of persons with legal rights and duties distinct from those of its constituent members (*ibid.* p. 10). One of the earliest cases of legal recognition of a collective entity in England and Wales arose from a problem related to the ownership of churches. Traditionally, the feudal lord erected the church on his estate and enjoyed property rights in it. He also had the authority to select the priest and the religious rites of the church. But the power of such lords had begun to diminish by the late thirteenth century. The question arose as to who owned the churches. A number of legal fictions were used at first but the ultimate solution was for the Church (*in abstracto*) to own the buildings, property and income which they generated. The highest officials of the Church could thence transact business in its name. The church had become a juristic person.

By the fourteenth century the concept had been extended to boroughs and towns. They were bestowed rights, including those of levying tolls and selling franchises, but they also had responsibilities, often to pay money to the Crown. The capacity to generate revenue required the status of a juristic person and this was the Crown's prerogative to grant. As Cullen *et al.* (1987) observed, these collective entities developed largely at the pleasure of the State and during this time the corporations often acted in quasi-governmental capacities by collecting tolls. This can explain the

frequently preferential treatment enjoyed by corporations. The corporation was a 'child of the State and in many instances performed the duties
of the State' (Coleman 1982b: 39–40).

The trading company emerged in sixteenth century England as a
commercial arrangement that allowed merchants to engage in joint
ventures. At first they resembled partnerships where the constituent
members acted legally as individuals but as their ventures grew larger they
traded as joint stock companies (Hadden 1977); at first for single
ventures and then later as permanent enterprises.

Although business was the *raison d'être* of these companies they were
also assisting the government from quite an early stage in their development. With burgeoning overseas trade and colonisation in the sixteenth
century, companies would operate in a political capacity in new territories
until the government could formally establish a colonial government
(Cullen *et al.* 1987: 112). Such companies were created by Royal Charter
based on the constitutions of the earlier boroughs and towns which had
been authorised to perform governmental functions such as the levying
of tolls. The government was generally keen to foster the symbiotic
relationship between itself and these companies as is evidenced by
legislation like the so-called 'Bubble Act' of 1720. The South Sea
company had been founded by statute in 1710 with the joint objectives of
exploiting the opportunities for trade with South America and serving as
a means of relieving the government of the burden of the national debt.
The 1720 Act declared unlawful the operation of unchartered joint stock
companies and was part of an effort to shore up the market for South Sea
shares by suppressing some of its competitors. A House of Commons
Resolution of 27 April, 1720 emphasised the effects of rash speculation by
drawing attention to the numerous undertakings which were purporting
to act as corporate bodies without legal authority, practices which
'manifestly tend to the prejudices of the public trade and commerce of
the Kingdom' (Gower 1992: 26). This Resolution was followed by the Act,
s.18 of which made the conduct of business along the lines described in
the resolution illegal.

The 1720 Act, however, produced a financial panic, causing the
collapse of many companies. The demand for charters declined rapidly as
a result of the panic and lawyers began to devise ways to circumvent the
Act. Companies were created with contractual agreements using a deed of
settlement modelled on the fourteenth century trust. The trust had
worked on the principle that trustees were obliged to administer the trust
property on behalf of the *cestui que trust* (beneficiary) and the trustees
were deemed to hold the property as trustees, a continuing and distinct
legal entity. These 'deed of settlement' companies shared the status of
corporations in that they both enjoyed the asset of transferable shares.
Unlike corporations, but like partnerships, the trust companies had no
distinct legal personality, although they could limit liability through
contract: *Hallet* v. *Dowdall* (1852) 21 LJQB 98.

Legal developments favouring companies

In their early stages of development, companies pioneered new areas of trade and governments had an interest in supporting these corporate activities. Much later, in the nineteenth century such principles were still at work. The rapid economic changes of industrialisation entailed many companies expanding very quickly. Many workers were sacrificed on the altar of frenetic economic expansion (Marx 1954 [1887]: chp 10; Engels 1969 [1845]; Ward 1962; Hobsbawn 1968). Deaths and serious injuries at work were prevalent in many industries, such as the great railway enterprises. There were in the early nineteenth century a growing number of civil actions against companies for compensation where workers had been injured in the most appalling circumstances. The number and gravity of injuries was such that if a doctrine of negligence allowing such claims had been clearly formulated at that time, the companies would have had to pay such huge sums in damages, or alternatively spend what they claimed were prohibitively high sums on safety, that they would have become inviable or insolvent. At this time, a number of legal doctrines were constructed which obviated the possible success of any such litigation.

One defence afforded to company defendants was that of *volenti non fit injuria* (no legal injury can be done to someone who volunteers to the risk). This defence meant that injured workers were not entitled to damages for injuries resulting from dangerous work to which they were deemed to have consented by accepting the employment. Thus even though it was 'his poverty, not his will, consented to the danger', (*per* Hawkins J., *Thrussell* v. *Handyside* (1888) 20 QBD at 364) it was often held that

> The master says here is the work, do it or let it alone … The master says this, the servant does the work and earns his wages and is paid but is hurt. On what principle of reason or justice should the master be liable to him in respect of that hurt? (*per* Lord Bramwell in *Memberry* v. *Great Western Railway* (1889) 14 AC 179 at 188)

Another defence protecting corporations was that of contributory negligence. Under this principle, until 1945, an injured employee or any other plaintiff could not sue for damages if s/he had contributed to his or her own injury by carelessness even of the smallest degree (Brazier, 1988: 238). As this could usually be proved against a plaintiff working often under great stress, many claims failed on this point.

A third type of shield given to corporate defendants in personal injury cases was the doctrine of common employment. Under this doctrine, an injured worker was not able to sue if his or her injury was actually inflicted through a co-worker (Brazier 1988: 282). Many injuries were of this sort even though the causation seen in a wider context was directly related to the conditions or system of work insisted on by the employer. As Fleming has argued (1983: 7), it was regarded by many judges as in the interests of an advancing economy to subordinate the security of individuals, who happened to become casualties of the new machine age, rather than fetter the enterprise by loading it with the costs of inevitable accidents.

The civil law was thus being developed to offer support and protection to companies. The policy was created on an *ad hoc* basis, judgement by judgement, not as part of any grand conspiracy but its effects were clear. As Gobert (1994a) points out, the same phenomenon was to be found in the law of contract where the courts invoked technical doctrines such as privity of contract to limit the scope of a company's liability (*Winterbottom* v. *Wright* 10 Meeson & Welsby 109). The doctrine of 'privity' entails that only those parties who make a contract can enforce or be bound by it – thus, someone who was to gain by a contract, although not a party to it, had no remedy if the agreement was not carried out by one of the parties.

Companies and the criminal law

The criminal law, as it touched corporations, was equally as sensitive to the needs of expanding business (Gobert 1994a: 397) but, for the early part of its history, the corporation lay outside the criminal law. 'It had no soul to damn and no body to kick' (attributed to Lord Thurlow, quoted in Leigh 1969: 4). If a crime was committed by the orders of a corporation, criminal proceedings for having thus instigated an offence could only be taken against the separate members in their personal capacities and not against the corporation itself (Stephen 1883: II, 61).

In 1701 Lord Holt C.J. is reported as having said that 'A corporation is not indictable but the particular members are' (12 Mod. p. 559). This was a consequence of the technical rule that criminal courts expected the prisoner to 'stand at the bar' and did not permit 'appearance by attorney' (a problem later solved by s. 33 of the Criminal Justice Act 1925 which allowed for a company to appear by representative). The old idea was supported by Roman Law. It was reasoned that as it did not have an actual existence, a corporation could not be guilty of a crime because it could not have a guilty will. Furthermore, even if the legal fiction which gives to a corporation an imaginary existence could be stretched so as to give it an imaginary will, the only activities that could be consistently ascribed to the fiction thus created, must be such as are connected with the purposes for which the corporation was created to accomplish. A corporation, could not, therefore, commit a crime because any crime would necessarily be *ultra vires* the corporation. Moreover a corporation is devoid not only of mind but also of body and therefore incapable of receiving the usual punishments: 'What? Must they hang up the common seal?' asked an advocate in 1682 (*R* v. *City of London* (1682) 8 St. Tr. 1039 at 1138).

The proliferation of companies in modern times and the extent of their influence in social life have caused the criminal law to bring them within its jursidiction. This incorporation within the criminal law has been arguably belated, careless and unsystematic but it has nevertheless occurred. As Turner noted (1966: 76)

> ... under the commercial development which the last few generations have witnessed, corporations have become so numerous that there would have been grave public danger in continuing to permit them to enjoy [the old] immunity.

This reasoning was also followed by Mr. Justice Turner in the course of his preliminary ruling in 1990 in the *Herald of Free Enterprise* case. He examined the history of corporate liability and noted (*R* v. *Alcindor and others, P & O European Ferries (Dover) Ltd* (1991) 93 Cr App R 72 at 83) that:

> Since the nineteenth century there has been a huge increase in the numbers and activities of corporations whether nationalised, municipal or commercial, whose activities enter the private lives of all or most of 'men and subjects' in a diversity of ways. A clear case can be made for imputing to such corporations social duties including the duty not to offend all relevant parts of the criminal law.

The first time corporations were brought within the jurisdiction of the criminal law (in 1842, see below) was for failure to satisfy absolute statutory duties. Thus the courts were not taxed with the problems of finding any mental element – in legal terms a *mens rea* – in a non-human entity. The terms *mens rea*, literally the 'mental thing', is taken from a longer latin formula hallowed within the criminal law which states that conduct is not criminal unless the mind of the person committing the conduct is blameworthy. In criminal law there are various types of *mens rea*, ranging from negligence to intention.

Developing commerce required that there should be no serious interruption or damage to parts of the economic infrastructure (such as roads, and bridges) which would impede the expedition of all sorts of commercial activities and thus be a cause of financial loss and annoyance to many enterprises. It was in this context that obligations were statutorily imposed on companies, and where the earliest prosecutions against companies would follow if they did not meet those obligations. In *R* v. *Birmingham and Gloucester Rly Co.* ([1842] 3QB 223) a company was prosecuted for failing to construct connecting arches over a railway line built by it, in breach of a duty imposed by the statute which authorised the incorporation of the company. It was argued that an indictment would not lie against a company but Mr. Justice Patterson rejected that claim, stating (1842 law report, as above, p. 232) that:

> a corporation may be indicted for breach of duty imposed on it by law, though not for a felony, or for crimes involving personal violence as for riots and assaults.

The prosecution there relied on non-feasance (not performing an obligation, as opposed to misfeasance – performing an obligation badly) as the basis of liability. Subsequently, the non-feasance/misfeasance distinction was dismissed as arbitrary and in *R* v. *Great North of England Rly Co* ((1846 9 QB 315), Lord Denman CJ confirmed that a company could be indicted for misfeasance. The company had obstructed a highway during its construction work on a railway, and had failed, contrary to a duty imposed on it by statute, to build a bridge for other traffic. Liability for omissions as in the *Birmingham* case (above) was now extended to liability for positive acts. Denman LCJ said (at p. 325):

> It is as easy to charge one person *or a body corporate*, with erecting a bar across a public road as with the non-repair of it; and they may as well be compelled to pay a fine for the act as well as for the omission. [emphasis added]

Disposing of an argument that it was unnecessary to prosecute the company when a culpable individual could be identified and proceeded against, the Lord Chief Justice said (at. p. 327):

> There can be no effectual means for deterring from an oppressive exercise of power for the purpose of gain, except the remedy by an indictment against those who truly commit it, that is, the corporation acting by its majority: and there is no principle which places them beyond the reach of the law for such proceedings.

During the last quarter of the nineteenth century, the number of annual prosecutions of companies rose, and those found guilty were fined. Delivering his opinion in a case in 1880 (*The Pharmaceutical Society* v. *London and Provincial Supply Association* [1880] 5 AC 857), Lord Blackburn stated, in passing, that a corporation can commit crimes for which it could be suitably punished. The courts agreed, however, that while companies could be criminally prosecuted they could not be prosecuted for offences requiring intent. In *R* v. *Cory Bros* ([1927] 1 KB 810) a coal company was indicted, *inter alia*, for manslaughter after it had instructed, during the 1926 miners' strike, that one of its fences should be electrified to prevent coal being pilfered. An unemployed collier was killed when he stumbled accidentally against the fence in the course of a ratting expedition. Mr. Justice Finlay held that the indictment could not properly lie against a corporation for a felony or for a misdemeanour involving personal violence.

If the criminal liability of corporations was to extend beyond this point, two difficulties had to be overcome. First, a corporation having no social duties was generally unable to form that state of mind which is required for the *mens rea* of crime. The only crimes it could commit were strict liability offences. The second problem was the means by which the 'mind' of the corporation could be identified or ascertained.

In 1944 a trio of cases were decided which were to have a lasting effect on this area of law. Indeed, Welsh has argued (1946: 346) that the effect was 'revolutionary' in the way that it established the notion that a company could have an ordinary *mens rea*. The reason for such a dramatic watershed in three decisions all within a few months of each other is not certain but Leigh has suggested (1969: 2) that it was in response to violations of wartime regulations. The cases established that a corporation could be guilty of a crime in circumstances where the principles of vicarious liability would not apply (Smith and Hogan 1996: 178–9). In these decisions we find the genesis of the doctrine of identification.

The offence in question, in the first case, *DPP* v. *Kent and Sussex Contractors* ([1944] 1 KB 810), was one under the Motor Fuel Rationing Order. The Divisional Court held that a company could commit a crime requiring intent to deceive. Mr. Justice Hallett states (p.158):

> With regard to the liability of a body corporate for . . . crimes . . . there has been a development in the attitude of the courts arising from the large part played in modern times by limited liability companies.

Giving judgement in the same appeal, Lord Caldecote said (at pp. 155–6):

> The real point which we have to decide . . . is . . . whether a company is capable of an act of will or a state of mind, so as to be able to form an intention to deceive or to have knowledge of the truth or falsity of a statement . . .
> Although the directors or general manager of a company are its agents, they are something more. A company is incapable of acting or speaking or even of thinking except in so far as its officers have acted, spoken or thought . . . the officers are the company for this purpose.

In the second case, *R* v. *ICR Road Haulage Ltd* ([1944] 1 KB 551), it was held that an indictment will lie against a company for common law conspiracy to defraud. Mr. Justice Stable said (at p. 556), referring to the decision in *R* v. *Cory Bros* (1927): '. . . if the matter came before the court to-day, the result might well be different'.

The last of the trio of cases, *Moore* v. *Bresler* ([1944] 2 All ER 515), followed the earlier decisions and a company was successfully prosecuted for using a document with *intent* to defraud.

Although the legal reasons for the decisions ('*rationes*' in legal language) in these three cases are far from clear they manage to surmount the theoretical difficulties of attributing *mens rea* to a company.

The observations of Hallett and Stable JJ were fully vindicated 21 years later in the unreported Glamorgan Assizes case of *R* v. *Northern Strip Mining Construction Company* (1965, *The Times* 2, 4, 5 February; *Western Mail* 4, 5 February). The defendant company was indicted for manslaughter. Neither eminent counsel (Mr. Philip Wien QC for the Crown; Mr. W.L. Mars-Jones for the defendant), nor the very experienced presiding judge Mr. Justice Streatfeild, appeared to have any doubt about the validity of the indictment. Indeed, Mr. Mars-Jones, for the defendant, directly conceded the propriety of such an indictment when he said:

> it is the prosecution's task to show that the defendant company, in the person of Mr. Camm, managing director, was guilty of such a degree of negligence that amounted to a reckless disregard for the life and limbs of his workmen.
>
> (*The Times*, 2 February, 1965)

Glanville Evans, a welder employee of the company, was drowned when a railway bridge he was helping to demolish collapsed and threw workmen into the Wye. The victim had been instructed to start the demolition work in the middle of the bridge. The man whom the company managing director had selected to supervise this demolition had no relevant training nor any substantial experience of this type of work. The Crown argued that the instructions given were an act of folly and would have inevitably led to the collapse of the bridge:

> there was such a complete disregard for the safety of the workmen that it goes beyond the mere matter of compensation and amounts to a crime against the state.
>
> (*The Times*, 4 February, 1965)

Although the company was found not guilty on the merits of the case, Leigh, writing in 1969, was clear that liability for manslaughter had been established as a crime for which a corporation could be indicted.

In *Robert Millar (Contractors) Ltd* [1970] 1 All ER 577, a company and its managing director were convicted following the death of six people on the M6. The convictions were not for manslaughter but for causing death by dangerous driving. Nevertheless, the case marks another development on the law's long road to the point at which it can condemn a corporate body for homicide. The managing director of a company in Scotland sent a heavy lorry on a journey to England. The court found that he must have known that the lorry had a seriously defective tyre. The tyre burst and the lorry crashed through the central barrier on the motorway hitting oncoming vehicles. The lorry was sent out in the dangerous condition because, against the protests of the driver, the director wished to avoid the lorry being out of commission for repairs with consequential disappointment to (and possible loss of business from) commercial customers. The judge imposed a modest fine and disqualification on the driver but he sentenced the managing director to nine months imprisonment and fined the company £750. Given the data presented in Chapter 4, indicating that over 1000 employees are killed each year, and tens of thousands sustain serious injuries in the course of their employment, such a ruling carries potentially great significance.

The problem of discovering the mind of the company

Following the decisions of the 1944 trio of cases, corporate intention was found by treating the *mens rea* of certain employees of the company as the *mens rea* of the company itself. It was not every employee whose *mens rea* was also that of the company, however. The test was wide and flexible, one of mixed fact and law (Burles 1991: 610). However, as a company has no physical existence and cannot think or act, a fiction has to be applied to convert the acts and thoughts of a human into those of the corporation thereby attributing personality to it. This is known as the identification principle and a variety of criteria and phrases for determining who in a company thinks and acts as that company have been suggested in the leading case of *Tesco Supermarkets Ltd* v. *Nattrass* ([1972] AC 153). Viscount Dilhorne (at 171) thought that it would have to be someone,

> ... who is in actual control of the operations of a company or of part of them and who is not responsible to another person in the company for the manner in which he discharges his duties in the sense of being under his orders.

In determining who are the people representing the 'controlling minds' of the corporation, a dictum of Lord Denning's, in *H.L. Bolton (Engineering) Co. Ltd* v. *T.J. Graham & Sons* [1957] 1 QB 159 at 172, was approved:

> A company may in many ways be likened to a human body. It has a brain and a nerve centre which controls what it does. It also has hands which hold the tools and act in accordance with directions from the centre. Some of the people in the company are mere servants and agents who are nothing more than hands to do the work and cannot be said to represent the mind or will. Others are directors and managers who represent the directing mind and will of the company and control what it does. The state of mind of these managers is the state of mind of the company and it is treated by the law as such.

This formula does not include all 'managers' since not all such persons 'represent the directing mind and will of the company and control what it does'. The wide and flexible test of the 1944 cases was disapproved and replaced by a far stricter one known as the 'controlling officer' test. In any event, it is a question of *law* whether a person is to be regarded as having acted as the company or merely as the company's servant or agent (*per* Lord Reid, in *Tesco, ibid* at 173).

Such a narrow test has had considerable implications for prosecutors (Burles 1991: 610). It means, in effect, that it is extremely difficult for companies to be convicted for serious crimes. A ruling from Lord Justice Bingham appears to make it virtually impossible for a company to be convicted for manslaughter because the way that responsibilities are distributed through a corporate body makes it extremely unlikely that the necessary fault will ever reside entirely in a single identifiable individual.

In his preliminary ruling in 1990 on whether a corporation could be properly indicted for manslaughter (arising from the charges brought against P&O European Ferries for the sinking of the *Herald of Free Enterprise*, above), Mr. Justice Turner said (p. 84):

> ... where a corporation, through the controlling mind of one of its agents, does an act which fulfils the prerequisites of the crime of manslaughter ... it as well as its controlling mind or minds, is properly indictable for the crime of manslaughter.

In order to establish that P&O itself was guilty of manslaughter, the

Crown had to prove that one of its directors was guilty of manslaughter. When the prosecution against five senior employees collapsed, the case against the company inevitably went too. Furthermore, certain restrictions on the criminal responsibility of corporations were set out in this judgement, precluding the aggregation of fault from several directors as being sufficient to incriminate the company. On this matter, Bingham LJ ruled that:

> Whether the defendant is a corporation or a personal defendant, the ingredients of manslaughter must be established by proving the necessary *mens rea* and *actus reus* against it or him by evidence properly to be relied on against it or him. A case against a personal defendant cannot be fortified by evidence against another defendant. The case against a corporation can only be made by evidence properly addressed to showing guilt on the part of the corporation as such (*R*v. *HM Coroner for East Kent ex parte Spooner* (1989) 88 Cr. App. R. 10 at 17)

The analogy with a personal defendant used by Bingham LJ seems inappropriate. Companies gain many benefits from the principle of aggregation. Indeed, the very notion of a separate legal personality being accorded to a group of people as a company is founded upon the principle of aggregation. With benefit comes responsibility. *Qui sensit commodum debet sentire et onus* (he who has obtained an advantage ought to bear the disadvantage as well). It is perverse to dispense with the principle of aggregation just at the point when its application would implicate the company in a serious crime.

This principle against aggregation applies in respect of serious crimes in general. This means that in any case in which it looks like a company (rather than an individual director or executive) should be prosecuted for fraud, or theft, or serious assault, the prosecution will face an immensely difficult task aggravated by a long, costly trial and a high risk of failure. If they opt, alternatively, for the prosecution of an individual director their task will be much easier and, if the case is successfully prosecuted, there will at least be some form of conviction on the public record.

The result of this framing of the law is that the rules work in a way which is more accommodating to corporations than to individuals.

Despite the public outcry that no-one including the company itself was convicted of any criminal offence following the disaster, what the prosecution did achieve was the admission by the Court that a corporate body is capable of being guilty of manslaughter. Although this success was welcome by many, the groundbreaking development of the law towards corporate manslaughter did not take place for a further five years.

On 8 December, 1994, OLL Ltd became the first company in English legal history to be convicted of homicide (Slapper 1997: JPIL 221). Peter Kite, its managing director, also became the first director to be given an immediate custodial sentence from a manslaughter conviction arising from the operation of a business. Both defendants were found guilty on four counts of manslaughter arising from the death of four teenagers who drowned off Lyme Regis while on a canoe trip organised by the defendant leisure activity company. Mr Kite was sentenced to three years imprisonment, and the company was fined £60 000. The Lyme Regis conviction, argues Slapper (1997), may well have a symbolic significance, and have a chastening effect on businesses which currently adopt a cavalier attitude to safety. How far it will affect the number of prosecutions in future is questionable. The case was arguably atypical of corporate homicide scenarios. The company OLL Ltd was small, so it was relatively easy to find the 'controlling minds'; the risks to which the students were exposed were both serious and obvious and also, critically, they were not technical or esoteric in any way (anyone can see the dereliction of duty involved in not providing competent supervisors, flares, a look-out boat, in not notifying the harbour authority, etc.). For the prosecution there was also the serendipitous evidence of the letter from the former employees which indisputably made the managing director aware of the risks in question; risks which, as the prosecution was able to show, were not subsequently addressed with any seriousness.

Since the Lyme Regis case, another company has been convicted of manslaughter, along with one of its directors, James Hodgson. Hodgson was imprisoned for twelve months and fined £1500, and the company, Jackson Transport (Ossett) Ltd, fined £22 000. The case arose from the death of a 21-year-old employee who died after being sprayed in the face with a toxic chemical while cleaning chemical residues from a road tanker. The case centred on allegations of inadequate supervision, training, and protective equipment (*The Safety and Health Practitioner*, December 1996, p3; cited in Slapper (1997)).

There are however, some offences the commission of which could hardly fall within the scope of employment of the 'controlling officer', like bigamy, rape and incest. The fact that a corporation cannot commit the offence as principal does not mean that it is incapable of committing it as an accessory. It is difficult to imagine a case in which a company could be held liable as a principal for dangerous driving but it may certainly be convicted as a secondary party (Smith and Hogan 1996: 252).

In 1972, immediately after the *Tesco* decision, the Law Commission considered the position of the law in this area. They examined possible reforms and questioned the moral justification for prosecuting corporate bodies, concluding by generally approving the law as it then stood, i.e. immediately post *Tesco* (Burles 1991: 611). This was at the very beginning of the process by which companies were brought within the jurisdiction of the ordinary criminal law. Between 1965 and 1995, 20 000 people were killed in incidents at work or in disasters like the capsize of the *Herald of Free Enterprise* and the King's Cross Underground Fire. In most of these cases, companies were to blame for allowing unnecessary danger, yet

there have only ever been five prosecutions for corporate manslaughter
and only two convictions (Slapper 1997: JPIL 224).

In its report *Legislating the Criminal Code: Involuntary Manslaughter*, The
Law Commission recommends a new offence of 'corporate killing' (see
Chapter 8, post and Slapper (1997) JPIL 223–4).

Conclusion

The law has advanced significantly from the time when one judge
(quoted above) noted that a company enjoyed immunity from prosecution as 'it had no soul to damn and no body to kick' (attributed to Lord
Thurlow, quoted in Leigh 1969: 4).

We have noted that since its early development from the Roman Law
principle of *societas*, the commercial corporate body has enjoyed significant legal privileges. Government found it useful to allow commercial
companies engaged in overseas trade and exploration to act on its behalf
– thus from the outset corporations had the advantages of various forms
of legal protection.

In the nineteenth century, a period of rapid economic development,
companies organising major projects like road building and the construction of the railways, could have been liable on a grand scale for the deaths
and injuries occurring within their industries. They *could* have been liable
(and thus deterred from engaging in such projects) were the ordinary
principles of civil liability to have been applied, but they were not liable in
a great many of the potential cases. This was because legal doctrines were
developed which had a notably artificial way of blocking liability.

One defence afforded to company defendants was that no legal injury
could be done to someone who volunteered to the risk. This defence
meant that injured workers were not entitled to damages for injuries
resulting from dangerous work which they were deemed to have consented to by accepting the employment. Another defence protecting
corporations was that of contributory negligence, by which even the
smallest element of carelessness on the worker's part barred him or her
from suing the company however grave its own negligence had been. A
third type of shield given to corporate defendants in personal injury cases
was the doctrine of common employment, under which an injured
worker was not able to sue if his/her injury was actually inflicted through
a co-worker.

The civil law was thus being developed to offer support and protection
to companies. The policy was created on an *ad hoc* basis, judgement by
judgement, not as part of any grand conspiracy but its effects were clear.

Gradually the law came to recognise that companies could be indicted
for crimes. At first this process involved only a recognition of corporate
crime where the offence in question arose from the omission to carry out

a positive duty imposed by statute, but, over time, the capacity of companies to commit most crimes was acknowledged in law. Although there are now many debates about the precise legal formulae that should be used to determine whether a company has behaved criminally (e.g. should we need to find at least one guilty mind at directorial level, or should we just judge the company by the outcome of its conduct?), the point of central importance is that companies are now seen legally (and socially) as units capable of crime.

Today, as we have noted, companies are socially ubiquitous and are regularly identified in newspapers, radio broadcasts, and television documentaries as responsible for crimes involving fraud, pollution, dishonesty, corruption, and offences against health and safety. They are, moreover, also now being prosecuted to conviction as culprits. In the following two chapters we examine the scale and cost of corporate crime.

Chapter 3

Mapping and measuring the extent of corporate crime

Introduction

In the first two chapters of this text we have sought to introduce corporate crime as a concept (Chapter 1), and to place both the development of this concept and the phenomenon which it attempts to signify in an historical context (Chapter 2). In this chapter, we begin to document empirically just what kinds of actions and omissions constitute corporate crime, and how much corporate crime actually occurs. More specifically, the chapter is devoted to a review of literature which has sought to measure and map the extent, nature and range of corporate crimes. We begin by referring to some of the key quantitative attempts at such mapping, before turning to discuss a more varied, and indeed richer, qualitative tradition. Through the material presented in these two sections, we seek to demonstrate that corporate crimes are widespread and pervasive; they are certainly neither peripheral to corporate activity nor, as some would have it (Bardach and Kagan 1982; Hawkins 1990, 1991), confined to a few irresponsible 'bad apples'.

We should also state at the outset of the chapter that our original aim in this chapter was to focus here upon work originating from, or examining, Britain. While we focus upon British work in this chapter, to have relied upon this exclusively would have made for a much shorter, more limited, chapter. In other words, one of the other facts that this chapter highlights in relation to corporate crime research is that it remains the case that the vast majority of work which exists on corporate and organisational offences continues to be North American in origin, and tends to focus upon this geographical context (Punch 1996: 52). Thus Levi's comment upon the relative paucity of work in this area in Britain, made in 1987, remains as accurate today as it did then: 'In Britain, business crime has been neglected by most academics and activists on the left as well as those on the right' (1987: xx). Thus while the following makes particular reference to British work, it will be clear to readers that much of what is discussed originates from, and more problematically is based in, US experience.

The extent of corporate crime: Sutherland and the quantitative tradition

Despite the fact that there have now been several attempts to assess quantitatively the extent of corporate crime, two studies are of paradigmatic importance. We shall begin by discussing these, before moving on to briefly note some other efforts at quantification of the incidence of corporate and organisational offending, turning them to examine some of the more recent, qualitative efforts in this sphere.

The first large-scale attempt at mapping the extent of corporate violations was, unsurprisingly given what was said in Chapter 1 relating to his pathbreaking work, undertaken by Sutherland. Sutherland examined decisions against the '70 largest manufacturing, mining and mercantile corporations' (1983: 13) – excluding public utility, transport, communications and petroleum companies – since their dates of origin. This analysis also examined decisions taken against the subsidiaries of these corporations (*ibid.*), though these are under-recorded given that many of these subsidiaries could not be identified (*ibid.*: 15); this latter point may be of particular contemporary significance in attempts to map corporate crime, given the trends towards fragmentation of corporate forms, the increased use of sub-contracting, strategic alliances, joint business ventures, and so on (Tombs 1995a), and we shall address these issues in greater detail in Chapters 7 and 8. Sutherland's focus is a limited one, examining violations in relation to restraint of trade, advertising, infringements of patent, trademarks and copyrights, and labour practices, drawing upon a range of publicly available sources. Thus he is clear that his record of decisions is substantially incomplete (1983: 14–15). Nevertheless, Sutherland's data revealed that each of the corporations had one or more decisions against it, the maximum being 50, the minimum being one (on the part of two corporations) and the average number being 14 (*ibid.* 1983: 15–18). We have already seen, in Chapter 1, that Sutherland would reject the objection that many of these decisions did not constitute 'real' crime because they had been taken by civil courts and administrative commissions. But he also noted that even if one limited the data set to decisions taken by criminal courts,

> it would show that 60 of the large corporations have been convicted in criminal courts and have an average of approximately four convictions each. In many states persons with four convictions are defined by statute to be 'habitual criminals'. . . .

> (*ibid.*: 23)

This latter observation is interesting in the light of developments in both the US and, more latterly, in the UK towards 'three strikes' laws, not least for the fact that such laws could, but do not, apply to corporate offenders (Geis 1996).

Sutherland's analysis is supplemented by a similar exercise in relation to the 'fifteen largest power and light corporations' (Sutherland 1983: 202), a group for whom he retains particular vehemence, referring to them as 'refractory and ungovernable' (*ibid.*: 201) and comparing their concerted efforts at manipulating political, regulatory and public relationships to Nazi propaganda (*ibid.*: 221). However, Sutherland reveals a range of adverse decisions against these corporations, noting that many of these cannot legitimately be used as firm proof of criminality, and that available data fails to 'provide an accurate index of the violations of law by these corporations' (*ibid.*: 205).

It was almost 30 years before there emerged any attempt to replicate the type of study undertaken by Sutherland. Although there was considerable US-based work on *white-collar* crime following Sutherland's initial statements on this subject, the issue of *corporate* crime was almost wholly untouched: academic research during the period up to the mid-1970s largely consisted of empirical studies of crimes by people of respectable status in particular occupational contexts (Geis *et al.* 1995: 4–5). Following this period was a post-McCarthyite, cold war decade during which there was 'an abrupt disappearance of social science interest in white-collar crime' (*ibid.*: 5), a silence broken with a return to interest in the 'crimes of the powerful' (Pearce 1976) which emerged in the context of the establishment of a radical, or critical, criminology. This latter development needs to be seen in a wider socio-political context, one in which there was an upsurge of a range of protests movements against 'big business and capitalist social relations that dominate in corporate America' (Kramer 1989: 147), these protests including the 'civil rights movement, organised labour, consumer advocates, women's groups and environmentalists' (*ibid.*: 146–7). Thus Katz has argued that the 1970s was a decade which saw the emergence of a social movement against white-collar crime (1980); of course, such an observation, even if accurate – and Katz's arguments are hardly uncontestable – relate specifically to the US, and certainly could not be applied to Britain.

In the mid-1970s, then, a large-scale empirical study of corporate crime was conducted by Clinard and others (Clinard *et al.* 1979; Clinard and Yeager 1980). When made widely available in published form, in 1980, Clinard and Yeager pronounced – correctly – this study to be 'the first large-scale comprehensive investigation of the law violations of major firms since Sutherland's pioneering work' (Clinard and Yeager 1980: 110). The study is based upon records of administrative, civil and criminal actions either initiated or completed by 25 federal agencies against 582 of the world's largest manufacturing, wholesale, retail and service corporations across a two year period (1975–76), though it did not extend to the numerous subsidiaries of any of these parent corporations. Of course, even if these corporations are among the largest, this figure of 582 is only a small sample of corporations in the US at the time of the study (estimated at two million; Young 1981: 324). A combination of the facts that their focus was upon formally recorded actions by 25 federal agencies, that the records of these agencies were incomplete (Clinard and Yeager 1980: 112), and that attempts to include state and local enforcement actions proved impossible (*ibid.*: 110), means that only a small proportion of detected violations are recorded in Clinard and Yeager's study. As the authors state, then, they are measuring 'minimal figures of government actions against major corporations' (*ibid.*: 112).

Despite these elements of under-recording, Clinard and Yeager found that,

> A total of 1,553 federal cases were begun against all 582 corporations during 1975 and 1976, or an average of 2.7 federal cases of violation each. Of the 582 corporations, 350 (60.1 percent) had at least one federal action brought against them, and for those firms that had at least one action brought against them, the average was 4.4 cases ... Only 33 (2.1 percent) of the actions instituted were later discovered to have been dismissed during the period covered by the study.
>
> (*ibid.*: 113)

These violations were of six main types:

> *administrative violations*   non-compliance with agency or court requirements, for example failure to obey an agency 'order to institute a recall or to construct pollution control facilities', and various 'paperwork violations';
> *environmental violations*   air and water pollution, violations of permits;
> *financial violations*   illegal payments, issuing of false statements/ information, various transaction offences, and tax violations;
> *labour violations*   discrimination in employment, health and safety violations, unfair labour practices wage/hour violations;
> *manufacturing violations*   mainly related to product safety, labelling and the provision of information, and product defects; and
> *unfair trade practices*   various competition offences, as well as false advertising (*ibid.*: 113–16).

The findings of Clinard and Yeager are similar to those of Sutherland, in that both studies provide clear empirical evidence that violations are widespread amongst even the largest and seemingly most 'respectable' of corporations. Other subsequent, somewhat similar, attempts to measure the incidence of corporate and organisational offending via quantitative analysis of large data sets have confirmed these albeit highly generalised conclusions. For example, Bilimoria (1995) reports upon a study of recorded filings (initiated proceedings) and violations (negative judgements) against 91 of the Fortune 500 in the three years between 1984 and 1986. (The sample was based upon selecting every fifth Fortune 500 company, the lack of published accounts reducing the original sample from 100 to 91.) Data on violations included unfair trade violations, product violations, environmental violations and labour violations (and was taken from corporate 10K statements and the Wall Street Journal Index). Of the 91 firms examined, 58.2 per cent were found to have at least one filing against them, and 25.3 per cent had at least one violation, in the three year period. Jamieson (1994) examined all recorded anti-trust charges against the America's Fortune 500 during the five year period from 1981 to 1985 (combining this with an attempt to explain the distribution of charges across these companies), finding that in this five year period there were 242 cases filed for antitrust violations which named 166 of the Fortune 500 companies, 277 times (Jamieson 1994: 40, and passim; see also Ross 1980).

Despite the importance and strengths of these quantitative surveys of recorded violations, there are also some problems or weaknesses with these that need to be noted.

First, given the nature of the sample corporations, then the surveys are biased towards larger corporations. Indeed, they tell us little or nothing about the distribution of offences amongst organisations; Braithwaite has noted that they have not proved very important for correlational analysis, tending to produce rather contradictory answers to questions about which types of organisations generate crime (Braithwaite 1995: 120). Further, these studies focus upon the incidence of offences on the part of the largest private corporations (as indeed does the vast majority of qualitative and quantitative work on corporate crime; Vaughan 1992: 128–9). While there are some theoretical reasons for expecting a greater incidence of offences on the part of larger corporations, there are also relevant factors pulling in the opposite direction (see Chapters 6 and 7). At the same time that there is certainly a need for an empirical and theoretical focus upon smaller companies, as urged by some more recent commentators (Croall 1989; Pearce 1990b; Sutton and Wild 1985), there are good methodological reasons why such surveys are likely to prove problematic, given the relative invisibility and sheer ubiquitousness of smaller business organisations.

Second, given that both Sutherland and Clinard and colleagues focused upon the distribution of offences amongst US-based companies, there is also a problem in simply extrapolating from this data to include corporations operating in other national jurisdictions; there may be material or cultural factors specific to US companies or the US economy and polity which affect the incidence of offending.

Third, the data used, and conclusions reached, by such surveys have a problematic relationship to time. The studies cited tend to take offences recorded within a given time period – for Sutherland, this was the life-time of the corporations in question, for Clinard et al. a two year period, for Jamieson a five year period, and so on. Thus they do not tell us about the annual volume of offending, which is the time period within which other crime data is usually organised. Nor do these data allow us to say anything about longitudinal trends in such forms of offending; and given that one key aim of providing data on crime seems to be to isolate and then attempt to explain differential crime *rates*, this is another aspect in which such datasets are inadequate. (These issues are explored further below, and in Chapter 4).

These points being made, the work of Sutherland and Clinard and colleagues remains enormously significant. One crucial effect of each was to demonstrate 'to a disbelieving world that the biggest and best companies are widely involved in criminality' (Braithwaite 1995: 120), so that both quantitative surveys had 'polemical significance' (*ibid.*). Thus of the conclusions reached and implications drawn by Clinard and colleagues, Young – despite being generally critical of the research – notes that 'All in all, the study shows crime to be endemic in business life. Indeed, it is a way of life' (Young 1981: 324). This work at least allows us, then, to conclude that corporate crime seems to be widespread and pervasive. As Sutherland himself emphasised, 'These crimes are not discrete and inadvertent violations of technical regulations. They are deliberate and have a relatively consistent unity' (Sutherland 1983: 227). Thus he argues that the criminality of the corporations within his study is 'persistent: a large proportion of the offenders are recidivist. Among the 70 largest industrial and commercial corporations in the United States, 97.1 percent were found to be recidivists in the sense of having two or more adverse decisions' (Sutherland 1983: 227).

In other words, based on this brief review of some quantitative evidence, corporate crime appears to be widespread and pervasive. That being said, the points noted above indicate that this type of work can be a starting point only. While 'the poverty of existing data sets' makes it 'doubtful ... that future scholars will be able to advance much on it' (Braithwaite 1995: 120), even the unlikely luxury of extensive data would only be of limited use given the need to move beyond empirical description of corporate offending. Reference to, and manipulation of, large data sets is of some use in understanding corporate and organisational offending, but to remain too wedded to such exercises is ultimately to become trapped within an empiricist social science.

The extent of corporate crime: the qualitative tradition

It is possible to identify three general types of qualitative studies of corporate crime, all of which utilise some form of the case study approach. These approaches – which take a particular offence, category of offences, or industry as their focus – are important since, as Braithwaite has argued, case studies are 'most likely to advance our understanding of corporate crime as a social phenomenon' (Braithwaite 1984: 7; Coleman

1987: 429). As we shall make clear in this section, this case study work does facilitate, but certainly does not constitute, the shift from description to explanation.

Case studies of crimes

The most specific level of corporate crime research, and indeed the basis upon which more generalised work relating to categories of offence and industry-wide studies has been based, is that which has been conducted in relation to *discrete crimes or groups of crimes*. Typically, these have been large-scale in nature, that is, involving significant amounts of financial loss, or large numbers of victims (most commonly, consumers, employees, or local residents), or with particularly symbolic political or popular effects. These studies go beyond stating the 'facts' of particular cases, but generally involve detailed post hoc social scientific reconstruction of events and processes surrounding a particular crime or group of crimes; somewhat differently, some of these studies are based upon intimate, after the event accounts by whistle-blowers or investigative journalists. The result is generally a detailed case history which facilitates under-standing of the processes by which corporate crimes emerge, occur, and are responded to.

Particularly of note here are the case studies of the Goodrich Brake Scandal, involving the falsification of testing data in order to meet deadlines for the production of braking systems for American airforce planes (Vandivier 1982); the Heavy Electrical Equipment Anti-Trust cases, 'flagrant criminal offences' involving a simple conspiracy to fix prices in which 29 corporations were implicated, including the two largest companies in the heavy electrical equipment industry, GEC and Westing-house (Geis 1967); the tragedies of Thalidomide (Knightley *et al.* 1980) and the Dalkon Shield (Finlay 1996; Mintz 1985; Perry and Dawson 1985), two of many case histories in which pharmaceutical companies both concealed and at the same time long contested evidence regarding the injurious 'side-effects' of their products, resulting in thousands of deaths, physical deformities and long-term illnesses; the leak of a cyanide-based gas at the Bhopal chemical plant, which was responsible for the greatest-ever acute and chronic loss of life associated with a single industrial event, not to mention the incalculable and enduring chronic health effects (Jones 1988; Pearce and Tombs 1989, 1993); the Savings and Loans Crimes, which have been referred to as 'the costliest set of white-collar crimes in history' (Pontell and Calavita 1993: 32), and for which the American taxpayer is likely to be paying well into the next century (Black *et al.* 1995; Calavita and Pontell 1995; Tillman *et al.* 1997); the decision to proceed with the production and sale of the Ford Pinto, despite knowledge within the company of an inherent design fault which would result in loss of life and serious injury, a fault which was not remedied following a cost-benefit calculation setting the costs of design changes alongside the costs of compensation for death and injury (Cullen *et al.* 1987; Dowie 1977); the explosion of the *Challenger* spacecraft, in which NASA and the private corporation Morton Thiokol Inc. were implicated in creating this 'disaster' (Kramer 1992; Vaughan 1996); and the development, nature and phases of implementation of the so-called 'Superfund' legislation in the US, a legislative programme to secure industry funded clean ups of polluted lands (Barnett 1994, 1995). Reference to, and discussion of, these, and other 'classic' studies, can usefully be found in collections of case study readers on corporate crimes (see, for example, Ermann and Lundman, eds 1982, 1992; Geis *et al.*, eds 1995; Hills, ed., 1987; and Pearce and Snider, eds 1995). In addition to this work, the vast majority of which either emanates from, or focuses upon, the United States, there has also been a limited amount of research on a number of cases which have a predominantly British element, such as: the Maxwell pensions saga (Bower 1995; Punch 1996); the Bank of Credit and Commerce International (Passas 1996); the fall of Barings Bank and the role of trader Leeson (Punch 1996); the illegal share dealings associated with the takeover bid by Guinness of Distillers, in which Morgan Grenfell and Woodmac were also heavily implicated (Punch 1996); the sinking of the gruesomely named ferry the *Herald of Free Enterprise* in Zeebrugge harbour, which killed 154 passengers and 38 crew, and resulted in a failed attempt to pursue a case of corporate manslaughter (Wells 1993, 1995; Bergman 1994); and the fire and explosion on the Piper Alpha oil installation, which killed 167 offshore workers (Woolfson *et al.* 1996; Whyte *et al.* 1996; Lavalette and Wright 1991). These latter cases are, for the most part, much less developed than the classic, mostly US based, case studies cited previously; but they do form the basis for what might prove to be a useful body of work on British-based corporate crimes.

Categories/types of crimes

Frequently, studies of corporate crimes take as their focus a group or type of offence. Such a categorisation was utilised by Sutherland and by Clinard and Yeager in their quantitative work, as we have seen, and has been adopted by many qualitative researchers in, as well as many commentators upon, corporate crime. The bases for such categorisation is usually a hybrid of the types of law at issue (antitrust, employment legislation, and so on) and the identification of victims (the natural environment, consumers, and so on). Amongst these various categorisations, four are perhaps most frequently used, namely: various forms of financial offences (fraud and theft, antitrust, tax evasion); offences against consumers; crimes against employees and employment protection; and various environmental offences. In essence, what we have here are *categories* or *types of corporate crimes*.

First, a variety of studies have focused upon a range of financial crimes.

This rubric clearly encompasses a vast array of offences, but includes the following: illegal share dealings, mergers, and takeovers; tax evasion; transfer pricing, namely the particular form of tax evasion whereby corporations operating across national boundaries are able to arrange transfers of funds internally – for example, by inflated or fictional payments for goods and services from one part of the organisation to another, thereby reducing tax liabilities in higher tax jurisdictions, increasing them in lower tax jurisdictions (clearly such activity is most likely in multinational conglomerates); bribery; and other forms of illegal accounting.

There is hardly a lack of cases of financial crimes in or affecting Britain which might form the basis of empirical and theoretical work – recent years have witnessed a series of high profile financial crimes, including, but not confined to, those involving the Sumitomo Copper Corporation and its relationship to Winchester Copper, Brent Walker, Barlow Clowes, Morgan Grenfell, Polly Peck, Barings, Natwest, the Maxwells and BCCI (Passas 1996; Lever 1992; Levi 1993a, 1993, 1995; Punch 1996; Buckle and Thompson 1995). More recently, there has emerged particular research interest in fraud against the European Union, some of which implicates corporations and in which there is clearly British interest as a member state (Clarke 1993; Passas and Nelken 1993).

However, there is relatively little work on financial crimes in the UK. What there is has been conducted by a small group of active researchers, most notable amongst whom are Michael Levi and Michael Clarke. In 1981, Levi examined the activities and control of the 'Phantom Capitalists' engaged in long-firm fraud, whereby bogus businesses are established as a means of obtaining large goods on credit from manufacturers. Later, Levi (1987) was to examine the nature, incidence and regulation of various forms of fraud, focusing largely on Britain but also with reference to Europe and North America (see also Levi 1993, 1995). At the time of writing, a new text is due to appear by Levi which promises to develop some of the themes of his 1987 work, in an attempt to estimate the extent of fraud, to examine its effects, and to consider how this form of crime is represented through popular media and understood by general publics (Levi and Pithouse, forthcoming; see also Levi and Pithouse 1992). Clarke's (1986) study of the City of London in general, and of banking, insurance and the stock exchange in particular, pays close attention to the context, nature and implications of regulatory reform. There have also been British based studies of tax evasion (Cook 1989; McBarnet 1991, 1992a, 1992b; see also Levi 1987). Beyond these examples, the vast majority of work has been conducted in the North America. Particularly noteworthy amongst the latter has been Shapiro's (1984) study of the 'wayward capitalists' engaged on securities fraud in the US, and examinations of antitrust violations. (See, for example, Bork 1978 and Jamieson 1994. Other studies of various financial crimes in the US include Auletta 1986; Simpson 1987; Stone 1991; Szockyi 1993. On Australia, see Grabosky, ed. 1992; on Canada, see Goff and Reasons 1978; for a comparative work on Britain and the US, see Freyer 1992.)

A second general area of crimes involves those which are committed directly against consumers. Examples here include illegal sales/market-ing practices, the sale of unsafe/unfit goods, such as adulterated food, cartel pricing and price leadership, false/illegal labelling or information, and the fraudulent safety testing of products. Of particular note in terms of the research in this area of corporate crime are early studies by Paulus (1974) on the regulation of 'pure food', Cranston's study of the enforce-ment of Consumer Protection legislation (1979), research by Hutter on the work of Environmental Health Officers (1986, 1988), and work on 'small businesses' and corporate crimes which has tended to focus upon trading standards and weights and measures offences (Croall 1988, 1989; and also see Croall 1992: 35–9, for some important insights drawn from an earlier piece of her own unpublished work in this area).

Thirdly, we can identify crimes arising out of the employment relation-ship, that is, crimes against employees (or potential employees in the case of recruitment and selection offences) by employers. These include cases of sexual and racial discrimination and other offences against employment protection; violations against wage laws; and violations against rights to organise, take various forms of industrial action, and so on. Of particular interest in the latter respect is the extent to which these types of crimes have been eradicated through the dismantling of regulations – thus while there is a rather flippant tendency to speak of the 1980s and beyond as the era of deregulation in the UK, while this is more accurately a period characterised by widescale re-regulation, there is no doubt that in the area of employment legislation deregulation has been thoroughgoing and has had profound effects (the effect of deregulation on the employment relationship has been documented recently in Ewing, ed. 1996).

Added to the above are a whole range of offences against employee occupational health and safety, such as failures to provide information and training, illegal workplace exposures, and failures to provide or maintain safe plant and/or equipment. This general offence category is of interest since there has been a relatively recent attempt to focus on British workplaces as a site of health and safety offences against employ-ees. Some of this has tended to focus upon the issue of corporate manslaughter, while other work has a somewhat wider focus. Never-theless, two classic sets of studies in this context, both emanating from Britain, are worth mentioning.

The first is a series of papers by Kit Carson on the 'conventionalisation' of factory crime in Britain (1970a, 1970b, 1974, 1979, 1980b). In these papers, Carson documents the emergence of a regulatory structure which was to prove crucial for the viability of early industrial capitalism in Britain. Part of this process (or, perhaps more accurately, series of struggles) whereby the first major intrusion of the criminal law into the 'private' sphere of work – the 'factory' – was subject to material and ideological initiatives to the point where what might have been marked out as an area of 'real' crime by legislation in fact came to form the classic instance of what Sutherland referred to as violations considered only to be *mala prohibita*. This work by Carson also prompted a critical response from Bartrip and Fenn (1980), who, writing from the Centre for Socio-Legal Studies, Woolfson College, Oxford, strangely presaged a later debate on regulation (see Chapter 8) by arguing that the failure to enforce the criminal law was explained by the constraints within which inspectors found themselves working. Carson's rejoinder demonstrated that Bartrip and Fenn's critique had in many respects provided unwitting support for his earlier argument (Carson 1980).

The second important study, also conducted by Carson, was his classic study of motivated regulatory failure in the UK offshore oil industry from its inception though to the early 1980s (1982). This focus was, as we have also already noted, expanded upon and brought up to date in the recent work of Woolfson and others (Woolfson *et al.* 1996; Woolfson and Beck 1997; Whyte *et al.* 1996; Whyte and Tombs 1998), even though their most common explicit focus was not on crime *per se*.

In addition to Carson's work on the factory inspectorate and on the regulation of offshore safety there has emerged a body of British work on the part of Bergman (1991, 1993, 1994), Pearce (1990a; Pearce and Tombs 1993, 1997), Tombs (1995, 1996), Slapper (1993) and Wells (1995a, 1995b), all of which has taken some aspect of health and safety crime as a key focus. In sum, this, added to the work of Carson and others, constitutes a surprisingly large body of British research on a particular aspect of corporate crime. Moreover, much of this work is relatively recent. There are perhaps several factors which might help to explain the relative upsurge in interest in health and safety offences as crimes which occurred in Britain in the latter part of the 1980s, and which is continuing. One reason is surely to be found in the fact that through his pioneering work, Carson marked out issues of occupational safety and health as legitimate criminological and sociological concerns. Second, and relatedly, was the enormous influence of Box's chapter on 'corporate crime'. This appeared in a book, *Power, Crime and Mystification,* which, for a long period, was 'the only student criminology text in Britain to incorporate such material' (Levi 1987: xx). And in this chapter, Box included discussion of health and safety crimes, and in particular referred extensively to, and indeed elaborated upon, the arguments based on occupational safety and health data made by Reiman (1979). A final reason for this particular area of interest might simply have been the surprisingly sharp upturn in recorded levels of occupational deaths and injuries that occurred in Britain from around 1980 onwards (Tombs 1990), followed in the latter half of the decade by a spate of large-scale disasters (Slapper 1993; Tombs 1995b; Wells 1995); each served to raise corporate offending in this sphere as a political issue, and surely served to highlight this as an area of academic concern.

A fourth, and final, category of offence is that of crimes against the environment, which would include illegal emissions to air, water, and land, the failure to provide, or the provision of false, information, hazardous waste dumping, and illegal manufacturing practices. In this area of environmental crimes more than in any of the other offence categories identified, there is a striking dearth of British based research. Certainly the enforcement of environmental regulations proved to be one of the earliest concerns of socio-legal researchers with an agenda to examine business regulation, based around the Centre for Socio-Legal Studies, Oxford (whom we shall discuss in Chapter 8). Thus Richardson and colleagues (Richardson *et al.* 1983), and then Hawkins (1984), both published major empirical studies of the work of regulators enforcing environmental law, a concern returned to by Yeager (1991) and more recently by another of the researchers associated with the Oxford School of academics (Hutter 1997). Beyond these works, there really is very little on environmental crimes *per se* emanating from Britain, an observation all the more curious given the stark contrast with the volume of North American work in this area (South 1998).

In the US in particular, there is a large and growing body of research evidence which attests to the fact that environmental crimes are routine and ubiquitous, focusing upon the dumping of hazardous wastes (Block 1993; Bullard 1990; Cass 1996; Szasz 1984, 1986c), crimes of environmental destruction, notably of forests and landscapes (Paehlke 1995), and crimes involving illegal emissions into land, air and waterways (Hyatt and Trexler 1996; Ross 1996; but from Britain, see Howarth 1991). These are only particular instances of a large body of work on environmental crimes more generally, including DiMento 1986; Edwards *et al.*, eds, 1996; Hofrichter 1993; National Institute of Justice 1993; Williams, ed. 1996). One particular aspect of this work has been to focus on the relationships between legitimate businesses and organised crime, for example in the sub-contracting from the former to the latter of the dumping of toxic wastes (Block and Scarpitti 1985; Ruggiero 1996). Amongst other issues, this latter focus raises key questions regarding the effects of, and corporate responses to, stricter regulation, to be addressed in Chapter 7.

Industry-specific case studies

Finally, in addition to, or one further aspect of, the above work is one further type of case study, that which takes as its focus a specific industry or sector. However, despite the fact that this type of work can do much to further our knowledge about both the extent and the causal dynamics of corporate crime, there remain few genuine *industry-wide case studies*.

Most notable amongst these are the following: a collection of articles examining the automobile industry as a criminogenic industrial structure (Farberman 1975; Leonard and Weber 1970; Nader 1965; Seid 1978; and see Needleman and Needleman 1979); a recent 'political economy' of corporate crime associated with the chemicals industries (Pearce and Tombs 1998); studies of the tendencies towards, and problems of regulating, crime in the financial services sector (Clarke 1986; Shapiro 1984; Levi 1981, 1987); a body of work on the (failures of) regulation of the UK offshore oil industry (Carson 1982; Coleman 1985; Molotch 1973; Woolfson *et al.* 1996; Whyte and Tombs 1998); and a series of texts and papers on crimes in and of the pharmaceutical industry (Braithwaite 1984, 1993; Finlay 1996; Peppin 1995). It is perhaps no coincidence that these industries have provided important objects of inquiry. Clinard and colleagues had found in their quantitative analysis of violations (Clinard *et al.* 1979; Clinard and Yeager 1980) that the industries in which companies were most likely to violate the law were oil, pharmaceuticals and the motor vehicle industries (Clinard and Yeager 1980: 119–22). The chemicals industry is one that is intimately related to both the oil and pharmaceuticals sectors, with most chemicals companies having significant interests in either or both of these other industries. Finally, a focus upon financial services is also an unsurprising one: there are good reasons for believing that in this sector more than most – given that its business is largely the circulation of various forms of financial assets – the opportunity structure for criminal activity and omission is greatest (on the importance of opportunity structures in understanding corporate crime, see Chapters 6 and 7).

The classic work of this industry case study genre is surely Braithwaite's (1984) study of corporate crime in the pharmaceutical industry. This provides a powerful documentation of the sheer range of crimes in which companies may be engaged or implicated. Braithwaite reveals common practices of bribery, negligent and fraudulent safety testing of drugs, unsafe manufacturing practices, antitrust violations, the illegal promotion of licit drugs, dumping and testing of drugs on 'Third World' populations, and various forms of financial illegalities (including fraud and transfer pricing) which he summarises simply as 'fiddling', each of which forms the subject of a chapter in this detailed study. Even within each of these general categories, then, there are a whole range of different forms of illegal activity and omission. Thus, in a later piece summarising some of the key findings of that earlier study of crime in the pharmaceutical industry, Braithwaite noted that:

> bribery is probably a larger problem in the pharmaceutical industry than in almost any other industry. Of the 20 largest American pharmaceutical companies, 19 had been embroiled in bribery problems during the decade before the publication of the book ... Product safety offences such as the sale of impure, over-strength, out-of-date or nonsterile products were also shown to be widespread. Anti-trust offences kept some of the wonder drugs financially out of the reach of most if the world's population for many years, causing countless lives to be lost needlessly. Misrepresentations in printed word and by word of mouth were common offences ... The pharmaceutical industry also had its share of tax offenders and fraudsters who duped

shareholders and creditors. But the most serious corporate crimes in the
pharmaceutical industry were, and still are, in the safety testing of drugs.

(1995: 13)

The significance and impact of Braithwaite's work was surely height-
ened by the almost simultaneous publication of two other texts on crime
and the pharmaceutical industry: Morton Mintz (1985) detailed the case
of the Dalkon Shield, while Stanley Adams provided a moving account of
his victimisation at the hands of the company on whom he 'blew the
whistle', namely Hoffman-la-Roche (1984). The combined effect of these
three texts was surely to inspire subsequent focus upon the industry. A
decade later, Peppin was to examine the industry from the point of view
of its particular victimisation of women. She documents the 'serious
adverse reactions, involving harm on a mass basis, [which] have occurred
when women's health needs have been targeted by drug companies'
(1995: 90). Thus she notes that '(d)evastating harm' has resulted from:
inadequate warnings of the risk of stroke and death from contraceptives;
poor labelling pertaining to the risk of toxic shock syndrome from
tampons; the marketing of diethylstilbestrol [DES]; AH Robins Co.'s
ignoring of warnings about the Dalkon Shield; and 'perhaps the best
known example', Thalidomide (*ibid.*: 90–1). Similar issues are addressed
in detail by Lucinda Finlay through studies of DES and the Dalkon Shield,
two products which, she notes, were developed not in response to disease,
but 'for use in healthy women to enhance what nature had provided or to
control the natural processes of reproduction' (1996: 59). Other well-
known case studies of pharmaceutical industry products have been
developed, including work on breast implants, weight loss products, MER
29 (triparanol), Thalidomide and Opren. Perhaps slightly less well-known
is the work of Abraham (1995), which examines the ways in which drugs
companies are able to produce scientific and regulatory decisions in their
favour, and that of Walker (1994), which charts the organised (and often
illegal) opposition of the industry against alternative treatments. Both are
important sources of material for any study of corporate crime in the
pharmaceutical industry. All in all, this work amounts to a significant,
indeed unique, body of literature on the crimes of a particular industry.

Conclusion: the state of corporate crime research

What are we to make of this overview of some of the academic research
that has been conducted into corporate crime? Several general comments
are worth making by way of a conclusion to this section.

First, despite the qualitative work reviewed briefly here being problematic in many respects (see below), it does, as a body of work, have two
important, and related, merits: it provides detailed insight into the
enormous range of offences in which corporations and organisations can

and do become implicated, from the well-known to the obscure, from the 'trivial' to the more obviously serious; and while Sutherland, Clinard and colleagues, and others sought to establish on the basis of quantitative evidence that *corporate crime is widespread and pervasive*, this qualitative work reinforces the fact that this offending results from almost every business activity, in almost every area of economic activity, amongst corporations and organisations of all sizes. While these points may seem relatively trivial, they are in fact of great ideological and material significance in the context of debates regarding the regulation and sanctioning of corporate and organisational offenders, and we shall return to them in Chapters 8 and 9.

A second general conclusion bears out a point that we have made several times in this text already. As this review has indicated, the overwhelming majority of corporate crime material both emanates from, and relates to, the US. We have attempted to focus upon British work in this section, but there is a far greater volume of work which is both North American in origin and focus. As we have also already noted, the US focus of much of this work raises the issue of the extent to which we can generalise any empirical and theoretical insights regarding corporate crime to the British context. But this is just one particular aspect of the more general problems of generalisability and reliability which beset qualitative work on corporate crime.

One of the key aims in addressing particular crimes by corporations, or groups of offences, or developing industry case studies, is to seek to make generalisations from particular instances. For example, in respect of industry case studies, the usual modus operandi in such studies is to take the actions and omissions of a number of the largest corporations within this sector as a basis for making more general points about the industry/ sector as a whole. This is understandable, is usually done on the basis of carefully provided rationales or justifications, but must also be recognised as having its own inherent problems as a modus operandi: that is, such work, as do all forms of case studies, raises the issue of generalisability. This is perhaps particularly acute in the context of considerations of corporate crime – for, given the politicised nature of crime discourses, crime research may have as one aim an impact on public policy, while this is rendered less likely as 'the use of a case study can be diminished by a belief that the findings may be idiosyncratic' (Bryman 1988a: 88).

However, while there are a number of technical responses to the problem of generalisability, some of which have been adopted by corporate crime researchers – such as studying a range of cases within a given population, replicating case study research, or selecting 'typical cases' – there are also good reasons for accepting that the 'problem' of generalisation need not be as great as some have argued. Indeed, Bryman has argued that representations of this 'problem' entail 'a misunderstanding of the aims of such research' (1988a: 90). In particular, rather than seeking to generalise from case studies to populations or universes – for example, from the crimes of some drugs companies to all pharmaceutical companies, or indeed to all manufacturing companies or even all private corporations – 'the issue should be couched in terms of the generalisability of cases to theoretical propositions' (*ibid.*). Thus case study data are significant when the researcher, or some other researchers, seek 'to integrate them with a theoretical context' (*ibid.*: 91). Indeed, while case study work has been invaluable in the corporate crime research tradition, there remains a tendency for these studies to be treated in relative descriptive isolation, rather than as forming the basis for theoretical interrogation and development (see Chapters 6 and 7); they provide some of the raw material of theoretical development, but have been all too frequently under-exploited in this respect.

In the context of corporate crime research, there is also a further aspect to the issue of generalisability. We have seen, particularly in the context of industry case studies, that certain industries have proven to be the focus for much more corporate crime research than others. Thus we have noted a focus upon oil, pharmaceuticals, and automobile industries. Does this mean, as Clinard and others claimed on the basis of their quantitative data, that these industries are the 'most' criminogenic of all industries, so that greater criminological attention to these is so justified? Or is it simply the case that an impression that these are industries are more criminogenic is *created* by the more concentrated focus upon these industries?

For us, this is not a question that is likely to be resolved empirically. In other words, we cannot conclude whether or not these are the most criminogenic of all industries on the basis of the qualitative evidence provided in these studies alone (nor, indeed, in conjunction with the quantitative evidence available). Any conclusion regarding the propensity or otherwise of businesses in certain industries to engage in criminality is not something which is likely to be proven on the basis of 'more and better' evidence (not least for the fact that such an empiricism leads one into the irresolvable problems of positivist and empiricist knowledge). Rather, alongside the kind of empirical detail which such case studies provide there must also be theoretical development regarding the nature and causes of corporate crime (though there is no doubt that each of the above studies does also seek to advance our theoretical understanding). We address such questions in Chapters 6 and 7.

Leaving aside the issue of the inherent criminogenicity, or otherwise, of these industries, one reason why they have been a focus of attention may simply be that, even if corporate crime in these industries is not easily studied, the fact that they are dominated by large, transnational actors may make them easier to study than sectors where medium or smaller sized firms predominate. By dint of their size and scope of operations, the former are more visible, and thus are more likely to have their activities tracked by journalists, activists, and so on. Their activities are more likely to be exposed by other corporations or organisations, given the sheer scale of inter-organisational transactions involved in such enterprises. Moreover, formal enforcement actions taken against companies within global reputations are more likely to attract publicity. Finally, all things being equal, the larger the company then the greater and more widely felt the consequences of certain types of illegality. Thus, for example, if a local market trader sells contaminated foodstuffs, then no matter how horrendous the consequences these are likely to be relatively localised; the same illegality on the part of a large food retailer will, logically, affect a larger and more widely spread number of victims. If a local garage sells second hand cars with known defects, the size of the garage/dealership means that a relatively small number of customers are likely to meet death or injury whilst driving those cars as a result of the defect; indeed, offending on a relatively local and low level, might not even be traced back to a particular defect, with all incidents of death or injury being viewed discretely, as 'accidents' (see Chapters 4 and 5). By contrast, if a multinational car manufacturer produces and markets a car with an inherent defect, it is likely both that more customers will be affected, and that the knowledge of those effects will spread to the point where there is an emergent sense both of victimisation to a crime has been committed, and of the identity of the offender.

Clearly, then, the use of case studies raise issues of generalisability which have historically (and continue to) beset work around corporate offences. Further, generalisability is intimately related to the methodological issue of reliability. This latter issue is exposed in a further, specific way in relation to qualitative work around corporate crime. Much of the work highlighted above, particularly that which is based in case studies of particular offences, is devoted to actually attempting to demonstrate – by way of criminological or sometimes more general sociological argument – that the events being described actually constitute a crime. In other words, such case studies often – though not always – refer to an event or set of events which have not been formally processed as crimes through any criminal justice system. In this sense, they bring into criminological discourse that which Tappan, and others, clearly wish to exclude. Further, they rely upon modes of argumentation – sociological rather than legal – and rely upon sources of evidence – investigative journalism and whistle-blowing rather than (what is in contrast represented as) 'hard' academic research – which invites charges of politicisation, polemics, and moralising (for a somewhat scathing attack around precisely such points, see Shapiro 1983). Again, we have raised these points previously. But this review of qualitative evidence, as with the brief references to quantitative data, indicates how pervasive such questions are to the entire enterprise of corporate crime research.

Finally, and perhaps relatedly, the review of qualitative research highlights the omissions and limitations of academic criminology with respect to corporate crime. It is possible to construct case studies of offences, types of offence, or offending industries, as we have indicated. However, to do this, one must often trawl for evidence and source material beyond the confines of the discipline of criminology. Thus much of the work cited above is not criminological in nature, and some of it only addresses crimes by corporations tangentially rather than centrally. Thus, for example, almost none of the work referred to above on the UK offshore oil industry focuses upon crime *per se*; but these are works which uncover, or provide a wealth of detail on, criminal activity and omission by corporations under study. Indeed, research on, and evidence concerning, corporate crime, needs to be collated from a range of disciplines which have no explicit concern with what Garland has called the Lombrosian or governmental projects, and out of which contemporary criminology has emerged (Garland 1994). Thus much of the work highlighted above has not been done by criminologists. Moreover, any attempt to provide an overview of research on corporate crime – and this holds for Britain to a much greater extent than the US, where there is a more empirically based tradition of researching white-collar and corporate crime within the confines of criminology – would need to make reference to a whole range of areas of disciplinary activity, with empirical and theoretical evidence regarding the nature and incidence of corporate crime being based in business, management and organisational studies, economics, history, political economy, politics, and sociology, and which makes reference to substantive areas of study such as industrial relations, business ethics and or studies in the social responsibility of business, studies of regulation, science-technology policy, studies of corporate failures, disasters and crises, and studies of social movements and activist politics. Previewing our later argument somewhat, there is at least an indication here that one of the consequences of an academic study of corporate crime is a more general exposure of the failings of criminology as a viable 'science' (Ruggiero 1998).

Chapter 4

Counting and costing corporate crime

Introduction

In the previous chapter, we referred extensively to academic studies as our guide to the extent and pervasiveness of corporate crime. The fact that a key focus of academic work has been to attempt to *establish* empirically the incidence of such forms of offending indicates that there is a relative paucity of official data; indeed, what is remarkable about official data is the extent to which these reproduce a skewed notion of what constitutes crime and the crime problem (Reiman 1979; Box 1983). In this chapter, we review the nature, and limitations, of official data on corporate crime. We then turn to a review of official and quasi-official estimates of the relative costs of corporate and street crimes, summarising the best available evidence regarding the (economic) costs associated with corporate offences; notwithstanding the poverty of such data, a point which in itself we shall discuss as being of no little significance, it is clear that, in economic terms at least, the costs of corporate offences far outweigh those associated with so-called conventional or traditional crimes. By way of illustrating the significance of some of these points, we then present a brief case study of occupational accidents and ill-health, focusing in particular on estimates of the extent of occupationally caused fatalities and the proportion of these which do, or might, constitute crimes. We then conclude with a series of arguments regarding the nature of corporate crime victimisation. If Chapter 3 has indicated that corporate crime is widespread and pervasive, this chapter demonstrates that such crimes have far greater economic, physical and social costs than those associated with traditional crimes.

Corporate crime and official statistics

Quite simply, measures used to indicate the scale of the crime problem do not include reference to measures of corporate offences. As Reiner notes, 'when mention is made of *the* crime statistics what is usually meant is the annual publication by the Home Office Research and Statistics Department of the volume Criminal Statistics: England and Wales, and more particularly . . . "Notifiable offences recorded by the police"' (1996: 186). While the categorisation of notifiable offences in Scotland is slightly different (Young 1992), it is equally useless for measuring corporate offences, as it too focuses overwhelmingly upon conventional crimes. Even a cursory examination of the notifiable offences for England and Wales reveals the extent to which they focus upon conventional as opposed to corporate crimes. The first category, *Violent Crime*, consists of violence against the person, sexual offences, and robbery. Second is *Burglary*, which includes burglary in a dwelling and burglary other than in a dwelling. Third is *Theft and Handling of Stolen Goods*, made up of a number of offences, namely: theft from the person; theft of pedal cycle; theft from shops; theft from vehicle; theft of motor vehicle; vehicle crime; and other theft and handling of stolen goods. Three final categories are *Fraud and Forgery*, *Criminal Damages*, and *Other Notifiable Offences*.

It is clear that the sub-category 'violence against the person' could include some forms of corporate crimes, though does not. Rather differently, the category *Fraud and Forgery* will include some corporate crimes, namely frauds not treated by the Serious Fraud Office. This category is broken down into 'Fraud by company director', 'False Accounting', 'Other Fraud', 'Forgery, or use of false drug prescription' and 'Other Forgery'. Yet this still does not allow us to say anything useful about corporate crime. First, while the two categories 'Other Fraud' and 'Other Forgery' are by far the biggest in terms of numbers of offences, these are also the most general, far too vague to be of any use. Second, there is no means of making the distinction based upon this data between occupational and organisational crime, a distinction which we referred to as significant in Chapter 1. The dangers of using such data as an index of white-collar crime, let alone corporate crime, are all too evident in Hirschi and Gottfredson's sloppy use of similar, official US data, as Steffensmeier ably demonstrates regarding their 'analysis' of the FBI's Uniform Crime Reports (Steffensmeier 1989; Hirschi and Gottfredson 1987).

None of this is to deny the problems with, and inadequacies of, crime statistics for so-called traditional crimes. Yet, whether we like it or not, there is no doubt that one of the key means of defining or representing the seriousness or otherwise of certain forms of criminal activities is through reference to quantitative data, so that 'numbers' remain predominant as a 'descriptive medium' (Maguire 1997: 139) of the scale and distribution of, trends in, and the nature of the crime problem. If, as Maguire notes, 'a salient feature of almost all modern forms of discourse about crime is the emphasis placed upon terms associated with its quantification and measurement' (*ibid.*), then it is hardly surprising that corporate crimes 'do not feature in . . . debates about the "crime problem''' (Nelken 1994a: 355; Green 1990: 27). This is one of the ways in which corporate crimes are organised off crime, law and order agendas (see Chapter 5).

We have noted consistently that in both academic and political terms, there is far greater scrutiny of corporate crime in the US than is the case for Britain. So it is of relevance to note that in the US, too, official data on corporate crime is grossly inadequate. Almost 20 years ago, a massive and thorough study conducted by Reiss and Biderman for the US Department of Justice pointed clearly to the enormous difficulties of measuring 'white-collar crime' (Reiss and Biderman 1980). The problems that these two researchers pointed to seem no less relevant today, and even more relevant in the context of the UK as compared to the US. Indeed, to attempt to arrive at some overall figure for even for the incidence of one group of corporate offences in the UK, namely fraud, would require examination, dissection and re-categorisation of data from a whole range of bodies, including, the Police, the SFO, the European Commission, the British Retail Consortium, the Association of British Insurers, the Association of Payment Clearing Systems, the Credit Industry Fraud Avoidance Scheme, the Audit Commission, the Charity Commission, the Inland Revenue, and HM Treasury (see Levi and Pithouse 1992: 231–2 for a brief list of the bodies involved in regulating fraud in Britain). And if this is the case with fraud – which, as we shall see (in Chapter 5), is amongst the corporate offences with the highest political and legal profile – then the situation with other corporate crimes is even more problematic.

Further, while there are enormous problems with official recording of conventional crimes, a key means of supplementing and correcting these has been the use of self-report or victimisation surveys. The British Crime Survey, for example, has proven an important adjunct to official statistics, to the extent that the Home Office now sponsor such a survey on a bi-annual basis. Yet while attempts to measure how much corporate crime exists cannot begin from official crime statistics, nor does the BCS attempt to include questions on offences by corporations and other organisations. It is of interest, and a useful indicator of political priorities attached to different forms of offending (see Chapter 5), that the Home Office has sponsored a victimisation survey on crimes *against* business in England and Wales (Mirrlees-Black and Ross 1995), while research into such crimes in Scotland is currently being sponsored by the Scottish Office. More generally, there is little attempt to generate more accurate corporate crime data via victim-based reporting. Now, there are some real reasons for this, which relate to the very different relationships between offender and victim that tend to characterise corporate crimes when compared with conventional crimes. In the former, victims are often remote in time and space from the offender; they are frequently diffuse; they are often unaware of their status as victims (we shall discuss these issues at greater length in Chapter 4). However, there have been some attempts to measure such victimisation. Most notably, the Second Isling-

ton Crime Survey included questions relating to commercial crime, and
to health and safety and pollution offences. While we shall not enter into
a detailed discussion of these results here (but see Pearce 1990a), it is
worth noting simply that they do, indeed, indicate widespread victimisation to corporate crime. For example, of those respondents giving
definite answers about their experience of buying goods and services
during the previous twelve months: approximately 11 per cent had been
given misleading information; 21 per cent believed that they had been
deliberately overcharged; and 24 per cent had paid for what turned out to
be defective goods or services. By way of comparison, the same survey
indicated that during the same period, approximately 4 per cent of
respondents giving definite answers had a car stolen, 7 per cent suffered
from a burglary and 7 per cent from an actual or attempted theft from
their person. This indicates that the incidence of commercial crime is
high both relatively and absolutely.

For 'official' data on corporate crimes, then, one must turn to
regulatory bodies and data which are dispersed across both national and
regional offices. However, even here there are problems with the data
that are available. By way of illustrating some of the difficulties entailed in
the use of such data, and the extent to which the picture they produce is
drastically incomplete, we present below a case study in measuring one
type of corporate crime, namely crimes against employees' health and
safety. Through this case study, we will indicate that while one must turn
to regulatory bodies for 'official' data on corporate crimes, there are
overwhelming problems in the use of such data. Two points require
emphasis. First, such data provides a (skewed) under-estimate of the
extent of health and safety crimes. Second, to arrive at a more accurate
picture, one needs to engage in a social scientific work. And the fact of
having to undertake such work in relation to official data, and invoking
other available, 'non-official' evidence, opens up researchers to the
charge of producing overly subjective, and 'non-scientific' work – the very
charges that Tappan made of Sutherland in the context of their celebrated debate on what constituted crime (see Chapter 1). Such a charge is
all the more likely to be made when researching issues which are both
marginalised but also some potential threat to powerful interests: as
Kramer has noted, 'powerful political and economic interests strongly
resist ... reformulations of criminality, and charges of bias are hurled at
"moral entrepreneurs" who don't pretend to be "value-neutral"'
(1989: 152).

Comparing corporate and street crimes: the economic costs

Notwithstanding the vast under-reporting of many forms of corporate
crimes, one further issue that needs to be addressed regarding attempts

to draw comparisons between corporate and traditional crimes. We noted earlier in this chapter that data presented by academics on corporate offending has a curious relationship to time; one aspect of this is that some data on corporate crimes (including some estimates of costs) collates offences across more than the one-year period within which data on traditional crimes is recorded. This difference has been used as a way of claiming estimates of corporate offending are inflated. Hirschi and Gottfredson, for example, complain that estimates of 'white-collar crime' compare crimes by 'an organisation with many thousands of employees over a period of many years with those committed by single individuals in a single year' (1987: 960). This is usually a further basis for rejecting corporate crime research as polemical and value-laden. However, it must be noted that such a rejection itself can be both 'self-serving' and confused (Steffensmeier 1989: 354 and footnote 7). Notwithstanding the fact that it is rather difficult to see what other option is open to those wishing to examine corporate crime, such complaints obscure the basic point that 'study after study has shown that most ... corporate crime just does not come to the attention of police agencies' (*ibid.*: 355, footnote 9). In other words, the corporate crime of which we know is almost certainly only a small proportion of that which takes place. Further, these complaints also obscure the rather peculiar nature of corporate crime when compared with conventional crimes – while much of the latter consists of inter-personal acts, the former often involve widescale victimisation, so that the issue of how many crimes are to be counted from a single event is raised. For example, had P&O European Ferries been convicted of corporate manslaughter following the Zeebrugge sinking, should the deaths of almost 200 people have been recorded as an equivalent for one conventional homicide?

All in all, then, the following provides a fitting conclusion to this brief section on the poverty of official corporate crime data:

> At present, there are substantial problems with virtually every known data source on the consequences of white-collar crime. Records and statistics maintained by offending organisations, for example, are unlikely to have this sort of information; and, if such information is maintained, it is unlikely to be available to outsiders. Records of enforcement and sanctioning agencies are more likely to have information about the nature of the offence than about its impact (except, perhaps, in very general terms).
>
> (Meier and Short 1995: 95; see also Sutherland 1983: 232–3)

The economic costs of corporate crime: some British estimates

If there are problems with the recording of corporate offences, then it is unsurprising that there are even greater problems when attempting to assess the costs – economic, physical, social – of such offences. That is, it remains difficult to speak with any degree of confidence about the consequences of corporate crime. And, again, although this also holds for conventional crimes, such difficulties are exacerbated in the context of the kinds of offences with which we are here concerned.

Hazel Croall has written that 'no attempt has been made to estimate or even guesstimate the total amounts or costs of white collar crime in either financial or human terms, or to compare this with conventional crime, as both are equally as unmeasurable' (1992: 42). While Croall indicates the enormous problems in any such exercise, she is only partially accurate. First, there have been attempts to engage in such comparisons in the US (see below), though certainly not in Britain. And, second, while there are enormous difficulties with any such measurements, we do not believe that both are 'equally as unmeasurable' – one important observation that we have made here, following others, is that there is much less data available regarding corporate crime than is the case for traditional crime. Yet nor do we accept the implication that no form of comparison can be made, though it is clear, as Croall implies, that no such comparison can be made with any degree of finality or certainty.

Thus there have been attempts to measure, or estimate, the consequences of corporate offences, though again it must be noted that almost all of these originate from, and relate to, the US. Such efforts are often couched in terms of a comparison with costs related to conventional offences, and such a comparison is also of interest for us here. There are two frequently used ways of developing such a comparison: one is to present estimates of the aggregate costs of each broad 'type' of crime; a second is to use more particular, and perhaps more reliable, but undoubtedly therefore more selective, points of comparison, through reference to the costs of particular instances of offending or broader categories of offence. We intend to concentrate *largely* on the former.

A starting point for any comparison of the aggregate costs associated with conventional and corporate offences respectively is an estimate of the former. If conventional crimes are more adequately recorded than is the case for corporate offences, this has hardly made the task of quantifying their economic consequences a straightforward one. Indeed, any overview of the variety of estimates produced attests to the difficulty of even this task – which in turn makes conducting a similar exercise for corporate crimes an even more daunting one.

There are many estimates of the costs of conventional crimes in circulation. And while most fail to define precisely what crimes (and indeed related processes) are being included for costing purposes, it becomes fairly clear on reviewing these that most researchers are not including corporate crimes in their calculations and estimates. The fact that this is not even made explicit is interesting in itself, a clear reflection of the distinction between 'real' crimes and corporate offences, a distinction reproduced even within the 'radical' work in this general sphere such as that by Taylor (1997).

Taylor refers to a Home Office Working Group estimate of the costs of crime for the UK which, despite being an 'incomplete account', makes it 'apparent that the costs of these criminal justice institutions in England and Wales must be at least £5000 million per year' (1997: 296). This figure includes the costs of compensation to victims of crime, the work of the police, the Crown Prosecution Service, criminal courts, the probation service, the prison service and the cost of Legal Aid. Aside from the fact that most of these figures do not include Scotland, they seem relatively inclusive, certainly when compared to some other estimates of overall cost. Taylor's estimate of £50 billion is comparable to an internal HM Treasury figure, which estimates the annual costs of crime as 'up to £50 billion' (personal communication, 7 March, 1998), but is somewhat in excess of other more recent figures (though this may be partly explained by its relative 'inclusiveness'). One figure in current circulation is that of £30 billion (which actually relates to 1993); the source of this estimate was an internal paper by Donald Roy of the Home Office Economics Unit, subsequently leaked to the *Sunday Times* (personal communication, 7 March, 1998). This figure included costs of prevention, criminal justice system, criminal damage, values transferred through thefts, fraud etc. and the value of 'life destroyed'. A second Home Office estimate puts 'Total expenditure on the criminal justice system in 1993/94' at 'over £9 billion', of which 'some £6 billion was accounted for by the police service' (Home Office 1997: 5); on this basis, the total cost of crime – that is, including the cost of 'loss and damage' – is in the region of £20 billion (*ibid.*; see also Home Office Research and Statistics Department 1995: 67, 74). Jon Bright, of the organisation *Crime Concern*, uses the estimates developed by the accountants Coopers & Lybrand to arrive at a figure of £16.7 billion, this including the costs of the criminal justice system (Bright 1997: 13). Bright also refers to the 1994 report *Counting the Cost*, to note that while 'the precise figure for particular crimes is difficult to quantify ... estimates have been made for burglary (£1 billion), car crime (£750 million) and crime against business (£5 billion)' (1997: 13). That same report, *Counting the Cost*, had estimated the annual cost of crime to be £24.5 billion, an estimate based upon 'government statistics, crime surveys and on the costs of lost and damaged property, policing, insurance and the cost of the criminal justice system' (Davies *et al.* 1995: 67). As one commentary has recently put it of such estimates, 'The moral is that, while the cost of crime must be high, no one has any real idea what it is' (*The Economist*, 8th June, 1996). Direct expenditure on criminal justice agencies in England and Wales seems to run at about £10 billion per annum; adding estimates of the costs of crime to this produces estimates anywhere up to about £50 billion.

How does this compare with the economic consequences of corporate crimes? While there is no data relating to the UK which we can use to make any direct comparison with the costs of traditional crimes (though see below, on the United States), what we *can* do is present some estimates of the costs of particular crimes of types of crimes in which corporate and organisational offenders are implicated.

The simplest starting place is with data on the activities of the Serious Fraud Office (SFO). The SFO was established by the Criminal Justice Act 1987, not insignificant in itself, since the SFO, and therefore the activity which it is designed to regulate, thus falls squarely within the context of crime and criminal justice (in marked contrast to almost all other law designed to regulate various corporate activities). The SFO was established to investigate cases of serious and complex fraud, that is, cases where: the facts and/or the law are of great complexity; or, sums of money in excess of £1 million are at risk; or, there is great public interest and concern for some other reason, for example, the identity of the suspect or the employment of a novel method of fraud (Serious Fraud Office 1989: 7). The conditions under which the SFO was established mean that it deals with only a tiny proportion of fraud, and thus of financial forms of corporate crime – and this is even more so now than at the time of its establishment, given that the original threshold of £1 million at risk was subsequently revised upwards to £5 million, and then to £6 million (Levi 1993: 75). Yet a large-scale, longitudinal survey of large UK companies has shown fraud to be widespread (Levi 1992: 175), so that serious fraud on this scale represents only a tiny proportion of all corporate fraud.

When the SFO was established, 'it was assumed that the Office would carry a caseload of about 60' (Serious Fraud Office 1989: 5). SFO Annual Reports generally note how many active cases the SFO are pursuing and attaches an estimate of the aggregate sums at risk in these cases. Thus the most recent Annual Report notes that at 5 April 1996, the SFO was investigating '70 cases with an aggregate value of alleged frauds in excess of £3billion' (Serious Fraud Office 1997: 16). Since its inception, the SFO has in any one year pursued between 39 and 82 cases, the aggregate value of which has ranged from £1.2billion to 'in excess of £5 billion' (Serious Fraud Office 1989, 1990, 1991, 1992, 1995, 1996, 1997). It is the sheer scale of the relatively few frauds investigated that makes comparison with street crimes and the work of the police difficult to sustain. At 4 April, 1994, for example, the SFO was investigating 48 cases at an aggregate value of over £5 billion. We should emphasise that this excludes the considerable sums at risk which comprise the work of the fraud Investigation Group: tackling frauds where at least £250 000 is at risk, its caseload has risen significantly since the mid-1980s (to 110 in 1991), with the sums at risk rising disproportionately (Levi 1993a: 10–14). One point of comparison here is the figure cited previously from Bright (1997), which costs all burglaries at £1 billion – 48 cases of serious fraud thus cost an estimated five times more than the crime which is central to representations of the crime problem! By way of further comparison, the most recent British Crime Survey notes that two-thirds of burglaries where there was loss involved sums of less than £1000, with almost one in five of these involving less than £100; the average net loss – including loss of earnings – was £370 (Mirrlees-Black et al. 1996: 42). Indeed,

In police terms, any crime involving more than a few thousand pounds is likely to be seen as 'serious'. Yet fraud occupies a different perceptual category, as if, once one passes a certain figure, the number of additional 'zeros' becomes irrelevant ... During 1990, in the whole of England and Wales, the police recorded 'only' 123 robberies, 419 burglaries and 819 thefts over £50,000, very few of which would have been significantly over that amount. Data from the [ABI] indicate that the costs of crime in England and Wales in 1990 totalled some £432m for theft of and from motor vehicles, £800m for burglary, and £500m for arson. The alleged frauds in any one of the most serious cases – those involving Bank of Credit and Commerce International (BCCI), Barlow Clowes, Guinness, Maxwell, and Polly Peck – approach or exceeded these figures, and in 1992, there were 21 SFO cases where more than £50m is estimated to have been involved. ...

(Levi 1995: 184)

One further aspect of this perceptual difficulty is the fact that while the aggregate costs of some corporate crimes are enormous, these costs can be so widely diffused across a wide range of victims that it is often unlikely there will be any recognition of their actual scale (see Box 1983: 31).

Levi's point is reinforced if we examine one recent group of offences, commonly now referred to – in highly de-sensitising terms – as 'pensions *mis*-selling' (on the particular forms of language used to represent corporate crimes, see Chapter 5). This series of illegalities is also interesting not simply because of the scale of the economic consequences of the offences, but because of the way in which opportunity and motivation for these illegalities were created by deregulation, privatisation and an ideology which combined a rolling back of state welfare and increased emphasis upon privatised welfare provision. Thus Clarke (1996) has documented how the gradual withdrawal of the Conservative Government from pension provision, coupled with deregulation of the retail financial services sector in the UK in the latter half of the 1980s (particularly with the Financial Services Act 1986), contributed to the 'biggest scandal of them all' in the sector. Pensions providers launched into a hard sell, targeting many public sector workers in well developed pensions programmes, wrongly advising many to cash in their contributions and transfer them to a new, private scheme about which they provided false and misleading information. Black refers to a survey conducted by the Securities and Investments Board which found that only 9 per cent of pensions companies had complied with legal requirements when originally advising on these pensions transfers (Black 1997: 178). Moreover, once exposed,

the industry proved extremely reluctant to admit wrong doing, even by way of over-selling, still less mis-selling. Enquiries by the supervisory regulator, the Securities and Investments Board in the early 1980s, eventually produced an estimate that 1.4 million people may have been mis-sold personal pensions and had a right to have their cases reviewed and awarded compensation as appropriate; the costs of this were estimated at between £2 and £4 billion.

(Clarke 1996: 14)

Indeed, despite the establishment of a timetable for reviewing and if necessary compensating for cases, the pensions providers have consistently missed deadlines, ignored cajoling and proven relatively resistant to government threats. While breaches had been first uncovered in 1990 (*Guardian*, 9 October, 1997), many of the offending companies – amongst whom were some of the UK's better-known and largest financial services retailers such as Abbey Life, Allied Dunbar, Co-op Insurance, Legal & General, Norwich Union, Royal Sun Alliance, Pearl Assurance, Prudential and TSB Life – had resolved less than 10 per cent of the cases under their respective review by 1997 (*Guardian*, 10 July, 1997). Incredibly, a survey by KPMG Peat Marwick of pensions advice given during 1991–1993, a period after the mis-selling had been first exposed, revealed that in 'four out of five cases' pensions companies were still giving advice which fell short of the legally required minima (cited in Black 1997: 178, and footnote 143).

By the end of 1997, the sum involved in this series of offences was consistently being referred to as £4 billion (*Financial Times*, 19 September, 1997) and involving two million or more victims (*The Times*, 20 September, 1997). Treasury Economic Secretary Liddell began resorting to consistent but apparently fruitless efforts to 'name and shame' the (41) most recalcitrant offenders (*Guardian*, 19 November, 1997). Early in 1998, the new Regulatory Body, the Financial Services Authority, cited new research which estimated the final costs as 'up to £11billion, almost three times the original estimate. The number of victims could be as high as 2.4 million' (*Guardian*, 13 March, 1998). *As the cost of one particular series of crimes, this figure of £11 billion – even if ultimately an over-estimate, and even though not an annual but a 'once-and-for-all' cost – dwarfs the costs of almost all estimates of all forms of street crimes put together.*

Of course, the above cost estimates 'prove' nothing. They are fraught with difficulty, involving various degrees of estimate and guesstimate (though, it must be added, much of this is on the side of under-estimation). These qualifications having been entered, it remains that the general direction of such estimates is clear: the economic consequences of corporate offences vastly outweigh those associated with the crimes normally associated with the crime problem (Croall 1992: 42–3). This general direction, or conclusion, is stunningly confirmed if we turn to mention briefly some of the estimates of the relative costs of crime which have been generated in the US over the past 25 years or so.

The economic costs of corporate crime: some US estimates

A recent review of the costs of crime in the US has been provided by Schmalleger (1996: 81–2), who uses Bureau of Justice Statistics, based upon its National Crime Victimisation Survey Data, to estimate 'Total losses all personal crimes' (rape, robbery, assault, personal larceny), 1992, at $4110 million, and 'Total losses all household crimes' (household larceny, burglary and motor vehicle theft), 1992, at $13 536 million.

These figures produce a combined total of $17 646 million, or $17.6 billion. These costs included 'losses from property theft or damage, cash losses, medical expenses, and amount of pay lost because of injuries or inactivities related to ... crime' (Schmalleger 1996: 81). A different estimate concluded that 'direct costs related to personal household crime averaged approximately $48billion annually' (Helmkamp *et al.* 1997: 4–5; Miller *et al.* 1996). Of course, such data does not include the costs of the criminal justice system. One recent estimate calculates the cost of this system in the US, including police and courts, at $100 billion (*The Economist*, 8 June, 1996). Taking these two data together, rough and no doubt incomplete as each is, we arrive at a figure of between $117.5 billion and $148 billion as the annual, direct 'cost of crime' in the US.

Now, since Sutherland's early work on 'white-collar crime', two points have generally been attested to: first, that providing estimates of the costs of corporate crime is difficult if not impossible (Conklin 1977; Punch 1996); second, that there is no doubt that the costs of such crime are almost beyond comprehension, certainly exceeding those associated with conventional crimes (for reviews, see Box 1983; Conklin 1977: 2–8, 1981: 4; Geis 1990; Hagan 1994; and see Wheeler and Rothman 1982, for some very specific data on this claim). Thus while Sutherland himself had claimed that 'The financial cost of white collar crime is probably several times as great as the financial cost of all the crimes which are customarily regarded as the crime problem' (1983: 9), he gave relatively little data in support of this claim, citing the costs of some particular crimes rather than providing any general estimates.

Thus, in summary,

> Most observers are quick to point out that the estimates they provide are conservative, and that the actual loss is probably far greater. There is agreement, however, that the annual cost from white-collar and corporate crimes is far greater than that from ordinary crime.
>
> (Meier and Short 1995: 82)

One of the earliest and most frequently cited estimates is that provided by Conklin in his 1977 text *Illegal But Not Criminal*. Conklin estimated there that the combined cost of the offences of robbery, theft, larceny and auto-theft in the US was between $3–4 billion, whilst various white-collar offences produced an annual loss of some $40 billion (Conklin 1977: 4). Conklin later produced figures which put the cost of 'white-collar crime' (a category not directly comparable with our own concern with corporate crime) as by far the greatest cost in terms of crime and the criminal justice system (1981: 45).

In the mid-1970s, the US Chamber of Commerce had estimated the direct cost of 'white-collar crime' at $41.78 billion annually (Meier and Short 1995; Helmkamp *et al.* 1997), an estimate later believed to be highly conservative and excluding many offence categories (Helmkamp *et al.* 1997, Meier and Short 1995). Congressman Conyers before Subcommittee on Crime of the Committee of the Judiciary in 1978 put the figure at $44 billion annually.

> Several observers since that time have pointed out that this estimate is very conservative and excludes a number of offences. Senator Philip Hart, as chair of the Judiciary Subcommittee on Antitrust and Monopoly, estimated that antitrust violations may illegally divert as much as $200 billion annually from the US economy.
>
> (Meier and Short 1995: 81; see also Helmkamp *et al.* 1997; Rodino 1978; Sparks 1978)

More recently, Reiman (1995, cited in Helmkamp *et al.* 1997) has attempted to update the US Chamber of Commerce's figures, producing an estimate of $197.76 billion annually which is 'calculated with the assumption "that the rate of white-collar crime relative to the population has remained constant from 1974–1991 and that its real dollar value has remained constant as well"' (*ibid.*: 4). Further, Barkan (1997) has estimated the annual cost of white-collar crime as $415 billion, compared to the annual estimated cost of street crime, $13 billion. The $415 billion is made up of losses from corporate crime ($200 billion), health care fraud ($70 billion) employee theft ($45 billion), and non-corporate tax evasion ($100 billion). The $13 billion street crime derives from losses from all reported robbery, burglary, larceny, auto theft and arson crimes in 1994 (cited in Helmkamp *et al.* 1997). Barkan's figures provide a comparison between street and 'white-collar' crimes which is beyond the range within which most other estimates of the comparative costs of 'white-collar' and street crime fall, and thus maybe somewhat less reliable (see below). However, taking his estimate for corporate crime, and setting this against street crime, we find that the former are more than 15 times greater than the costs of the latter in the US.

A recent paper produced under the auspices of the National White Collar Crime Center (Helmkamp *et al.* 1997) provides a concerted effort to calculate the monetary costs associated with white-collar crime in the US. Having noted the poverty of existing official data sources (in particular, the FBI's UCR and the Department of Justice's National Incident Based Reporting System), the authors bring together a whole range of estimates of the relative costs of white-collar as opposed to conventional crime, and end up with a range within which estimates of these relative costs fall. The fact that these authors break down their category of white-collar crime provides us with some opportunity to isolate those cost estimates which relate only to corporate crimes; thus, despite the fact that the authors use a broad definition of white-collar crime, and certainly obscure the distinction between occupational and organisational crimes, we can avoid the over-estimate of the costs of corporate crime which would be the result if we simply took their figure for white-collar crime as synonymous with the former.

However, it should also be emphasised that the authors state that 'because the economic cost of white-collar crimes involving activities such as threats to health and safety, unsafe products and workplaces, and the environment are more difficult to estimate, they are not addressed in this study' (Helmkamp *et al.* 1997: 5). Thus, 'Only those white-collar crimes committed in the United States, where monetary loss was mentioned or estimated' (*ibid.*) are included. In other words, these authors omit from their calculations a massive array of corporate crimes to which – as our example of costs associated with UK health and safety offences indicates – there are enormous economic costs attached. In this respect, any calculation of the costs of corporate offending based upon these authors' estimates is likely to be a considerable under-estimate. Finally, these authors are clear that their estimate of loss 'does not account for the full impact' these crimes have on their victims, so that costs such as higher taxes, increased costs of goods and services, higher insurance premiums, and costs of maintaining regulatory and justice systems are excluded (*ibid.*: 11–12).

Turning to the particular categories of offence used, we can ignore those under the headings employee theft, cargo theft, insurance fraud and credit/debit card fraud, since these will cover mostly occupational and/or individual offences. We should also set aside the costs of computer-related/high-tech crime, check fraud/counterfeiting, health care fraud, rebate and coupon fraud, mortgage fraud and telecommunications fraud; the latter will include both individual and corporate offences, but are presented in a form which makes it impossible to distinguish what proportion of costs is the result of corporate offences. Much the same can be said of the offence categories of money laundering (the estimated annual costs of which are $100–215 billion) and arson-for-profit (amounting to $1.5–2 billion annually), each of which are likely to have a substantial corporate element (Helmkamp *et al.* 1997: 10).

By contrast, some categories are unequivocally indices of corporate offences, amongst these being the following.

First, consumer/personal fraud, defined by the authors as 'fraud against consumers'. The annual amount lost by virtue of consumer and personal fraud ranges from approximately $40 to $100 billion' (*ibid.*: 7).

Second, 'corporate tax fraud', which 'costs the US between $7 to 50billion annually' (*ibid.*: 5). Indeed,

> corporate tax fraud costs the public at least five times more than burglary, larceny and welfare fraud combined ... The GAO estimates that two-thirds of all US corporations fail to report some of their income and that tax cheating accounts for about one-third of all income lost to tax fraud. All of corporate America pays less in taxes than the amount paid by families in New York, California and Ohio combined.
>
> (*ibid.*)

Third amongst the categories listed by Helmkamp and colleagues which is of particular interest for us is 'corporate financial crime':

There are many different offences which fall within the category of corporate financial crime. These offences include antitrust violations, bribery, price-fixing, false and misleading advertising, organisational fraud and deception, kickbacks, and pollution law violations. Corporate financial crime is estimated to cost the public between $200 and $565 billion annually.

(*ibid.*: 9)

If we take the cost estimates provided for the three categories upon which we have focused as corporate crimes – consumer/personal fraud, corporate tax fraud and corporate financial crime – we arrive at an overall estimate for a limited set of corporate crimes costing the US economy between $247 billion and $715 billion annually. The figure cited by consumer activists during the first half of the 1980s, namely that corporate crime costs the US economy $200 billion a year (Bilimoria 1995; Gautschi and Jones 1987), falls within the lower end of this range, if adjusted for inflation. Any of these figures clearly exceeds that of $117.5–148 billion for street crimes cited above.

However, all of these sums pale into relative insignificance when set alongside the costs of particular crimes, such as those now referred to as the 'Savings and Loans' (S&L) crimes, and generally acknowledged as the costliest crimes in history. These crimes – now well documented (see above) – have been estimated as costing US taxpayers $1.5 trillion (Pontell and Calavita 1993). To put such figures into perspective, we should note that even the GAO's early mid-range estimate of $500 billion (cited in Pontell and Calavita 1993: 32) was, at the time, a dollar amount that exceeded the Gross Domestic Product of any national economy outside the G-7. Again by way of perspective, Schmalleger notes that the cost of just one S&L collapse – that of the Lincoln Savings and Loan Association – 'cost taxpayers ... around $2.5 billion' (Schmalleger 1996: 340). While not all S&L failures were the result of crimes (about 80 per cent were), and while some might have involved occupational as opposed to, or alongside, corporate offending, it is still the case that such estimates are of both a unique and incomprehensible magnitude.

One thing is clear. The costs of corporate crime far outweigh those associated with conventional crime. Helmkamp and colleagues conclude that the economic costs of white-collar crimes fall within a range of between 10 and 35 times greater than the costs of street (personal and household) crimes. White-collar crime, on these authors' definition, is a broader category than corporate crime. On the other hand, it excludes many of those corporate crimes – such as health and safety crimes, environmental crimes – which have large if almost incalculable costs.

Recording and costing corporate crime: a case study in health and safety

The aim of this brief case study is to illustrate in some detail some of the points already made in this and the previous chapter. In particular, a focus upon occupational fatalities as crimes allows exploration of a number of key issues relevant to all forms of corporate crimes, namely: the extent to which corporate crimes are under-reported; the social processes which contribute to such under-reporting; and the economic and physical costs associated with corporate crimes. However, even in the context of a case-study such as this, the key issues can only be treated relatively briefly; they have been examined in much greater detail in Tombs (1998, forthcoming and Slapper 1993, forthcoming).

Counting deaths at work

Published confirmed figures for fatal injuries at work, for the year (April) 1994 to (March) 1995 reveal that a total of 376 fatal injuries were reported under the Reporting of Injuries, Diseases and Dangerous Occurrences Regulations (RIDDOR) 1985, to all enforcement authorities. This figure is a 'record low' (Health and Safety Commission (HSC) 1996a: 79) for the recorded number of fatal injuries. Yet despite the Health and Safety Executive (HSE) claim that data on fatal injuries is 'virtually complete' (HSC 1996b: 1), this data is actually far from complete. Many more people are killed by working than is indicated in what we shall call this 'headline' figure.

First, it does not include deaths or injuries arising out of the supply or use of flammable gas, despite the fact that these are reportable to HSE as occupational incidents; for 1994/95 there were 36 fatalities reportable under RIDDOR (the lowest number on record). Second, this figure excludes fatal injuries that occur in the course of sea fishing and those arising out of transport and communications work under the Merchant Shipping legislation (HSC 1996b: 102). In 1994 (a calendar year) these contexts accounted for 26 deaths and one death respectively (Marine Accident Investigation Branch, Department of Transport, personal communication, 4 September, 1997). Adding these figures to the HSE's 'headline' figures produces a total of 439 workplace deaths.

Yet these figures are still a massive under-estimate. First, and perhaps most significantly, fatal injury data recorded by HSC/E excludes all deaths which arise while driving in the course of employment (Slapper forthcoming; Tombs 1998). Yet there is evidence that there are here a high number of work-related deaths which quite properly should be included in annual HSE fatal injury statistics. In fact, records of road traffic deaths are compiled by the Department of Transport, and it is this Department which publishes the relevant annual data. Thus if someone is 'at work' in a motor vehicle when they are killed the death will not be processed by the HSE.

There are many occupations which cause employees or the self-employed to be driving all or some of the time: cab, bus, coach and lorry drivers; postal and other delivery workers; district nurses; van drivers (including plumbers, builders etc.); commercial sales representatives; members of the emergency services; and maintenance engineers. Excluding travel to and from work – which now constitutes a fifth of all vehicle use (Royal Commission on Environmental Pollution 1995: 10), and forms part of injury data in many European countries – recent OPCS (Office of Population, Censuses and Surveys) statistics note that over 1.8 million workers drive each day as the main part of their job. There are three million company cars on the roads in Britain travelling a total of 63 thousand million miles a year. One estimate of the risks involved in such work was produced by the insurance company General Accident (GA): in 1989 it calculated that there was one death or serious injury per 41 company cars (Maryon 1993). More recently, a series of publications by the Royal Society for the Prevention of Accidents (RoSPA) have, on the basis of conservative assumptions, attempted to estimate road traffic deaths involving people at work (Bibbings 1996; RoSPA 1997a, 1997b; see also *Hazards* 1995, 52: 6). For 1994, RoSPA calculated 877 deaths (Bibbings 1996: 21), so that driving in the course of work activity may produce a greater annual risk of fatality than coal mining (RoSPA 1997a). A subsequent publication has claimed that 'as many as a thousand people die every year in occupational accidents on our roads' (RoSPA 1998: 7). The omission of such data from the fatal injury statistics is a glaring one. Interestingly, it is one upon which the HSC has refused to act – both during and after recent reviews which led to changes in reporting requirements and the coverage of health and safety law, both RoSPA and the Chartered Institute of Environmental Health Officers made unsuccessful submissions to the HSC that road accidents should be reportable under health and safety law (Bibbings 1996: 7; *Hazards* 56, Autumn, 1996: 5); any such changes had been opposed by industrial representatives on the grounds that they would be 'burdensome' (Bibbings 1996: 7).

If we add the RoSPA figure (above) of workplace deaths on the roads for 1994, namely 877, to those arising from the supply or use of flammable gas (36), deaths that occur in the course of sea fishing (26), and those that arise out of transport and communications work (1) under the Merchant Shipping legislation (HSC 1996b: 102), the grand total of deaths at work rises to 1316. This is of rather a different order to HSE's headline figure of 376.

Yet these figures for fatal accidents are still under-estimates. A second general reason for the under-recording of official occupational fatalities, is the system of death registration and classification. One study of this system (Slapper 1997) suggests that the annual figure for deaths through incidents at work could be higher than the official figure, quite apart, that is, from the exclusion of people at work who are killed in road traffic incidents.

As a consequence of the historic duty of the Coroner, before a death can be registered, a valid certificate giving the cause of death must be completed and signed by a registered medical practitioner who attended the deceased during his/her last illness. The cause of death, so certified, must be shown to be entirely natural. In every other case the death must be reported to the Coroner and, if a death is shown to be 'violent or unnatural', the Coroner is required by law to conduct an inquest. The evolution of this 'fail-safe' system (Burton *et al.* 1985: 2) provides that the registration of every death shall be subject to scrutiny. The reason for the notification system is that:

> certain types of accident and disease (usually, but not invariably, industrial in
> origin) are considered to be so serious that notification of their existence
> must be given to relevant Government bodies for the purpose of investigation
> and research.
>
> (Jervis 1993: 289)

Thus deaths arising out of or in connection with work must be so reported: S.I. 1985 No. 2023 – The Reporting of Injuries, Diseases and Dangerous Occurrences Regulations, reg. 2(1).

There is no higher duty imposed on doctors than upon any other person at common law to report a death to the Coroner although, by virtue of their profession, doctors may be considered to be well placed to know which deaths should be reported and in practice the vast majority of cases are reported by doctors and the police. It is arguable therefore that the system stands or falls on the co-operation of the medical profession.

Two recent studies (Start *et al.* 1993 and Start *et al.* 1995) highlighted the inability of both hospital clinicians and general practitioners to recognise some categories of reportable deaths. Buchanan and Mason (1995: 145) argue that this is due to ignorance of the law and is the product of the minimal medico-legal teaching in English medical schools and of the free interchange of doctors from civil law jurisdictions of the European Community. The dangers of failure to recognise a notifiable death undermines the safeguards provided to society by the Coroner system and may cause administrative difficulties, unnecessary distress for bereaved relatives and 'cases may evade medicolegal investigation altogether because they are not recognised as death due to unnatural causes' (Start *et al.* 1993: 1038).

The first study indicated that individual clinicians at all grades showed a variable appreciation of the different category of cases which should be reported with consultants consistently performing less well than their junior staff. When asked to assess medical histories and whether the resulting death should have been reported, anything up to 60 per cent in individual cases were wrong. Furthermore,

> most, but worryingly not all, clinicians reported the cases involving allegations

of negligence, death in police custody, criminal death, suicide, and industrial disease. Deaths resulting from accidents were often unrecognised and many clinicians did not seem to know that such deaths are reportable to the coroner, no matter how long a time had elapsed between injury and death.

(Start *et al.* 1993: 1039)

Even when the lapse between an injury and consequential death is a period of many months, the matter could still be within the jurisdiction of English homicide law. The old rule that a prosecution had to be brought within a year and a day of the relevant attack was abolished by the Law Reform (Year and a Day Rule) Act 1996 (Slapper 1996).

In a second study involving general practitioners (Start *et al.* 1995), only 3 per cent recognised those deaths which should be reported for further investigation in all the case studies. Some doctors held disturbing misconceptions in relation to the Coroner system which could have a wide range of outcomes, from serious crime going undetected, to loss of industrial pension or other appropriate compensation for relatives. Deaths from industrial or domestic accidents were recognised as cases requiring referral by fewer than half of general practitioners.

Both studies, indicate that certifying doctors consider only the eventual cause of death rather than the sequence of events leading to death (Start *et al.* 1995: 193). Although some of the unreported reportable deaths would be picked up later by other doctors signing cremation forms, by the local registrar of births, deaths, and marriages, or by coroners' officers when contacted for advice, other cases may receive no further attention.

A third general source of under-reporting is in the unreliability of data relating to those in self-employment. It might be argued that these have little or nothing to do with *corporate* crime, but in this context we need to remember that self-employment is increasingly created by corporations requiring this status of those who were formerly direct employees. Many serious injuries sustained while the victim is at work can result in death months later but are not classified as deaths arising out of work. We know that there is substantial under-reporting of serious injuries at work. On the basis of analysis of data from the 1990 Labour Force Survey, HSE concludes that

only a third of reportable non-fatal injuries to employees are being reported, with marked variations between industrial sectors (from under a fifth in agriculture and only a quarter in the services sector to two fifths in manufacturing and construction and four fifths in the energy sector).

(HSE 1993a: 83)

The HSE further concludes that 'For the self-employed, only one in twenty reportable injuries are reported' (HSE 1993a: 83). Now, in the context of a consideration of occupational fatalities, the self-employed sector is sufficiently large for even a tiny fraction of its fatalities and major injuries to be numerically important. According to figures from the

Department of Employment, there are about three million workers in this category.

Major injuries can occasionally be the cause of death many months later. Such deaths would technically be classifiable as deaths arising from work for HSE purposes; they would also be prosecutable as manslaughter. It appears that a considerable number are not reported to (and thus not recorded by) the HSE. Taken together, this data suggests that the official annual figure of work accident fatalities may be an underestimate. The 'dark figure' of deaths at work may, therefore, be higher than the officially recorded statistic.

Even if we set aside the social process around death registration which creates under-reporting of occupational fatalities, and even if we set aside the problem of the unrecorded numbers of deaths whilst in self-employment, we return to our calculated figure of 1316 occupational fatalities for 1994/95. Yet even this does not exhaust the numbers of those killed as a result of work activity per annum; to this must be added data on deaths arising from occupationally caused fatal illness. Here existent data is much less useful (HSC 1996a: 86). The most reliable source is maintained by HSE, based upon copies of death certificates that are forwarded to them. These cover a small number of occupational diseases, namely asbestosis, mesothelioma, pneumoconiosis, byssinosis and some forms of occupationally caused alveolitis; in other words, these are illnesses with the clearest possible occupational causes, most of them in fact related to exposure to asbestos.

There are obvious reasons why doctors and coroners are unlikely to record occupational causes on death certificates. First, there is rarely any material advantage for any party to do so; second, save for the most well known conditions, there is likely to be a lack of knowledge of occupationally caused illness; third, and perhaps most significantly, it remains the case that GPs and coroners often fail even to consider occupational causes, so that they do not enquire into the working history of those with fatal illnesses, except perhaps in a highly cursory way. This is even more likely to hold for women, who are still less likely to be considered as paid workers.

With all of these qualifications tending towards gross underestimation in mind, it is nevertheless possible to turn to the available evidence from death certificates. Data for 1994/95 (which remains provisional), records 1409 deaths caused by asbestos exposure (mesothelioma- and asbestos-caused lung cancer) in workplaces and 293 deaths due to occupationally caused lung disease other than asbestosis (that is, pneumoconiosis, byssinosis and some forms of occupationally caused alveolitis) (HSC 1996b: 158).

Even within the specified categories of diseases, this data only includes a small proportion of relevant deaths. The HSE itself suggests that there are at least as many deaths from asbestos-caused lung diseases as there are from mesothelioma, that is, 1200–1300 per annum (HSC 1996b: 68). Further, HSE is currently formally revising upwards the data on mesothelioma; at the time of writing one private communication suggests that a figure of about 5000 will be released for the most recent annual total of mesothelioma deaths. And of course such categories themselves are only a small proportion of workplace-caused fatal illness and, even if accurate, would not represent the numbers of occupationally-caused fatal illnesses: 'most of us will die of a common form of death ... if your job causes you to die from heart disease, you will be one, statistically insignificant death, lost among thousands in the general population' (*Hazards*, 1995, 51: 11).

Thus, for example, trade union research suggests that upwards of 10 000 people die every year from work-related medical conditions (Bergman 1991: 3) and some research puts the figure at up to 20 000 (GMB 1987: 5). These deaths result from multifarious chronic conditions and diseases, such as carcinoma arising from exposure to radiation, mesothelioma from construction work and pneumoconiosis from working in mines. In many cases it seems clear that employers knew of the risks to which their employees were being exposed. On current law, manslaughter could be proven against an employer where he or she (or the company) had shown 'indifference to an obvious risk of injury to health' or had an 'actual foresight of the risk coupled with a determination to run it'.

The asbestos industry provides some clear examples of appalling suffering and death caused to thousands of people through exposure to the pernicious dust when ample evidence, known to employers, demonstrated the health dangers. Asbestos was implicated in causing industrial disease as far back as the 1920s. There is documentary evidence that from the 1930s the English firm (and world leader in asbestos production) Turner and Newell set out to flout laws designed to protect workers. Recent research studies, by Professor Julian Peto, have shown that cancers from asbestos exposure are set to rise for the next 30 years to about 9000 a year (*Guardian*, 25 November, 1994). The potential wrongdoing here is on an enormous scale.

Nevertheless, even confining calculations to the two figures for occupationally caused fatal illnesses provides a total of 1702 deaths which are unequivocally recorded as occupationally caused. To this figure, can be added that for deaths from fatal injuries, namely 1316. This provides a total of 3018 occupationally-caused deaths in one year, notwithstanding that this is a gross under-estimate.

As some indication of the scale of these deaths, comparison might be made with annual homicide totals. In terms of popular definitions of violence and its place within social problems of crime, law and order, homicides retain a significant place in popular consciousness, even if the actual number of such deaths is relatively small. In 1994, the year most directly comparable with the HSE data, the number of homicides – that is, recorded deaths by murder, manslaughter or infanticide – in England, Wales and Scotland was 834 (in the ten years between 1985 and 1994, the number of homicides ranged between 700 and 850 per annum) (personal communication, Crime and Criminal Justice Unit, Home Office, and Scottish Office Statistical Bulletin, 1995). Thus the combined figure of 3018 recorded occupational fatalities is about four times the number of recorded homicides (834). Similarly, were we to use data on manslaughter as a more accurate comparison with occupational fatalities, then we find that there is a similar discrepancy. Over any 12-month period, the number of deaths at work is, on average, about two and a half times the number of cases resulting in convictions for manslaughter (excluding 'diminished responsibility' cases – those under s. 2 of the Homicide Act, 1957). Thus, over the decade 1979–1989, the number of annual convictions for manslaughter (excluding s. 2 cases) fluctuated between 99 (1989) and 192 (1987). The number of people killed at work over a 12-month period – restricting ourselves to the HSE headline figure – is notably higher, for example: 558 during 1987/88, 730 during 1988/89, 681 during 1989/90 and 572 1990/91 (HSE 1988, 1989, 1990 and 1991). When one considers that these accidents only relate to the working population which is less than 50 per cent of the whole (Box 1983; Williams 1994), it does give some idea of the extent of the problem of occupational deaths.

This does not, of course, mean that one is four times more likely to be killed at work than to be the victim of homicide. Such a calculation does not actually compare like with like, a point obscured by the otherwise powerful arguments of Reiman (1979: 65–72) and Box (1983: 25–9). For if this data represents the relative scale of the 'social problems' of deaths at work and homicide, a 'social problem' does not equate with a crime, law and order problem. In order to address any distortions inherent in social definitions of the latter, it is necessary to know what proportion of deaths at work are related to crimes on the part of managements or employers, since all the homicides are, by definition, the result of crimes.

Counting safety crimes

Determining what proportion of workplace deaths are attributable to employers' health and safety crimes is, given the paucity of available data, a difficult exercise, and one in which assumptions certainly must be made. However, these assumptions can be made in a way which, contra Nelken (1994) and Shapiro (1983), need not descend into mere moralising (Levi 1994: 300).

One means of calculating what proportion of deaths are the result of criminal offences by employers might be to resort to prosecution or other enforcement data. However, the reluctance of the HSE to resort to formal enforcement action is well-documented (Bergman 1991, 1993; Slapper

1993; Pearce and Tombs 1990, 1991). Moreover, the use of formal enforcement action, always a matter of last (and very reluctant) resort by HSE and its inspectorates, is now being further abandoned, as HSE redefines itself formally as much more of an advisory and educational body than any form of police force for industry (HSC 1996b: 38; HSC 1997; Tombs 1996). In fact, less than 40 per cent of workplace deaths from fatal injuries are followed typically by a prosecution (Bergman 1994). However, there is some available evidence which allows some comment to be made on the scale of criminal activity and omission involved in the causation of workplace deaths.

First, there exists a series of special investigations into groups of fatalities undertaken by HSE in the 1980s. These are an invaluable source of data given that many fatalities, and the vast majority of non-fatal injuries, are never subject to any detailed investigation. Of particular significance is that the findings from these separate investigations proved remarkably consistent. It was found that managements bear primary responsibility for the 'accidents' under investigation. Of 1186 fatalities which occurred between 1981 and 1983, investigation concluded that site managements were responsible for 73 per cent of these (HSE 1985a); 78 per cent of 106 fatal maintenance accidents in general manufacturing could have been prevented if reasonably practicable precautions had been implemented (HSE 1985b); an analysis of 326 fatal accidents between 1980 and 1982 concluded that 83 per cent could have been eliminated by taking reasonably practicable precautions (HSE 1985c); of 502 fatal and major injuries investigated in the chemical industry, site management were found wholly responsible for 68 per cent, and in 75 per cent of these site management were 'wholly or partly responsible for failing to take all reasonably practicable precautions to prevent an accident' (HSE 1987); similar investigations concluded that managements were responsible for approximately two out of three deaths in general manufacturing (HSE 1983), for three out of five farm deaths (HSE 1986) and for 70 per cent of deaths in the construction industry (HSE 1988).

These investigations sought to determine underlying causes rather than allocate 'blame' or legal responsibility. But their conclusions are of some use in clarifying the location and level of responsibility entailed in their incidence, even if they clearly cannot be taken as legal judgements (Bergman 1994). Further, we can set these conclusions against the relevant legal test of responsibility, which is that managements must do 'all that is reasonably practicable' to eliminate a risk or prevent an accident/injury. This standard of reasonable practicability – long criticised by some for explicitly allowing an element of economic cost-benefit analysis (Moore 1991) – is the minimal duty of care that is required by health and safety legislation in the UK, and sits at the heart of the Health and Safety at Work (HASAW) Act 1974, being written into its key General Duties (ss. 2 and 3). Thus it appears, on best available evidence, that in the majority of 'accidental' injuries examined by HSE, most of them producing fatalities, managements were in contravention of the General Duties (ss. 2 and 3) of the HASAW Act. We should also bear in mind that this Act is a criminal statute, whether or not the HSE choose to enforce it as such through legal proceedings (Bergman 1991; Tombs 1989). The HSE reports further demonstrate that the criteria for reckless manslaughter appear, *prima facie*, to be present in many of the cases which, if they are prosecuted, are only charged as regulatory offences under the HASAW Act 1974. It is evidence of this kind which prompts one writer to state that 'There is much evidence to suggest that a very high number of the 18 151 deaths occurring within a commercial setting during the last 27 years were classifiable, at least prima facie, as instances of reckless manslaughter' (1993: 425; see also Slapper forthcoming).

A second body of relevant data is to be found in the form of the now considerable stock of detailed material within reports which resulted from Commissions of Inquiry into a whole series of disasters that occurred in the UK (mostly in the latter half of the 1980s). Slapper has recently provided a useful catalogue of these (1993: 424; see also Harrison 1992; Wells 1993) and has rightly noted that in each case 'the relevant companies have been inculpated by the evidence (and with some official enquiry report) in contributing in some significant way to the cause of death' (Slapper 1993: 424). Indeed, such was the weight of evidence relating to corporate misconduct that the combination of these disasters and official reports led to the re-emergence of arguments for corporate manslaughter in the UK (Tombs 1995; Slapper 1993), arguments eventually taken up (albeit inadequately) in the form of proposals by the Law Commission (Law Commission 1996; Cahill 1997), and (it seems) by the Labour Government (*Guardian*, 3 October, 1997).

Finally, there exists a series of Accident Investigation Reports (again, HSE) comprising one-off but highly detailed examinations of particular incidents, usually resulting in one or a small number of fatalities. Again, in each case, despite there rarely following any prosecution (let alone for manslaughter or unlawful killing) these reports usually provide more than enough evidence to point to clear contraventions of the General Duties of the HASAW Act (Tombs 1989).

Each of these bodies of evidence points to the clear conclusion that in the majority of cases of workplace fatalities there is at least a criminal case to answer. Unfortunately, there is no comparable evidence that can be brought to bear on the causation of occupational (fatal) illness as exists for occupational injuries. However, given that the evidence on management responsibility for occupational fatalities points to consistent and basic managerial 'failings', there is absolutely no reason to believe that occupational health is likely to be managed any more effectively. (In fact, the current HSE campaign under the slogan *Good Health is Good Business* is one manifestation of its certainty that health is managed even more poorly than safety.) Further, there is much less scope in the context of health, rather than safety, for responsibility (organisational and legal) for fatalities to be blurred through charges of worker carelessness, apathy, stupidity and non-compliance, so that claims of collusion in the context of ill-health are even less likely to be grounded in reality than they are in the case of safety (Tombs 1991); while workers might be able to mitigate the effects of mismanagement in the context of their safety, they are much less likely to be able to do so with respect to their health. Matters of occupational safety are often related to physical hazards, which are (potentially at least) more 'obvious'; health hazards, by contrast, often operate 'silently', cumulatively and gradually. While occupational health is not occupational safety, the differences mean that it is reasonable to expect greater numbers of deaths from occupational ill-health to be attributable to managements than fatal accidents.

This general attribution of responsibility also holds in the case of deaths at work whilst driving. Superficially, incidents such as these may seem to be a clear case of individual responsibility. However, there is clear evidence that in the majority of cases, employers are failing to meet their legal duties to provide safe systems of work, and to reduce risks 'so far as is reasonably practicable', where they are requiring employees to drive as part of their employment.

David Crichton, the UK Commercial Underwriting and Claims Manager for GA, contends that management style and lack of training contribute to the death toll. He remarked that:

> Even a matter such as tight schedules or giving sales reps too big an area can have an effect on driving standards. Drivers and managers are ever optimistic about the time it will take to get from A to B and this can result in speeding and aggressive driving.
>
> (quoted in Maryon, 1993)

RoSPA cite key causal factors in fatality and accident rates as including: the failure to consider safer, alternative means of transport or indeed routes; the setting of unsafe schedules, journey times and distances; failures to maintain vehicles adequately; failures to invest in vehicles with additional safety features; and the lack of specialised training on offer for regular drivers (RoSPA 1998).

Professor Horne, Director of the Sleep Research Laboratory at Loughborough University, has shown that the economy seems to influence road traffic behaviour as the quality of driving in a geographical area where he has conducted research has worsened with the recession. Between 1989 and 1993 accidents on the M5 involving driver fatigue have increased by 275 per cent, company car drivers being the largest group of victims. Horne and the Automobile Association consider that the recession has led to more drivers, in fear of their jobs, travelling hundreds of miles without a break (*Safety and Health Practitioner*, September 1993). He has written (letter to authors, 5 December, 1994) about research he is currently engaged in that:

Our own work specifically looks at driving fatigue and we find that there is a substantial surge of sleep-related accidents between 5 and 7 in the morning. Many of these drivers are either on their way to work or are coming home after night shifts. In particular, I think that people driving home after their first night on shifts are very vulnerable to falling asleep at the wheel if the drive entails more than 20 minutes on a dull road.

A review by the International Transport Workers Federation (1987) sought to identify the main factors in work-related road traffic deaths. It found that long working hours was one very common factor. The accident rate rose where drivers had been on the road for more than five hours. The accident rate rises steeply with driving duration. There were two and a half times as many accidents where the driver had been driving for 13 hours (with short breaks) than where the driver had been on the road for less than ten hours. Many long distance lorry drivers are effectively required by employers to be on the road for longer than EC regulations permit. More recent British trade union research has strikingly confirmed the tenor of these findings (see, for example, T&G 1997).

On the basis of the above discussion, it should now be clear that there are enormous problems in determining how many people die as a result of being at work, and there are even greater problems reaching a figure amongst this group that can be considered to result from criminal activity or omission on the part of employers. Yet for all the assumptions in, and incompleteness of, the above, it is absolutely certain that the scale of deaths caused by working activity is both enormous and largely obscured. Moreover, on the basis that the most conservative estimate for workplace deaths was about four times greater than homicide, that suggests that at least two out of three fatal injuries appear to occur as a result of criminal acts or omissions on the part of employers, and that employers are more rather than less likely to bear responsibility for deaths from occupationally-caused illness. It is also absolutely clear that *deaths from safety and health crimes far outnumber deaths from homicide.* Yet while the former do not impinge upon popular representations of the crime, law and order problem, the latter are a key element of these.

Costing safety crimes

Finally, it is possible to say something about the costs of occupational safety and health crimes, though here, as with all of the exercises in costing crimes cited previously in this chapter, we are in the realm of guesstimate. There have recently been efforts to estimate the costs of accidents and ill-health at work in Britain. Now, contrary to the claims of Reiman and Box, we cannot simply take occupational fatalities, injuries, or ill-health as synonymous with crimes. On the other hand, as we have noted, there are good reasons for believing that some two-thirds of recorded injuries are the result of illegality on the part of employers;

moreover, there are at least good conceptual reasons for accepting the claim that in the event of ill-health caused by work, this is even more likely to be the result of legal violation on the part of an employer than is the case with an injury (Tombs 1998). Moreover, the data presented below does not take into account occupational fatalities and accidents occurring on the roads which, as we have seen, constitute by far the greatest source of occupational fatalities; in this context, it is worth noting that the Department of Transport has calculated that the average cost of *one* fatal road accident in 1994 was £913140 (cited in RoSPA 1998: 11). Notwithstanding these qualifications, recent estimates of the costs of injuries and ill-health are of interest in any discussion of the costs of corporate and street crimes.

Two recent studies in the UK have attempted to quantify the costs of occupational accidents and ill-health. The first, produced by the Accident Prevention Advisory Unit (APAU) of the Health and Safety Executive (HSE), concluded that costs arising from accidents involving injuries, damage, disruption and production losses represented: 37 per cent of annualised profits; 8.5 per cent of turnover; 5 per cent of operating costs; or the equivalent of closing down the production process for one day a week (HSE 1993). Further, considering the costs of occupational accidents and ill-health at the level of the British economy as a whole, these costs were put at 2–3 per cent of Gross Domestic Product. More recently, a second HSE-sponsored report concluded that the overall cost to British employers of ill-health and accidents at work ranged somewhere between £4–£9billion per year; this is equivalent to 5–10 per cent of all UK trading companies gross trading profits in 1990 (Davies and Teasdale 1994). If accidents and ill-health cost 'the British economy' between £4–9billion per annum, then some two-thirds of this figure might be attributed to safety and health *offences*, that is, between £2.6–6billion. Moreover, it is worth noting that these figures are likely to be significant under-estimates, due to the restricted definition of accidents (HSE 1993: 2, 4; Cutler and James 1996: 757, 759) and of illness caused by working conditions (Davies and Teasdale, 1994: 17–18) that were used in the studies.

Conclusion: corporate crime and victimisation

If there is little doubt that the costs of corporate crimes exceed those associated with street crimes, then it is crucial to add that the economic and physical costs of such crimes may actually be their least inimical element. It is beyond dispute that many of the corporate crimes with which we are concerned in this text have enormous physical consequences: unsafe pharmaceutical products, illegal emissions into the environment, unsafe working conditions, unfit food products, and so on, kill, maim and render sick, both chronically and acutely, thousands of citizens. These physical costs far outweigh those associated with all forms of traditional crime. Yet before closing this chapter, it is worth specifying in a little more detail who the victims of corporate crimes are most likely to be. In this way, we will demonstrate that aside from economic and physical effects, corporate crimes have pernicious and destructive social consequences.

In the previous chapter, we presented a brief overview of some areas in which corporate crimes occur, and what form(s) these take. Such an overview, based upon a division into various categories of (types of) offence, is of some use as both a presentational and an analytical device. However, we should beware of *reifying* any such distinctions between different types of corporate offences, since any divisions are somewhat arbitrary and if overstated may obscure general similarities between them, for example in terms of causation. Any such reification might also obscure important features regarding the consequences of corporate crime.

Now, there is no doubt that on one level, different types of corporate offences have different respective victims (even if these are not always identifiable; see Chapter 5). Certainly Sutherland had written as if different types of offence had different types of victims, stating that the corporations which he studied had 'committed crimes against one or more of the following classes of victims: consumers, competitors, stock-holders and other investors, inventors, and employees, as well as against the state in the form of tax frauds and bribery of public employees' (Sutherland 1983: 227). More recently, Dee Cook provides greater detail on the range of victims who suffer as a result of (what she labels) 'white-collar crimes', noting that

> victims of commercial fraud may be investors, pensioners, pension funds, competitors, and entire banking systems; victims of price-fixing may be consumers, legitimate businesses and tax payers; victims of corporate crime may be employees, investors, competitors and all who depend on the integrity of global economic systems. In the case of pollution and safety violations we are all potential victims of environmental disasters.
>
> (1997: 65)

In the final sentence of that quotation from Cook, there is an important issue being raised. For it is difficult to conceive of any form of corporate crime which does not ultimately impact negatively upon us as victims. While there is an important truth to this observation regarding the ubiquitous nature of corporate crime victimisation, two points of clarification must be made.

First, there is an obvious sense to the claim that 'we' are all victims where we are speaking of crimes against the environment, or even of certain kinds of crimes against consumers, for we are all exposed to the environment and we are all consumers, to greater or lesser extents. But it is perhaps less obvious why 'we' all experience victimisation in the case of economic/financial crimes and health and safety crimes against employees. If we take the former, however, then offences which entail tax evasion clearly deny income to the Treasury and thus affect Government revenues and, ultimately, both local and national provision of services and rates of direct and indirect taxation (Cook 1997: 100). In the case of various forms of apparently inter-organisational crimes – for example, illegal share dealings – then if one or some organisations are victims of these offences, then the costs of this victimisation will be dispersed throughout and beyond that organisation. Thus it may be the case that much corporate and organisational crime is directed against other corporations and organisations (Wheeler and Rothman 1982: 1418; Coleman 1987: 431), but we need to bear in mind that the costs of victimisation will be borne by shareholders (which include those who pay into pension schemes, those who take out insurance, those who own TESSAs, PEPs, and so on), or by Council Tax payers, by direct (and indirect) employees of the organisation-as-victim, and by consumers of any ultimate good or service provided by that company, even if any or all of these groups are unaware of their status as victims. Similarly, while there are 'obvious' victims in the case of health and safety offences against workers, the effects of such victimisation spread far beyond the offending organisation. These costs are borne widely in financial terms through higher prices for goods and services, health and welfare provision, and un- or under-employment. As Woolfson and Beck have recently noted, 'most of the costs of accidents do not fall upon employers. The primary costs are borne by insurance, injured employees' families, and, to a large degree, the welfare state' (1997: 15; see also Atiyah 1997: 108–13). Further, in the case of any form of corporate crime, there are also social costs in terms of the decline of people's quality of life, one aspect of which might be diminishing levels of trust and confidence that we place in organisations with which we interact. (Indeed, for some writers, this abuse of trust is the defining characteristic of 'white-collar crime'; see, for example, Shapiro 1990, and Chapter 6 of this text.)

Second, these considerations need further refinement. Thus while it is at one level accurate and, we believe, important to point out that 'we' are all, ultimately, victims of corporate crimes, it is crucial to be sensitive to the fact that speaking from societies riven by cleavages of class, gender, race and ethnicity, degrees of able-bodiedness, and age, then it is also non-sensical beyond a certain level of abstraction to speak of 'we'. This can be starkly illustrated with respect to the effects of environmental pollution, much of which constitutes crime, since environmental risks are frequently represented as the most ubiquitous of all. Thus, according to one currently dominant trend in social thought, we are now living in an era characterised as a risk society, where risks are ubiquitous and cannot be escaped by anyone (Beck 1992: 22, 53; Beck et al. 1994). On one level, this is accurate as an indication of the qualitative shifts in the nature or risk introduced by chemical, nuclear, and bio-technologies. On the other hand, there is clear evidence that environmental risks are borne to a disproportionate extent by those experiencing the harshest effects of other forms of social and economic inequality. As Welsh has put it,

> the idea that there are global risks which are 'somehow universal and unspecific' recognising none of the social categories which have stratified societies ... is only true at the level of rational abstraction used in global risk assessments.

> (1996: 20)

Thus we are in perfect agreement with Fagan, when he writes that 'the dynamics and dimensions of risk society look remarkably similar to the class society' which risk theorists claim has been transcended (1997: 16). Thus there is now a significant body of evidence which points consistently to the unequal distribution of environmental risks in the United States, so that there is agreement on the association between class, racial and ethnic composition of geographical areas and exposures to environmental pollutants (see Bryant and Mohai, eds 1992; Clark *et al.* 1995; US General Accounting Office 1983; Gould 1986, Stretesky and Lynch 1997; see also Bullard 1990; Hofrichter ed. 1993), while it is clear that environmental risk is highly unequally distributed on a global scale (see, for example, Hofrichter, ed. 1993; Williams, ed. 1996). Although there is at present little work within 'environmental justice studies' in the UK, nor indeed in Western Europe, there is no reason to expect that environmental effects are differentially distributed in these geographical contexts.

Similar observations regarding the unequal distribution of victimisation to corporate crime might be made beyond the realm of environmental crimes. We would argue more generally that to the extent that some forms and levels of pollution, some forms of workplace hazards, some living conditions involve corporate violations of law, then corporate crimes clearly have effects which are over-determined by class, gender, race-ethnicity, and other social cleavages. They are not randomly distributed.

This is further illustrated throughout the body of work on crimes associated with the pharmaceutical industry, since this clearly points to the particular victimisation historically experienced by women. This gendered victimisation to corporate crime follows from the construction of women as reproducers, so that women are differentially victimised by the products of the pharmaceutical industry (Szockyi and Fox 1996). But there are also class and ethnic dimensions which overlay these gendered aspects of victimisation. For example, Finlay notes that one of the reasons why DES victims were able to mobilise effectively was due to the 'demographics' of the drug. DES was an expensive drug, one dispensed largely by private physicians as opposed to those serving public hospitals or clinics:

> Most of those who were exposed to DES are middle- or upper middle-class,

white, well-educated women. The characteristics of the affected population, which came to be known as DES daughters, later contributed to their grassroots activism, pursuit of medical information, and inclination to file a large number of lawsuits. The injured women had the education to do research and become involved in their own medical treatment; and they are from a racial and economic group that tends to regard legislatures and courts not with alienation and distrust but with the expectation that they will produce justice.

(1996: 67–8)

This work on the crimes of the pharmaceutical industry also documents the extent to which women experience victimisation as producers: that is, in addition to being targeted as the consumers of unsafe 'medical' or cosmetic products, they are victimised in the labour market and within workplaces through a range of illegal exclusionary and discriminatory practices (*ibid.*). Indeed, while women work in sectors which are increasingly being recognised as particularly unsafe and unhealthy, representations of hazard have traditionally been associated with male occupations; indeed, despite the fact that research, largely conducted by men, has mostly ignored women's occupational health and safety issues (Szockyi and Frank 1996: 17), trends in data indicates that those areas in which women are over-represented, notably services, are those which exhibit both persistently high, and rising, rates of injuries and ill-health (see Craig 1981; Labour Research Department 1996).

More generally, where workers are victims of health and safety offences, these are most likely to be those in poorest protected and most poorly paid occupations rather than those working in 'inherently' dangerous occupations. This point has been made by Carson, and more recently by Woolfson and colleagues in relation to the UK offshore oil industry (which has drawn upon labour from the unemployment 'blackspots' of Scotland and Northern England). That there are gender and ethnic, as well as class, dimensions to this unequal victimisation is evidenced in the work of John Wrench (Wrench 1996; Lee and Wrench 1980; Wrench and Lee 1982; see also Boris and Pruegl, eds 1996). Understanding victimisation to corporate crime, and differential responses to and public knowledges of this victimisation, thus requires an understanding of various forms of class-race-gender articulations.

Corporate crimes have redistributional effects. One way of viewing corporate crimes is to understand them as a means by which the private corporation is able to externalise some of the actual costs of production. The benefits of this externalisation accrue largely to those who own and control the capitalist corporation. The costs are borne disproportionately by those most dependent upon the social wage. Moreover, the effects of these inequalities operate as a double-bind. For not only are the most disadvantaged members of any social order likely to be those who are most vulnerable to suffering the impacts of corporate crime, but where these are the direct victims of such offending then they are also those least likely to possess the social, economic and technical resources to act upon that victimisation. Corporate crimes do more than rob from the poor to pay the rich: they exacerbate the structures of inequality and vulnerability which capitalism systematically generates. In this sense, they are the most offensive and egregious of illegal acts. It is surely for reasons such as this that commentators have referred to crimes by corporations as 'more abominable' than so-called street crimes (Geis 1990: xv), exacting an enormous toll in terms of 'physical, economic, political, social and human suffering and damage', with far greater economic, physical and social costs than street crimes (Box 1983: 25–34; Reiman 1979).

Chapter 5

Crime, law and order agendas: the (in)visibility of corporate crime

Introduction

Fifteen years ago, Steven Box described a 'collective ignorance' regarding the extent and nature of corporate crime (1983: 16). In the intervening period, while some varieties of corporate crime have undoubtedly been hoisted on to social, political and legal agendas, most notably some forms of 'economic' crimes, corporate offences against (so-called) social regulation (for example, health and safety crimes by employers resulting in occupational deaths, illegal pollution of land, air and waterways), remain largely absent from such agendas.

In this chapter, we consider reasons for the fact that corporate offending remains relatively invisible within crime, law and order agendas. Specifically, the chapter addresses a number of mechanisms through which the discourses of crime, law and order, and the 'collective ignorance' regarding corporate crime are created and maintained, these being: ideologies of business; media representations of crime, law and order; the nature of victimisation; causal complexity; and, finally, methodological problems.

'Crimes', law and politics

We do not intend to discuss formal political and legal agendas at any length here. The ways in which these have historically been constructed have been partly addressed in our discussion of what constitutes corporate crime (Chapter 1), and our discussion of the development of the corporation and law regulating corporate activity (Chapter 2). The construction and impact of such agendas will be further considered when we discuss the regulation (Chapter 8) and sanctioning (Chapter 9) of corporate crime. Suffice it to say here, however, that it is clear that both formal politics and the law play crucial roles in the production and maintenance of dominant definitions of crime, law and order. At the political level, this is the case in terms of particular policies – such as various resourcing for various enforcement agencies – and in the subject matter of the formal politics of crime, law and order. The political rhetoric of crime, law and order also largely excludes corporate crimes. Cries of 'zero tolerance', 'three strikes and you're out', mandatory sentences, being 'tough on crime and tough on the causes of crime', 'short sharp shocks' and protecting and furthering the rights of victims have all been deployed in the context of street or traditional crimes, even though they are perfectly applicable to corporate offending (see, for example, Etzioni 1993; Geis 1996; Lofquist 1993). The collective ignorance is reinforced.

If we turn from formal politics to law and legal regulation, we find that at every stage of the legal process, law tends to operate quite differently with respect to corporate crimes than in the context of 'conventional' crimes. Thus an examination of the very framing of the substance and parameters of legal regulation, its enforcement, the ways in which potential offences and offenders are investigated, the prosecution of offences, and the use of sanctions following successful prosecution, point consistently towards the conclusion that most forms of corporate and organisational offences are relatively decriminalised.

Of course, our argument in this chapter is not to imply that corporate crimes can be treated homogeneously; we are guarded against this by the insights of Sutherland and Bonger, to the effect that certain forms of corporate crimes are more likely to be subject to effective regulation than others (see Chapter 1). Indeed, a key exception to this formal political focus on street crime to the exclusion of corporate crime is to be found in the case of financial crimes, and in particular serious frauds. There are very good reasons why financial crimes, of all forms of corporate crimes, have attracted particular political and legal attention (see Levi 1993; Snider 1991; Tombs 1995).

Economic illegalities, certainly those within and between corporations, may be inimical to the 'effective' functioning of, and also maintenance of legitimacy for, contemporary capitalism (Pearce 1976). Moreover, 'economic regulation' may help to provide a 'predictable and controlled business environment' (Szasz 1984: 114), which is significant given the persuasive argument that corporations often commit crime through attempting to control their operating environments, seeking predictability and stability (Box 1983; see also Chapter 7). Thus research from North America claims that the regulation of economic crimes is likely to be more successful than the enforcement of social regulation (Snider 1991), and more recently has documented how deregulatory initiatives have been targeted at 'social' as opposed to 'economic' regulation (Snider 1997; see also Chapter 8). Thus it is interesting that while recent years have witnessed popular and political controversy in Britain regarding the failings of the Serious Fraud Office, the Securities and Investment Board and, more generally, the DTI in cases such as BCCI, Blue Arrow and

Guinness, there has been no similar level of scrutiny nor outcry with respect to the failings of, for example, the Health and Safety Executive or the Environment Agency, or other agencies in the sphere of 'social' regulation.

Thus certain economic crimes have been subjected to some Government attention, and indeed one of the first acts of the new Labour administration was to announce plans to reform radically financial regulation via the introduction of a new regulatory body which would effectively assume the functions of the Securities and Investments Board, the Bank of England, the Investment Management Regulatory Organisation, the Personal Investment Authority, the Securities and Futures Authority and nine professional bodies currently performing (self) regulatory functions (*Guardian*, 21 May, 1997: 18; *Observer*, 25 May, 1997: 7, 9).

Why have such forms of illegalities received this political and regulatory attention so recently? Punch has argued that changes in the 1980s created new opportunities for business deviance, and that the abuses which were generated led to public debate on controlling the 'new business world' (Punch 1996: 39), a debate which 'brought business deviance to the forefront of the socio-political stage' (*ibid.*). Crucial here, then, was both government promotion of deregulation, and the fact that 'business deviance began to undermine ... business's own long-term interests for relatively healthy, predictable and trustworthy economic relations' (*ibid.*: 41).

On such activity, Levi argues that there is a multinational convergence in prosecution which arises 'largely because of the risks that fraud is posing to popular capitalism, to investments in securities markets, and to deposits in financial institutions, as well as because of the fear of the infiltration of organised crime into business' (1993: 79). For these reasons, Levi claims that we are witnessing more than just 'a cynical political exercise', and that there has been 'a genuine shift of official opinion that the moral and economic, as well as the political, seriousness of commercial fraud had been insufficiently appreciated hitherto' (1987: 285; see also Punch 1996: 41).

These arguments are persuasive up to a point. Not only are various circulation activities crucial to the effective functioning of capitalism, and indeed to any popular legitimacy that is attached to capitalism, but it is also clear that many more of us both perceive and to some extent do have some personal stake in the probity of financial dealings. That is, despite the fact that popular capitalism is much more illusory than real, there are larger numbers of (albeit very small) shareholders now than 20 years ago; many of us have monies invested in pensions, in PEPs, in TESSAs, in endowment policies, and so on, all of which either creates the reality or the belief amongst many of us that we have a stake in the effective and clean functioning of markets. Perhaps more important in renewed efforts to combat serious frauds was the so-called 'Big Bang' in the City, a series of changes designed to attract overseas financial capital to London, so that maintaining the confidence of large-scale overseas investors was crucial. As Black has stated,

> support for 'tough regulation' and 'effective enforcement' increases when the regulation is aimed at an industry where investor confidence is vital, and which is trying to promote itself as an international centre of finance.
>
> (1997: 56)

However, it is important not to exaggerate, nor to represent simplistically, the current nature of serious fraud regulation in Britain.

First, we should remember that when the Serious Fraud Office was established in 1987, it was designed to investigate cases where: the facts and/or the law are of great complexity; or, sums of money in excess of £1m are at risk; or, there is great public interest and concern for some other reason, for example, the identity of the suspect or the employment of a novel method of fraud (Serious Fraud Office 1989: 7). In other words, the SFO was established partly for symbolic reasons – the novelty of any offence would presumably be incorporated within 'complexity', the first rationale, indicating that the more precise point of interest was high profile cases defined in terms of well-known defendants.

Secondly, it should also be clear that the conditions under which the SFO was established mean that it deals with only a tiny proportion of fraud, and thus of financial forms of corporate crime – and this is even more so now than at the time of its establishment, given that the original threshold of £1million at risk was subsequently revised upwards to £5million and then to £6million (Levi 1993: 75). Yet a large-scale, longitudinal survey of large UK companies has shown fraud to be widespread (Levi 1992: 175), so that serious fraud on this scale represents only a tiny proportion of all corporate fraud.

Third, despite the high political profile attached to, and symbolic nature of, the establishment of the SFO and some of its work, it is relatively poorly resourced. Total funding for the SFO for 1996–97 was £16.69 million (Serious Fraud Office 1997: 33). At April 1997, the SFO had 166 permanent and 44 temporary staff on its payroll (*ibid.*: 24), and currently have 12 seconded police officers (personal communication with SFO 22 August, 1997). Resourcing at such levels 'is tiny compared with the size and complexity of the losses it is required to investigate ... and the funds available to some of the corporations and individuals it is investigating' (Levi 1995: 183).

Fourth, we should be wary of treating fraud, even 'serious fraud', as an homogenous category, when it in fact is a term that refers to a heterogeneous range of activities, on the part of various actors and organisational forms, involving victimisation of diverse kinds (Levi 1987; Levi and Pithouse 1992). In this respect, it is worth noting the point made by Levi and Pithouse, who claim 'a certain irony' (though on the basis of the preceding, this seems not to be particularly ironic, in fact all too predictable), that:

much of the increased media and regulatory attention to 'white-collar crime' during the 1980s has occurred in precisely those areas of fraud like insider dealing and the making of multiple share applications which – however politically 'sexy' in the context of financial services deregulation and privatisation issues and the status of offenders – probably have the least effect on the emotions and/or the pockets of real individuals who cannot afford their loss.

(1992: 245)

We should certainly be wary, then, of exaggerating the extent to which even the regulation of some forms of financial/economic crime has become a real (as opposed to symbolic) political priority (see, for example, Weait 1995). However, it is clear to us that the regulation of economic crimes is likely to be more rigorous than is the enforcement of many forms of so-called social regulation, such as occupational safety and health or environmental protection legislation (Snider 1991). The latter is likely to be relatively ineffective since it may impinge upon 'the most minute details of production', rendering such regulation fundamentally 'antagonistic to the logic of firms within a capitalist economy' (Szasz 1984: 114). That being said, it is undoubtedly the case that some forms of social regulation can be functional for capital, albeit under certain conditions, for some companies, over limited periods of time (Mahon 1979; Snider 1991; Tombs 1995).

There is no need to enter into detail on these issues here, but enough has been said to make it clear that we cannot treat corporate crime as an homogeneous category; it is equally clear, however, that it would be inaccurate to treat 'traditional' crime in a similar fashion. Thus the argument here is one of a general relative contrast.

Ideologies of business

One key contributing factor to the collective ignorance regarding corporate crimes is that to point to such offending, to render it visible, requires speaking of legitimate formal organisations as (potential) offenders; crucially, in most instances, it requires speaking of business organisations as offenders or criminals. There are enormous difficulties in the use of such language (see, for example, Lacey 1995: 21, note 34).

It is a truism that business organisations are legitimate organisations. They perform socially useful and socially necessary functions. They create necessary goods and services, employment, taxation revenues, shareholder dividends, and so on. Now, this is not to say that business activity could not be organised differently from current capitalist forms – it clearly could be (Pearce and Tombs 1998: 34–82) – but it is to accept that the business *per se* is not criminal. However, the effect of this truism is one that is vastly exaggerated and has consequences in terms of our 'knowing' of corporate crimes. First, the legitimacy of business organisations is often represented as standing in contradistinction to those objects of 'traditional' crime concerns; most of those who end up being processed through the criminal justice system are treated as some form of burden upon society in a way that business organisations are not. This is intimately related to a second point. Where business organisations engage in criminal activity, then this is represented and/or interpreted (not least by many academics; Pearce and Tombs 1990, 1991) as side effects of their core, legitimate activities, a clear contrast with representation of many forms of conventional criminality, within which various manifestations of pathology remain predominant. In fact, there are good reasons for accepting that criminality is endemic to business activity within corporate capitalism. We shall address the theoretical arguments in support of this latter claim in the following chapters of this book (but see also Pearce and Tombs 1998). The empirical basis for such a claim is undermined by the type of data presented in Chapter 3, all of which points to the conclusion, as we have noted, that corporate crime is widespread and pervasive. Alongside the notion that crime is a side-effect of legitimate business activity stands a third, and closely related, claim: namely that where business organisations are involved in criminality, then this is mostly trivial, consisting of illegalities which are *mala prohibita* rather than *male in se*. Such a claim was one focus of criticism in Sutherland's early work on 'white-collar crime', as we have seen, and remains difficult to sustain either empirically or theoretically (Pearce and Tombs 1990, 1991; Wells 1993); nonetheless, it retains a popular predominance (and, unfortunately, some academic support; see Chapter 8).

Of course, it should be noted that these distinctions between business organisations and traditional criminals, and in particular the legitimacy that attaches to business organisations, are far from static. Indeed, since the early 1980s, Britain has witnessed a generalised and often very conscious construction of a pro-business ideology, one of a very particular form within which the concept of free enterprise has been resurrected in the context of a struggle to reassert neo-liberal hegemony (Pearce and Tombs 1998). An element of this is of course a particular version of law and order from which business offences are largely excluded (Brake and Hale 1992: 134). We need to emphasise here that the crucial signifier is '*free* enterprise' rather than simply 'enterprise' – that is, business activity increasingly free from (illegitimate) regulation. It is no coincidence, then, that the reassertion of this ideology has been accompanied by very conscious, if highly selective, efforts at deregulation (Tombs 1996). Such has been the effect of this ideological and material assault on ('social') regulation that the recently elected Labour government has, far from seeking to challenge it, sought to embrace it positively, seeking to establish its pro-business credentials, and dovetailing perfectly with its explicit adoption of highly conservative assumption regarding appropriate modes of 'crime control' (Brownlee 1998).

The mass media

Images of crime, law and order within the mass media both reflect and in turn reinforce dominant social constructions of what constitutes the crime problem in contemporary Britain, within which 'traditional' or street crimes are central. Before entering the detail of our argument around this claim, we should emphasise that we are not claiming that there is no attention to corporate offending. On this point, we should note Levi's words of caution, when he stated that,

> the British and American television viewer or reader of the quality or even some of the 'tabloid' national press might find ample daily evidence to refute the assertion – still repeated in many key criminological texts (Box 1983) – that because of the 24 hours news cycle and the fact that they are owned by 'big business', white-collar crime receives little or no attention in the media. This was an over-simplification even when Box wrote it, but despite the growing concentration of the Press, it is even less true in the mid-1980s.
>
> (1987: 11)

He later claims that 'conventional notions of media neglect of white-collar crime and fraud are now *passé*, even if they were ever wholly true' (Levi and Pithouse 1992: 229). Now, Levi is correct to warn against over-simplification here, even if he is rather unfair in his characterisation of Box's own claims on this matter (see Box 1983: 17, 53, 64). But he is, for us, wrong if he is implying that corporate crimes are accurately represented as a phenomenon, or fairly represented alongside conventional crimes. Despite the fact that some corporate crimes are represented via mass media, this does not obviate, and in some ways actually reinforces, the fact that dominant representations of crime, law and order issues within various forms of media have the effect of obscuring or removing corporate crimes from such discussions.

If we examine the treatment of crime, law and order in the broadcast media, the relative invisibility of corporate crimes is immediately clear. A survey of fictional treatments of crime issues across any of the terrestrial or satellite TV channels would reveal a preoccupation with 'cops and robbers', that is, with various aspects of (albeit fictionalised) street crimes. Such is precisely the stuff of classic series such as *Dixon of Dock Green, Z Cars, The Sweeney, Starsky and Hutch* and *Hill Street Blues*, their more contemporary counterparts, such as *The Bill, Homicide, NYPD Blue*, and *Due South*, and the range of crime-based movies shown across TV channels. This is not to imply that there are not occasional treatments of corporate crimes – though where corporate crimes are the subject of fictional broadcasting, these crimes are likely to be financial crimes (*Wall Street* being the famous example; but see Denzin 1990) – but they are extremely rare. In other words, precisely *contra* the claims of Levi, who refers to particular types of programmes 'on abuses of power by business-people or politicians' (Levi 1987: 10; Levi and Pithouse 1992: 239), the issue is one of the overwhelming, reinforcing mass of images rather than particular exceptions. Thus, over 20 years ago, Chibnall documented carefully how discrete areas of crime reporting could converge to produce 'blanket' conceptualisations regarding 'law-and-order' (Chibnall 1977); more recently, Randall has noted that while there is coverage of 'business illegality' in the media, there is relatively little attention to this with the effect that it becomes 'buried' (Randall 1995: 112–13, and passim). As Mathiesen admirably puts it in his recent discussion of the role of the Synopticon in modern capitalist societies,

> with regard to the media, the total gestalt produced by the messages of television is much more important than the individual programme or even type of programme ... The total message inculcates a general understanding of the world, a *world paradigm* if you like.
>
> (1997: 228–30, original emphasis)

Now, one reason for this generalised bias in fictional broadcasting may be the claim that many forms of corporate crime do not make for very interesting television, particularly where the crimes involved are based upon acts of omission: not testing certain hazardous substances; falsifying data required by a regulatory body; meeting to fix markets or prices; not acting upon information about the obvious and serious risks of ferry turnaround times; not meeting standards of maintenance on industrial plant; training pensions sales-staff in the techniques and languages of mis-selling, may not, on the face of it, make for very gripping television. However, we should be aware that traditional crime is just as intrinsically uninteresting, only made worthy of drama through fictionalisation, so that, for example, televisual images of policework bear little or no relation to the ways in which most police officers spend most of their time. In fact, there are no real reasons why dramatised accounts of corporate offending need be any less (or more!) interesting than those of conventional crimes – certainly the documented accounts of 'normalised deviance' within NASA in the lead up to the fatal *Challenger* launch decision (Vaughan 1996), or Goodrich's decision to conceal problems with its aircraft brakes and to proceed on the basis of falsified testing data (Vandivier 1982), or the Heavy Electrical Price-Fixing Conspiracy (Geis 1967), or BA's 'Dirty Tricks' campaign against Virgin employees (Gregory 1994), would all make for viewing just as intrinsically interesting as many forms of fictionalised crime drama.

These latter examples are all, of course, drawn from actual case histories. Indeed, if one turns to non-fictional programming, there is perhaps more extensive coverage of corporate crime within the overall diet of crime, law and order issues. Thus there are certainly treatments of corporate crime amongst the classic documentary series such as *Panorama* and *World in Action*, and more latterly *Dispatches*, *Network First* and *First Tuesday*. Also of note here is the odd coverage of some forms of corporate crime amongst consumer issues programming such as *Watchdog*, *The Cook Report* and even *That's Life*. Nevertheless, any focus on corporate crime is vastly outweighed by the steady stream of non-fictional treatments of traditional crime issues. More important here than frequent one-off documentaries is the cumulative effect of *Crimewatch, Crimefile, Police Five*, and so on. Indeed, amongst the latter it is worth noting that *Crimewatch* attracts a mass audience – and this has an almost exclusive focus upon conventional crimes within a format based around 'documentary reconstruction', using the drama of fiction to represent particular crime events (Schlesinger and Tumber 1994: 248–70). What the latter also illustrates is the media focus upon, and reproduction of, fears around what Stanko has called 'stranger danger'. One effect of the fuelling or production of such fears is at the same time to focus attention away from familiar or other apparently innocuous contexts – thus we tend not to concern ourselves with guarding against victimisation when we visit a local shopping centre, are contacted by a new, privatised water or gas supplier, or receive literature from a private pensions or insurance provider. And corporate executives are equally aware that they are relatively unlikely to be viewed as potential offenders: while it is ironic, it is on one level unsurprising that at the same time that as the Chief Executive of Britain's largest private pensions provider – the Prudential – was launching a television and poster advertising campaign featuring himself as the 'trusting face of the man from the Pru', the company was more heavily implicated than any other in the offences related to pensions mis-selling, and was 'named' as one of the most recalcitrant companies in terms of failures to settle urgent cases (*Guardian*, 17 November, 1997).

This imbalance in the coverage of 'crime' in the broadcast media is also reproduced through daily newspaper coverage of crime, law and order issues, where conventional versions of crime, law and order predominate. To claim that that corporate crime is not covered in daily newspapers would be inaccurate. But a cursory examination of recent crime, law and order reporting in a number of national newspapers suggests a number of clear, if at this stage highly provisional, conclusions.[1]

First, the sheer volume of coverage of conventional crimes vastly outweighs that of corporate crimes. Second, where corporate crime *is* treated in mainstream print media, such coverage is less rather than more prominent than treatments of conventional crime. Corporate crime is less likely to be reported within the mass circulation tabloids than it is in the broadsheets; and within broadsheets, corporate crime reporting has a lesser profile than that of conventional crimes, being located in specialist sections rather than in earlier news and features pages. Third, corporate crime is also treated in more specialist rather than popular contexts (a point which Levi himself notes: 1987: 10). Amongst the broadsheets, corporate crime receives by far the greatest volume of coverage in the *Financial Times* (see also Stephenson-Burton 1995) but this is a publication which has a specialist rather than general readership and stands tenth out of eleventh in overall circulation tables for national daily newspapers (the circulation of the *Sun*, for example, is about 13 times greater). Fourth, and as should be clear from some of the previous points, where corporate crimes are addressed in the print media, these tend to be financial/economic crimes – that is, those kinds of activities which have been subject to some recent political and regulatory attention (see above) and upon which academics are most likely to focus (see below).

Further, while specialist sections of broadsheets *do* cover aspects of corporate crime, they tend to do so in a way that does not treat these as crime, law and order issues. There are various ways in which this latter effect is produced, and indeed these are common both to print media and the broadcast media considered above. First, representations of corporate crimes tend not to treat them as *corporate* crimes. Most notably, corporate crimes are considered via personalities, and it is the dominance of individual, 'respectable' figures that renders them newsworthy (Levi and Pithouse 1992). Relatedly, such crimes are considered newsworthy for their very abnormality. In other words, they may become individualised, which at the same time has the effect, in many instances, of obscuring their actual causes – beyond individual idiosyncrasy, character or pathology – and thus their normality and routineness. Moreover, to focus upon the individuals involved in such crimes is to obscure the corporations, structures and systems within which, and on behalf of which, they are likely to have offended.

If the corporate origins and nature of corporate crimes are often obscured in their reporting, then so is the fact that they are *crimes* (see Reiner 1997: 196). In support of his claim that there has been a considerable increase since the 1960s in media coverage of 'business crime', Levi himself refers to 'the cult of *expose machismo* in media cycles that favours the making of programmes on abuses of power', not least because 'scandal sells' (Levi 1987: 10, 12). Now, the terms 'scandal' or 'abuse', the latter in particular common currency when referring to corporate crimes (Tumber 1993), are no doubt highly critical; but abuse is a term which carries with it implications of (im)morality rather than legal offence. Moreover, where crimes are treated as scandals (or exposés, and so on), this again serves to emphasise their novelty or rarity. In these ways, the normality of corporate crimes, and their location within (and commission on behalf of) a particular organisational form – the corporation – is again obscured.

The term 'scandal' is one instance of the more general way in which particular forms of language are central to the production and reproduction of crime, law and order issues. Language carries with it particular connotations of causation (and thereby appropriate modes of prevention and regulation) and effects (seriousness). Wells has noted the potency of different forms of language attaching to different types of criminal activity:

> The word 'fraud' is an anaesthetising generic term for a number of offences including theft. If we do not call a white-collar thief a thief then we should not be surprised that it sounds a little odd to talk of a corporation stealing (or

wounding or killing). The idea is difficult to contemplate because our image
of the thief is of an individual physically taking the property of another. There
is a conflict between the images, reinforced by the choice of language, of
different types of offence and offender and the possible categories into which
they could legally be placed.

(1993a: 10)

Thus, she continues,

Through the use of language different messages and meanings are
communicated. 'Mugging', 'joyriding', 'shoplifting', 'glassing', 'vandalism' are
examples of the many colloquial terms in use for conveying the social
meanings of behaviour; each has an equivalent legal term and definition. The
social vocabulary for corporate harms is less well-developed.

(*ibid.*: 12)

Thus if we take as an example occupational safety and health crimes, it
is clear that the vast majority of these remain cast as 'accidents', which is
likely to mean that there has been little or usually no investigation of their
circumstances, nature and relationship to law and legal duties. The
language of 'accidents' is one which focuses upon specific events,
abstracting them from a more comprehensible context (Scheppele
1991). It evokes discrete, isolated and random events, and carries with it
connotations of the unforeseeable, unknowable and unpreventable,
despite the fact that any examination of a range of incidents reveals,
common, systematic, foreseeable and eminently preventable causes and
consistent locations of responsibility. Similarly, both the languages of
accident and illness invoke events or phenomena in which victims are
implicated, via their carelessness, apathy, or lifestyles (bad eating, lack of
exercise, alcohol or tobacco use, and so on; Tombs 1991).

Finally, the term 'accident' carries with it implications regarding
intentionality, or the lack of it, which are crucial in the context of safety
and health crimes. Thus Goldman notes that what she calls 'accidentality
terms',

provide us with an account of the mental element – intention, will, desire,
deliberation, purpose, etc. – in some event. When describing some incident or
process as an 'accident', or having 'occurred/been done accidentally' rather
than 'deliberately' or 'intentionally', we conflate information not just about
causation, and perhaps (if pertinent) degrees of culpability and fault to be
imputed, but also about the element of consciousness that intruded into the
event.

(1994: 51–2)

There is no doubt that some of this language is the result of conscious
corporate manipulation, both generally and in relation to specific events
(Wells 1993: 40). This is hardly surprising given the privileged access to,
and indeed the ownership of, all forms of mass media by large corporate
interests. The concentration of ownership, the internationalisation of
media and communication markets, the role of advertisers and sponsors,
and consistent gnawing away at public broadcasting systems by corporate

capital all affect the content of various media forms (Bagdakian 1997; Curran and Seaton 1988; Lorimer 1994; McChesney 1997; Tumber 1993). As Wells notes, and as is particularly of relevance given the nature of victimisation in the case of many forms of corporate crimes, the further removed the harms they cause are from the public experience, then the easier is such manipulation (1993a: 40).

To say this is of course not to claim that this effect is one that can be characterised as any simplistic determining or controlling; we would not deny that, 'even in the area of business and financial coverage, the mass media, whilst still having a role in reproducing dominant ideology, do at times provide a more open terrain' (Tumber 1993: 347). Levi himself has pointed to the role that the media can and do play in exposing some forms of corporate crime, not least through drawing attention to the plight of victims (see Zedner 1997: 593).

Indeed, the use of particular forms of language need not be understood simply, or perhaps even largely, as the result of conscious manipulation, since 'The social construction of behaviour and events results from a complex interaction between a number of factors, including cultural predispositions, media representations, and legal rules, decisions, and pronouncements' (Wells 1993a: 13). What we can conclude is that, all in all, the media both reflect, and help to construct, dominant conceptions of crime, law and order, from which corporate crimes are largely excluded. As Hillyard and Sim have recently stated,

> it is important not to postulate a deterministic position in terms of the relationship between the mass media and popular consciousness but as a range of sociological work has demonstrated that relationship exists and is built on a system of power which has the capability to define in as well as define out what is newsworthy, important and relevant.
>
> (1997: 57)

Even academics who tend to deny the obscuring of corporate crime within mass media in fact help to reproduce this. For example, a recent text examining 'The Media Politics of Criminal Justice' contains one half page consideration of 'white-collar crimes', and at least one other one-line reference to these crimes amongst its almost 300 pages (Schlesinger and Tumber 1994). One of these two references was the claim that 'white-collar crimes' had been found to be 'slighted to a lesser degree', that they 'received basically the same display as street crime stories', and that the 'cases concerning fraud and insider dealing in the late 1980s ... [have] given white-collar crime a prominent position in the media' (Schlesinger and Tumber 1994: 185).

The nature of victimisation

It has recently, and rightly, been noted that victimology has become a key growth area in criminology and law (Mawby and Walklate 1994). A key element of victimology is the uncovering of unrecorded crime. But there are good reasons for believing that while such techniques are of some use in the context of 'conventional' crimes, they are less useful in attempting to gauge the incidence of corporate crime and victimisation. Most fundamentally, this is so due to the fact that most forms of corporate crimes are distinct from most forms of conventional crimes in terms of the victim-offender relations which are involved. Crucial here is what we can best term the issue of 'proximity'. In many forms of traditional crime there is, or must at some point be, a degree of proximity between an offender and victim: this is most obviously the case with regard to personal assaults, robberies and so on; but it also applies to theft of and from motor vehicles and to burglaries, in the sense that even if absent from a dwelling or car at the time of the theft or robbery, the victim does have some proximity in time and space to these as owners, residents, drivers, or passengers. By contrast, in the case of corporate crimes, there are frequently enormous distances between offender and victim, in terms of both space and time. This has important implications in terms of awareness and proof of victimisation. There are a variety of reasons which lead to this conclusion.

First, many victims of corporate crimes are unlikely even to be aware of their status as victims (Croall 1989; Meier and Short 1995). There are two different types of this lack of awareness. On the one hand, we might be aware of some unfavourable personal circumstance but not that we have been the victim of any type of legal offence. For example, most of us are unlikely to think of our workplace as a causal site when suffering some form of illness, and even less likely to consider unhealthy conditions in terms of illegality on the part of our employer. Where our child suffers from breathing difficulties, we may think in some generalised way about the state of our local environment (for example, poor air quality), but are unlikely to concretely consider ourselves as possible victims of illegal emissions from local taxis, buses, vans, and so on. Similarly, in the event of accidents – be these major or minor – ideologies of the accident-prone worker are so prevalent that workers often routinely place blame upon themselves, as a result of their carelessness or bad luck (Tombs 1991). Where representations of self-blaming or collusion are resisted, victims of safety and health crimes may still be unaware of the legal status of what they have experienced – that is, they may have a sense that they are victim of an injustice, or a wrong, but not a criminal offence on the part of an employer. On the other hand, we may be completely unaware of our status as victims. For example, it is unlikely that when people buy port products that they might stop to think of themselves as victims of a long-running, global lysine cartel (Palast 1998); when buying glass products they are victims of a long-standing soda ash cartel amongst leading European chemicals companies (*Chemistry & Industry*, 1991: 2); when buying white or other electrical goods in Britain in recent years, most of us will not have stopped to consider that these might be cheaper, or that there might be more genuine choice, were it not for price-fixing or the creation of illegal barriers to market entry amongst manufacturers and retailers (*Guardian*, 21 May, 1997, 31 May, 1997, 31 July, 1997); when choosing meat products in the most well-known high street stores, we do not expect labels to mislead by under-stating the percentage of water added to the product (*Guardian*, 29 October, 1997).

A second general issue in relation to corporate crime victimisation is the ability, or most people's perceptions of their abilities, to seek redress. That is, where victims of health and safety crimes *are* aware of their status as victims, actually acting upon this awareness is often extremely difficult (again, see Croall 1989). Indeed, an informed understanding of the extent of these difficulties may actually act as a disincentive against reporting or acting. This might be manifest in rationalisations invoking bad luck or being more careful in the future, and uttering platitudes such as 'win some, lose some' or 'once bitten, twice shy', and so on. Yet even where victims might seek redress, either independently (via civil law, for example) or through an enforcement agency, then distances in time and space between victim and offender(s), and thus of proving an offence has occurred even where – as is often the case – the offender is identified are likely to prove overwhelming obstacles.

Thus many who comment upon the problematic nature of identifying corporate crime make a useful comparison with many forms of conventional crimes. In the case of the latter, it is argued, the fact of a crime is rarely an issue; what is at issue, and what consumes agency (here, police) resources is identifying an offender. In the case of many forms of corporate crime, however, problems frequently arise in quite the opposite way. That is, there is very often little problem in identifying an offender (Clarke 1990), although we should note that this is not always the case, not least given the (apparent) complexity of some forms of organisational structures (more on this below); here, the issue is actually establishing whether any offence has occurred. This involves quite a different set of problems and processes to those commonly found with respect to conventional crime.

Crimes related to occupational and environmental exposures are classic examples here. Thus if workers are aware that a skin rash, breathing problems, nausea, headaches and so on are likely to have a primary cause in working conditions, an enormous burden of proof rests with them. And proof in such instances must make reference to scientific discourses, this raising the location and role of expertise and experts, and the fact of unequal access to these, be they toxicologists, pharmacologists, epidemiologists, and so on. Proof also requires that highly unequal access to legal expertise – an inequality likely to be exacerbated given current proposals regarding legal aid (Dyer 1997; Woolf 1996) – be overcome. Finally, also at issue here is what Becker was referring to via his notion of a 'hierarchy of credibility' (1967), whereby he seeks to demonstrate how power is rather more significant than 'truth' in producing credible statements.

However, there *are* instances where identifying an offender to the point where such identification can be proven in law can be difficult, to say the least. Even if one is aware that a particular condition can be caused by workplace exposures – for example, the well-known diseases associated with exposure to asbestos fibres – then there can remain enormous difficulties in locating exposures to a *particular* workplace or employer, at a *particular* time. The fact that many industrial diseases take long periods to develop – sometimes as much as 40 or 50 years – makes pursuing (let alone proving) a case against a particular employer very difficult, this compounded where a worker has been employed by different companies over the course of a working life (Health and Safety Commission 1996a: 63). Two recent cases, one relating to environmental exposure to asbestos, which found against Turner & Newall, and the other which resulted in a judgement against the former National Coal Board, are paradigmatic instances of the general process being highlighted here.

Two test cases against Turner & Newall were won in October 1995, each of which related to environmental exposure to asbestos dusts during childhood, whilst living in the vicinity of a T&N subsidiary's factory in Leeds. The struggle for workers' compensation for asbestos-caused diseases is a long and well-known one (see, for example, Brodeur 1985), and in many ways represents the classic history of corporate denial, deception, falsification and concealment of evidence, only to be followed by defeat in the face of overwhelming evidence (not least in the form of dead bodies). Indeed, the legal struggle over environmental exposures represents what has been called the third-wave of asbestos litigation (Wikeley 1997). It is interesting in the light of this history that T&N representatives were still claiming, during these recent test cases, that the company did not know of environmental risks to local residents. Also of interest is that the crucial documents required to expose the fact that the company did have such knowledge – internal documents dating back to 1943 – only came to light following an action taken by Chase Manhattan Bank over use of asbestos in the construction of its headquarters, an action itself prompted by claims made against Chase Manhattan for compensation for asbestos related diseases (*Guardian*, 28 October, 1995: 2). It is perhaps instructive that it took a large, powerful corporation to succeed (in exposing illegal activity) through the use of disclosure legislation where groups of activists had failed for years (Wikeley 1997: 270).

The second set of cases worth noting here are those in which six miners won damages in January 1998 as a result of a test case of negligence against the NCB for failing to take reasonable steps to minimise the 'creation and dispersion' of coal dust through available techniques, and as such exposed miners to a trigger for bronchitis and emphysema. The hearing began in October 1996, and was 'the longest running industrial injury action' in British legal history. More than 100 000 former miners are expected to make similar claims, as will the families of those miners who have died since their claims were first registered. (Almost half of those who had registered claims have died since that registration.) The Coal Board were aware of research in the 1970s which showed that exposure to coal dust leads to bronchitis and emphysema (*Guardian*, 24 January, 1998: 2, 7).

Szockyi and Frank summarise the generalised problems illustrated by these two sets of cases:

> Victims of corporate crime engage in a long struggle to gain recognition of their victims status. The causes of the victim's injuries are hidden from view. Family, friends, and the official agencies of government may presume that the injury is just a random happenstance rather than a consequence of corporate misconduct. The individual who has been harmed must first overcome this presumption in order to be treated as a crime victim. The victim must then establish evidence that the corporation in question was responsible for the injury or health problems *and*, in many cases, that the corporation acted unreasonably and unlawfully. Only rarely will an act of corporate victimisation be unambiguously determined to be the result of a crime.
> (Szockyi and Frank 1996: 8, emphasis in original)

Despite the common complexities involved in the struggles to win the two groups of cases discussed above, in one sense they were still less problematic than some efforts to pursue legal actions against corporations. For some attempts to pursue legal cases against corporations must also confront one further layer of legal complexity, which arises as a result of (apparently) complex organisational structures. The existence of subsidiaries, autonomous sub-units, strategic business units, and so on, all appear to create legal difficulties in tracing lines of decision-making and accountability. Most famously, a key element of Union Carbide's defence against any criminal and civil actions following the Bhopal disaster was the claim made from Union Carbide Corporation head offices in Danbury, Connecticut, that the plant at Bhopal was managed, in respect of safety as in all other respects, by local management, and that it was owned by Union Carbide India Ltd, a distinct legal entity (see Pearce and Tombs 1998). Similarly, Woolfson and colleagues describe the attempts by families of the 11 men who died when the Cormorant Alpha crashed into the sea during a routine two-minute flight taking offshore workers from oil rig to accommodation barge. When families of the deceased men began to seek compensation against Shell and Exxon in US courts, Shell took out an injunction to prevent this, ensuring that compensation be sought in Scotland. Shell warned that 'violation of this court order ... could result in the families and survivors concerned being subject to bodily imprisonment' (Woolfson *et al.* 1996: 422). In a move completely echoing that of UCC in the Bhopal case, Shell argued that American litigation was inappropriate because Shell UK was an independent, British company. The matter was eventually settled out of court (*ibid.*: 416–25).

If we strip away many of the excessive claims regarding globalisation, we can still accept that significant numbers of companies are organised across national borders; this means that the issue of locating control can be problematic, and will become more so if cross-national operations really are increasing. Finally, even within national jurisdictions, the apparent increasing complex organisation and fragmentation of businesses, as well as the increased prevalence of contracting out and 'self-employment', problems of locating causality and lines of accountability and responsibility are likely to be exacerbated (Keane 1995; Tombs 1995).

Further, there is a real sense in which those individuals and groups most likely to be victims of corporate crimes are those who are least able to recognise their status, or act upon this recognition. As we noted in Chapter 4, those most likely to suffer the effects of illegal environmental emissions – to land, air or waterways – are often the most vulnerable members of any society – that is, risks of victimisation to many corporate offences are not randomly distributed. For example, victims of safety and health crimes are much more likely to work in smaller rather than larger workplaces, or to be self-employed or on short- or fixed-term contracts, to be non-unionised, and receiving relatively low levels of pay; in other words, safety and health crimes remain relatively invisible partly because patterns of victimisation exacerbate what have been called, in another context, structures of vulnerability (Nichols 1986). Similarly, consumers most likely to suffer the effects of illegally prepared or stored foodstuffs, or most likely to buy illegally defective (i.e. unsafe or unfit) goods, are those at the lowest end of the economic spectrum, for whom there is little opportunity to 'pay for quality' (where quality is, unfortunately, often equivalent to legal and safe). Those most likely to have fallen prey to the illegal sales methods used by pensions companies were those who were least sophisticated in terms of knowledge of financial products, and had a misplaced faith in their ability to handle such affairs independently (Black 1997: 143), a point surely partly explained as a rationalisation given that most of these victims would not have been able to secure access to independent financial advice, since this access is more likely the greater one's income and wealth. In this way, victimisation processes in relation to corporate crimes may not be dissimilar to those of other forms of crime, where it is perhaps more appropriate to conceive of victimisation as part of day-to-day existence, a process rather than an event (see Maguire 1997: 172).

Causal complexity

There are other aspects to complexity which render corporate crimes relatively invisible, not least being those related to the complexity in commission or causation. While the force of these points should be noted, we should recognise at the outset that this very notion of complexity is a socially constructed one. 'Complexity' is partly constructed through legal processes, such as the nature of the burden of proof has been placed upon a particular set of (potential) offender-victim relationships. It is partly constructed through regulatory structures, so that some forms of corporate crimes may actually seem much more complex than they 'really are' simply because of the fragmented, under- or over-lapping, and often downright confusing responsibilities spread across different regulatory bodies. And complexity is also intimately linked to resource issues, so that differential representations of complexity can be used as a means of attracting enormous resources to 'fight' crime – as in the trade in illegal substances – or as a means of rationalising regulatory withdrawal.

These points being made, it is certainly the case that some forms of corporate crimes involve complex planning, perhaps most notably in the commission of financial crimes. This complexity is partly a consequence of the transnational nature of some corporate crimes, which also renders effective regulation problematic (see Chapter 7). Thus Levi notes that 'almost all serious securities frauds involve extraterritorial informational needs on the part of national agencies' (1993: 79); for example, 80 per cent of cases investigated in London 'have some cross-border aspects' (*ibid.*: 80).

Similarly, Braithwaite has stated of transnational pharmaceutical industry crime that:

> the offences that we are discussing are complex to start with, before one adds the problem of international jurisdictional tangles. There is the complexity of the books – paper trails through the finances and the raw scientific data that are difficult to follow. Then there is the scientific complexity of cutting-edge technology ... Then there is organisational complexity.
>
> (1993: 14)

However, while there is no doubt that many forms of corporate crimes are complex in their causation, it would be unwise to exaggerate this aspect of corporate offending. It is frequently the case that corporate crime arises from very simple acts of commission or omission – the failure to adequately test or label substances, the failure to train or inform employees, the failure to meet basic standards of environmentally-protective engineering standards, and so on. Relatedly, then, the calls for non-jury trials to be introduced to deal with serious fraud cases (see Levi 1993a: 187–93), a call precisely based in assumptions of complexity, or the decision in the 'McLibel' case to try to a judge rather than a jury on the grounds of scientific complexity (Vidal 1997: 89–93), are actually erroneous. For what is at issue in such cases is exactly that which is at issue in the vast majority of cases involving a whole range of other forms of alleged illegal activity – namely assessments by 12 members of the public regarding the veracity and consistency of conflicting versions of events and phenomena.

In other words, we would be wise not to exaggerate the reality of what may seem to be enormous legal and technical complexities in the context of corporate crime, even though there are particular legal issues which pertain to some forms of such crime. In fact, there are two other issues that are of greater relevance here than causal complexity *per se*, but which can be confused with complexity.

The first is the carefully constructed and legally protected corporate veil behind which corporate structures, decision-making, lines of accountability and responsibility remain largely hidden from public scrutiny, a veil which often serves to confound legal challenge. Organisational complexity is often a means of confounding legal scrutiny or challenge. As Snider puts it graphically, 'Acts tend to be hidden in a vast organisational matrix that impedes surveillance or the attribution of responsibility. Records are hard to find, easy to doctor, and highly manipulable; and few signs of criminality are visible to external observers' (1993a: 79). That this complexity is more apparent than real, however, is clear in the sense that once one shifts to an internal level, organisations seem not to find insurmountable problems in distributing the 'goods' which accrue from their organisational activities. As Braithwaite wryly observes,

> When Corporations want clearly defined accountability, they can generally get it. Diffused accountability ... is in considerable measure the result of a desire to protect individuals within the organisation by presenting a confused picture to the outside world.
>
> (1984: 324; see also Pearce and Tombs 1998: 120–2)

Second, is the problem of intentionality. This is intimately related to complexity, to the extent that what may appear to be issues of organisational complexity may in fact be an effect of the inapplicability of common notions of intentionality to corporate crimes. As Black *et al.* have recently commented,

> white-collar crimes are often well-disguised by the complex business transactions within which they are woven. Indeed, the difference between a crime and ordinary business activity often rests on the issue of intent – a subjective state notoriously difficult to ascertain.
>
> (1995: 29–30)

Thus when we are dealing with corporate crime we are dealing with corporate actors (and all the obscurity thereby entailed) rather than individuals, and relatedly with a body to which traditional, individualised notions of intention sit rather uneasily. The problem of grafting individualised notions of intention onto corporate entities was well illustrated in the failed attempt to prosecute Townsend Car Ferries Ltd and a number of its directors for manslaughter when the *Herald of Free Enterprise* capsized. Against pressure from the coroner, the jury at the inquest returned a verdict of unlawful killing. On appeal, The Queen's Bench

Divisional Court supported the coroner's view that there was insufficient evidence to prosecute Townsend Car Ferries Ltd, but accepted in principle the concept of corporate homicide provided that 'both the *mens rea* and *actus reus* of the offence could be established against those that were *identified* as the embodiment of the corporate body itself' (*Times Law Report* 1 October, 1987). After intense and continued pressure by the Herald Families' Association (Dover Port Committee, 1988), the Director of Public Prosecutions (DPP) issued eight summonses for manslaughter arising out of the tragedy. P&O European Ferries (Dover) Ltd (formerly Townsend Car Ferries Ltd) and two of its directors, two of its captains, the Bosun, an assistant bosun and the Chief Officer were charged with manslaughter.

In the trial the argument proceeded on a charge of reckless manslaughter and turned upon an interpretation of the legal doctrine of identification. According to this, those who work for a corporation are distinguished as being either its 'hand or brain', that is its ordinary servants or its 'directing mind and will' (Leigh 1969; Lacey *et al.* 1990). This latter notion informs the principle of identification, which in law requires that at least one controlling officer must be found personally guilty of manslaughter (Slapper 1993; Wells 1993); English law does not provide for the aggregation of the actions of different controlling officers (Moran 1992; Slapper 1993), even though this is possible in other jurisdictions (Slapper 1993), not least within US federal law (Wells 1993a: 118–20). The presupposition in the trial was that one or more of the directors and 'directing minds' had been personally reckless as to the drownings, that is, that somebody had ignored an 'obvious and serious risk that the vessel would sail with her bow doors open, when trimmed by the head, and capsize'. The judge dismissed the case against the directors and the company and the DPP withdrew its case against the other defendants.

There is a further point to make regarding intention, one made originally – to the best of our knowledge – by Reiman in a simple but striking fashion. Reiman contrasts the motives (and moral culpability) of most acts recognised as intentional murder with what he calls the indirect harms on the part of absentee killers, by which he means, for example, deaths which result where employers refuse to invest in safe plant or working methods, where manufacturers falsify safety data for new products, where illegal discharges are made of toxic substances into our environment, and so on. Reiman notes that intentional murderers commit acts which are focused upon one (or, rarely, more than one) specific individual, a point which we know holds for contemporary Britain, despite moral panics about 'stranger danger'; thus in such cases the perpetrator – whom in many respect fits our archetypal portrait of a criminal – 'does not show general disdain for the lives of his fellows' (Reiman 1979: 60). Reiman contrasts such forms of intentional killing with the deaths that result from 'indirect' harms. For Reiman, the relative moral culpability of the intentional killer and the absentee killer is quite distinct and, he argues, contrary to that around which law operates:

> Our absentee killer intended harm to no-one in particular, but he *knew his acts were likely to harm someone* – and once someone is harmed, *he* (the victim) is someone in particular. Nor can our absentee killer claim that 'he was not himself'. His act is done, not out of passion, but out of cool reckoning. And precisely here his evil shows. In this willingness to jeopardise the lives of unspecified others who pose him no real or imaginary threat in order to make a few dollars, he shows his general disdain for all his fellow human beings ... We are left with no moral basis for treating *indirect harm* as less evil than *one-on-one harm.*
>
> (1979: 60–1, original emphases)

Thus, Reiman concludes, the former is less likely to represent some generalised threat to others than is the latter. For Reiman, and his point is a convincing one, indifference is at least if not more culpable than intention, and ought to be treated as such by any criminal justice system.

Yet the greater moral culpability that is attached both legally and popularly to acts of intention can also allow those implicated in corporate crimes to rationalise away the consequences of their actions. The case of the Ford Pinto is well-known and has been well-documented within literatures on corporate crime and business ethics. When the Ford Pinto was released in 1970, Ford executives knew that it was likely to explode from a rear-end collision. They calculated that appropriate safety measures would cost $135 million, but that prospective law-suits would be unlikely to top $50 million. Between five hundred and nine hundred people lost their lives and thousands of others suffered debilitating and painful burn injuries. They were never successfully prosecuted for their actions (Dowie 1977; Cullen *et al.* 1987), although successful civil suits did proceed against the company.

Despite clear evidence of the crudest form of cost-benefit analysis being used to justify proceeding with a design which was likely to result in death and injury, Lee Iacocca, who had been CEO at Ford Motor Company at the time of the design of the Ford Pinto, was later able to invoke the fact that there was no intention to kill to evade moral culpability:

> Whose fault was it? One obvious answer is that it was the fault of Ford's management – including me ... But there's absolutely no truth to the charge that we tried to save a few bucks and knowingly made a dangerous car. The auto industry has often been arrogant, but it's not that callous. The guys who built the Pinto had kids in college who were driving that car. Believe me, nobody sits down and thinks: 'I'm deliberately going to make this car unsafe.'
>
> (Iacocca 1986: 171–2)

The rather obscene consequences of the strange legal prioritisation of intention over indifference were also illustrated in the only legal action to follow the recent outbreak of *E.coli* amongst Lanarkshire residents, resulting in 20 deaths and more than 400 people ill, many of whom continued to suffer the effects of the poisoning long after originally contracting it. John Barr and Sons were fined £2500 for failing to ensure equipment was kept clean and failing to ensure that food was protected against contamination. The contaminated meat sold at the butcher's had been identified as being at the centre of the *E.coli* food poisoning outbreak in Lanarkshire in November 1996. John Barr entered into a plea bargain: he pleaded guilty in return for charges of selling contaminated food which lead to 'a number of persons' contracting *E.coli*, and dying, being dropped. Sheriff Cameron noted that the episode had brought notoriety and financial loss on the butcher's, resulting in a 40 per cent loss of business: 'However, the court has to mark its displeasure at the lapses which form the complaint to which the firm has now pleaded guilty' (*Guardian*, 21 January, 1998: 7). Clearly John Barr did not intend to kill any of his customers. But for an experienced butcher to fail to ensure that equipment was kept clean and to ensure that food was protected against contamination at least indicates indifference to the consequences, which one must accept might have been food poisoning and death. One might respond by saying that this consequence was not a likely one, that the butcher (and those who died) were 'unlucky'; but such consequences are at least foreseeable. And it is difficult to see how such a context differs from the 'poor luck' which results in a driver having drunk three pints of beer being involved in a road accident in which a death results. Perhaps there are two real differences. The first is that the driver, in driving after drinking three pints, was not seeking the benefit of economic profitability, perhaps making her/him *less* morally culpable; the second is that most people in Britain in the 1990s would accept that the 'poor luck' of the driver was irrelevant to the moral and legal responsibility which attaches to her/him for the resultant death.

This latter example is a useful comparison since it provides a well-known illustration of a point that should be borne in mind, namely that popular and legal notions of the importance of intentionality can shift. Thus it is possible to identify a recent historical, and continuing, criminalisation of road traffic accidents where drivers are found to have more than legal amounts of alcohol in the bloodstream. Indeed, here, moral opprobrium seems increasingly to be attached precisely to the fact of indifference rather than any intention. As Reiman also notes, 'if the criminal justice system began to prosecute – and if the media began to portray those who inflict *indirect harm* as serious criminals – our ordinary moral notions would change on this point ...' (Reiman 1979: 61, original emphasis).

In our view, then, issues related to both organisational complexity and intention actually present themselves as problems because of the individualising nature of bourgeois law. Thus, our understandings of what constitutes complexity are socially constructed. As such, neither is immutable, and neither actually present insuperable technical legal problems. For example, while in Britain the charge of corporate manslaughter remains a highly difficult one to pursue successfully, there are no insuperable problems intrinsic to law to the effective criminalisation of such offences, as Bergman (1991, 1994), Slapper (1993) and Wells (1995a, 1995b) have demonstrated; what is commonly lacking is political will, itself related to particular representations of 'law and order' and what constitutes real crime. Thus while English law does not provide for the aggregation of the actions of different controlling officers (Moran 1992; Slapper 1993), this is possible in other jurisdictions (Slapper 1993), not least within US federal law (Wells 1993a: 118–20). Such initiatives indicate that the corporate veil can be pierced and the issue of intention resolved. They also indicate that we should be very wary of any claims based upon the abstraction of what appear to be technical, legal difficulties from the contexts within which such understandings are culturally produced, and produced not in randomised ways, but in ways intimately related with power. As Lacey has written, 'technical difficulties of proof . . . may themselves be produced or exacerbated by exercises of economic power or ... cultural understandings' (Lacey 1995: 23; see also Wells 1995a, 1995b).

Conclusion: academics and obstacles to knowing

None of the various mechanisms noted above whereby corporate crimes are rendered relatively invisible, and through which particular versions of crime, law and order are produced and maintained, are particularly remarkable in isolation. What is crucial, however, is *their mutually reinforcing nature*, so that in their combination they have powerful effects in terms of reproducing social constructions and also erecting obstacles to knowing about corporate crime.

In the face of obstacles to knowing, one group to whom we might look are academics. Yet as we have argued in previous chapters, the record of academics in relation to corporate crime, particularly those within the discipline of criminology, is hardly an impressive one. One set of factors which might partially explain this 'record' – and reinforce our relative ignorance of corporate crime – are of a methodological nature.

As we have already seen in a previous chapter (3), one type of methodological problem relates to the nature of official data which is collected and available. However, in addition to these particular concerns relating to the inadequacies of official corporate crime data is a more general series of methodological problems encountered in attempting to examine the nature of these forms of crime.

One methodological problem likely to be encountered is that of access to offenders (and sites of offending). Of course, access to offenders is problematic for researchers of conventional crime. Yet in comparison with offenders or potential offenders in the context of corporate crime, conventional crime researchers are dealing with the relatively powerless which, whether we like it or not, renders such work immediately more feasible than dealing with, and seeking to focus upon, the relatively powerful. Indeed, as Reed has noted, 'the inner sanctum of the company boardroom and the senior management enclaves within corporate hierarchies still remain a largely closed and secretive world' (1989: 79, cited in Punch 1996: 4).

Of course, while methodological issues such as gaining access from the 'outside', the role of gatekeepers, the co-operation of the researched, and so on are common across social research (Bryman 1988b), the extent to which they may, or do, prove problematic varies context by context. Thus the argument being made here is that in general there are good reasons to expect it to be more difficult to research the relatively powerful, where such research involves access to the powerful themselves.

Where access *is* successfully negotiated, the possibilities of deliberate obfuscation on the part of the researched is greater where one is dealing with individuals who are often well-educated, possessing highly developed social skills, socialised into particular business ideologies and corporate cultures, and so on. Researching corporate crime often requires access to data that the offenders themselves possess, and jealously guard, be these internal financial or other forms of records, minutes, memoranda regarding safety standards or knowledge of health hazards, or knowledge of conversations. It has been suggested that in the context of studying corporate crime, ethnographic forms of research are 'very difficult because much of the work of managers is carried out in offices, behind closed doors, composed of phone-calls, memos and other correspondence' (Punch 1996: 43).

Vaughan has usefully summarised some of these problems when discussing 'limited access to data about the internal dynamics of organisational life':

> Documentation of misconduct within an organisation prior to an enforcement action or public investigation is and always has been difficult for researchers to obtain. After a violation has become public knowledge, an offending organisation is understandably reluctant to have a sociologist located in its midst, and evidence documenting internal activities that is obtained by social control agents is not always admissible in judicial proceedings, let alone open to perusal by social scientists ... we are constrained by missing data: critical conversations never recorded; records undiscovered, distorted, destroyed ...
> (1992: 132)

One of the consequences of these methodological problems is a tendency to rely upon whistle-blowers and investigative journalists. Nelken has claimed that this opens academic work based upon such sources to concerns regarding 'accuracy, frequency, or representativeness' (1994a: 356). Equally, material relating to corporate crime that is made available on a case-specific basis, as is often the case, raises the problematic issue of representativeness and our (in)ability to generalise (Punch 1996), although, as we noted in Chapter 3, some argue that this concern regarding the value of case studies is more apparent than real (Bryman 1988a).

Finally, and perhaps paradoxically, there is one further methodological problem regarding the study of corporate crime: such work tends to reflect a bias towards larger corporate actors, rendering smaller businesses relatively invisible (Croall 1989). In other words, while there are numerous difficulties entailed in the study of larger corporate actors, one is at least likely to know of their existence, to be able to glean some publicly available data, and so on. However, there is evidence that much corporate crime actually occurs at the level of small businesses, yet is not studied since it goes largely unrecorded, not least because the business organisations themselves are not registered with relevant authorities, such as the Inland Revenue, the Health and Safety Executive, the Environment Agency, and so on.

Even if we accept these very real problems, however, they under-explain the relative lack of attention paid amongst academics to corporate crime. Given the economic, social and intellectual capacities/resources to bring to the empirical and analytical fore hitherto neglected social problems, their record is not particularly impressive. There is, of course, academic work (mostly, but not entirely, North American), which does focus upon corporate crime. We have referred to some of this in previous chapters, in considering issues of definition and measurement. We now turn to two chapters considering arguments regarding the causes of corporate crime. Here, it becomes apparent not simply that there is a relative poverty of theoretical work on corporate crime *per se*. But, supporting the arguments of this chapter, it is also of interest that almost all of the concepts and modes of enquiry/analysis developed within traditional academic criminology are either relatively inappropriate for, or have not been used in, the analysis of corporate crime.

Note

1. These points regarding the coverage of corporate crime within the print media are based upon a preliminary analysis of crime, law and order reporting within a number of national newspapers – the *Sun* and the *News of the World*, the *Mirror* and *Sunday Mirror*, the *Guardian* and the *Observer*, the *Daily* and *Sunday Telegraph*, and the *Financial Times* – over a six-week period. Material gathered from these sources is in the process of being subjected to a detailed content analysis of the relative coverage of corporate and conventional crime, undertaken by Steve Tombs and Dave Whyte.

Chapter 6

Accounting for corporate crime: corporations and pathology

Introduction

Fifty years ago, Edwin Sutherland observed that standard criminological theories were inadequate to account for white-collar crime. Most such approaches sought to compare criminals with non-criminals and to discover in the former some sort of biological, psychological or social pathology which would account for their offending. These theories would obviously not transfer well to the realm of white-collar crime. Sutherland (1949: 257–8) said that you could suggest only in a jocular sense that:

> the crimes of the Ford Motor Company are due to the Oedipus Complex, or those of the Aluminum Company of America to an Inferiority Complex, or those of the U.S. Steel Corporation to Frustration or Aggression, or those of Du Pont to Traumatic Experience, or those of Montgomery Ward to Regression to Infancy.

We have indicated in earlier chapters that there now exists a significant body of work around the phenomenon of corporate crime, our preferred term; but, as we have also noted, the greater part of this work concerns either case studies or arguments concerning law and its enforcement. There is a relative dearth of academic work which attempts to theorise and account for patterns of offending, despite there being some recent contributions in this field. (See, for example, Fisse and Braithwaite (1993), Wells (1993), Pearce and Tombs (1998) and Slapper (forthcoming); two brief pieces which indicate the key elements of any such theorising are Coleman 1987, and Vaughan 1992.)

What is also clear, however, and this reflects a point made in the previous chapter regarding the general lack of attention which criminologists have paid to corporate crime, is the fact that most of what constitutes criminological theorising has signally failed even to attempt to account for corporate offending. But there have been some attempts to include corporate crime with general theories of crime causation, while others have taken elements of criminological theorising and attempted to use this to interrogate the causational aspects of corporate crime. This chapter sets out to examine some of the most prominent or widely written-about endeavours in criminological theory which have sought to explain corporate offending by reference to organisational factors. The theories we examine here have quite divergent approaches to accounting for corporate crime. Of interest for this chapter is the extent to which corporate offending can be explained by aspects of criminological theory, and to what extent it is possible (or indeed desirable) to develop a general theory of crime which can account for corporate offending. In this chapter, our concern is with 'explanations' that focus upon intra-organisational factors.

Beyond atomised individuals

One question which presents itself at the outset of investigating organisational pathology is how organisations can be seen as distinct from the people who form them.

It can be argued that organisations *per se* neither think nor act (Coleman 1987). Such a contention, however, misses the important point that organisations are more than just the aggregate of individuals who constitute them. Organisations are a collection of roles and functions which are occupied by a series of people. Thus the personality and moral code of any particular executive or director can be seen as much less significant in determining the outcome of doing the job than the structural pressures bearing on the appointment (Coleman 1982a).

The irrelevance of particular individuals in the structure and functioning of business needs to be stressed, especially given the tendencies towards individualised forms of explanation within contemporary societies. Thus, as Coleman points out, in management training programmes in many firms there is a game commonly used as part of the programme called the 'in-basket game'. Management trainees are asked to imagine that they unexpectedly replaced the previous plant manager over the weekend and are confronted with the unanswered mail in their predecessor's in-basket. The challenge is to respond appropriately to each letter. A few of the letters are personal, and the trainees are expected to be able to distinguish between those which are intended for the plant manager *as* manager. The aim of the exercise is to be able to make the transition between one manager and another unnoticeable – to make the manager *as a person* irrelevant to the functioning of the plant.

Sometimes the structural occupational pressures on the incumbents of some important corporate roles can have devastating effects. The consequences of an unhealthy culture infecting and taking over an organisation are neatly exposed in the essay 'Ethical Dimensions of the Challenger Disaster', in which Boisjoly, Curtis and Mellican (1995) look at the sequence of events which led to the deaths of seven astronauts aboard the space shuttle *Challenger* in 1986. They argue that in large organisations the individual is no longer 'the locus of power and responsibility'. Rather, the organisation itself is the acting unit which can overwhelm personal standards of ethical conduct. Thus:

> it is no longer the character and virtues of individuals that determine the standards of moral conduct, it is the policies and structures of the institutional settings within which they work and live.
>
> (1995: 208)

Sutherland and differential association theory

Once again, our starting point is with the work of Sutherland (1945, 1949), whose work in this context remains of enduring significance today, not least because it was the first attempt to develop a general criminological theory to encompass both 'conventional' and what he termed 'white-collar' crime. Sutherland argued that the reason why white-collar offending is very low when contrasted with the criminality of blue-collar workers is that wealthy and powerful units in society are able to participate in legal process in ways which control how crimes are defined and enforced.

Some of Sutherland's analysis extends to conduct such as the crimes of individual executives, stockbrokers and so forth, which is outside the scope of a book like this on organisational and corporate offending. Nevertheless, we examine his contentions here because much of his thinking is applicable to our theme. Sutherland argued that the conventional picture of crime dwelt on the individual offences of people who were generally poor and working class. Thus, he argued, a false picture of non-criminality was created. Official reports and statistics gave the impression that corporations and wealthy, powerful people do not commit crime. Embezzlement, falsified company accounts, bribery of public officials, fraudulent advertising and other business crimes were not part of the subject matter of criminology. Sutherland's motivation was (1949: v) 'an attempt to reform the theory of criminal behaviour' rather than a campaign for social reform.

Sutherland argued that it was pointless to look at the ordinary criminal statistics in order to measure the extent of white-collar crime because white-collar criminals are very rarely processed by the criminal justice system. He accounted for this by reference to the class bias of the courts and the power of the élite to influence the implementation and administration of the law:

> This class bias affects not merely present-day courts, but also, to a much greater degree, affected the earlier courts which established the precedents and rules of procedure of the present day courts.
>
> (1940: 7)

Sutherland argued that in contrast with white-collar offenders, ordinary criminals are dealt with by the police and the criminal courts. Alleged white-collar criminals are separated from the stigma of this system from the outset. They are left to be dealt with by inspectors who issue various warnings and orders before taking out proceedings, and, where proceedings are successfully brought, the resultant sanctions are fines often at a level which for business makes the penalty the equivalent of a parking or speeding fine.

At the centre of Sutherland's thinking about white-collar crime is the idea that any reliable theory of crime must be able to account for all types of crime. He considered that the crime of the upper and lower social classes were substantially similar (1949: 7):

> (The) crimes of the two classes differ in incidentals rather than essentials.
> They differ principally in the implementation of the criminal laws which apply to them.

Sutherland argued that the range of conventional criminological theories all focused upon the pathologies of the lower-class people who committed conventional crime and were thus unsuitable theories to elucidate the causes of white-collar crime.

Looking at individual offenders (people or corporations) criminal behaviour could be explained, he argued, by the fact that the offender had absorbed a preponderance of criminal norms over non-criminal ones. Taking a step back from this immediate explanatory factor, Sutherland also argued that 'differential association' could be explained by reference to anomie and culture conflict theories. Passas (1990) has applied the theory of anomie to the activities of corporations in an economic setting (see Chapter 7).

From the early to the middle twentieth century there was an exponential growth in the number of businesses (in the UK as well as the USA). All sorts of dubious practices were emerging and neither the public nor judges, nor even governments, had any *a priori* fixed standards by which to judge the new practices. While these standards were being fixed, a 'normlessness' or anomie developed. Anomie theory applied to white-collar crime concerned the indeterminate standards of proper business practice which were a consequence of the fitful advent of government control.

Sutherland also contended that where many publicly inimical business practices did arise, the clash between the commercial culture in favour of these behaviours and any governmental culture against them was often won by the better co-ordinated and thus stronger commercial community.

Sutherland argued (1949) that ordinary and white-collar crime could be explained by the same principles. Sutherland advanced a theory, one that has come to be known as 'differential association theory', which he claimed could explain all types of crime. Criminality was learned in association with other offenders, and resulted from an excess of received opinions ('definitions') favourable to law violation over attitudes unfavourable to violation. He stated (1947: 6–7) that:

> Criminal behaviour is learned in interaction with other persons in a process of communication ... When criminal behaviour is learned, the learning includes (a) techniques of committing the crime, which are sometimes very complicated, sometimes very simple; (b) the specific direction of the motives, drives, rationalisations, and attitudes ...

Not everyone who comes into contact with criminals becomes a criminal. Sutherland, therefore, argued that the type of interactions that would be likely to lead to conversions could be judged by looking at the frequency, duration, priority and intensity of the contacts. This theory of 'differential association' is not now widely regarded as of particular use in understanding the origins of organisational crime. Braithwaite (1985: 3) describes the theory as something verging on 'a platitudinous restatement of social learning theory'. If people or organisations are criminal because they mix with and learn values from other criminals, we still do not understand from where those 'other criminals' have derived their criminality. Where and why does the deviance emerge? Even refinements to Sutherland's work, like that of Glaser (1978) who includes the influence of television and cinema amongst the sources of influence upon potential criminals, do not substantially address the social origins of the criminality in question. Glaser (1978: 127) argues that his 'differential-anticipation theory' assumes that a person will try to commit a crime

> wherever and whenever the expectations of gratification from it – as a result of social bonds, differential learning, and perceptions of opportunity – exceed the unfavourable anticipations from those sources.

There is much traditional criminological theory, following Sutherland, based upon notions of learning from a subculture. Wolfgang and Ferracuti (1958), for example, wrote of a 'subculture of violence'. Looking at passion homicides, they argue that the immediate cause of such killings were the ideas of the subculture about expected modes of behaviour. In some subcultures it is regarded as appropriate to respond with lethal force to certain insults or personal violations. Not to do so would be seen as unacceptable by other members of the group. It is thus the *ideas* and *codes* of particular social groupings, like subcultures, which are the real and immediate causes of crime. There are many other variants of subcultural theory in a similar vein; see, for example, the gang theories of Cloward and Ohlin (1960), and Cohen (1985).

It may well be that organisational offending is boosted by key personnel in any given company being occupationally obliged to periodically mix with their counterparts from other organisations, many of whom have an amoral approach to business success (for examples, see Punch 1996: x and *passim*; Jamieson 1994). Such a phenomenon, however, could, only explain the proliferation or perpetuation of a problem not its social origin.

Hirschi and Gottfredson and human nature theory

Hirschi and Gottfredson have also ventured to put a 'general theory of crime [which] accounts for the frequency and distribution of white-collar crime and at the same time [as] it accounts for the frequency and distribution of all other types of crime, whether they be rape, vandalism, or simple assault' (1987: 950).

The writers contend that as with ordinary common crime, the white-collar offender seeks personal benefit, and that the setting is not relevant to the cause of crime. The usefulness of a category of 'corporate crime' (used in this text and elsewhere see Chapter 1) is also dismissed as irrelevant:

> Thus, although Sutherland tabulated his crime data on firms ... and ridiculed explanations of their behaviour based on individual pathology, he continued to explain corporate crime with the theory of differential association, and he consistently equated the behaviour of the corporation with the behaviour of the people in positions of power within it.

Hirshi and Gottfredson state that this sort of crime is no different from crimes committed by individuals in any other group or organisational setting where those in authority decide how their inferiors should behave, or, at least, set them targets which they can only really fulfil by breaking the law.

To explain the causes of white-collar crime (including by their definition the organisational crime which is, they argue, attributable to the deviance of individuals) and ordinary crime, the writers put forward a 'General Theory of Crime' which they base upon classical assumptions about human nature. They begin their argument by looking at crimes rather than criminals, and state (1987: 959) that because 'versatility in offenders is an established empirical fact' all crimes must share common properties that make them appealing to potential offenders. They assert that:

> In our view, the concept of human nature that best organises the data is that found in the classical assumption that human behaviour is motivated by the self-interested pursuit of pleasure and the avoidance of pain. Crimes are events in which force or fraud are used to satisfy self-interest ...

Crime, they say, is simply the easiest way of some people satisfying their desire to maximise pleasure and minimalise pain, to gain certain ends rapidly, certainly and with minimal effort. Features of criminal events that enhance their pleasure or minimise their pain can be part of the reason why they are committed. To be maximally pleasurable, events should take place immediately, and force and fraud can help produce results rapidly. Force and fraud also help events become certain and ensure a minimum of effort. They conclude that 'Crimes, including white-collar crimes, therefore require no motivation or pressure that is not present in any other form of human behaviour' (*ibid.*: 959). Criminality is thus seen as the tendency of individuals to pursue short-term gratification in the most direct way with little consideration for the long-term consequences of their acts.

There are several highly contentious elements to the arguments of Hirschi and Gottfredson. One problem with their analysis is that, even if we accept – which we do not – that they are correct in arguing that 'white-collar' crime does not require a unique set of principles to explain it, it *does* have a much more deleterious effect upon society than ordinary crime (Box 1983; Slapper 1993; Jones 1988; Ermann and Lundman 1992) and is therefore worth keeping as a distinct area of study for its value as a comparator with ordinary crime (see Chapter 4 of this text). Corporations exercise an enormous influence over social affairs and it is much more important to understand their crimes than those crimes committed by the church, or by elderly people, to mention examples given by Hirschi and Gottfredson in their contention that white-collar crime is just one of innumerable possible divisions of crime with no significance in relation to the general cause of crime.

Another controversial element in their argument is their use of the term 'human nature' when discussing the impulses which prompt criminality. What are these 'tendencies'? Do we all have them? Are they hereditary? Are they treatable with social or chemical therapy? Hirschi and Gottfredson are disturbingly quiet on these questions, other than to say that 'indicators of such a tendency [to commit crime] include impulsivity, aggression, activity level and lack of concern for the opinion of others'. They declare that

> people high on this tendency are relatively unable or unwilling to delay gratification; they are relatively indifferent to punishment and to the interests of others. As a consequence, they tend to be impulsive, active, and risk-taking.
>
> (1987: 959)

They argue that criminal tendencies in people do not lead ineluctably to crime regardless of the setting in which an individual is placed because he or she may be able to satisfy desires in non-criminal ways. The really disputable part of their writing, however, is the implicit notion of innate pathologies. It seems that the theoretical consequence of this notion is one of crime being attributable to the personal weaknesses of an aggregate of impetuous people.

It is possible to argue (although Hirschi and Gottfredson do not) that human beings have survival instincts as part of their nature, but as rational and mutually-dependent beings we recognise that co-operation, peacefulness and mutual aid are, generally, better routes to survival than unbridled violence in pursuit of individual aims. It is possible to differentiate between 'human nature' and 'human behaviour' (although Hirschi and Gottfredson do not) and to recognise that a key factor determining social conduct is the type of society into which we are born. The rules of the game in any society are more important than our 'nature'. Our behaviour is influenced by our environment. The peaceful and co-operative communities of various Amazonian tribes or the Kalahari bushmen (Coleman 1987) have long established histories of reproducing generations of peaceful, ingenuous and co-operative people, whereas communities racked with violence (Wolfgang and Ferracuti 1967; Levi 1994) or fraud (Punch 1996; Levi 1987) tend to reproduce people inured into the same practices.

Accepting such assumptions about the social causes of crime would render it unnecessary for psychologists or biochemists to screen people to discover whether they were 'high on a tendency of impulsivity and aggression'.

Hirschi and Gottfredson support their General Theory of Crime by reference to various data sets which show that demographically the distribution of white-collar crime and ordinary crime by reference to age, sex, and race are very similar. One weakness with this analysis is that the 'white-collar crimes' selected by the authors for comparison with ordinary crime like murder are fraud and embezzlement. In many ways the latter are not the same sort of wrong as much corporate and organisational crime. The category 'fraud' includes all sorts of petty individual crimes like social security ruses and falsifying documents in taking out loans. Again, 'embezzlement' is a crime usually committed by individuals, and is a wrong *against* a corporation.

Steffensmeier (1987) notes that the studies all show that persons arrested for fraud and forgery do not qualify as white-collar criminals. The evidence (Daly 1986; Giordano *et al.* 1981) indicates that most arrests for fraud and forgery are not occupationally-related but rather involve passing bad cheques, credit card fraud, theft of services and welfare fraud. One analysis of 1981 and 1986 police files in Pennsylvania (Steffensmeier 1987) found that less than 2 per cent of all arrests for fraud and for forgery were for a white-collar or an occupational crime. Similarly, the sort of embezzler who becomes a criminal statistic is more likely to be a club treasurer or cashier than a high status individual.

Hirschi and Gottfredson bring together a wide range of authors and texts under the label of 'cultural theories', like Sutherland's 'differential association' theory, and argue that these are misguided because they concentrate on particular crimes and seek causations which cannot be generally applied across a variety of ordinary crimes. Underneath this contention is the assumption that all crimes are sufficiently similar to warrant a general explanation. The authors point out, for example, that according to cultural theory, the longer a person is normalised into a particular culture, the more likely they are to absorb its values. They then put forward evidence that in relation to the two white-collar crimes they have selected as examples (fraud and embezzlement), more offending occurs at the younger end of the age range than at the older section.

It can be argued that some of this reasoning is flawed by a mis-understanding of 'cultural theory'. Hirschi and Gottfredson say that:

> Since our theory permits no propensity distinctions among types of offenses, it is perfectly general, and is once again directly contrary to cultural theories, with their view that crimes have unique, specific cultural motives.

> (1987: 971)

It is inaccurate to say that cultural theories try to find 'unique, specific cultural motives' for crime like white-collar crime. Mostly what such examinations have sought to do is to explain the psychological and cultural phenomena which allow otherwise law-abiding people to end up doing things in the course of their work which cause large-scale social harm. The *motive* for such offenders might be exactly the self-interested concern advanced by Hirschi and Gottfredson, but the way in which it is materialised is a different matter and an understanding of that key process (*how* good people come to do bad things at work) is an important issue.

Techniques of neutralisation

While one cannot reduce (criminal) phenomena to the actions, omissions and motivations of individuals, the latter question – *how* good people come to do bad things – is nevertheless a relevant one. In *Delinquency and Drift*, an influential work published in 1964, Matza argued that many delinquents do in fact recognise their behaviour as morally wrong but neutralise its iniquity in their own minds. Using concepts similar to the ones used by the law to go to mitigation of sentence (self-defence, provocation, diminished responsibility), the delinquent will come to see himself or herself as 'guilt-less'. There is much evidence of this phenomenon. Yochelson and Same-now (1976) found that even hardened and persistent offenders were unwilling to admit that they were criminals. Similarly, Cressey (1953) found that embezzlers were unlikely to conceive of themselves as criminals. They held positions of trust and had to live like very respectable people. They therefore found ways of interpreting their criminal conduct as merely borrowing from the money over which they had control. Matza and Sykes (1957) – in relation to juvenile delinquents – propound five 'tech-niques of neutralisation': denial of responsibility ('It wasn't my fault'); denial of injury ('they can afford it'); denial of victims ('they had it coming'); condemn the condemners ('everyone is crooked anyway'); and the appeal to higher loyalties ('I did it for the gang'). Similarly, another study found that police officers who used illegal force justified this on grounds of necessity, saying the force was needed for them to carry out their duties (Westley 1953).

Techniques of neutralisation can be seen in operation in many areas of organisational crime. Such techniques do offer an insight into the motivation of individuals if we understand individuals within a 'structural framework of enablement and constraint' (Clegg 1989: 146). To say that vocabularies of motives are structurally offered (Mills 1956) is to argue that motives and reasons for individual conduct do not originate within individual actors, but are structurally available, within 'bounds of normalcy' (*ibid.*). Somewhat differently, techniques of neutralisation may act as post-hoc rationalisations of, or justifications for, action. In this way, they may not necessarily explain why people within organisations commit crime (although in some cases they can go very far in such an explanation), but reference to such techniques does help in the understanding of how the wrong can be sustained and repeated by people who are not insensitive nor amoral in other parts of their life.

Gioia (1992) has explained how senior executives in a corporation can come to have their own ethical standards and inclinations overcome by the organisational demands of their work. Gioia was a key executive in the Ford Motor Company in the 1970s just before the scandal of the Pinto broke into public knowledge.

On 13 September, 1978, Ford Motor Company was indicted in Indiana, USA for reckless homicide. A Grand Jury decided after three days of deliberation that Ford was to be tried as a responsible party for the deaths of three teenagers who were burnt to death when their Ford Pinto burst into flames following a low-speed, rear-end collision. Many people had died in similar incidents all over the USA. Dowie has stated that 'by conservative estimates Pinto crashes have caused more than 500 deaths' (1977: 14). These were dreadful deaths. The subcompact car was popular with young mothers. Some of the people who were killed were burnt to death in a matter of minutes with their children, in too much pain to get out of the vehicle. Others did manage to escape on fire but were usually too badly burned by the time help arrived to be able to survive. Dowie (1977: 13) recounts one case where a mother was in a Pinto with her 13-year-old son. They entered a merge lane and the car stalled. Another car hit hers at the rear at about 28 mph. The gas tank ruptured and vapours mixed quickly with the air in the passenger compartment. A spark ignited the mixture and the car exploded in a ball of fire. The mother died in agony a few hours later in an emergency hospital. Her son survived although his whole body is scarred and he has a surgically constructed nose and ear, albeit poor ones because he had so little unburnt skin from which grafts could be made.

Fighting strong competition from Volkswagen for the lucrative smaller car market, the Ford Motor Company rushed the Pinto into production in much less than the usual time. The normal time span from conception to production of a new car model is about 43 months, whereas the Pinto Schedule was set at 25 months (Dowie 1977: 16). The man behind this project was a young executive, Lee Iacocca, who had been 'head-hunted' from General Motors to become the Chief Executive Officer at Ford, and then gained a reputation after the enormous success of his first project – the Mustang. Ford engineers discovered, however, in the pre-production crash tests of the Pinto that rear-end collisions would rupture its fuel system very easily. Because assembly-line production was already tooled (i.e. the factory plant and machinery to be used in making the cars) when engineers found this defect, a decision had to be taken at the highest levels within the company that production should nonetheless proceed. Heightening the anti-safety pressure on Pinto engineers was an important goal set by Iacocca known as 'the limits of 2 000'. The Pinto was not to weigh an ounce over 2 000 pounds and not to cost a cent over $2 000. An engineer gave evidence that Iacocca enforced these limits 'with an iron hand', so even when a crash-test showed that a one-pound, one-dollar piece of metal stopped the fuel tank from being punctured as it was pushed against the differential housing, it was rejected as extra cost and extra weight (Dowie 1977: 17). The engineer remarked that: 'This company is run by salesmen, not engineers: so the priority is styling, not safety'. The company was prepared to go to any lengths to retain and expand its share of the car market.

One piece of evidence led by the prosecution in the Ford case concerned the company's prior convictions. The court heard (Cullen *et al.* 1987: 282) that in February 1973 Ford had been convicted of 350 (sic) criminal counts of filing false reports to the Environmental Protection Agency and was fined a total of $7 million. The crimes occurred in 1972 when the company performed unauthorised maintenance on test vehicles and submitted falsified data certifying that the emission levels of its 1973 models (including the Pinto) met the standard prescribed by the 1968 Clean Air Act. This was a straightforward case of lying in order to make financial gain. The cost to the environment and the people who would, to varying extents, be poisoned was dismissed.

The actual homicide trial resulted in the company being acquitted. The defendant was probably acquitted because it managed to raise a doubt about the causation of the three deaths in question. It contended that the vehicle in which the three victims were travelling was hit at a speed in excess of 50 mph, a collision in which many types of vehicle suffer a ruptured fuel tank and would burst into flames. Vehicles were not legally obliged to be structurally able to withstand a collision in which they were hit at 50 mph. For this account to be true, however, the victims' vehicle would have had to have been stationary at the moment it was hit in the rear, whereas several eye-witnesses testified that the victims' vehicle was moving when it was hit. Ford adduced 'scientific' evidence to support its contention that the Pinto in question was hit by something travelling at more than 50 mph, but the tests which showed this had been conducted in their own grounds by an expert to whom they paid $22 000 (Cullen *et al.* 1987: 265–307).

Dennis Gioia worked for Ford at its World Headquarters in Dearborn,

Michigan. He became the company's Field Recall Coordinator and thus responsible for recalling cars that had safety defects. Gioia recounts graphically how on two occasions he, along with others on a committee, had the opportunity to recall the Pinto but decided not to do so. There were various general factors which pressed upon him and others not to make a recall of the car including the fact that there was an oil crisis.

> The effects of the crisis had cast a pall over Ford and the rest of the automobile industry. Ford's production line, with the perhaps notable exception of the Pinto and the Maverick small cars, was not well-suited to dealing with the crisis. Lay-offs were imminent for many people. Recalling the Pinto in this context would have damaged one of the few trump cards the company had . . .
>
> (1992: 145)

Most important, however, in his decisions not to recall the model of car whose defective design resulted in so many unnecessary deaths, was the way in which Gioia's personal ethics were subordinated to the clinical decision-making processes of the company. In retrospect Gioia admits that there were some signs indicative of the Pinto's dangerous design but he (and others) did not recognise these signs in a way which would have led them to recall the vehicle. People doing his sort of work were compelled to use 'schemata' and 'scripts' in their occupation in order to work efficiently. A schema is 'a cognitive framework that people use to impose structure upon information, situations, and expectations to facilitate understanding', and a script is a specialised type of schema which provides a cognitive framework for understanding information and events 'as well as being a guide to appropriate *behaviour* to deal with the situation faced' (*ibid.*: 151–2).

There were hundreds of decisions to be made by him all the time in a fast-paced routine which involved an enormous quantity of data ('an overwhelming information overload', p. 153). Individualised investigations could simply not be made in every case. It was in this setting that the Field Recall Coordinator came to receive several reports of Pintos which had burst into flames, and suffered the occasional moral or emotional flinching at the horrible outcomes, but failed to recall the vehicle because the data received did not fit existing templates of a dangerous automobile.

Bowles (1991) has identified mechanisms by which large corporations can persuade executives to subordinate their personal codes and moralities to organisational imperatives. They operate in a 'subculture of structured immoralities' (Mills 1956: 138, cited in Box 1983: 54). This phenomenon is comparable to the concept of a 'subculture of delinquency' used by Matza (1964).

In his work *Delinquency and Drift*, Matza had contended that for most of the time delinquents keep fairly normal routines. They were not constantly offending. Traditional criminological theories which sought to differentiate 'criminals' from 'non-criminals' by reference to some key psychological or biological condition were, Matza argued, erroneous because they could not account for the fact that offenders only offended periodically, and (in most cases) eventually drifted away from crime and into conventional lifestyles. Matza argued that 'drift' occurred in the spaces within the social structure where control was loosened so a person was free to respond to whatever forces came along – forces for rectitude or forces for delinquency.

Comparing the theories of Mills and Matza, Box states that both consist of precepts and customs that are delicately balanced between convention and crime; both posit objectives that may be obtained through crime but also other means; both allow crime but it is not demanded or necessarily considered the preferred path, and both consist of 'norms and sentiments' which are beliefs that function as the extenuating conditions under which crime is permissible.

> Thus, these subcultures respectively enable corporate officials and lower class adolescent males to commit crimes without too many pangs of conscience; through their sanitising prism, each subculture softens criminal acts so that they assume the appearance of 'not really' being against the law, or it transforms them into acts required by a morality higher than that enshrined in a parochial criminal law.
>
> (1983: 54)

Braithwaite and elements of conventional criminology

One important contemporary attempt to provide a general explanation of crime that can illuminate both organisational and ordinary crime has emerged through some of the work of John Braithwaite (1985, 1989, 1993). Braithwaite has attempted to draw together from conventional criminology elements of strain theories, aspects of labelling theory, sub-cultural theory and control theory and, in conjunction with his considerable empirical research, to put together an integrated theory of crime. The key to his attempt to synthesise elements from varied parts of criminology is the notion of 'differential shaming – the shaming from organisational cultures of compliance versus the shaming from subcultures of resistance to regulatory law' (1989: 333). However, we are not concerned with Braithwaite's attempt at synthesised explanation *per se*, more with the insight that he offers on the utility of existent elements of criminological theory in explaining corporate crime.

Subcultural theory, control theory, and the theory of 'tipping points'

There are many subtle progressions of reasoning in Braithwaite's argument, but before we address these it is important to highlight his central idea. He argues that the distribution of organisational crime in society depends on the availability of legitimate and illegitimate opportunities to achieve organisational or departmental (what he terms 'subunit') goals; the extent to which hostile industrial policing of organisations causes them to become recalcitrant and foster 'subcultures of resistance to law' (something we examine later in Chapter 8); and the extent to which organisations without resistant subcultures exercise informal controls (control theory) which expose offenders to shaming.

In this analysis, control theory works only where there are more definitions favourable to compliance than definitions favourable to non-compliance. Thus subcultural and control theory accounts are posited as having differential explanatory power, depending on where an organisation is along the 'differential association continuum'. Thus, according to Braithwaite, where all parts of a corporation and the corporation as a whole have good legitimate opportunities to achieve their goals, the main determinant of whether it will commit crimes is how far its personnel are controlled by organisational systems. But if its opportunities for legitimate gain are blocked then the corporation will be more likely to offend and the situation will worsen if the state authorities then respond to its offending not with a policy of 're-integrative shaming' but with such an uncompromising shaming that the corporation is completely alienated. This is a contentious analysis and, again, something that we examine later in Chapter 8.

Some writers (e.g. Gross 1978) have approached the construction of a theory of organisational crime by grounding it in organisational theory. Braithwaite instead adapts elements from traditional criminology. His basic reasoning about organisational crime can also be applied to the criminology of individuals. Nevertheless, he does not reject explanations of organisational crime which are based upon organisational theory. He regards them as important because general theories like the one he posits 'will explain only modest proportions of the variance in particular types of crime' (1989: 334). Braithwaite concedes that if his theory works it will explain why, how and roughly what distribution of organisational offending will occur in different circumstances but only a detailed analysis of any given organisation will be able to conclude whether the chances of it offending are high or low.

Using opportunity theory (Merton 1957; Cloward and Ohlin 1960), Braithwaite argues that organisational crime is more likely to occur when an organisation (or an organisational subunit) suffers major blockages of legitimate opportunities to achieve its goals, and where it has the opportunity to commit crime. This, though, on its own is insufficient to explain organisational crime because not all companies with blocked opportunities commit crime to improve their situations. It is at this point in his reasoning that Braithwaite introduces subcultural theory – the exercise of informal social control within a company to secure non-compliance with the law.

Where companies face blocked legitimate opportunities they may develop a subculture of law-breaking. Geis's study (1967) of price-fixing in the heavy electrical equipment industry is a good illustration of the way new executives in a company were socialised into the business of illegally conspiring with competitors to fix consumer prices.

This subcultural theory, however, contrasts with control theory (e.g. Hirschi 1969) which concerns the use of formal controls to secure compliance with the law. Where people in organisations are being pressured by both sides – by subcultural forces for non-compliance and control forces for compliance – what decides which way the people go? Braithwaite posits as a 'theory of tipping points' the principle of differential association (Sutherland and Cressey 1966): when definitions favourable to violation of a law exceed definitions unfavourable to violation of the law, violation of the law will occur. Then Braithwaite comes to the crux of his reasoning:

> The challenge for a theory of organisational crime is to give greater specificity of content to the social conditions in which the stake in compliance will predominate and to the social conditions which tip the balance to a stake in noncompliance. I submit that the variable which plays this role is shaming.
>
> (1989: 340)

He maintains that there are two types of shaming: reintegrative shaming and stigmatisation. The former allows those doing the shaming to keep bonds of respect for the offender and focuses on the evil of the deed rather than the evil of the actor, allowing for forgiveness. The latter makes no attempt to reconcile the offender to the community and 'degradation ceremonies are not followed by ceremonies to decertify deviance' (*ibid.*: 341).

Labelling theory

Subcultures of resistance develop in organisations when they are stigmatised by the authorities: 'when organisations are treated as irredeemably crooked, they are more likely to become crooked'. If they are 'pushed around' by the state authorities in a way they regard as unfair their irresponsibility may grow 'because a sense of injustice abrogates the moral bond of the law' (Braithwaite 1989: 343). This is taken from criminological 'labelling theory' (Becker 1964) most neatly summed up in the proposition that 'social control leads to deviance' (Lemert 1967: v).

Nelken (1994a) has noted that the labelling approach has been comparatively neglected in the study of white-collar crime even though it could be seen as particularly relevant given the relevant recency of many laws regulating business, the sharp swings between political projects of regulation and deregulation and the divergent views of different groups as to the appropriateness of criminalisation. Nelken's work *The Limits of the Legal Process: A study of Landlords, Law, and Crime* (1983) is one of very few works to have examined the processes of labelling and de-labelling in relation to business misconduct.

His work shows that although the Rent Act 1965 was passed following widespread disgust at the misconduct of corporate commercial landlords, those actually apprehended for landlord crime under the Act were immigrant landlords with small properties who were involved in disputes with their tenants. It was possible, but often a serious challenge, to bring company landlord misconduct within the scope of the Rent Act 1965. The Act had focused upon misconduct like 'harassment' of tenants by landlords who wanted the former evicted, whereas the real mischief committed by company landlords who wanted their tenants out was much more subtle. Thus whilst practices like harassment and illegal eviction (which were mainly used by individual landlords who were resident in the same premises as their tenants) were criminalised, abuses of Improvement Grants where property is not improved for the benefit of existing tenants (a company landlord malpractice) were not criminalised. The legislators knew this and were apparently quite lenient on company landlords because they wanted to retain a large privately-rented sector as publicly-rented accommodation could not meet total demand. It was thought by some key legislators inappropriate to frighten private company landlords out of the residential market by conferring too many rights on tenants. Additionally, Nelken shows abuses of company landlord power were not seriously dealt with under the Act because they were perceived by the various state and local government officials (whose job it was to operate the provisions of the Rent Act) as being closely similar to ordinary business behaviour and therefore excusable under social axiom.

Nelken's work manages to combine both a close-up detailed account of how the Act came to be passed and why some malpractices were 'labelled' as crimes while others were passed over, with a wide-angle focus on the political and economic factors which gave a setting to and helped shape the behaviour of all of the actors in this historical drama. He refers to 'the necessity to draw both on structural and interpretative approaches in order to provide a convincing account of the emergence and implementation of the law' (1983: 211).

He recognised the necessity to draw on both structural and interpretative approaches in order to provide a convincing account of the emergence and implementation of law, arguing that 'proponents of structural approaches now readily admit that any examination of the structural constellation of forces cannot be used to read out the emergence or content of a given piece of legislation, whilst those who adopt an interpretative perspective are obliged to concede that the negotiation of meaning is biased in favour of structurally powerful groups' (*ibid.*: 211). Nelken argues that such an approach, combining an understanding of both 'negotiated meaning' and the 'structural constellation of forces', allows us to identify what he refers to as a 'coherence without conspiracy' (*ibid.*: 212).

Organisational structure

According to Braithwaite, in most organisations definitions favourable to compliance with the law hold sway even though it would often be more rational (economically) for them to break the law. Here, Braithwaite suggests, control theory will help us to understand the problem: 'we should never underestimate the moralising social control within complex organisations' (1989: 349). The tighter the managerial control over work practices, the less likely there is to be organisational crime. In his study of five American coal mining companies with outstanding safety compliance records, Braithwaite (1985) found that the companies were characterised by clearly defined accountability for safety performance, rigorous monitoring of that performance, and good systems for communicating to workers and managers when their performance fell below standard.

In contrast, criminogenic companies are defined in Braithwaite's view by their 'concerted ignorance' and cultures where the senior managers say 'get it done but don't tell me how you do it'. Some companies in the pharmaceutical industry have 'a vice president responsible for going to jail'. But the diversity of corporate cultures is attested to by the fact that other pharmaceutical companies have adopted a structure which ensures that the chief executive is given dangerous knowledge. Thus, some companies will insist that any decision to overrule the recommendation of a quality control manager (that, for instance, a certain medicine is unsafe) cannot be taken by the production manager without the consent of the chief executive. How far corporate crime can be accounted for by factors internal to any given corporation, as opposed to endemic features of the corporate structure and of capitalism, is addressed in detail in Chapter 8, with particular reference to the work of Braithwaite and colleagues.

There is no doubt that corporate crime needs to be partially understood with respect to the organisational characteristics of different corporations, and any full-blown theory of corporate crime needs to take account of various aspects of organisational form and structure. The nature of internal accounting procedures, the relative power of different units and sub-units within an organisation, the extent to which certain kinds of activity are sub-contracted out, the 'clout' (and indeed protection) afforded to compliance staff, to workers, to whistle-blowers, organisational culture and indeed the different cultures of different parts of a corporation, the ways in which Standards Operating Procedures are developed, monitored and revised, the precise forms of lines of accountability and responsibility within corporations, the nature and extent of internal communications mechanisms, have all been shown to have some bearing on either the extent or potential for corporate crime (see, for example, Braithwaite 1989; Braithwaite and Fisse 1987; Fisse and Braithwaite 1993; Keane 1995; Tombs 1992, 1995a; Vaughan 1983, 1996).

Yet, while we need to recognise that different organisational forms can attenuate or exacerbate the tendency to criminal activity or omission on the part of the corporation, we should be wary of allowing a focus upon such forms to obscure the necessary features of a corporation operating within a capitalist social order, namely the need to maximise profitability, a feature to which we have pointed in Chapter 1, and which we further consider in Chapters 7 and 8. Thus precise organisational forms are largely effects of the tendency to achieve this goal, contingent elements of the essential nature and rationale of the corporate entity.

Shapiro and the 'social organisation of trust'

One of the key reasons for examining the particularities of organisations is that these structural and cultural features can greatly affect the distribution and availability of opportunities for illegality within an organisation. That is, different organisational forms do offer varying opportunities for corporate crime, and indeed distribute these differentially. The intra-organisational distribution of opportunity is also a consideration for Shapiro, who focuses upon the (differential) levels of opportunity and temptation to commit crime in different social situations (Shapiro 1990). Her analysis may also be of some help in the consideration of several aspects of organisational and corporate offending. In a paper entitled *Collaring the Crime, Not the Criminal: reconsidering the concept of white-collar crime*, she seeks to distinguish between 'role-specific norms' and 'the characteristics of the occupants of these roles'. Fraud, for example, is a crime which can be committed by working class people on welfare support as well as by company officials and stockbrokers (Levi 1987), so, if one is keen to understand the causes of the crime, a focus on the social status of the offender is not as significant as a focus on the nature of the crime.

Shapiro (1990) looks at the 'social organisation of trust' and the way that trust is differentially distributed throughout the occupational hierarchy. Senior personnel and high-status officers are generally bestowed with more trust than others in commerce and industry and yet they have considerable opportunities to abuse that trust; *and* their offending can result in greater losses than when people at the lower end of an organisation's hierarchy offend in the course of their employment to achieve organisational goals.

Shapiro's argument (see also 1985, 1987) proposes that the nature of the roles people play in organisations and companies are more important to appreciate for an understanding of occupational offending than their personal characteristics or social status. She states that 50 years after Sutherland's pioneering work:

> it is time to integrate the 'white-collar' offenders into mainstream scholarship by looking beyond the perpetrators' wardrobe and social characteristics and exploring the modus operandi of their misdeeds and the ways in which they establish and exploit trust.
>
> (1990: 363)

The thrust of her theory is that in modern capitalism there is in commerce and industry an almost universal use of the 'principal–agent' relationship. Businesses and business people have to engage the services of all sorts of experts to perform for them: lawyers, stockbrokers, accountants, computer experts, investment managers *et al.* These people, as agents, have to be given a certain amount of trust and freedom to exercise a professional discretion over what they are doing. They have, thus, good opportunities to misuse their powers. All principals can do to protect their interests is to select their agents with care, and try to build into the agreement alignments between the interests of principal and agent like performance fees and profit-sharing plans. Worse than simple agency agreements are the fiduciary relationships which proliferate in business. Whereas agency agreements are relatively symmetric (where the principal, at least technically, retains the right to direct the agent on what to do) in fiduciary relationships 'one party is at the mercy of the other's discretion' (Weinrib 1975: 7, cited in Shapiro 1990: 15).

According to this analysis, therefore, the weak point or defect in organisations which permits and sometimes (in conjunction with other personal or social forces) triggers criminality is the opportunity to breach trust. Shapiro argues that ordinary robbers steal directly from their victims by threats or actual violence. Trustee 'robbers' become *confidence* men, women and organisations and induce victims to part with their money or property with lies and misrepresentations rather than brute force.

> Ordinary burglars steal by break in or trespass. Instead of cultivating mechanical technology to break into a secured building, trustee 'burglars' cultivate social technology to become trusted organisations or insiders in organisations rich with opportunity for exploiting their positions for personal or corporate advantage.
>
> (1990: 350)

Many of the agents Shapiro refers to are, in fact, organisations like banks and investment firms, and are dealing with hundreds of principals. In this setting, with such complexity, it is often impossible for the principals (many of which are themselves organisations) to keep a watchful eye over what the agents are doing. The agents can therefore shape the nature of the relationship and this will often result in one which is conducive to crime. Shapiro observes:

> ... agents such as banks, municipal governments, charities, publicly-held companies, or pension funds collectivize the discrete interests of dispersed, multiple, and often changing principals. These 'collective' agents, therefore, remain insulated from the preferences, demands, incentives, or surveillance of each discrete principal and relatively unresponsive to them ... so agents rather than their principals often design the agency contract.
>
> (1990: 349)

Conclusion: beyond pathology, beyond criminology?

One major problem with attempting to explain corporate offending in terms of some form of pathology afflicting the corporate entity is the sheer complexity of variable factors – a complexity which is arguably even more fraught than that surrounding an individual offender. As Punch has observed, it is very difficult to understand why some companies under certain circumstances choose to adopt deviant solutions to business problems because analysis has to touch on:

> societies, markets, the organisational structure of corporations, the division of labor in managerial work, regulatory regimes, and the mechanisms that lead businessmen to break rules. But the more complex the variables, the more difficult and debateable it is to link with any degree of certainty environmental and structural features to human behaviour. Each case, for instance, can be seen as rich in context, if not unique, and can appear to defy comparison. ...
>
> (1996: 215)

On these grounds, we would not expect any particular theoretical framework from criminology to account satisfactorily for all forms of violation within the wide range of corporate offending. Nevertheless, several of these theories do shed light on many aspects of when, why, and how corporations come to offend.

A second general issue with explanations rooted in some aspect of organisational pathology is simply the fact that, as is clear from the work surveyed in Chapter 3, corporate crime is widespread and routine – that is, it is produced by 'normal' rather than pathological organisations. This is not to deny that there are not propositions in the above literatures which are of some use in understanding, perhaps even determining the likelihood of, corporate offending in different scenarios. Thus, following Braithwaite's objection (1985: 6) to 'platitudinous generalisations' in criminological explanation, Punch notes the illusion of any 'encompass-ing framework that explains business crime and deviance' (1996: 244). These latter comments may say as much about the places in which the 'search' for that all-encompassing explanatory framework has been conducted – namely, criminology and sociology – as about the possibility of such explanatory power being developed *per se*. In the next chapter, we move somewhat beyond criminology, and to the margins of what constitutes sociology, in the search for explanatory power. There, we examine how far an understanding of the nature of corporations within a capitalist social order, based around accumulation, amorality, and the reduction of relationships between men and women to relationships between mere things, namely commodities – phenomena and processes accessed through the lens of political economy – can help to explain the phenomenon of corporate crime.

Chapter 7

Accounting for corporate crime: corporations and political economy

Introduction

If, in traditional criminology, there have been numerous attempts to explain criminal behaviour by reference to economic factors – for example, to establish correlations or causational links between general economic conditions and crime rates (Box and Hale 1982; Castellano and Sampson 1981), between unemployment and crime rates (Simon Field 1990; Nagel 1977), and between inequality and crime (Merton 1957; Cloward and Ohlin 1960) – there is now a developing literature which makes similar efforts with regard to corporate offending. This chapter reviews the contours of this literature, focusing upon argument both within and beyond criminology. As in previous chapters, we place a particular focus upon occupational safety and health crimes, whilst recognising that there may be *some* peculiarities with regard to these forms of corporate crime.

While our focus here is on macro-level considerations, we should emphasise that the explanation of corporate crime, no less than adequate explanation of any other social phenomenon, cannot remain simply at this level, just as it cannot be reduced to the level of individuals and their micro-level interactions. The most sensitive forms of explanation of course attend to individual–society relationships, and it is in this tradition that there have emerged some useful theoretical efforts around corporate offending within criminology.

Anomie and corporate crime

A useful starting place for this chapter is with the work of Merton, and his well-known use of the concept of anomie. Merton noted (1957) that the culture of any society defines particular goals which it elevates as worth striving for. For Merton, in American society the acquisition of wealth has always been seen, by conventional thought, as a noble and virtuous pursuit. Wealth is seen in many quarters as emblematic of personal worth. Social status is more commonly measured by, for example, a person's standard of living than it is by her/his standards of knowledge, skill, kindness, and so on.

In modern society, the goal of acquiring wealth has been given great emphasis. Indeed, those who acquire wealth illegally are often represented as enjoying a much better life than those who slog away in a compliant manner. For those whose social position makes it difficult in the extreme to gain much by the proper 'institutionalised means', there may be a great pressure to offend. Merton referred to as 'anomie' the contradiction between the culture to acquire wealth and status and the social structure which effectively shuts off any such realistic possibility for many parts of the general population. Under such pressures, Merton argued, people could take one of five options, depending upon how they regarded the cultural goals and the institutionalised means of achieving them, namely: conformity, innovation, ritualism, retreatism, and rebellion. In what he terms 'stable societies', he argues that most people opt for conformity, where they accept the cultural goals and the institutionalised means of achieving them. Most crime in society, however, takes the form of innovation. Here, people remain faithful to the cultural goal of acquiring wealth but they find that they cannot succeed by institutionalised means. They thus use illegitimate methods to acquire wealth.

This is not the place to enter into the details of Merton's claims, nor his revisions of these, nor the many criticisms which his work has prompted. Nevertheless, it is worth noting that while Merton's work vastly under-explained conventional crime, it may have some force in helping us to understand some forms of both white-collar and corporate offending, despite his lack of concern with either phenomenon. Thus many commentators have noted that if the resort to illegitimate means to acquire wealth is a feasible response to the lack of availability of institutionalised means, this might help to explain some high status offending. For example, Vold and Bernard note how Merton's schema does not only apply to ordinary criminals:

> Businessmen may devise different forms of white-collar crime entailing fraud and misrepresentation, or they may cheat on their income tax.
>
> (1986: 190)

Indeed, it is worth pointing out that the term 'anomie' is derived from the sociology of Durkheim. Merton's use of that term is rather different to that of Durkheim. Yet while Durkheim was not primarily concerned with crime *per se*, his original formulation of the concept anomie does state quite clearly that this structurally caused phenomenon might be an explanatory factor in high status as opposed to lower-class crime. In the following passage, Durkheim is referring to suicide, which he took as an instance of crime, and we can legitimately read this term as crime for our purposes:

> Poverty protects against suicide because it is a restraint in itself. No matter how one acts, desires have to depend upon resources to some extent; actual possessions are partly the criterion of those aspired to. So the less one has the less he is tempted to extend the range of his needs indefinitely. Lack of power, compelling moderation, accustoms men to it. Wealth, on the other hand, by the power it bestows, deceives us into believing that we depend upon ourselves only. Reducing the resistance we encounter from objects, it suggests the possibility of unlimited success against them. The less limited one feels, the more intolerable all limitation appears ... wealth, exalting the individual, may always arouse the spirit of rebellion which is the very source of immorality.
>
> (Durkheim 1897/1979: 254)

This is surely one instance supporting the claim that Durkheim's study of suicide contained important raw materials for a fairly complex form of social-psychology (Pearce 1989). Moreover, Durkheim's claims in this passage, of how wealth, power and an enormous freedom to act can engender an antipathy to any attempted hindrance of that freedom, namely law, conjure up for us images of Gordon Gekko in *Wall Street* or the 'Masters of the Universe' in *Bonfire of the Vanities*. Where wealth, risk-taking, enterprise and individualism were encouraged in both Reagan's America and in Britain of the 1980s and 1990s, we can find an insight into the social-psychology of high status offenders such as Milken, Boeskey, Leeson and company in Durkheim's claims, made almost a century ago.

The work of Merton, albeit reformulated, and Durkheim's treatment of individual–society relationships, one tiny element of which we referred to above, are both of relevance for us in that each offers insights on the phenomenon of individual offending within organisational or corporate settings through reference to extra-organisational, that is societal or structural, factors. Thus one can only understand Merton's arguments if one examines both the dominant values within, and the distribution of institutionalised means for achieving these across, a given social order. The locus of explanation is not in fact any individual, but the structural positioning of individuals.

Now, following Durkheim, and Merton, if anomie provides some insight into the offending of business-people, then Box argues that such a schema can also be applied to corporations. Indeed, Box claims that while many of the well-known criticisms of Merton's arguments are valid, many of these criticisms lose their force if this form of analysis is applied to corporate crime (Box 1983: 35). Box's argument takes as the defining characteristic of the corporation that it is a goal-seeking entity, this goal being profit, 'at least in the long run' (*ibid.*). For Box, this makes the corporation inherently criminogenic, since

> it necessarily operates in an uncertain and unpredictable environment such that its purely legitimate opportunities for goal achievement are sometimes

limited and constrained. Consequently, executives investigate alternative means, including law avoidance, evasion, and violation and pursue them if they are evaluated as superior to other strictly legitimate alternatives.

(*ibid.*)

In a novel development of Mertonian strain theory, Box argues that in seeking to pre-empt or mitigate the uncertainty introduced into their operating environments, in particular by competitors, governments, employees, consumers and the public, corporations tend towards law violation. While corporate motivation to illegality must of course be translated into reality – and thus is mediated – by real men and women who face differential opportunities, have different personal values and ethics, possess greater or lesser degrees of ingenuity, authority and social power, Box's simple formula is nevertheless a helpful one. Certainly, for example, we know that many markets are awash with hundreds or thousands of companies competing with each other continuously. One corporation's competitive advantage through, say, product differentiation, is relative failure for many other companies, and thus for the human beings who depend on them as a source of income. In these circumstances, it is not difficult to see why there is industrial espionage, labour and environmental violations via cost-cutting, fraudulent advertising, customer poaching and so forth. And in less competitive markets, even in oligopolistic ones, corporate crime can occur when those who control (even if they do not own) the relevant enterprises stand to gain by such corporate offending; in this context, it is important to bear in mind that there are no quantitative limits set on profit maximisation, so that there is never quite an entirely satisfactory level of profit, dividend return, market share, and so on (it is precisely this latter fact which both apologists for and critics of capitalism alike claim is the key to its innovative and dynamic nature).

A more recent, but similar, attempt to elaborate upon the concept of anomie, drawing directly upon the work of Merton, is that of Passas (1990), who links deviant behaviour to the disjunction between institutionalised aspirations and the accessibility to legitimate opportunity structures. Although Merton saw these phenomena as confined to the lower classes, Passas argues that there is no compelling reason why anomie theory cannot be applied to high-class and corporate deviance.

> As the meaning and content of success goals vary from one part of the social
> structure to another, similar difficulties in attaining diversely defined goals
> may be faced by people in the upper social reaches too; they are, therefore,
> far from immune to pressures towards deviance.

(1990: 158)

Passas attempts to consolidate anomie theory with points made by theorists operating in diverse, often conflicting, orientations or perspectives. His analysis suggests that the central proposition of Merton's theory and the insights of the other theorists are not mutually exclusive, but quite compatible and, to a certain extent, complementary. Each illuminates part of the same social phenomenon. The structure of contemporary societies is inherently conducive to anomic trends.

Passas identifies one of the processes leading to deviance as 'structurally induced problems and strains'. The pressure to succeed exists for business and organisations in terms of maximisation of profit, growth and efficiency. These goals may have to be obtained *by all* or *any means* particularly when the continuation of the corporation is at stake and the corporate actors realise that the attainment of their own ends depends largely on the prosperity of the firm. Structural pressures and strains may be applied both to those at the top as well as their subordinates and the employment of deviant methods may be the only possible way of dealing with problematic situations, or may be perceived as such.

Deviant behaviour may be further promoted and maintained, he argues, through processes of interaction leading to widespread rationalisations which 'excuse' and 'justify' illegal practices. Anomic trends may then ensue, as the use of profitable and effective but illegal techniques become widespread and convey the impression that in order to be successful, business cannot always be entirely compliant with the law. Thus, given the existence and legitimation of such practices, more of them can occur even in the *absence* of compelling pressures.

The processes which result in deviance and anomie thrive in an environment dominated by concerns of cost and benefits and are reinforced by the structural pressures generated within a capitalist mode of production. Sometimes the connections between market pressures and corporate crime are easily seen. Companies often end up committing crimes or making terrible reckless errors because they are desperately endeavouring to acquire, retain or re-gain a significant slice of the market. Car ferries on the England-to-the-continent route, for example, were often to be found setting sail with their bow doors open before the 1987 Zeebrugge disaster in which 192 people were killed when the *Herald of Free Enterprise* capsized after flooding through its open bow door. The reason why ships sailed before the huge door was closed was that the routes were plied by several shipping companies in bitter competition with each other, and so there was a premium on 'turn-around time', that is, the time it took for a ferry to dock, unload, reload and set to sea.

Although his analysis concentrates on free market capitalist societies, Passas makes the point that the problems discussed can also be found in state capitalist command-economy countries. There are no ready-made solutions available. Anomic trends could be disrupted and minimised through mechanisms of social control, but, he argues, additional contradictions leading to a relative immunity of upper-class individuals and legitimate corporations, sustain and perpetuate such an anomic climate affecting (at least, potentially) the whole society. He suggests that, contrary to claims made by some scholars, corporate deviance seen as a product of existing cultural, structural and economic demands, is at least as serious a problem as ordinary, predatory street crime and that it has significant implications for the social order.

Capitalism as social structure

Merton (1957) described as a 'Copernican revolution' the change in the sociology of knowledge that came when scientists began to look for explanations not only of 'mistakes' but also of the 'truth', explanations of what was socially held to be true, plausible or valid knowledge. Aubert has noted (1952: 263) that there are some fairly obvious reasons why the origin and function of deviant behaviour have been the main focus of scientific attention, 'to the neglect of the complementary phenomenon of norm-conformity and pressure to conform. It seems somehow "natural" to ask why the deviants become deviants, and not why the conforming majority conform ...'. We can take this notion and apply it to corporate offending. Rather than just gaze at those entities which offend (or at least those which have been caught offending and then prosecuted) it might be quite illuminating, Aubert suggests, to focus on the general run of other companies to look at what pressures they are under, how close their conduct comes to violating law, and if we can conclude anything from why we think or know that they are not offending.

Thus the economic and political environments surrounding companies – their 'social structure' – can become as useful a source of knowledge about corporate crime as understanding offending corporations per se. As Aubert observes:

> What is theoretically important is that white-collar crime seems to be one of those phenomena which are particularly sensitive to – and therefore highly symptomatic of – more pervasive and generalizable features of the social structure.
>
> (1952: 264)

Crucial elements of that social structure for corporations include the nature of the market(s) in which they operate, the general state of the economies in which they do business, the dominant ideologies within any social order in which they function, and the nature of regulation and enforcement to which they are subject. Account must be taken of each of these macro-level phenomena in attempts to 'explain' corporate crime.

Markets and industry structure

There are various ways in which it is possible to argue that market forces are criminogenic. It is important to emphasise that not all such arguments derive from left-of-centre or critical research, from which one might expect a general antipathy to free markets. For example, the classic study of criminogenic market forces conducted by Leonard and Weber (1977) is based upon a general commitment to free market principles. In summary, their argument is that it is when the market is allowed to develop in a particular way – in particular where too much power is reposed in a few major corporations who dominate a market – that crimes are 'coerced' by such a structure.

Their study focuses on car manufacture in the USA: 'one of the most solidly entrenched oligopolies among United States industries'. The gist of their contention is that because only three gigantic corporations (Ford, Chrysler, and General Motors) are responsible for virtually all vehicle production in the USA, they are able to dictate very unfavourable terms to individuals or companies who seek car dealerships. The result of this is that car dealers, in order to survive economically, come under immense pressure to commit various crimes like cheating customers on servicing, and making false statements when selling second-hand cars.

They note that all crime can be better understood 'when the conditions affecting the performance of occupational duties are known' (1977: 420). For them the relevant conditions in the automobile industry are (1) the concentration of manufacturers, and (2) the very high entry barriers, namely costs of capital, patents, advertising, and economies of scale (see also Pearce and Tombs 1998, on the structural features of the international chemicals industries).

Car dealers are technically independent business-people but they very rarely have sufficient capital to own the value of property involved in the dealership. The manufacturers are happy to supply the extra investment to the 'right' people. In the franchise agreement, the dealer contracts to sell and service the manufacturer's vehicles. If the minimum sales quota is not met, the dealer's franchise is subject to cancellation. No dealership has ever been cancelled, however, for failure in relation to the supply of spare parts and servicing. Dealers are therefore pressured to be sales-oriented and to down-grade service.

Leonard and Weber cite many examples of the illegal and unethical conduct that abound in this industry. We are asked to consider fraud in the sales of new cars, accessories not ordered but forced on buyers, used cars sold for new, engines switched in cars, excessive finance charges, repair overcharges, fake repair diagnoses and many other abusive practices. In order to sell the number of new cars required of them by the manufacturer, the dealers have to drop their prices to such low margins that they could not survive without engaging in unlawful practices in order to make money:

> what appears to the public as unethical or criminal behaviour on the part of
> dealers and mechanics represents 'conditioned' crime, or crime stimulated by
> conditions over which the dealer or mechanic has but little control. Perhaps a
> better phrase would be 'coerced' crime, since it results from the coercion of

strong corporations whose officers can utilise the concentrated market power
of their companies to bend dealer and mechanic to serve company objectives.
(1977: 416)

Leonard and Weber follow Taft in describing automobile manufacturers as 'socially dangerous people' since they function as 'causers of
the causes of crime'. Taft describes 'socially dangerous people' as those
who, 'not technically criminal themselves, nevertheless create conditions
which result in crime' (Taft 1966: 15–23).

Corporate policy can thus produce extensive low-level offending. The
Big Three motor companies, as they are termed by Leonard and Weber,
offer the mechanics in the dealerships a 'flat-rate' – standard times set for
repair jobs. If changing a fuel-pump is pegged at half an hour then the
mechanic will get the same payment even if the work is done in 15
minutes. Designed as an incentive for mechanics to improve productivity,
the system in fact promotes quick and often shoddy work, and the use of a
new part even where a repair could be carried out, because repair takes
longer than replacement. In another example, one of the Big Three was
found to be paying prizes to whichever of its dealerships managed to
spend the least in honouring warranties!

Leonard and Weber acknowledge macro-economic criminogenesis
only to a very limited extent: 'Taft feels that the social system compels the
business institution to be exploitative. It is our opinion that additional
economic factors must be taken into account' (1977: 421). They see the
absence of true competition as the reason for much offending. They say
that 'the need is for a market structure in each industry to allow
competitive forces rather than government to do the regulating'
(1977: 421).

This is a highly contentious view. As we have noted, there are also
persuasive, and completely contrary, claims to the effect that it is
competition, not oligopoly, that produces corporate crime. In the following chapter, we shall note that there is a great deal of evidence that
corporate crime increases in deregulated industries. Indeed, as Coleman
has noted, perhaps the most heavily researched question within the area
of corporate crime causation has been 'the effect of market structure on
crime', yet the results of both quantitative work (such as the use of large
datasets discussed in Chapter 3) and qualitative research has produced
largely contradictory findings on this point (Coleman 1987: 428). The
conclusions of theoretical and empirical work around the relationship
between market or economic conditions and corporate crime is equally
conflictual. For example, in a review of such work, Snider notes that while
there is evidence that falling profits and recessionary conditions do seem
to produce increases in corporate crime, 'the most crime-prone industries – pharmaceutical, oil, and automobile companies – have also been
among the most consistently profitable' (1993a: 75).

Two points are worth emphasising here. First, notwithstanding the fact
that the relationships between markets and corporate crime remains

indeterminate, Leonard and Weber's analysis is useful since it is one approach – and there are others – which at least sensitises us to the need to examine market structure as one factor conducive to, or indeed compelling of, criminal activity on the part of corporations. Second, from the point of view of a valid explanation, there is no reason why both competitive and oligopolistic markets should not produce corporate crime – a realist, as opposed to a positivist, epistemology would lead one to expect, rather than question, the fact that one effect can have different causes.

Finally, it is worth referring briefly to well-known work by Needleman and Needleman (1979), work which examines aspects of organisational practice and both market and industry structure which may be more or less conducive to crime. In many respects, this work is complementary to that of Braithwaite (particularly) and to Shapiro, each referred to above. It is worth focusing upon here, because while discussions tend to focus upon either intra- or extra-organisational aspects of corporate offending, Needleman and Needleman (as have others since) present an analysis which links both types of features, clearly important given that there are a whole range of factors external to particular organisations which influence how organisations operate, are structured, staffed, and so on.

Their argument is that whereas sociological interest in the criminogenic features of organisational structure has tended to focus on 'crime-coercive' systems that compel their members to commit illegal acts as a price for being a member, attention should also be focused upon 'crime-facilitative' systems. In this latter model of criminogenesis, system members are not circumstantially forced to break the law but are presented with extremely tempting structural conditions – high incentives and opportunities coupled with low risks – that encourage and facilitate crime.

Needleman and Needleman start with the idea that some organisational systems like those to be found in some parts of industry can – by economic, legal and normative features of their internal structures – be criminogenic (Leonard and Weber 1970). Crime-coercive systems force members into criminal activity by 'Godfatherism', that is by confronting them with 'an offer they cannot refuse'. They cite Farberman's study (1975) of the automobile industry in which it is shown how franchised automobile dealers, under pressure from a car manufacturing oligopoly to turn over large inventories of new cars at fixed, low-profit margins are forced, in order to remain in business, to sell second-hand cars for cash in order to evade tax, and falsely diagnose car problems for other customers in order to carry out expensive but unnecessary repairs. They also cite Denzin's study (1977) of the liquor industry as one illustrative of organisational mechanisms that compel law breaking. Denzin showed how distillers, who themselves break antitrust laws through price agreements, impose sales quotas on their distributors. In order to meet these quotas, the distributors entice retailers to buy premium items by throwing in some 'off the invoice' items, and they cover themselves by keeping double books or reporting fictional warehouse thefts. The retailers in turn, in order to keep a high volume of business, must fix prices between themselves.

Crime-facilitative systems, by comparison, work on the basis of temptation and incentives. Needleman and Needleman draw their illustrations from the securities industry. Estimates of the level of loss from securities theft and fraud in the USA were as high as $50 billion at the time they addressed the issue (1979: 521). Fraudulent dealing in securities takes at least two forms. The first is the 'conversion' (changing the apparent ownership) of stolen or counterfeit stocks or bonds into negotiable instruments that will be accepted and traded by banks. The second form of fraud involves the creation of fake securities from scratch, basing their value on fictional companies. From a detailed study of the Senate Hearings on the securities industry, they extract three structural features of the securities industry that work to facilitate fraud: the pattern of legal liability, the industry's traditions of commerce, and the incentives for market flow.

Needleman and Needleman's first factor tempting crime in the securities industry is the way business is carried on according to the legal framework. Banks and brokerage firms can take advantage of a privileged legal status known as 'holder in due course' which gives them a clear legal title to any securities they have purchased 'in good faith' even if these were stolen. Thus, in effect, unless the seller indicates to the purchasing bank that the securities are stolen, the bank is pretty safe in buying almost anything. The banker is under no obligation to check the validity of anything he or she buys (*ibid.*: 523).

The second crime-facilitative factor advanced by Needleman and Needleman is the tradition of commerce in the securities business. The authors cite, as example, the use of trust in modern banking. Bankers relate to large depositors as important men and women.

> Apparently the idea of subjecting large depositors to close questioning and checking, on the chance that they might be crooked, strikes many bankers not only as a poor business move but also as impolite. Without some compelling reason, it would be an improper way of doing business. Bank secrecy laws, particularly on the international level, are built on this tradition of trust, protecting the privacy of depositors presumed to be important and honourable. This feature of the industry, of course, makes it possible for con men ... to take advantage of the banker.
>
> (*ibid.*: 525, quoting from US Senate Hearings)

Since Needleman and Needleman made that observation there have been many events which corroborate their view. See, for example, the collapse of the bank BCCI, *Independent, The Times,* 9 May, 1997; Passas 1996; Punch 1996: 9–21; Smith and Hogan 1996: 560).

The profit-motive and the commodification of social relationships

Beyond the consideration of market and industry forms, an even more fundamental and less tangible issue of potential explanatory significance *vis-à-vis* corporate crime is that of the structural necessities of contemporary capitalism. The first and foremost of these, we argue throughout this text, is the demand for profit maximisation. The paramount economic priority of companies is to be profitable, and to this end business is predominantly based upon the making of amoral calculations (see Chapter 8). The essence of this amorality was long ago thrown into sharp relief by Lord Lauderdale, who sought to deny chimney girls and boys a right to life by arguing that neither morality nor ethics had anything to do with market efficiency (Strange 1982; Easton 1984; Moore 1991). A quite different, but perfectly compatible, illustration of capitalist amorality, here in its contemporary manifestation of 'enterprise', was provided recently when, during a recent drought, water supplies had been simply exhausted in some parts of England, at least two groups of young men were discovered trying to *sell* buckets of water to old, housebound people. Their conduct may be regarded as morally repugnant but it was not illegal and it was, in a strict sense, within the province of what has been described as 'enterprise culture'.

The claim that capitalistic activity is amoral is not to deny that individual business-people may care about collateral issues such as doing business ethically, although, of course, 'doing business ethically' may simply be a strategy developed to secure competitive advantage, market growth and profitability; but, overall, business operates according to the code of profitability rather than in accordance of any particular morality. Certainly, although companies can afford to occasionally run into debt, condone certain losses and discount certain items, these must be only intermittent and temporary. The quest for profit is a continuous and vital part of business operation: a business needs profit like a swimmer needs air.

The results of a recent survey, in which two journalists visited the business advisers of four high street banks, become relatively unsurprising in the light of these points. The journalists, aided by headed letter paper, assumed the identities of people wishing to set up accounts for a white supremacist party, a magazine for drug dealers, a company dealing in chemical weapons and a pornographic magazine specialising in schoolgirl outfits. Only the Co-operative Bank refused to deal with any of them, this bank having dramatically increased market share and profitability in recent years precisely through developing an 'ethical' stance towards doing business. The bogus White British party, which introduced itself as 'a good old fashioned right-wing party – you know, like in the thirties' was told by one bank's business adviser that his bank had no 'ethical worries', and he even suggested that a club/society account would make financial sense. An account for the magazine 'Pipe and Rocks – a magazine for the hardcore drug dealer' was well received at one bank where the business adviser even suggested selling it at night clubs and record shops (*Guardian*, 12 May, 1995).

In addition to the amorality of capitalist corporations, the prevailing ideology of any given society also affects the extent to which corporate crimes are produced and indeed are more or less acceptable. Certainly a value system which prioritises, indeed valorises, the taking of risks, and even produces techniques whereby the taking of such risks can be deemed to be acceptable, is likely to be one which accepts a level of corporate illegality as 'normal'. Work practice is governed by a state of affairs characterised by William Morris as 'modern commerce – the counting-house forgetful of the workshop' (1947, 1877: 35). This pressure was directly conceded by Dr John Cullen, the Chairman of the Health and Safety Executive, when he stated:

> The enterprise culture, the opening up of markets, and the need to survive competition place businesses under unprecedented pressure ... the scale and pace of technological change means that increasing numbers of people – the public as well as employees – are potentially at risk.
>
> (*Guardian*, 4 March, 1989)

Now, as many business people often claim, from the launching of a company onwards the process of running a company is constantly beset with a variety of risks (e.g. Barclays Bank, 1997 – Will customers materialise? Will rival firms adapt and block the development of a newcomer? A new business risks losing all of its capital outlay). Companies are relentlessly having to remain 'competitive' by keeping their expenditure as low as possible. Clearly, many companies today will not knowingly jeopardise the lives of their customers or the general public but there are enough documented instances of such risks apparently being knowingly taken to demonstrate the compelling pressure of commercial competition.

Vehicle manufacture again provides illustration. When in 1978 the Ford Motor Company was indicted in Indiana, USA for reckless homicide following the deaths of three teenagers, evidence was led in the case which demonstrated that Ford was aware of the danger posed by the Pinto car but had used a cost-benefit calculation to decide that the vehicles should be left, unaltered with their owners. It would have cost less than $11 per car to remedy the defect but calculations had shown that subsequent insurance claims resulting from the number of people predicted to be killed and maimed would be $49.5 million whereas it would cost $137 million to recall and alter all the Pintos it had sold. The calculation was made on the basis that a life was worth $200 000. Rather than produce the figure itself, Ford had, in conjunction with other motor companies, procured the Highway Traffic Safety Administration to make the necessary calculations and in 1972 it did so estimating the price at $200 725 (Dowie 1977: 20). This sort of cost-benefit analysis, which relegates human life below the considerations of profit, is not peculiar to Ford Motor Company or to recent developments. It is a feature endemic to the system of commerce.

The way that the economic imperatives of commerce can prompt decisions which imperil life was commented upon by Max Weber. In 1904 he observed that:

> After their work, ... [Chicago] workers often have to travel for hours in order to reach their homes. The tramway company has been bankrupt for years. As usual, a receiver who has no interest in speeding up the liquidation, manages its affairs; therefore, new tramcars are not purchased. The old cars constantly break down, and about four hundred people a year are thus killed or crippled. According to the law, each death costs the company about $5,000 which is paid to the widow or heirs, and each cripple costs $10,000, paid to the casualty himself. These compensations are due so long as the company does not introduce certain precautionary measures. But they have calculated that the four hundred casualties a year cost less than would the necessary precautions. The company therefore does not introduce them.
>
> (quoted in Swigert and Farrell 1980: 166)

The Pinto case is infamous for a variety of reasons, not least for the highly unusual fact that the calculations which had been made actually came to light; but the fact that we rarely learn directly of such calculations should not lead us to underestimate their prevalence. As Swigert and Farrell note (1981: 176), cost-benefit analysis is not unique to the Ford Motor Company. Corporate profits depend upon a rational calculation of income and expenses. It has also been argued that consumer safety regulations themselves encourage such calculations:

> when, therefore, the prosecution said that Ford had made a conscious choice to 'trade' cost against safety, the answer is that this is precisely what the tort law ... establishes as the limit of its legal obligation ...
>
> (Epstein 1980: 19, cited in Swigert and Farrell 1981: 176)

According to cost benefit analysis, if the cost is greater than the benefit, the prospective project should not proceed. It can be seen as the quintessential calculation of capitalism. The analysis is also not significantly different from the formula used in the United States to determine whether the defendant has been negligent: the defendant is guilty of negligence if the loss caused by the accident, multiplied by the probability of the accident's occurring, exceeds the burden of the precautions that the defendant might have taken to avert it – the so-called 'Hand formula' named after the judge who devised it (*United States* v. *Carroll Towing Co.*, 159 F.2d 169 (2d Cir. 1947)). Posner (1972: 69) notes that this is an economic test. The burden of precautions is the cost of avoiding the accident. The loss multiplied by the probability of the accident is the cost that the precautions would have averted. If a larger cost could have been avoided by incurring a smaller cost, efficiency requires that the smaller cost be incurred. Quite openly then, a company can decide on how safe its workers, passengers or consumers will be using a cost calculation in conjunction with human conscience. Accessible, and excellent, critiques of the practices and assumptions of cost-benefit analysis are provided by Moore (1991) and Nichols (1997).

A society in which the social production of goods and services is dominated by commercial considerations will be likely to generate a certain human sacrifice. These are portrayed as people who die for the greater good of the majority. What originates as a necessary consequence of the economic structure is translated into a social axiom. The problematic force, then, is social – it originates systemically – and the decisions, made by individuals, which endanger life are results of the underlying, hypostatic grammar of economic reasoning which underlies capitalism. Capitalism relentlessly reduces all forms of social relationships into economic ones; in this sense, the development of capitalism is synonymous with the commodification of all forms of human life. We are cautioned against seeing the origin of economically motivated recklessness in individuals by Marx who noted (1887, 1954: 257) that all the life lost in industry does not depend on the good or ill will of the individual capitalist but rather on external coercive economic laws.

He goes on to examine cases where individual capitalists with a conscience pricked by the suffering of children in their factories could not behave any more compassionately to their 'hands' because to do so would jeopardise their position *vis-à-vis* their competitors. In a footnote (*ibid.*), for example, Marx notes that in the beginning of 1863, 26 firms owning extensive potteries in Staffordshire, including Josiah Wedgwood & Sons, petitioned for better legislation to govern the employment of children because 'Much as we deplore the evils before mentioned, it would not be possible to prevent them by any scheme of agreement between the manufacturers . . .' (Children's Employment Comm., Rep. 1, 1863, p. 322)

Nichols (1984) has observed that, at the time of the Robens committee's examination of health and safety law (1972), the considerations of profit maximisation and cost cutting, along with unquestioned assumption of the legitimacy and thus maintenance of managerial authority, were put before safety by employers. This is not just because employers enjoy membership of a modern equivalent of Dickens' 'Association for the Mangling of Operatives', nor is it simply a result of the employers' callous disregard for the welfare of workers and the public interest. Rather such consequences are a logical outcome (Moore 1991) of an economic system which reduces working men and women to the commodity 'labour power' (Marx 1878/1949). This inevitability is recognised by the Organisation for Economic Co-operation and Development (OECD) (1989). There is widespread agreement in OECD member countries on the need for government regulation to play a major role in this area. It acknowledges that:

> protection against work accidents has historically tended to be the first area of government intervention into the workplace. Such intervention has been based on the belief that the predominance of the private market would lead to socially unacceptable levels of occupational injury, disease and death.
>
> (1989: 6)

The legal framework of protection and compensation has historically upheld the primacy of free markets and managerial authority (Moore 1991; Posner 1972) which originates within nineteenth-century master and servant legislation. Thus, working class moves for forms of joint control over safety have been fiercely opposed by the state and employers. Such forms remained very rare until the Health and Safety at Work etc. Act 1974, and even then the legislation did not permit the scarcely unreasonable trade union request to be able to stop work in situations of extreme risk. This has now just (in 1993 legislation) been achieved 160 years after the first factory legislation in 1833. Employees now have the right not to be dismissed or subjected to detrimental treatment on the grounds that they left or proposed to leave their place of work, or any dangerous part of the workplace, 'in circumstances of danger which he or she reasonably believed to be serious and imminent' and which the employee could not reasonably have been expected to avert (ss. 22A (1)(d) and 57A (1)(d) of the Employment Protection (Consolidation) Act, 1978 as amended by the Trade Union Reform and Employment Rights Act 1993).

The idea that the servant was fair game for any risk to which the master wished to expose him or her, and consented to danger by virtue of a contract, is thus partly eroded. The 'employee' now has a similar nominal and civil status as his or her 'employer', but this change has itself been used as the basis to decriminalise certain lethal risk-taking with the lives and limbs of workers. Now, following from the new, 'civilised', cordial employment relations in some workplaces where managers and workers all wear the same smart company clothes and eat together in the same staff canteens, the inherently lawful, virtuous nature of the relationship is accentuated whenever anything goes drastically wrong. However grave are the faults exposed in an investigation, the company will be able to stress the respect which it is accorded in the community and the esteem in which it is held by its personnel.

We should note here (as we have in other chapters) that the social valorisation of corporations and corporate activity tends to produce a highly distorted gaze in the wake of potential illegality on their part, both popularly and in law. Frequently the response to such illegality is to focus upon the actions or inactions of relatively powerless individuals located at or near the site of the event in question (Tombs 1991). Events following the railway crash at Clapham Junction station on 12 December, 1988 provide one such relatively well-known example. A crowded commuter train ran into the rear of a stationary train just south of Clapham Junction station. The death toll was 35, with an additional 500 people injured, 60 of them seriously. The immediate cause of the disaster was a loose wire in a relay controlling signal which allowed the display of a yellow light instead of a red one. A senior technician had re-wired this particular signal two weeks earlier as a part of the Waterloo Area Resignalling Scheme (WARS), and had left the old wire hanging loose which was his usual practice. In fact, British Rail standard procedures required the old wire to be cut back and removed or tied back. The Report of Anthony Hidden QC (Hidden 1989) on this disaster clearly reveals the way in which culpability can be traced back from individual error, through lax and indifferent management, to wider economic issues (Field and Jörg 1991). The technician himself could be the sole target of blame for having violated a departmental instruction, 'S.I. -16' which stipulated that disconnected wires should be insulated and secured. Nonetheless, another departmental instruction demanded that an 'independent wire count' be conducted by the technician's supervisor or the area Testing and Commissioning Engineer after the work had been completed. These procedures did not operate. The technician could not recall any occasion in which his work had been checked in this way. Some of his mistaken techniques had been long-standing ones which had never been corrected or even discovered by BR management.

The violation of S.I.-16 takes on a different meaning when it is discovered that the technician received very little proper training and never even received a copy of the instruction in question; neither was his supervisor aware of the requirement for an independent wire count. The area Testing and Commissioning Engineer did not realise that he had overall responsibility for ensuring that the necessary testing was carried out. All this ignorance was attributable to failures of management to communicate with its employees. The wire count instruction had been issued with no accompanying explanation, training or monitoring. The WARS was worked on a tight schedule, dependent upon high levels of overtime. These levels were never monitored. In the 13 weeks before the accident 28 per cent of the workforce had worked seven days a week, and another 43 per cent had worked 13 days out of 14. One witness told the inquiry that staff were 'shell shocked by the pressure of work'. A situation which Moore (1991: 23) notes can only be described as 'paradoxically bizarre, in as much as workers were forced to work to the point where they were almost comatose from nervous exhaustion while installing a system designed to improve safety'. The technician in question, who was under great personal financial pressure, had taken only one day off work in the preceding three months. Such levels of overtime had been going on for years at BR. Writing over 120 years earlier (in 1866), Marx addressed a similar incident:

> A tremendous railway accident has hurried hundreds of passengers into another world. The negligence of the employés is the cause of the misfortune. They declare with one voice before the jury that ten or twelve years before, their labour only lasted eight hours a-day. During the last five or six years it had been screwed up to 14, 18 and 20 hours, and under a specially severe pressure of holiday-makers, at times of excursion trains, it often lasted for 40 or 50 hours without a break. They were ordinary men, not Cyclops. At a certain point their labour-power failed. Torpor seized them. Their brain ceased to think, their eyes to see. The thoroughly 'respectable' British

jurymen answered by a verdict that sent them to the next assizes on a charge of manslaughter, and, in a gentle 'rider' to their verdict, expressed the pious hope that the capitalistic magnates of the railway would, in future, be more extravagant in the purchase of a sufficient quantity of labour-power, and more 'abstemious', more 'self-denying', more 'thrifty', in the draining of paid labour-power.

(1954/1887: 242)

In the Clapham incident the technician made a mistake (possibly a worse one than he was routinely making) through exhaustion and ignorance. He was tired because he had been overworking as the only means of securing a 'normal' living wage, so his error tracks back to the economy. He was ignorant because of lax management, and this is attributable (Field and Jörg 1991) to the low priority that safety was accorded within BR for commercial reasons. Yet the distorted gaze (legal, political, social) which incidents such as that at Clapham generally attract, both results from, and at the same time reinforces, the legitimacy afforded to commercial activity within a class-based, capitalist social order. As we have argued in Chapter 5, the definition of crime attaches itself much more easily to working class men and women than it does to corporations and their senior staff. As a London magistrate once remarked, the standard middle-class definition of crime is 'the sort of thing I don't do'. Much the same thing is postulated by corporate concerns and their political and legal public relations agents. Karl Mannheim observed that:

There is implicit in the word 'ideology' the insight that in certain situations the collective unconscious of certain groups obscures the real condition of society both to itself and to others and thereby stabilizes it.

(1936: 36)

The more powerful the group, the less likely will its misdeeds be perceived and classified as crimes. As an old Polish proverb has it: if you are caught stealing a chicken you are branded a common chicken thief, if you steal a Kingdom you will be hailed as a King. This exculpation of corporate entities is further facilitated by the criminal law as it evolved and was adapted and sustained to deal with individual offending. After four centuries of development, corporate liability in criminal law only begins in substance in the 1940s. Since then there have been several jumps forward culminating in the latest proposals from the Law Commission to legislate for the crime of corporate manslaughter (see Chapter 2).

The research of one of the current writers (Slapper 1999) found that in case studies of deaths at work (in incidents from all over the country, and over a three year period), 60 per cent of the deaths were directly attributable to the pressures of the profit-system economy. Thus, the work practice being used, the disregard for safety equipment or training, were the result not of ignorance but of an unwillingness or inability to pay the necessary extra in order that the work would be safe. For example, in one London case (1999: 253), a man and his partner were doing work in which they were not properly qualified or experienced. They did not have suitable equipment. The man's son told an inquest that his father was a metal craftsman who having been made redundant from a regular job several months before the incident, had teamed up with a friend and workmate, to do self-employed repair and construction work, sometimes, as in this instance, for large companies. In a twist compounding the economic setting of this fatality, the deceased's friend, very distressed, gave evidence to the inquest about how the accident had occurred: the deceased was on a roof trying to re-claim some asbestos sheeting which was to be used elsewhere on the site when he had fallen through a skylight and crashed some 15 foot below, smashing his head on a concrete floor. The two men were only doing this work because their real skills were made economically 'redundant'; the large company only engaged their services because they were less expensive than engaging a specialist firm; and, ironically, the work in question was reclaiming old asbestos for use elsewhere because this was cheaper than the purchase of new asbestos. It has been argued that the predominant factor in determining law, practice and policy in relation to deaths at work is the balance of class forces within any given social order (Carson 1979, 1982; Pearce 1976; Pearce and Tombs 1998; Slapper 1999; Tombs 1995b).

Relatedly, it is of interest that economic rationales are frequently used to determine precisely what constitutes legal obligations or duties of care in respect of commercial activity. In 1968, Mr. Justice Stanwick produced a judgement which noted that economic considerations are an important element in determining the nature and extent of some legal duties (*Stokes v. Guest, Keen & Nettlefold (Bolts and Nuts) Ltd* [1968] 1 WLR 1776 at 1784 B–C). The phrase 'reasonable practicability', at the heart of the Health and Safety at Work Act, precisely invites definition on the basis of economic – or rather commercial – criteria (Whyte and Tombs 1998). Further, such definitions are often loaded by reference to something called the 'national interest' (*ibid.*). Thus at the close of the Ford trial, after the jury had heard evidence of the company's cost-benefit analysis which was coldly prepared to countenance the burning of people as a cheaper option than a mass re-call and re-fit exercise, Jim Neal, attorney for the company said:

> If this country is to survive economically, we've got to stop blaming industry and business for our own sins. No car is now or ever can be said to be safe with reckless drivers on the road.
>
> (Cullen *et al.* 1987: 291)

Balancing safety and cost is a similar operation to balancing the control of crime and cost. The problem of reducing crime levels is often a question that hinges on resources and a political balance: *certain* sorts of crime could perhaps be substantially reduced or even eradicated if there were to be enough of an inroad into civil liberties.

The level of safety at work operates on a similar way to that in rail, sea and air travel: cost and expediency are balanced against known dangers, their chances of materialising, the number of people who would be hurt in the event of such materialisation and the gravity of injury to them. As Asquith LJ put it in one case:

> As has often been pointed out, if all the trains in this country were restricted to a speed of five miles an hour, there would be fewer accidents, but our national life would be intolerably slowed down. The purpose to be served, if sufficiently important, justifies the assumption of abnormal risk.
>
> (*Daborn* v. *Bath Tranways Motor Co., Ltd & Trevor Smithey* [1946] 2 All ER 333 at 336)

A case study in the economics and politics of human life: ferry safety

Recent controversies in the context of ferry safety provide an interesting area for case study, illuminating the relationships between law, economy and politics as these intersect around the preservation or sacrifice of human life. The precise nature of the negotiation between commercial interests and best safety practice has been recently exposed in relation to the safety of 'roll-on, roll-off' ferries (so-called because lorries drive in through the bow and out through the stern at the destination). Bow door safety became an issue constantly returned to by campaigning bodies and the news media.

In 1985 a paper presented at a conference held in London, by the Royal Institute of Naval Architects, detailed the urgent need for design changes in roll-on, roll-off ferries in the wake of the capsize of the vessel *European Gateway* off Harwich in 1982. Six people were killed in that incident. Several senior members of the Institute are recorded in the minutes of the conference as urging quick change to the design of roll-on, roll-off vessels before an even larger scale of incident occurred. One address from a senior Institute member blames 'commercial pressures' for stopping ship owners and governments from insisting on the installation of transverse bulkheads, and ends thus:

> The question must still be asked: what happens if a vessel of this type carrying 1000 passengers instead of 34 suffers a similar accident?
>
> (Royal Institute of Naval Architects 1986: 63)

Two years later, when the *Herald of Free Enterprise* capsized on 6 March, 1987 because it sailed with its bow doors open, 192 people lost their lives. Following the prosecution for manslaughter of P&O European Ferries (Dover) Ltd in 1990 in the aftermath of the disaster, several reports resulting from marine engineer studies recommended that all large ferries should be installed with bulkheads in the lower deck. If this huge open area which houses lorries and cars is not partitioned at intervals any water entering this deck causes rapid instability and means that the vessel will sink very quickly in a matter of minutes. The installation of bulkheads would provide a critical extension of perhaps 30 minutes – retarding the destabilisation – to allow passengers and crew to get into lifeboats. Shipping companies could adapt the existing ships but they have not done so on grounds of expense. The companies all insisted that the alterations that they had made in the light of the Sheen Report on the *Herald* disaster (like closed-circuit television enabling the bridge to check the bow doors are closed before sailing) were sufficient.

P&O were aquitted of the formal charge but were publicly exposed as being more concerned with making profits than with some aspects of passenger safety. After the tragic loss of nearly 200 lives and the public chastisement entailed in the criminal trial at the Old Bailey, there would be good reason to imagine that the company (and others watching the trial, who might have whispered 'there but for the grace of God go I') would be shaken into scrupulous safety consciousness. Such a belief would be mistaken. There was considerable pressure on companies to change their policy but to no avail.

Shipping interests seemed to have considerable influence on the political process. After the Zeebrugge disaster, the Prime Minister, Margaret Thatcher announced that:

> It is the fundamental design of the ferry that I understand is the problem.
> That is a factor that will have to be looked at very quickly because public
> confidence has been severely jolted.
>
> (*The Times*, 8 March, 1987)

The factor was indeed examined very quickly and immediately rejected. Three days later the Secretary of State for Transport, John Moore, told the House of Commons: 'I have no evidence to support the view that the disaster was due to the design of the ship' (*Hansard* [Commons] Vol. 112, No. 1410, Col. 21, 9 March, 1987).

The Department of Transport was represented at the 1985 conference and was furnished with a full report of the research demonstrating the perils of open vehicle-decks, so it seems inexplicable that just 18 months after his department had been explicitly warned (by the most suitable body in Britain to do so) of danger to ferry passengers, the minister could claim to the House of Commons that he had 'no evidence' that the design of the ferries was unsafe.

There followed repeated public statements of concern (e.g. Bergman, 1990a & b, 1993) that nothing was being done to correct what had been identified as a serious contributory factor (the undivided vehicle deck), and to require all ferries to install bulkheads. Once again however nothing was done. Meanwhile, relatives of the *Herald* victims expressed fury when the chairman of P&O European Ferries, Sir Jeffrey Stirling, was ennobled in Mrs Thatcher's resignation honours. This, notwithstanding the observation of Mr Justice Sheen in his official report that P&O was a company in which:

> All concerned in management, from the members of the Board of Directors down to the junior superintendents, were guilty of fault in that all must be regarded as sharing responsibility for the failure of management. From top to bottom the body corporate was infected with the disease of sloppiness.
>
> (Report of the Court, No. 8074. Dept. of Transport, 1987, para. 14. *M. V. Herald of Free Enterprise*)

The news of the new peerage was treated with dismay by some newspapers. One headline ran: 'It's Lord Zeebrugge' (*Daily Mirror*, 21 December, 1990).

Following Zeebrugge, the United Nations body, the International Maritime Organisation (IMO) convened a special conference and eventually passed the Safety of Life at Sea Regulations (SOLAS 90). Regulation 8 of SOLAS 90 states that all roll-on, roll-off ferries must be able to stand upright long enough for passengers to evacuate. Although this applies automatically to vessels built after April 1990, it does not apply to those built before that date. This is a remarkable compromise with safety, but one which is normal in the commercial world. If a parent found that a brand of toy he or she had just bought a child was unsafe and put the child at serious risk, the parent would be most unlikely to say 'well keep that one but I shan't be getting you another one of those!' Clearly, the dangerous toy would be taken from the child. The only justification for keeping the old ferries without bulkheads, once the newer safer design had been stipulated for post-1990 vessels, is a commercial one. The cost of installing such bulkheads, if it was to be passed on to passengers, would increase fares by between 18 and 19 pence per ticket. In an age of great competition between ferry companies (and air and train travel) this, apparently, according to the operators, makes a significant difference to the fortunes of the operators. The standards agreed as suitable in SOLAS 90 have been repeatedly postponed. They will now not be fully operative until 2005.

The contradiction between this postponement and best safety practice was put to Dr William O'Neill, President of the IMO, during the television interview in 1992 (*Checkout*, Channel 4, 24 June, 1992). He answered the questions put to him thus:

Q. It does look like some of the member countries, and in the end enough to carry the day, basically felt that safety standards cost too much.

A. No. I don't think that they felt that safety standards cost too much. I think that they felt the *level* that was prescribed might have been more than they were willing to apply to the existing ships. But the safety standards are still improved. They are still elevated. So the acceptance of increased safety standards is still there.

Q. But commercial interests won out?

A.   No. Commercial interests did not win out.

Q.   But if safety cost too much then commercial interests won out.

A.   No, no. Commercial interests had their part to play in the decision-making process.

While relatively unsafe ferries plied their trade into and from British ports, the government and the IMO were allied to commercial interests. In another telling television interview in the documentary mentioned above, Lord Caithness, then minister responsible for shipping, was asked whether he would be prepared to publish a list of all the ferries that had thereto conformed *in full* with the SOLAS 90 standards, that is, had fitted bulkheads. The minister replied to the camera that he would have no objection. Then, in an extraordinary turn of events, a voice was heard off camera asking for the film to be stopped. The film, perhaps unknown to the minister, was not stopped, so the viewer saw a man in a suit clasping a batch of paper walk on to the set and talk in grave tones to the minister. The documentary then cut to what was a re-take of the original question. This time the minister said that he would *not* publish such a list (despite the fact this would assist British travellers to select the safest ferries) because it would prejudice the business interests of some British operators whose foreign rivals (from northern and western Europe) would gain from such disclosure. This was the second take:

Q.   In an era of open government can we have your assurance that the details of which ships comply to SOLAS 90 will be published?

A.   I think that every country ought to do that.

Q.   And will you do it?

A.   I think that every country ought to do that and it can only be done effectively on a complete basis with every country doing it. *It isn't going to be beneficial* by just one country doing it because it puts at a severe commercial disadvantage that country. [emphasis added]

Here the minister sees the interests of passengers and commerce as identical whereas there is a clear conflict. It obviously *would* be 'beneficial' to customers to be able to make properly informed decisions about the safest ferry to travel on, even if the shareholders of British operators were not best pleased that passengers were choosing to travel on ferries operated by foreign firms.

Then, the *Estonia* capsized in the Baltic sea on 28 September, 1994, killing over 900 people (small children were not registered as passengers so the toll could have been significantly over 900). Water entered the vessel through defective bow doors. Most of these people died in the vessel because they did not have sufficient time to get on to the upper deck. Had the ferry been fitted with bulkheads the sinking would have been delayed long enough for everyone to have escaped from the ship (*Guardian*, 29 September–4 October, 26 October, 1994).

Following the sinking of the *Estonia*, Dr O'Neill made several contributions to news stories (e.g. *Independent*, 8 November, 1994, p. 3) in which he emphasised that the matter of the compulsory installation of bulkheads would be urgently reviewed. No new research was cited by the President of the IMO, so he was evidently responding to nothing more than the huge death toll: 900 grieving families and world alarm over ferry safety evidently spoke more eloquently to him than all the cogent evidence from naval architects and safety groups which he had been repeatedly given in the wake of Zeebrugge, and which he had repeatedly rejected.

Six weeks after this sinking, a report from the Department of Transport's Marine Safety Agency discovered that of the 107 roll-on, roll-off ferries it had inspected, bow door faults were found in one in three vessels (*The Times*, 8 November, 1994). In October 1994, only one ferry operating in British waters had bulkheads, and this was operated by a Belgian company, Ostend Lines.

The chrematistic pressures of commerce evidently prevail over the most obvious and urgent, if time-consuming and interruptive, dictates of safety.

Safety *versus* cost?

So clearly and widely is it now recognised that the engines of industry and commerce are primarily controlled by financial factors that these have been reverted to by health and safety regulators as the key to promoting compliance with occupational safety and health law. This is of particular interest, because it represents a clear admission – whether wittingly or not – on the part of regulatory bodies that it is the cost of compliance which is the major propulsion towards crime. One response to this recognition might be to adopt enforcement strategies based upon raising the costs of non-compliance, namely a deterrence-based approach. In contrast, the response of the Health and Safety Executive is to appeal to the economic self-interest within corporations, arguing that being safe and healthy – that is, meeting legal requirements – is good for the bottom line.

Perhaps this rather curious turn is also a recognition that the very essence of corporations – seeking profit-maximisation – makes them relatively immune to other forms of regulation: appeals to companies for humane working practices; threats (but little actual use) of criminal proceedings; educational campaigns; equipping workers with the right knowledge; and all sorts of negotiated compliance strategies have still left a high toll of death and injury, much of which is produced by crime. Thus in a recent publication (HSE 1994b), one of a several on the same theme (HSE 1991c, 1993b, 1996; Davies and Teasdale 1994), the Health and Safety Executive estimates that £16 billion is lost to the British economy each year through accidents and ill-health at work. The loss to industry is calculated at £360 a year for every worker. More than 2.2 million people suffered from ill-health which was wholly or partly caused by work and 750 000 of them took time off as a result, leading to the loss of 11.5 million working days. Work-related illnesses forced 70 500 people to stop work permanently. While calculations can vary somewhat – we cite some alternative figures in Chapter 4 – the message to owners of industry is, essentially, take better safety precautions for your workers (in training, equipment and procedure) because it will cost you more if they are killed and injured than the sum you will have to spend to avoid such occurrences. This replicates the *Hand formula* (above) used in the USA to determine whether a defendant has been negligent. Frank Davies, chairman of the Health and Safety Commission, was quite explicit in his admonition to employers: 'Accidents hurt your profit and loss account' (*Guardian*, 10 February, 1994, p. 6). The title of the HSE's campaign to effect compliance with occupational health legislation is no more subtle: 'Good Health is Good Business'. Even compliance with the law is reduced to a commodifiable process.

The headline of a newspaper story (*Independent*, 24 November, 1994, p. 6) examining the provisional findings of the Health and Safety Commission research (before the report was published) captured the import very succinctly: 'Profits "at risk from accidents at work"'. Company losses through accidents were between eight and 36 times greater than insured costs. The report followed a detailed study of accidents and illnesses at a construction site, a creamery, a transport haulage company, a North sea oil production platform and an NHS hospital, each of which had a previously established above average record of safety. It calculated that the construction firm lost £700 000 a year through accidents and ill-health, the creamery almost £1 million, the transport company £196 000, the hospital £400 000 and the oil production platform £3.7 million. The relevant costs include the payment of compensation to injured workers or relatives, replacing staff involved in an accident and repairing damaged equipment. It estimates the direct cost to employers of accidents and work-related ill-health at between £4 and £9 billion, equivalent to 5–10 per cent of all British-based company profits.

The preservation of human life and welfare is not the abiding, supreme governing principle of capitalism. Human welfare is a desideratum that prevailing ideology suggests must be sought as far as commercial considerations make this a realistic, achievable goal. Each year at least 400 people are killed and 50 000 seriously injured at work in Britain. Most of these are avoidable. They occur through economically-related causes concerning training, supervision, equipment and working environment. The degree of moral culpability (measured by the criminal law's criteria of gross negligence and recklessness as these apply to the crimes of manslaughter and serious assault) from which the commercial carnage results is strikingly similar to that of conventional crime. There is, though, a pressure for what is engendered by commercialism as a regular toll of mayhem not to be regarded as endemic crime. If that became too sharp and commonly accepted a social perception the cost would be twofold: it would be grist to the legitimation crisis mill (Habermas 1976: 33–94) and it would undermine a core part of the ideology of the market system, namely that a system which is posited on the promotion of social good by the pursuit of individual gain in a competitive economy (Smith 1776/1976: 456, para. 9) best promotes the public interest. Smith argued famously that:

> As every individual, therefore, endeavours as much as he can both to employ his capital in support of domestick industry, and so to direct that industry that its produce may be of the greatest value; every individual necessarily labours to render the annual revenue of the society as great he can. He generally, indeed, neither intends to promote the public interest, nor knows how much he is promoting it. By preferring the support of domestick to that of foreign industry, he intends only his own security; and by directing that industry in such a manner as its produce may be of the greatest value, he intends only his own gain, and he is in this, as in many other cases, led by an invisible hand to promote an end which was no part of his intention. Nor is it always the worse for society that it was no part of it. By pursuing his own interest he frequently promotes that of the society more effectually than when he really intends to promote it. I have never known much good done by those who affected to trade for the public good. It is an affectation, indeed, not very common among merchants, and very few words need to be employed in dissuading them from it.

In the context of promoting safety, it is clear from the general history of factory legislation (Marx 1887/1954; Carson 1970a, 1979, 1980b) that the public interest is not best promoted by Smith's nascent laissez-faire policy. On the contrary, the evidence suggests that, in the same way as there is a constant downward pressure on wages from capital, there is a constant downward pressure on the expense of safety. Smith's dichotomy between, on the one hand, the shameless pursuit of individual interests, and, on the other hand the altruism of 'those who trade for the public good', is as irrelevant now as it was at the time that he penned these false alternatives (see Pearce and Tombs 1998).

The regulatory structure and the production of 'crime'

While we consider questions relating to regulation and punishment at length in the following chapters (8 and 9 respectively), it is also important here to address regulation in the context of understanding the *causes* of corporate crime. That is, if we accept that corporations are inherently criminogenic, then one of the key variables in explaining why particular crimes occur, and why particular corporations engage in illegalities at particular points, is some sense of opportunity to do so. And, as Coleman has noted,

> A knowledge of the pattern of the state's enforcement efforts and the likelihood and severity of the punishment for different offences is therefore important to our understanding of the attractiveness of various opportunities.
>
> (1987: 426)

One route into the terrain that needs to be covered if any understanding between regulation and corporate crime is to be reached is set out by Kramer:

> We need ... to develop an understanding of the political economy of corporate violence; we need to know how and why a corporate capitalist economy systematically generates such violence, and why the state in a capitalist economy is so impotent in its attempts to control these acts. We need also to understand how organisational environments, goals, and structures relate to corporate violence.
>
> (1983: 167)

A helpful starting point in the context of the questions raised by Kramer is a brief history of the state's response to death and injury incidental to employment. As we have stated, the social incidence of corporate crime can be linked to the efficiency of the regulatory structure. The first piece of health and safety legislation came in 1802 in response to the appallingly inhuman condition in which child apprentices were worked in the mills (Carson 1979; Engels 1845/1969: 170–81). The Health and Morals of Apprentices Act prohibited the employment of children for more than twelve hours a day and provided for the eventual cessation of night work by children. Some rudimentary provision was also made for the physical and intellectual well-being of these children with minor requirements concerning clothing, sleeping arrangements and their education. A further Act of 1819 fixed the minimum age for working in a cotton factory at nine years, and prohibited the employment of those under 16 for longer than 12 hours a day (excluding meal times). By 1831 these rules were extended to night working. As Carson notes, these measures were almost wholly ineffectual because enforcement was left to the Justices of the Peace who, if they carried out any inspections, were evidently quite uncritical and perfunctory in their checks. In view of the fact that these people shared the same class status and clubs as those whom they were supposed to police, this reluctance may not be surprising (Field 1990). Looking at the possibility of making violations of safety legislation punishable as an ordinary crime, a Royal Commission in 1833 rejected the idea with the conclusion that such a change would: 'create a serious objection to the investment of capital in manufacturing industry in this country' (Carson 1979: 42).

Instead, the Act decided that the appropriate sanctions would be a relatively low level of fines with an additional cushion that where the magistrate found that a violation was neither wilful nor grossly negligent the defendant could be discharged or given a minimal penalty. The ensuing legislation did create four inspectors and a number of superintendents to work under them but they were under instructions to be 'in communication exclusively with employers, with the view of making the law acceptable to them' and it was not long before the inspectors were reporting that the new law *was* being generally adhered to. Carson notes that the enforcement policy here came close to 'an outright conspiracy' (1979: 43). Before the final phase of the 1833 legislation was to come into effect, bringing 12–13-year-olds within the law, the factory inspectorate were actually persuaded by mill owners to oppose such a change on the grounds that it would make life impossibly difficult for them; a consideration which appears to have held greater sway than the interests of the thousands of children who were being worked to death.

Legislation was drafted to postpone the change but it was not promulgated. One of the problems of enforcement was that the owners of industry tried, in periods of economic adversity, to improve their performance by cutting labour costs and by extending the hours worked. This was not just restricted to the poorer less reputable firm. According to witnesses (Carson 1979: 50; Marx 1887/1954: 232), masters even admitted quite openly that it was easier to pay the occasional mitigated fine than to incur the costs involved in obeying the law or lose the profits accruing from its violation. Sixty-eight per cent of all fines imposed between 1836 and 1842 involved sums of £1 or less, £1 being the minimum stipulated fine, although it could be less in exceptional circumstances. The state of affairs today is very similar. The level of penalty an employer can expect for serious infringements is relatively low, although of course the absolute average is higher today. Thus, while 'generally pathetic levels of fines continue to follow successful prosecutions' (Tombs 1995b: 353), by 1997/8 the provisional, 'adjusted' penalty for a health and safety offence was £3886 (HSC 1998: 178). Also similar is that today, as in the nineteenth century, there remains very little chance of being inspected, with one inspector to every 690 registered premises – not counting the estimated 40 per cent of sites and premises which do not register (Whitfield 1992). Estimates vary as to the frequency with which a company can expect an inspector's visit: from once every ten years (Hutter 1993) to once in four or five years (Nelken 1994a; Tye 1989).

Having gained the advantages of legislation which, although creating criminal wrongs, contained only regulatory offences, the employers were then afforded the additional advantage in the policy, developed by inspectors, of only prosecuting when there was evidence that there had been a *mens rea* of intention on the part of the employer, for example, the offence in question was committed in violation of an earlier warning from the inspectorate.

Carson concluded that the operation of the law developed in this way in order not to constrain the economic development taking place in the nineteenth century (1979: 57). In his later study of the high death rate in the North Sea oil fields, he notes that by the middle of the 1970s the rate of 'accidental' death in the oil industry was 11 times higher than that for construction, nine times higher than that for mining and six times higher than that for quarrying. His evidence indicates that the accidents were not simply what is only to be expected when an industry undertakes hazardous operations at the very frontiers of technology but rather the result of factors like poor communication, failure of equipment, poor working practices and lack of safety precautions. Throughout the 1970s the British government was under considerable pressure to extract North Sea oil as rapidly as possible for economic reasons including a pressing balance of payments problem. The government was heavily dependent on the expertise and resources of the major transnational oil companies who would only act quickly if they were left relatively unhampered by any requirement for costly and time-consuming safety precautions. The government eventually acceded to their demands about the legislative framework in which the companies were to operate. Carson concludes that most of the 106 deaths which had occurred up to December 1980 could have been avoided if the 'political economy of speed' had not been allowed to prevail over the 'political economy of employees' lives'. He was struck by the parallels between the history of North Sea oil safety and that of the earliest efforts to impose statutory controls upon the operations of the 'dark satanic mills' of the nineteenth century. In both periods there were 'immutable laws of capital' which rendered it imperative that regulation should be minimised (1982: 302).

The amoral nature of the operation of commerce is a sine qua non of capitalism, and always has been. Witness the following extract from a factory inspector's report from 1841:

> It is certainly much to be regretted that any class of persons should toil 12 hours a day, which, including the time for their meals and for going to and returning from their work, amounts, in fact, to 14 of the 24 hours ... Without entering into the question of health, no one will hesitate, I think, to admit that, *in a moral point of view*, so entire an absorbtion of the time of the working classes, without intermission, from the early age of 13, and in trades not subject to restriction, much younger, must be extremely prejudicial, and is an evil greatly to be deplored ... [emphasis original]
>
> (Leonard Horner, Reports of Insp. of Fact. for 31 Dec., 1841, cited in Marx 1877/1954: 264)

The code of conduct being followed by business is not a moral one. Nevertheless, it offends the moral sensibilities of many, but the immorality of the ravages it caused to children did not, in itself, call the conduct to a halt. It was only when moral indignation and philanthropic reforming zeal were joined by parallel desires for change from the owning class who recognised that some regulation was in their best long-term interests (Marx 1887/1954: chp 10; Engels 1969; Carson 1970a, 1979) that the legislation became feasible.

Marx wrote about how, at every legislative restriction on the factory owners, many industrialists strove to do the most that they could to undermine or limit its intended effect. The 1833 Factory Act left it optional with the factory owners during the 15 hours, from 5.30am to 8.30pm, to make every 'young person' and 'every child' begin, break off, resume, or end his 12 or 8 hours at any moment they liked, and also permitted them to assign to different persons, different times for meals. The factory owners, far from using the discretion with any compassion, immediately resorted to a 'system of relays' which completely thwarted the inspectors' attempts to check who, if anyone, was being overworked. They ensured that 'the labour-horses were not changed at fixed stations', but were constantly re-harnessed at changing stations (1887/1954: 266). Later, the 'lynx eye of Capital' discovered that while the Factory Act of 1844 did not allow five hours work before mid-day without a pause of at least 30 minutes for refreshment, it prescribed nothing of the kind for work after mid-day,

> Therefore, it claimed and obtained the enjoyment not only of making children of 8 drudge without intermission from 2 to 8.30pm, but also of making them hunger during that time.
>
> (1887/1954: 272)

There were often good economic reasons for factory and mill owners to support some of the reforms restricting the working day if they believed that the legislative requirements would be manageable and would detrimentally affect their smaller rivals. There is even an example of the smaller firms helping to fund agitation by workers in the larger firms to promote legislation for a nine-hour day when the smaller firms saw this as being in their economic interests (Marx 1887/1954: 257, n.2).

There were other reasons why the owners of industry lent support to legislation relating to control over working conditions, but, critically, these reasons are related to the economic interests of that class rather than moral or humanitarian case for change. For one thing, in the interests of preserving the working class from being over plundered, the Factory Acts were necessary, in Marx's words, to 'curb the passion of capital for a limitless draining of labour-power' (1887/1954: 229). He reflects that:

> Apart from the working class movement which daily grew more threatening, the limiting of factory labour was dictated by the same necessity which spread guano over the English fields. The same blind eagerness for plunder that in the one case exhausted the soil, had, in the other, torn up by the roots the living force of the nation.
>
> (*ibid.*)

That the working class was in danger of being pummelled so badly that its wealth-creating ability would be significantly reduced is corroborated by medical data concerning epidemic illness and the declining physical condition of military recruits (*ibid.*). Capitalists were also prevailed upon with two further economic arguments against over-working their servants.

First, that this would shorten the life, and therefore duration of labour-power, of a worker; that the rate at which workers need to be replaced would increase; and, therefore, that the cost of the social reproduction of labour-power would increase (*ibid.*: 253). Second, that 'all work and no play' would reduce the ingenuity, dexterity and general productivity of workers (*ibid.*: 261).

There is evidence to suggest that another factor lending support to regulation (apart from the pressure of reformers, and the enlightened economic self-interest of certain capitalists) was that it assisted in the discipline and regimentation of the workforce. The emphasis on regularity and uniformity, upon records of machinery operation, upon times of entry and departure from the mills, all helped inculcate 'habits of obedience' (Thompson 1967; Carson 1979). Similarly, the efforts of the early factory inspectors to impress upon employers that the provisions relating to the education of children in the 1833 Act should be complied with, helped to disseminate awareness of the advantages that might accrue to labour discipline from education of the factory children (Carson 1979: 45). The results of one survey of employers showed that those who had installed schools enjoyed an enhanced level of what the inspectorate labelled the 'habits of subordination'.

Conclusion: explaining corporate offending?

As we have argued in this chapter, corporate crime can only be understood in the context of wider political economy. One essential feature of corporate existence across all political economic contexts is the need, at least in the long run, to maximise profitability, and it is impossible to disassociate this fact from the incidence of corporate crime. However, it is also clear that there are aspects of particular political economies which need to be taken into account in understanding the particular incidence of criminal activity on the part of corporations.

Thus any full-blown theory of corporate crime would both encompass a range of elements and levels, and seek to represent the articulation of these elements and levels. Such a theoretical task would entail a transcendence of the confines of both criminology and sociology. Key aspects of any such analysis would integrate understandings of the general state of national and the international economy, the nature of markets, industries, and the particular products or services with which particular corporations are involved, dominant ideologies and social values, formal political priorities and the nature of regulation, particular corporate structures, the balances of power within these, the distribution of opportunities within and beyond these, and corporate cultures and socialisation into these. Even this cursory indication should demonstrate that a truly comprehensive theory of corporate crime – even the basic elements of which are beyond the scope of this text – would take account of all of these phenomena.

One criminologist who has urged this sort of analysis is Coleman (1987), who has attempted to integrate etiological research on white-collar crime on the basis that criminal behaviour results from 'the confluence of appropriate motivation and opportunity' (1987: 406). His starting point is the interactionist theory of motivation basic to most of the social psychological research on white-collar crime. Nonetheless, he argues, that while interactionist theory can help us understand white-collar crime in terms of the offenders' symbolic construction of their social worlds it ultimately fails to explain the *causes* of crime. Coleman argues that the origins of symbolic motivational patterns are to be found in the social structure of industrial capitalism and 'the culture of competition' to which it gives rise.

Coleman notes that there are various causes which 'motivate' people to carry out white-collar crime. Directors of companies can use various 'techniques of neutralization' (Matza and Sykes 1957) to allow themselves to maintain a non-deviant self-image by breaking law they regard, for example, as unfairly burdensome on business. One of those in the American heavy electrical equipment price-fixing case said: 'If I didn't do it, I felt someone else would. I would be removed and somebody else would do it' (Geis 1967: 84). Even so, notes Coleman, explaining how someone gets his or her criminal behaviour through interacting with others who have criminal values does not explain the genesis of criminality in those others. All one ends up with is a theory that says that criminals are produced by other criminals. The important inquiry concerns where types of criminal conduct originate:

> The answer to this question must ultimately be found on the structural, not the social-psychological, level, and the failure of interactionist theorists to root their analysis in the political economy of industrial capitalism.
>
> (1987: 161)

Coleman traces the seventeenth and eighteenth century burgeoning of the social idea that wealth and success should be the central goals of human endeavour, and that the best results for society will come from the aggregate efforts of individuals struggling in a selfish manner to make the best for themselves, even at the expense of others. This eventually leads to an almighty and over-arching grand idea of competition as an axiomatic desideratum, the correlate of which is the terrible fear and consequence of failure. This is not a natural part of human nature, and Coleman cites various anthropological studies (Dentan 1968; Lee 1979) to show how human beings can and do live in uncompetitive, co-operative communities.

For us, a society with a strong competitive *ethos* (whether or not this is an accurate reflection of reality (see Pearce 1976)), a socially developed fear of failure (which permeates both individuals, and the *ésprit de corps* of corporate bodies), an increasing commodification of all human relationships and practices, an ever increasing number and frequency of transactions (Vaughan 1983) which at the same time are less open to public scrutiny, and a capitalist economy constantly pushing people with targets to hit, promotions to seek and demotions to avoid, recessions to try to survive, and so on, can thus be seen as a society likely to engender corporate crime. Where certain sorts of crime, like corporate crime, are scarcely policed, rarely prosecuted and hardly ever punished with severe sanctions, the structure of the criminal justice system also contributes to the facilitation of corporate crime as an option for achieving business goals.

Chapter 8

Regulating corporations?

Introduction

Perhaps more than any other substantive area related to corporate crime which we address in this text, the discussion of regulation can be one which only summarises a selection of some of the key theoretical approaches, concepts, empirical findings and debates. Studies of regulation have proven something of an academic growth area in recent years and there are now enormous theoretical and empirical literatures spanning criminology, socio-legal studies, political science, sociology, economics and business/management studies. Some possible reasons for this seemingly exponential expansion of interest are worth noting in themselves.

First, it might simply be the case that there has slowly emerged a general recognition of the prevalence of corporate irresponsibility, misconduct and crime; the issue of how the corporation can be controlled – and we should be clear that this is what regulation entails (Mintzberg 1996) – has been increasingly posed by empirical events. Related to this is simply the intensifying scale and spread of corporate activity. As we have noted in an aside in a previous chapter, it is certainly the case that many of the arguments regarding the globalisation of economic activities are exaggerated; moreover, as a phenomenon, globalising capitalism is hardly new – both Marx (Marx and Engels 1848/1977: 39), and Durkheim (1897/1979: 255–6), for example, each pointed to the ineluctable logic of capitalism to expand its operations, ever seeking new markets, as well as sources of labour and raw materials. However, it is the case that the break up – and subsequent 'liberalisation' – of the Soviet Union, coupled with the ability of corporations to operate within and with the huge Chinese economy, have greatly augmented the playing field upon which corporations can operate in the past decade. Moreover, and relatedly, it must also be acknowledged that the sheer number of corporations who operate across national borders (even if there are few truly global companies) is now huge, thus raising the issue of the mobility of capital. By this, we mean the ability of capital to respond to real, or even threats of, greater regulation in one state or national context by relocating its operations to a less regulated state or nation. Again, perhaps for obvious reasons (the threat of relocation provides enormous leverage for corporations in pre-empting tighter regulation), the ability of corporations to relocate is often exaggerated – location decisions are based upon much more than the level of health and safety or antitrust legislation, for example, while some operations are easier (technologically and politically) to shift from one place to another than are some others. It is phenomena and arguments such as these that mean that regulation of corporations, not least those which are transnational, proves to be a particularly difficult problem for governments, academics and communities alike.

A further reason for an upsurge in concern about regulation is that to the extent that privatisation has swept across the industrialised and industrialising world in the past two decades, then problems of regulation raise themselves quantitatively and qualitatively. In quantitative terms, privatisation simply means that there are more corporate actors to be regulated, thus raising the scale of the task for regulators and states; *more* regulatory activity is needed. In qualitative terms, newly privatised industries sectors raise *new* problems of regulation; for example, where once the state, through direct ownership, was able to exercise some control over its electricity and gas industries, or telecommunications, or rail, and so on, the passing of these operations to private corporations has opened up new regulatory problems which have seen states struggle with the intractable problems of allowing private corporations to pursue profit maximisation whilst attempting to force upon them the need to meet certain social needs – the provision of electricity to households where bills cannot be made, bus and postal services on loss-making rural 'routes', investment in clean water technologies where these require massive up-front investments which have not immediate or short-term pay-offs for private owners, and so on (see Prosser 1997, for a discussion of such regulatory issues in the context of newly privatised industries in Britain).

This indicates a final reason for a growing concern with regulation – namely that expressed through the phrase 'Quality of Life'. Essentially, some have argued that one consequence of the post-war boom in Western industrialised economies in general, but in Britain in particular, was to deliver universal provision of basic services and goods – access to education, shelter, employment or means of subsistence when un- or under-employed – the meeting of such basic needs leads to populations shifting their concern from access to the necessities of life to the quality of life. Thus concerns shift from the right to work to the right to a safe workplace; from women's access to employment to 'equal pay for equal work' in employment; from mass house-building to the preservation of rural landscapes and the flora and fauna therein. This argument is problematic in the sense that it assumes that most people *did* in fact win access to work, housing, education, in the context of the 'post-war settlement' (Jessop *et al.* 1988); moreover, even if we assume that one aspect of this settlement was widespread (though not universal) access to such forms of state/social provision, then it is certainly clear that such access is less widespread now than it was 20 years ago, prior to the crisis of the British state in the 1970s and the collapse of this settlement (*ibid.*). These reservations entered into, however, it is reasonable to argue that in the meeting of certain needs, new, 'higher' needs are developed (Marx and Engels 1845/1985: 49); thus to the extent that as 'pro-regulatory groups' (Snider 1991; see below) win concessions in certain areas, then they are likely to extend their demands to other aspects of life.

Regulation, then, raises an enormous range of complex issues which go right to the heart of debates about the nature and role of corporations, about economic activity, and about the very nature of contemporary economies, states and societies. For the purposes of this text in general, however, and this chapter in particular, our focus will be necessarily be much narrower, though we will refer to these latter issues in a final section. We begin with an extended discussion of arguments around compliance-oriented enforcement techniques. These are dominant amongst regulatory agencies, and this dominance is used by some in the context of a debate often cast – misleadingly – in terms of the stark choice of 'punish or persuade' (Hopkins 1994: 431; Braithwaite 1985) to argue that these techniques of persuasion are *necessary* in the context of regulating corporations. We argue that despite the superficial plausibility of claims that seeking compliance through persuasion is the most appropriate regulatory strategy, such a claim does not stand up to empirical nor theoretical scrutiny. We then turn to assess a set of arguments which have some similarity with, but much greater adequacy than, these claims regarding enforcement techniques – namely the work of Braithwaite and others around self- and enforced self-regulation. In the course of this critical assessment, we argue that one of the virtues of this work is that it sets out a range of regulatory options, how these might relate to each other, and the conditions of existence of both compliance-oriented and more 'punitive' regulation, which in the latter case is a principle of deterrence. We conclude by arguing, following others, that regulation needs to be understood through reference to the dynamics of macro-political economy, within which the micro-dynamics of regulation negotiations can be more adequately interpreted; some of the basic contours of this political economy approach are sketched out in the concluding section of the chapter.

Compliance-oriented enforcement

There are numerous studies that document the extent to which a compliance-oriented approach to the enforcement of regulations is the predominant one amongst regulatory bodies. For example, there are useful empirical studies/research on the enforcement practices of consumer protection officers (Cranston 1979), the Department of Energy (Carson 1982; Woolfson *et al.* 1996) and the Offshore Safety Division (Woolfson *et al.* 1996; Whyte *et al.* 1996; Whyte and Tombs 1998), on Environmental Health Officers (Hutter 1988), on the *modus operandi* of the Factory Inspectorate (Carson 1970a, 1970b; Dawson *et al.* 1988) and other HSE inspectorates (Hutter 1993, 1997), the Inland Revenue (Cook 1989), and on the enforcement of various aspects of pollution/environmental legislation (Richardson *et al.* 1983; Hawkins 1984; Weait 1989).

What, then, is a compliance-oriented approach? Perhaps the classic statement of a compliance-oriented approach to regulatory enforcement is to be found in Keith Hawkins's *Environment and Enforcement* (1984). Here, it is claimed that there are two different ways in which police work can be done, namely by 'sanctioning strategies' with a 'penal style' which is 'accusatory and adversarial', or through 'compliance strategies' with a 'conciliatory style'. The former applies a punishment for breaking a rule and doing harm but is less concerned with producing '[c]onformity with the law'. Such strategies are typically followed in situations where 'deviance has a categorical, unproblematical quality', particularly if involving 'personal harm', where 'law breaking is essentially a discrete activity' and 'unpredictable', and where 'enforcement relations tend to be compressed and abrupt'. The goal of a 'compliance strategy', on the other hand, is to 'prevent a harm rather than punish an evil', aiming thus for 'social repair and maintenance' at minimum cost. Enforcers respond to problems 'negotiating future conformity to standards which are administratively determined'. Compliance enforcement is marked by 'an extended, incremental approach' where any ultimate prosecution is viewed by the enforcement agent as 'a sign of failure'. Enforcement tends towards compliance when victims are 'distant, diffuse and indeterminate' and where the deviance itself is a state of affairs allowing 'the development of social relationships between rule-enforcer and rule-breaker'. Hawkins refers to 'unfenced machinery, substandard housing, adulterated food, drunkenness' and 'vagrancy, prostitution or mental disturbance'. Overall what 'prompts a sanctioning rather than a compliance response is not who does the law enforcement so much as the sort of behaviour which is subject to control' (*ibid.*: 1–8). Thus a compliance-oriented approach is essentially one of persuasion and bargaining.

Before discussing compliance-oriented enforcement, several points need to be made regarding the literature which documents this as the regulatory norm.

First, this work focuses almost exclusively upon what has come to be known – misleadingly (Pearce and Tombs 1998) – as social regulation; that is, regulation aimed at forcing upon private businesses the consideration of certain social ends, often represented as being in some public interest, particularly with regard to the protection of consumers, employees, local publics and the natural environment. Generally (though not entirely) excluded from such work are considerations of regulatory bodies which oversee probity and compliance in financial markets, competition, various transactions between corporations and between corporations and governments, determination of prices, and so on. One recent, notable, exception is a study of regulation of the financial services industries, which argues that this industry has moved towards a system of mandated self-regulation, a system very similar to that described below as enforced self-regulation (Black 1997).

Second, it is worth noting that many of the studies of corporate crime that we referred to in Chapter 3 are in fact studies which take regulation as their primary focus. Including these within any list of studies of regulatory activity, we arrive at an impressive body of literature.

Third, we should note that there is an enormous body of work which is US-based, much of which reaches the same conclusions regarding the prevalence of compliance-oriented enforcement amongst regulatory bodies. Indeed, one recent text has gone so far as to argue that there is evidence of a convergence of enforcement styles across enforcement bodies, jurisdictions, bodies of law, and so on: Hutter claims that there is an extensive body of evidence from Australia, Britain, the Netherlands, Sweden and the US, that regulators favour compliance-based methods; what is more, she claims, this emerging preference extends to financial regulation and certain areas of policing (1997: 243).

Fourth, there is an important distinction to make regarding the range of the work which considers compliance-oriented enforcement. As we have noted, almost all studies of enforcement in Britain (and many beyond Britain) endorse the claim that such a practice is predominant amongst regulators. This is not to say that more punitive regulatory methods have not been used, even if this has been relatively rare in Britain (see, for example, Pearce and Tombs 1997, for some instances of these), by far the exception than the rule. Indeed, in many respects, Britain is the classic site of compliance-oriented regulatory enforcement, as one aspect of a more generally consensual or cooperative regulatory structure, more so than, for example, Germany, Sweden or the US (other national contexts which have been subject to research; see, for example, Brickman *et al.* 1985; Kelman 1981; Peacock ed. 1984; Vogel 1986). However, amongst the British literature on compliance-oriented enforcement, we perceive a crucial distinction. For some, while describing the prevalence of such techniques, these are seen as problematic, over-accommodationist, ensuring that regulatory goals are set too low, and affording too little protection for workers, consumers, local residents, and so on (Carson 1982; Pearce and Tombs 1998; Woolfson *et al.* 1996). These latter studies typically suggest reforms whereby greater elements of punitive enforcement are recommended on the part of regulators. None of these studies claims that compliance-oriented enforcement can or should be abandoned, all argue that it is problematic to the extent that it is the predominant regulatory technique; in the crude terms set out above, all argue for rather more punitiveness, rather less persuasion, within the regulatory mix. By contrast, there is a rather different body of work which not only *describes* compliance-oriented enforcement, *but also argues that this is the most effective, most appropriate, most desirable and/or only feasible mode of enforcement.* A second feature which distinguishes this work from that which is more critical of compliance-oriented techniques is that much of this is conducted with the support – and all that this entails in terms of access, availability of insight, and so on – and sometimes funding from the regulatory agencies under examination. Much of this work is associated with the Centre for Socio-Legal Studies, Woolfson College, Oxford, and includes the work of Black, Genn, Hawkins, Hutter, Jamieson and Richardson and colleagues. A third distinguishing feature is that whilst much of the critical research on compliance-oriented enforcement is either Marxist or radical in origin, the work associated with Woolfson College works within a rather different epistemology – much of this is in fact based within a micro-, or interactionist, sociology. This form of social science is one of attempting to 'make sense' of situations as perceived or understood by participants.

Fifth, we should note that within this latter literature on compliance-oriented enforcement, the term 'compliance' is being used to identify 'one of the two strategies by which *regulators* may seek to bring the regulated into conformity with the law' (Hopkins 1994: 431); in fact, compliance 'more conventionally' refers to 'the behaviour of the *regulated* in conforming with relevant regulation. Thus the aim of *both* strategies employed by regulators, punishment and persuasion, is to bring about compliance by the regulated' (see *ibid.*: 431–2). We should not be misled by the common counter-posing of the term compliance *against* that of punitive enforcement that the former techniques seek to ensure compliance with law, while the latter seek only to punish for violations; each approach seeks compliance. Where most writers on regulation are in agreement is that what is at issue is the appropriate combination of techniques, and the emphasis amongst these, whereby compliance can be achieved (often referred to as the 'regulatory mix').

Finally, we should make clear that we do not intend in this chapter to review the range of works that demonstrate the pervasiveness of a compliance-oriented enforcement. Indeed, adequate reviews of such work are available elsewhere (see, for example, Rowan-Robinson *et al.* 1990). That this is the dominant form of enforcement is clear. Rather, we will subject to extended critique the latter body of work, which we shall refer to here as the 'compliance school'. We address this work partly because it is so influential in British studies of and debates around regulation, and partly because we find many of its elements highly problematic. Two further prefatory points should be entered. First, we cannot here address all of this work in any detail, and thus we will partly obscure some of the nuances peculiar to the work of each of the particular writers within this rubric. We shall use the work of Hawkins as largely representative of this work: he is widely cited as having produced the classic statements of this genre, generally acknowledged in texts and papers written within it, and is the General Editor of the series in which many of the key texts of the genre appear (namely, the *Oxford Socio-Legal Studies* series). We shall also draw upon some of the theoretical underpinnings upon which Hawkins himself draws, namely those of Bardach, Kagan and Scholz, three American writers whom have elsewhere been characterised as members of this school (Pearce and Tombs 1990, 1991). Second, we should thus note that those whom we will characterise as working within the compliance school have not readily accepted this label, nor indeed some of the criticisms made of them which we set out below.[1]

The compliance school

In addition to describing a compliance-oriented approach as that which regulators adopt, those working within the compliance school also seek to provide reasons for why this is the most appropriate regulatory style – that is, they shift from description to prescription, from the empirical to the normative. In sum, the proponents of a 'compliance' (as opposed to a 'policing') regulatory strategy argue that the nature of corporate illegalities calls for different forms of regulation than is the case for other kinds of law breaking. Businesses and particularly corporations are not, as many would have it, typically 'amoral calculators', but rather 'political citizens' who may indeed sometimes err but more because of 'organisational incompetence' than deliberate wrongdoing. Thus they need advice rather than chastisement: regulatory agencies should act as consultants rather than policemen (Kagan and Scholz 1984: 68). Although some corporations sometimes act as if they are 'amoral calculators', this is neither necessary nor typical; where regulations are violated, this is usually the result of factors other than pure economic calculation. Corporations can and do have a primary commitment to act in a socially responsible fashion, are not essentially criminogenic, and will not cease to commit violations because of attempts at deterrence (Kagan and Scholz 1984: 67–8; see also Hawkins 1984: 110; Hutter 1988: 45–7, 80; Richardson *et al.* 1983: 125–49). To accept a view of the corporation as an amoral calculator entails a corresponding view of the most appropriate regulatory response to such corporations, namely, 'strict enforcement of uniform and high specific standards, backed by severe penalties', with regulatory officials acting quite literally as 'policemen' (Kagan and Scholz 1984: 72). Legal infractions by business are unsuitable for criminalisation. Regulatory agencies tend to try and achieve 'compliance' through persuasion rather than a 'policing' strategy which uses legal sanctions against businesses and executives found to be in breach of the law. This normative arguments rests upon a number of theoretical and empirical bases. In the following sections, we set out each and subject them to critical attention.

1. Corporations as amoral calculators?

In their essay 'The Criminology of the Corporation and Regulatory Enforcement Strategies', Robert Kagan and John Scholz distinguish three different 'popularly-held' images of the corporation, each of which is said to provide a different explanation for regulatory violations, and each of which requires a particular regulatory response. These are that the corporation can be seen as an amoral calculator, as a political citizen, or as organisationally incompetent (Kagan and Scholz 1984: 67–8). *Amoral calculators* are 'motivated entirely by profit-seeking', and 'carefully and competently assess opportunities and risks. They disobey the law when the anticipated fine and probability of being caught are small in relation to the profits to be harnessed through disobedience. Non-compliance stems from economic calculation' (*ibid.*: 67). The firm as *political citizen* is

> ordinarily inclined to comply with the law, partly because of a belief in the rule of law, partly as a matter of long-term self interest. That commitment, however, is contingent. Business managers have strong views as to proper public policy and business conduct. At least some law breaking stems from principled disagreement with regulations or orders they regard as arbitrary or unreasonable.
>
> (*ibid.*: 67–8)

The *organisationally incompetent* is 'inclined to break the law', but 'Many violations of regulations are attributed to organisational failure – corporate managers fail to oversee subordinates adequately, to calculate risks intelligently, to establish organisational mechanisms that keep all operatives abreast of and attentive to the growing dictates of the law' (*ibid.*: 68).

The assumption that most corporations are not in fact amoral calculators – in other words, that their adherence to regulations is not conditional upon their interpretation of either their own short term or longer term self-interest – is common in the work of all those associated with the compliance theories of regulation. Perhaps its clearest and most explicit expression is to be found in Bardach and Kagan's *Going by the Book* (1982). In this text, these authors actually attempt to quantify the proportion of all corporations which are amoral calculators, or, 'bad apples'. In fact, they assume, 'for analytical purposes', that 'bad apples' 'make up about 20 per cent of the average population of regulated enterprises in most regulatory programs' (*ibid.*: 65). Indeed, they add that, 'This distribution almost certainly overestimates the proportion of bad apples in most regulatory programs, but it does square roughly with

what commentators have said and with much regulatory practice ...'
(*ibid.*).

Central to the argument of many of these commentators, then, is the
notion that while some corporations at some times act as if 'amoral
calculators', there is no necessity in their acting thus, and in fact most
corporations at most times do not act thus. Where regulations are
violated, such violations are the result of factors other than pure economic calculation on the part of the corporation (Hawkins 1990: 452–6).
*Corporations can and do have a primary commitment to act in a socially
responsible fashion, are not essentially criminogenic, and will not cease to commit
violations because of attempts at deterrence* (see also Hawkins 1984: 110;
Hutter 1988: 45–7, 80; Richardson *et al.* 1983: 125–49). Were we to accept
the view that the corporation is essentially an amoral calculator, then we
would also have to accept that the most appropriate regulatory response
to such corporations is 'strict enforcement of uniform and high specific
standards, backed by severe penalties', with regulatory officials acting
quite literally as 'policemen' (Kagan and Scholz 1984: 72).

The claim that corporations are not amoral calculators has some
appeal, not least due to the power of the ideologies of business, to which
we referred in Chapter 5; but in our view, it is an unsustainable one. One
obvious issue that this question raises however is how we *know* to what
corporations actually have a commitment and, indeed, what corporations
really are?

One option is to ask the people within them, their employees, but
perhaps more crucially their middle and senior level managers who take
the decisions or non-decisions out of which corporate crime may be
produced. However, to view corporations as amoral calculators is not to
claim that the individuals who hold positions of power and take decisions
within them will all act criminally; again, this is clearly not (always) the
case. The question of whether or not corporations are amoral calculators
is not reducible to, and cannot be resolved by reference to, the individuals nor their personal preferences, morals, motives, rationalisation,
justifications, and so on.

A second option is to look at the outcomes of corporate activities and to
seek to understand the extent to which these outcomes were the result of
amorally calculative decisions. If we were to do this we would need to be
aware that, despite the caricatures offered by some (Hawkins 1990, 1991),
to argue that corporations are amoral calculators is *not* to claim that
rational (or amoral) calculation necessarily means that all regulations are
ignored by corporations, nor that any particular corporation will in
practice succeed in either a correct interpretation of what is rational, nor
be able to act in accordance with that interpretation. Corporations will
clearly, at times, act 'irrationally'. Indeed, what the compliance school call
'incompetence' and 'political citizenship' are both perfectly compatible
with a concept of corporations as amoral calculators. Thus Hawkins is
partially correct when he notes that it is possible to find incidences of

non-compliance where there was 'an apparent failure of people to calculate' (1990: 455): of course it is possible to find such incidences! But this does not, as he claims, invalidate the argument that corporations strive constantly towards rational calculation (and, incidentally it is also based upon the view that organisational actors can be understood through the actions of individuals, a view which we, following others, find untenable, as we have argued in previous chapters).

A third option is to examine these decision-making processes themselves. One problem raised by such an option is the extent to which data is ever available to allow us to reconstruct decision-making processes. Moreover, there is a greater epistemological problem entailed in such reconstruction: for the danger is that in reconstructing in detail the micro-processes of such decision-making, analysis becomes *confined* to understanding the situation as participants themselves understood it – that is, one falls foul of a key failing within micro-sociology in general, and interactionist sociology in particular. Through such a sociology, one may lose touch with broader social, economic and political contexts which structure and influence decision-making in organisations. To the extent that studies are painstaking in their micro-empirical details – such as Vaughan's generally excellent recent text on the *Challenger* space disaster (Vaughan 1996) – they are perhaps more prone to understanding the reconstructed situation in ways that are likely to cast decision-making processes as 'normal' in that they are entirely comprehensible, and certainly not viewed as deviant, from the point of view of the actors themselves in a particular situation at a particular time (see Tombs 1997).

Fourth – and much more promisingly – we might ask a question which demands an answer grounded in theory as well as empirical data. Thus, contra the claim of Hawkins, we fundamentally disagree that 'the extent to which business calculates is an empirical question' (Hawkins 1990: 454). We need to ask a key theoretical question – namely, *what is a corporation?* – without which empirical observation is at best of little use, at worst positively misleading. To ask this is also to ask a subset of questions such as: what are the conditions of existence of a corporation; what is its 'room for manoeuvre'; what is the legal constitution of the corporation; what are its practical and legal obligations to whom and so on, questions which we have partly considered in Chapter 2 (and see Pearce and Tombs 1998). If we were to do this we would find that the claim that corporations can do anything other than attempt to maximise long-term profitability is theoretically untenable (Pearce and Tombs 1997, 1998). For a variety of legal and structural reasons, capitalist corporations can be nothing other than rational, amoral calculators.

The first reason is that the managers of corporations have a legal obligation to act in the best interests of their shareholders. By and large, this excludes acting ethically or socially responsibly, unless it can be demonstrated that to act thus is actually congruent with profit maximisation (which it may well be in certain economic and political conditions; see Tombs 1993). It is instructive here to recall that it was precisely the emergence of a disjuncture between owners and controllers of corporations – the advent of so-called managerial capitalism – that prompted a series of concerns within economics, political sociology and business/management studies as to how to ensure that managers retained profit maximisation as their key operating criterion; and it was this which forced Friedman to argue that the social responsibility of business is to make profits. In that famous argument, Friedman noted how managers were only employees, and that it would be immoral for them to act morally, if acting morally meant acting in ways which prioritised some (social) end over the economic end of profit maximisation. Thus it is of interest that Glasbeek's withering critique of the social responsibility movement – once developed both theoretically and empirically – cites approvingly Friedman's cry that 'If businessmen do have a social responsibility other than making maximum profits for stockholders, how are they to know what it is' (Friedman, cited in Glasbeek 1988: 380). Glasbeek's argument clearly highlights the empirical and theoretical weaknesses in any claims that corporations can do anything other that seek to maximise profitability. Moreover, as he notes, and as we have seen Chapter 2 of this text, the corporate form itself, and the construction of the legal protections of limited liability in particular, is a legally created fiction whereby some of the costs and risks associated with this profit-maximising can be minimised, avoided or passed on to others, that is, 'a convenient means by which to dodge responsibility' (Glasbeek 1988: 385). This form is 'Clever, certainly, but not very socially useful' (*ibid.*).

Second, we must of course recognise that the goal of profit maximisation may be obscured, not always readily apparent, so that some observers might falsely perceive corporations as actually operating on the basis of some other goal. For example, as we have noted above, corporate managers may not always calculate successfully; it is easy, but misleading, to examine *post facto* a series of decisions taken by a corporation, out of which profit maximisation is not the outcome, and to conclude that profit maximisation could not then have been the intention. That is, we must not confuse outcome with intention. That corporations do not always act in profit maximising ways is something we know – it is something which business and management schools try to correct through teaching the techniques of successful calculation and operationalisations of these – but this is not the same as saying that profit maximisation was not what was intended.

Third, corporate managers may make their calculations regarding profitability using different criteria, methodologies, time-spans, and so on, and these differences have real and important effects in terms of outcomes – for example, all things being equal, longer term calculations will result in greater compliance with the law than short-term ones. Indeed, corporations may calculate that it is in their profit maximising interests to represent themselves as not amoral calculators, as acting ethically, or socially responsibly, precisely as part of these calculations. But that they must act in a calculating, hence amoral, fashion does not seem to us to be open to dispute.

2. Corporate crimes and real crimes

As we have seen, it is also argued by the compliance school that there are unique features pertaining to corporate illegalities which distinguish them from so-called 'traditional crimes', and thereby necessitate a particular type of enforcement attitude or response, namely that of seeking compliance through persuasion rather than through the threat of sanctions. There are, it is argued, several differences between corporate crimes (or *illegalities*, as the compliance school would have it) and traditional crimes. Now, as we have argued throughout the preceding chapters of this book, but most particularly in Chapter 1 *via* reference to the debate between Sutherland and Tappan, in Chapters 3 and 4, where we provided indicators of the extent and costs of corporate crimes, and in Chapter 5, where we considered processes by which corporate crimes are organised off law and order agendas, the claim that 'Corporate Illegalities' are not 'Real Crimes' is powerful, pervasive, but highly misleading.

First, the compliance school claim that the offenders are different. If corporations are not viewed as amoral calculators, if it is recognised that crime (or, rather, illegality) is the peripheral side-effect of essentially legitimate, productive and socially useful activity, then this must be taken into account when regulating. In the case of pollution, for example, Hawkins notes the need 'to preserve a fragile balance between the interests of economic activity on the one hand and the public welfare on the other' (Hawkins 1984: 9). This representation of different types of offenders, and how this relates to 'fundamental differences' in respective appropriate regulatory techniques, is given its clearest expression in Kagan's essay, in which he claims that the police

> often deal with explosive or emotional situations, with offences that stem from desperation, rage, or pathology ... with a predominantly lower class population of individuals, in situations in which normal social controls, restraints of conscience, or concerns for preserving reputation and property have broken down. The organisations they police, such as narcotics networks, are literally beyond the law, with little incentive to comply with it. Police deal, in short, with the virtually ungovernable. Policing essentially involves the use of force (or the threat of force) to bring order to anarchy, to pacify the warring, or punish the undeterrable.
>
> The business enterprise that regulatory inspectors deal with, even the worst of them, live in a much less anarchic world. They are organised entities with property to protect, customers and goodwill to retain. They are embedded in a web of market considerations and liability laws that, however imperfect, impose some constraints and compel rational responses to long-term as well as immediate incentives. The basic task of regulation, therefore, is not

pacification or punishment but, to use a dictionary definition, 'to adjust' behaviour – to change incentive structures, to plug gaps in existing control systems, to bring hidden risks or externalised harms to a higher level of salience on the plant manager's crowded agenda.

(1984: 59–60)

Of course, again as we have noted in Chapter 5, the distinction between 'traditional' criminals and corporate offenders is not an entirely illusory one – it is powerful precisely because it does contains both real and ideological aspects. The distinction describes certain aspects of reality in that business is an activity which has certain socially-useful consequences. But it remains largely inaccurate in that it implies that the corporation can have a primary commitment to act in a socially responsible manner; it is inaccurate in that illegalities are considered to form a marginal rather than an inherent element of business activity; and it is inaccurate in its acceptance of business's own definitions as to what constitute 'reasonable' regulations. Moreover, to the extent that it also imports negative stereotypes of lower class criminals as pathological, ungovernable and so on, as in the passage from Kagan, above, then it is not only misleading but, in our view, somewhat dangerous.

A second set of arguments advanced to justify non-punitive modes of regulatory enforcement centre around the problematic applicability of *mens rea* in many cases of regulatory violations, an inherent injustice in the use of a standard of strict liability, and a claim that most regulatory offences involve acts or omissions which are *mala prohibita* rather than *mala in se*. Thus, typically, regulatory violations differ from 'traditional' or 'consensual' crimes in that the former are 'morally problematic' (Hawkins 1984: 11), lack 'self-evident moral blameworthiness' (Jamieson 1985: 30) or are characterised by 'moral ambivalence' (Hutter 1988: 10–11). Third, to these arguments is also often added the practical caveat that problems of establishing guilty intent or liability are compounded in the case of regulatory deviance, since such deviance occurs within an organisational framework (Richardson *et al.* 1983: 56–7). Such arguments are predictably reinforced by the fact that many regulators and the judiciary in practice displace standards of strict liability, utilising commonsense standards of moral culpability in their place. Fourth, these commentators also state that the victims of regulatory deviance may sometimes be (i) difficult to distinguish, (ii) remote in time and space from the casual act(s) or omission(s), and (iii) colluders in the illegal act(s) or omission(s) to which they fall victim.

On these latter claims, we have argued in previous chapters of this text that the distinctions between what is *mala prohibita* and *mala in se* are in many respects contingent, subject to change, and often based upon a curious inversion of intention and indifference in any moral hierarchy. Further, on the problems of distinguishing victims of corporate crime, while these are, as we have noted in Chapter 5 in particular, certainly real, they are in essence technical problems of linking victims to agents and, as technical problems, should not be made into insuperable obstacles. It is possible – in law and in its enforcement – to clarify legal responsibility in and around corporations. The issue of collusion is both a red herring and somewhat offensive – while victim-blaming is commonplace in response to corporate crime, it rarely stands up to any scrutiny, serving only to divert attention from the real causes of any particular crime (see Wells 1993a, 1995b; Tombs 1989 and 1991). It is unfortunate for academics to reinforce such unfounded, if highly functional, claims.

Once confronted, it is clear that this set of assumptions which is used to underpin the distinction between 'traditional' and 'regulatory' offenders, and the different regulatory responses engendered by this distinction, is highly problematic, thus weakening the distinction itself and the arguments against the 'policing' of industry.

3. Strict enforcement as counter-productive?

These authors, however, do not only argue that corporations are not amoral calculators, and that their offences are inherently distinct from traditional or real crimes. They also argue that to adopt an enforcement strategy based upon strict enforcement, what they call the 'Regulator-as-Policeman-Strategy', will be more than simply ineffective; rather, it is likely to produce quite the opposite response to that which is intended. Thus, in setting out the 'limits' of the 'Regulator-as-Policeman-Strategy', Kagan and Scholz argue that the devising of specific rules and their subsequent strict enforcement engenders rigidity and legalism, and ultimately produces 'counterproductive tendencies' (1984: 73).

It is interesting to note here that Kagan and Scholz do accept that, where the 'Regulator-as-Policeman-Strategy' has been put into practice, it has in fact produced 'measurable results' (*ibid.*: 72). However, they present two explicit objections to that strategy.

The first, and less significant, objection is that such an enforcement strategy engenders rigidity and/or legalism. Legalism and bureaucratisation in turn generate what Bardach and Kagan have called 'regulatory unreasonableness' – 'the imposition of uniform regulatory requirements in situations where they do not make sense' – and 'unresponsiveness' – 'the failure to consider arguments by regulated enterprises that exceptions should be made' (Bardach and Kagan 1982: 58). This is a claim which found a ready political audience, but is empirically and conceptually sloppy. Here the regulatory inspector is represented in caricature, as something akin to an automaton, compelled towards the prosecution of each and every violation detected. Such a representation is negative and stereotypical – it precisely echoes Thatcherite and Reaganite 'anti-statist' rhetoric, within which regulators were consistently cast as clipboard carrying, grey suited, checklist-ticking wielders of red-tape (precisely the images that were used at Conservative Party conferences by both Peter Lilley and Neil Hamilton in apparently hilarious diatribes during speeches on deregulation). Moreover, as a representation both of what police actually do, and as a version of a more punitive enforcement strategy, it is highly misleading (see Pearce and Tombs 1990, 1991, 1992, 1998).

The second objection posed by Kagan and Scholz is the tendency of such an enforcement strategy towards the 'stimulation of opposition and the destruction of co-operation' (1984: 73). In the first place, business may respond to strict enforcement by resorting to legalistic counter measures, which would force the inspectorate to expend further resources on particular cases, and thereby divert resources from other areas such as basic inspection; secondly, firms regulated 'strictly' might in fact organise politically and attack the agency at the legislative level, so that indiscriminate reliance on a legalistic enforcement strategy can jeopardise the agency's legal mandate, its funding, and its very existence (*ibid.*: 74).

It is interesting that at this point there is a recognition not simply of inequalities of power, but of power operating at a macro, indeed political, level. These are important points to be made regarding the consequences of stricter regulation even if such realities are rarely explicitly articulated within this body of work, at least not in the language of power *per se*. But what is the implication of this point, as presented? In *reductio ad absurdem*, the argument is that enforcement is always entirely contingent upon the acquiescence of the regulated. Of course, this is not the case. Moreover, to speak of stimulating opposition is to assume that corporations are ever reconciled to external regulation. The crucial point is surely that the extent to which the regulated can mount effective opposition, the extent to which it can frustrate and undermine inspectorial activity both locally and indeed at the national political level, is intimately related to the macro political economy and the ways in which the latter is reflected, mediated and resisted at local levels. For example, experience of the past quarter of a decade in Britain, since the passing of the Health and Safety at Work Act and establishment of the HSE, indicates that factory inspectors are much less prone to such opposition where they are operating in workplaces with strong trades unions, within a relatively supportive material and ideological political context, and during periods of relative economic prosperity, as opposed to attempting to enforce law in non-unionised workplaces, where macho management prevails, within a political context in which the discourses of deregulation are predominant, and in an economy in recession or downturn (see, for example, Grunberg 1983, 1986; Tombs 1990, 1996). In other words, if we are to make sense of the claim by Bardach and Kagan that a punitive enforcement strategy is counter-productive, then we must address questions of power and also questions of macro-level political economy; we cannot address such questions on the basis of micro-level analyses of relationships between regulators and firms, nor within any interactionist sociology in general. The compliance school fails to consider macro-level questions of power, as even some sympathetic to compliance-oriented arguments have noted. As Weaitt has noted, the danger of 'concentrating upon what enforcement officers do' is that 'we remove ourselves from the legal and political context in which they do it' (Weait 1989: 69; see also McBarnet 1981).

Indeed, a shift to a macro-level political economy reveals that recent deregulatory movements in Britain and the US have not been occasioned by a simple 'backlash' to 'regulatory unreasonableness', as the compliance school have claimed (Hawkins 1990: 448, 452; Hutter 1997: 244). In fact, it is terms precisely like 'regulatory unreasonableness' and 'backlash' which have been used as justifications by British right-wing ideologues who have always wanted to roll back the state and whose arguments, to a limited extent, have been somewhat cynically adopted by corporate capital; their use is justified, whether consciously or unintentionally, by much of the social science of the compliance school (Pearce and Tombs 1998; and, on the US, see Woodiwiss 1990). Thus in the last two decades there has been a general, but by no means universal, push towards deregulatory or (ever) more conciliatory regulatory strategies, towards the (selective) limiting of state control, and towards the freeing of business from the meddlesome interventions of bureaucrats (that is, inspectors). As Snider has put it, during this period 'nation after nation has unmade corporate crime by repealing regulatory statutes, firing staff, dismantling monitoring and data gathering machinery' (1997: 6); and it is important to emphasise that these trends have been particularly marked in Britain, which is a state with a long (perhaps the longest) history of highly conciliatory regulatory approaches across a whole range of areas of regulatory enforcement.

Such phenomena are much more explicable in terms of efforts on the part of international capital and dominant states to create a neo-liberal economic and social international order that facilitates the growth of a transnational capitalism and imposes severe constraints on those states seeking to pursue national development, whether in a corporatist capitalist or more socialist manner (Gill and Law 1988). When accounting for shifts in forms and modes of regulation in particular nation-states, we need also to take into account that the relations between the capitalist class and other classes and social groups in these different states vary (cf. Pearce 1976), and that the particular form of state restructurings, forms of class compromise, and related to these changes in regulation, also vary. None of these factors are even hinted at by reference to terms such as *backlash* or the *stimulation* of *opposition*.

Moreover, it is clear that in a particular set of political and economic circumstances, enforcement strategies that stress consultation and conciliation all too easily end up with agencies endorsing the industry's own evaluation of what is reasonable and usually allow companies to negotiate their way out of penalties for violating even these agreements (see Carson 1970a, 1982; Pearce and Tombs 1998; Snider 1991; Whyte and Tombs

1998). This is precisely why governments who seek deregulation or wish to 'lift the burden off business' portray regulatory agencies as over-powerful/over-zealous (see Tombs 1990 and 1996 on this process in the context of health and safety regulation in Britain), thus legitimating attempts to either abolish or emasculate these agencies, demanding that they stop 'punishing industry' and seek 'its co-operation instead' (Hawkins 1990: 452). Such claims reflect the power of capital, not its inherent 'reasonableness'. Indeed, these aspects of compliance-oriented approaches also raise the issue of either capture and/or agency corruption. These issues are interestingly juxtaposed in the work of Hutter. Hutter endorses a compliance-oriented enforcement approach, arguing that compliance must be seen as processual, explaining regulatory enforcement via the interactionist notion of a 'career':

> regulatory agencies are typically – but not inevitably – in long term relations with the regulated, whose compliance is of ongoing concern (Bardach and Kagan, 1982). The relationship between the agency and the regulated is reflexive, with each party adapting and reacting to the moves and anticipated moves of the other (Hawkins and Hutter, 1993). Enforcement is often serial and incremental (Hawkins, 1984), and the whole process of enforcement may usefully be characterised as a 'career'.
>
> (1997: 195, references in original)

Elsewhere, Hutter had stated of this enforcement process, that

> The failure to implement fully the 1974 [Health and Safety at Work Act] provisions relating to employee-inspector relations may also be located in the regulatory traditions of the inspectorates. FI [Factory inspectorate] and RI [Railways Inspectorate] have, in common with so many similar agencies, traditionally adopted a co-operative, accommodative enforcement approach. Securing compliance, rather than punishment, is the main objective of this approach and the preferred methods to achieve these ends are conciliatory. The main actors in this approach are employers, managers and inspectors, not employees ... The evidence seems to be that the involvement of the workforce with management and regulatory officials can be effective ... The evidence of this paper suggests that it is important to pay attention to the social and political contexts within which enforcement takes place ... Ironically, it may also raise questions about the accountability of legal actors who may, for whatever reasons, fail to comply with the law themselves.
>
> (1993: 465–6)

In these quotations there is a perfect illustration of how more sensitive analyses within the compliance school can point to tensions within their own position, and indeed can signal the need for (but cannot develop) a more general political economy of regulation and regulatory enforcement. Prior to a consideration of the elements of a political economy of regulation and regulatory enforcement, we turn to a different, but in some ways similar, set of arguments about appropriate modes of regulatory enforcement.

A case for (enforced) self-regulation?

Rather different to those studies of regulatory enforcement practices which conclude that the most effective means of enforcement is compliance-oriented are arguments, pursued most coherently by Braithwaite and others, for enforced self-regulation. However, prior to addressing the latter arguments in some detail, it is worth noting that there are some similarities between these and those of the compliance school.

First, the work of Braithwaite and others – particularly in their use of the notion of enforcement pyramids (see below) – places compliance-oriented strategies as the first, and predominant, regulatory option. One point of interest is that Hutter's recent work on the enforcement strategies of the Industrial Air Pollution Inspectorate, the Factory Inspectorate and the Railways Inspectorates, to which we referred immediately above, argues that such enforcement pyramids are actually the most accurate characterisation of how these regulators currently operate (Hutter 1997: 227, 229, and *passim*). Second, both arguments for compliance-oriented enforcement and for (enforced) self-regulation make claims that corporations need to be understood as other than rational, amoral, calculating entities (though this is either tempered, or somewhat has a somewhat contradictory place within, some of this work, certainly in that of Braithwaite). Third, both sets of arguments have been labelled 'co-operative models' of regulatory enforcement – the essential element linking them here is their under-estimation of, or failure to theorise adequately, corporate power (Snider 1991, 1993a).

The academic case for self-regulation has been put most cogently by Braithwaite, working with various colleagues, and most succinctly in a 1987 article entitled 'Self-Regulation and the Control of Corporate Crime'. As set out in that piece, the argument for self-regulation begins by stating baldly its basic premise:

> We know that it is unrealistic to expect that our generation will see the public resources devoted to corporate crime control approach anywhere near those expended on crime in the streets. Thus, the relevance of assessing how much private enforcement might contribute to corporate crime control.
>
> (Braithwaite and Fisse 1987: 221)

In other words, Braithwaite and Fisse explicitly state that in the absence – now or in any feasible future – of effective regulatory resources, there is a need to consider other forms of regulatory enforcement. In considering the possibility that corporations might effectively self-regulate, or engage in effective 'private policing', Braithwaite and Fisse raise perhaps the central question: why should corporations devote resources to such activity? The answer offered is threefold: first, because corporations can and do act as moral rather than purely economically rational actors, and thus have some commitment to compliance; second, because many corporations are concerned with their reputations, their good name, and 'self-respect'; and third, to pre-empt 'the less palatable alternative' of external regulation (*ibid.*: 221–2). It is worth noting that these arguments are very close to Mintzberg's claims that trust is necessary in attempts to 'control' corporations, though he adds, tellingly, that in dealing with corporations, trust is required since, no matter which other strategies can be brought to bear, 'managers will always retain a great deal of power' (Mintzberg 1996: 404).

We should note that as Braithwaite and Fisse define self-regulation here (1987: 222), this is distinct from deregulation. The latter term is often itself used very loosely, but in the context of corporate crime 'deregulation' refers to a removal of laws designed to regulate the corporation, or perhaps the explicit withdrawal from the enforcement of existing laws. Nevertheless, it is important to note that while the intention of Braithwaite and others may well be to argue for effective self-regulation, rather than deregulation, the uses to which academic work may be put clearly exhaust the intentions of authors; thus the production of ideas validating self-regulation in an era of deregulation are likely to have been seized upon by proponents of the latter.

Braithwaite and Fisse argue that self-regulation has many advantages over external forms of regulation. Private police have a greater technical and social capacity to inspect, and can achieve greater inspectorial coverage in terms of frequency and depth of inspections than could ever be achieved by an external inspectorate, who are responsible for hundreds, usually thousands, of workplaces or businesses (*ibid.*: 222–4). The 'Essential Requirements' of an effective self-regulatory system combine structural features – mechanisms, procedures, systems – supported by aspects of an organisational culture, which in their combination produce a tendency towards compliance. Thus companies which effectively self-regulate: invest clout in, and provide top management support for, compliance staff; clearly define accountability for compliance performance, placing this on line managers; ensure that performance is carefully monitored, and that managers are told when standards are not met; design systems whereby compliance problems are effectively communicated to those with power to act upon them; develop programmes of training and supervision for compliance (*ibid.*: 225–40). In general, 'companies must be concerned not to put employees under so much pressure to achieve the economic goals of an organisation that they cut corners with the law' (*ibid.*: 240–2).

For all this, however, these authors are clear that there is a sixth principle of effective self-regulation that underpins the other five: namely that companies, and managers, must have the motivation and willingness to effectively self-regulate. Bearing in mind the claim that corporations have reasons to self-regulate based upon the fact that they are moral rather than rationally calculating actors, Braithwaite and Fisse's response to this 'fundamental problem of self-regulation' is an interesting one:

we believe companies can be so motivated both from their internal
deliberations as moral agents and, *more importantly, from external pressures
calculated to make effective self-regulation an attractive policy.*

(*ibid.*: 242, emphasis added)

Indeed, these authors are clear at one point that a system of self-
regulation is which needs to be avoids the 'naive assumption that we need
to rely *only* on the goodwill of business' (*ibid.*: 225, emphasis added).
Thus, 'Direct regulatory enforcement – by prosecution, licence suspen-
sion, adverse publicity, or other means – is one outstandingly important
way of putting pressure on companies to self-regulate' (*ibid.*: 244). In
reality, then, these authors are proposing self-regulation within the
context of a pyramid of regulatory options, the next available option
being enforced self-regulation (Braithwaite 1982; Braithwaite and Fisse
1985). By enforced self-regulation, Braithwaite and colleagues mean a
requirement made of a corporation to develop a tailored set of rules by
which it intends to secure compliance with law. Any proposals would need
the approval of an external regulator, an approval which may entail a
series of negotiations. Subsequently external regulators would oversee
not compliance, but the functioning of a company's own internal
compliance/inspectorial function. In this way, the costs of regulation are
largely passed on to the company; the potential of punitive intervention
remains, where evidence of sustained non-compliance emerges, with the
result being 'flexible, particularistic standards and enforcement' which
are the results of negotiations between regulators and individual companies (Ayres and Braithwaite 1992: 102–16). This strategy is an attempt
to transcend the 'delay, red tape and stultification of innovation' that
detailed government regulation can, it is claimed, engender (Ayres and
Braithwaite 1992: 106).

Indeed, Braithwaite further argues that regulatory regimes should
move towards goal-oriented rather than prescriptive legislation:

When the state negotiates the substantive regulatory goal with industry,
leaving the industry discretion and responsibility of how to achieve this goal,
then there is the best chance of an optimal strategy that trades off maximum
goal attainment to least cost productive efficiency.

(*ibid.*: 38)

In fact, what is being proposed here is a system of goal-based regulation
to which many regulatory bodies in the UK now seem to be shifting (see
Hutter 1997; and see Scott 1995, on fragmentation and consolidation).
However, some evidence from recent studies of trends in regulatory
enforcement Britain indicates that where regulatory agencies shift
towards goal-based regulation (and, indeed, where legislation is explicitly
developed around this notion), then the effect is to lower standards of
compliance. That is, goal-based regimes create at least two types of (from
our perspective, undesirable) opportunities for corporations: first, at the
level of the individual corporation, to argue in favour of the lowest

common denominator; and, second, at the level of the trade association, to impose definitions of what constitutes feasible compliance across a given industry. For sure, each strategy is already commonly used by corporations; but each becomes much more utilisable once particular (that is, prescriptive) requirements are removed, and where these are replaced by goals, such as the maintenance of standards of 'reasonable practicability', the definition of which are at once much more liable to direct contest by powerful corporate actors. In other words, the use of 'goal-setting' as opposed to prescriptive regulation has the effect of further shifting an already highly unequal balance of power between the regulators and the regulated further in the favour of the latter (see Whyte *et al.* 1996; Whyte and Tombs 1998; Woolfson *et al.* 1996; Woolfson and Beck 1997).

If there are problems with both self-regulation and enforced self-regulation, particularly where these are explicitly allied to goal-setting, we should be clear that the work of Braithwaite consistently argues that compliance is more likely where regulators have at their disposal a range of credible enforcement techniques which allow an escalation in severity of sanctions in response to unco-operativeness on the part of the regulated. Thus Braithwaite frequently resorts to setting out the enforcement process via a pyramid, where non-compliance at the lower levels leads to the invoking of ever more interventionist or punitive modes of enforcement on the part of regulators (see, for example, Ayres and Braithwaite 1992). In essence, Braithwaite is arguing for a sensitive enforcement strategy based on the principle of deterrence.

Deterrence and regulation

It is certainly important to point out, as do Braithwaite and colleagues, that such an enforcement process can only effectively function where any sanctions that are formally at the disposal of regulators are credible ones – that is, that such sanctions are used in the face of non-compliance.

> the greater the heights of punitiveness to which an agency can escalate, the greater its capacity to push regulation down to the cooperative base of the pyramid.
>
> (Ayres and Braithwaite 1992: 40)

Thus a deterrent, potentially punitive regulatory strategy can be cost-effective in that '*the bigger the sticks, the less they* [the regulators] *have to use them*' (*ibid.*: 40–1). This seems to be based upon the view that corporations *do* make explicit calculations regarding the costs and benefits of compliance/non-compliance. It is interesting that Braithwaite's enforcement pyramid, as indeed is the efficacy of particular elements of this – not least effective self-regulation – is in fact based upon both a principle of deterrence and the rational, calculating form of corporate entity that

such a principle entails. Despite claims about the potential for corporations to act morally, Braithwaite and colleagues can only propose their
arguments for self-regulation and enforced self-regulation on the basis of
a recognition of the 'whip' of credible, external enforcement, that is, a
regulatory system based upon deterrence. Thus, to the extent that
corporations behave 'morally' (that is, comply), then they do so only as a
means of pre-empting more punitive enforcement, that is, out of amoral
calculation.

For us, however, it is for precisely this reason – this recognition of the
rational, calculating nature of corporations – that we depart from any
promotion by Braithwaite and others of self-regulation, even as (only) a
first element of any regulatory strategy. For a variety of reasons, this faith
in the ability of corporations to self-regulate is misplaced. Detailed
critiques of the notion of self-regulation, in practice and in principle,
have been set out elsewhere (Smith and Tombs 1995; Tombs 1992).
Suffice to say here that, for us, self-regulation, whether enforced or not, is
likely to fail. First, we know on the basis of historical record that
regulations and regulatory agencies have been established because most
employers have simply *not* been self-regulating. Second, we also know that
corporate executives can and do falsify records, not least to deceive
regulators; if self-regulation is a means of pre-empting external regulation, then there is no reason why the practice of self-regulation should
not be used cynically to continually keep regulators at bay. Third, as
Braithwaite, Fisse and others know, the structures, mechanisms and so on
of self-regulation can be highly cynical; there is no reason why the
structural elements of this system – for whistle-blowers, for training
programmes, for supervision – cannot be put into place but used simply
symbolically (see Whyte 1998). Fourth, both the removal of pressures
upon middle-managers to prioritise and the ability of internal inspectors
to act in ways which are perceived to be opposed to the short-term
interest, are highly contingent; such 'freedoms' are only possible under
certain limited conditions for certain limited periods of time. Fifth, and
perhaps most problematic of all, is that arguments for self-regulation in a
hostile economic and political climate are likely to be expropriated, by
dominant economic and political forces, and used in ways that differ
markedly from the intentions of those who had originally espoused them;
thus such arguments are often re-presented as arguments for deregulation, as has been the experience in both the US and the UK in recent
years (Pearce and Tombs 1990, 1991; Snider 1991).

A key merit of the work of Braithwaite and others, then, is that it points
to the need to consider the potential for a regulatory strategy organised
around the principle of deterrence. It has long been accepted by most
criminologists that deterrence fails when aimed at individual 'street'
offenders. However, some have argued that corporate illegality offers a
sphere in which deterrence is much more likely to be effective. This is
clearly the implication of Sutherland's characterisation of the corpora-

tion as coming 'closer to economic man and to pure reason than any person or any other organisation' (Sutherland 1983: 236–8), a view of the corporation which, as we have argued, we find persuasive in as much as it represents that which corporations are capable of, and strive towards, even if they do not always achieve this level of rationality and calculability. It is these very features of the corporation which render it potentially liable to deterrence-based sanctions (Croall 1992: 147).

However, the applicability of deterrence theory in the context of corporate crime has been contested by others, certainly by those who do not cast the corporation as a rational, calculating entity. Thus the compliance school have argued that deterrence and more punitive modes of enforcement are neither desirable nor feasible. Yet ironically on this specific point of deterrence, even within such work there are recognitions both that most firms try to get away with violations of safety law (Hawkins 1990: 450), and that the vast majority of firms comply with regulations only if they believe that those transgressing regulations will be detected and sanctioned (Bardach and Kagan 1982: 65–6). Further, while Braithwaite and colleagues have been much more convincing in pointing to the limits of any regulatory strategy based upon deterrence (Ayres and Braithwaite 1992; Braithwaite *et al.* 1993; Braithwaite and Makkai 1991, 1994), their work also indicates that for at least for certain kinds of economic actors, the use of deterrence is an effective means of achieving compliance (Braithwaite *et al.* 1993; Braithwaite and Makkai 1994). Indeed, Braithwaite and Geis have argued that 'the discredited doctrines of crime control by public disgrace, deterrence, incapacitation, and rehabilitation can be successfully applied to corporations' (1982: 293). This general proposition is itself based upon the arguments that 'corporate crime is a conceptually different phenomenon from traditional crime' (*ibid.*: 294). Thus corporate criminals may be 'among the most deterrable types of offenders . . . they do not have a commitment to crime as a way of life, and their offences are instrumental rather than expressive' (*ibid.*: 302–3). Indeed, in relative terms they 'usually have a good deal more than their fair share of the world's goodies, and they will be reluctant to risk losing what they have' (Geis 1996: 258).

We agree that deterrence is fundamentally flawed both as a practical strategy, and indeed at a conceptual level, when directed at 'street' or 'traditional' crime, a view commonly expressed within criminology, and which finds its most thorough and eloquent expression in the work of Mathiesen (1990). However, deterrence has a rather different potential with respect to corporate crime. There are four aspects to this rather different potential, which we present in relation to Mathiesen's cogent rejection of the principle and practice of deterrence.

First, many corporate crimes tend not to be one-off acts of commission, but are actually ongoing states or conditions – for example, maintenance of false records or the provision of false information to an external agency, chronic exposures due to faulty plant, an absence of legally required guards or other forms of protective hardware, collusive relationships between companies, a failure to provide information or training, false product labelling, and so on. Moreover, the identification of the criminal (that is, the corporation) is usually much less problematic than is the case with street crime. In other words, detection and 'clear-up' rates are very different issues in the context of (many) corporate as opposed to street crimes. What Mathiesen (1990: 54–7) refers to as the '*low detection risk*' of crime (and see also the claim made by Braithwaite and Geis 1982: 294–6) – one of the factors which in his analysis renders general prevention (deterrence) unworkable – does not generally apply in this context. We would not argue that this is the case for all forms of corporate crimes, however. For example, some financial crimes may be very difficult to detect (Mathiesen 1990: 68, 71–2), though even here some argue, convincingly, that detection is much more likely than in the case of traditional crimes (Levi 1987). What is crucially pointed to here is that for those crimes which are ongoing states, then *detection is dependent upon a proactive inspectorial strategy*. Of further significance is that once a corporate crime has been detected then, rather differently to the case of many traditional crimes, 'apprehending a suspect . . . is almost always easy with corporate crime' (Braithwaite and Geis 1982: 296–7).

Second, then, the requirement for a proactive inspectorial and regulatory strategy raises the issue of enforcement resources. Certainly, as in all social activities, there is a minimal level of resource required to make regulation effective, as opposed to merely gestural or symbolic. More specifically, adequate resources are required to maintain routine, or preventive, visits, and to prepare prosecutions. We are thus led to a (familiar) demand for greater (here, regulatory) resources in the name of crime control. Again, however, it is worth distinguishing the contexts of corporate and street crimes. Since many corporate crimes do not pose the same problems of detection as street crimes, then greater regulatory resources *would* increase detection (Levi 1987: 281–4; Croall 1992: 154–6); this is quite distinct from the relatively marginal effect of increased resources for policing on levels of traditional crime. Moreover, this is often an increase from a very low level: for example, the Offshore Safety Division, established following the loss of 167 men in the Piper Alpha disaster, is unable to make surprise inspections visits to offshore installations because it does not have its own helicopter – instead, it has to contact oil companies, days in advance of any inspection, seeking to find spare seats on its own flights to a particular platform. Nevertheless, certainly in the context of safety, health and environmental crimes, significant increases in funding for relevant regulatory agencies are unlikely to emerge in any voluntary fashion upon dominant political agendas in Britain – yet the emergence of what Sutherland called 'organised public resentment' can have effects in this respect, even in highly unfavourable climates. Witness, for example, the increased resources for the Health and Safety Executive for the UK under the third

Thatcher government (Tombs 1995b), or the renewed funding for the US Environmental Protection Agency in its Superfund enforcement under the Bush administration (Barnett 1994).

Third, a further objection raised by Mathiesen to the principle of general deterrence – namely that the 'message' of deterrence is not communicated to those who need to receive it (Mathiesen 1990: 58–69) – is also largely inapplicable in the context of corporate crimes. Certainly, the symbolic effects of punitive sanctions against highly visible corporate offenders is one that should not be too easily dismissed (see Chapter 9). Moreover, those who own and control corporations know all too well what is required of them in law and of any likely developments in law and regulation; they play formal – as well as informal and covert – roles in the development of such law, and influence its interpretation. And they are well aware of changes in enforcement or sanctioning practices on the part of relevant regulators.

Fourth, in the context of corporate crime deterrent forms of sentencing should not serve to exacerbate social inequality, as seems to be the case for traditional crimes (Mathiesen 1990: 72, 97, and *passim*). Indeed, as we have argued in Chapters 3 and 4, corporate crime results in massive economic, social and physical costs which are disproportionately borne by the weakest and most vulnerable members of society; thus any more effective regulation and prevention of such crime is likely to be more rather than less egalitarian in its consequences. Indeed, given these costs and effects, equal justice demands a punitive response to corporate crime (Geis 1996: 247, and *passim*).

Taken in combination, the above points indicate that deterrence as a principle informing enforcement activity and the sanctioning of corporate crime has considerable potential. And there is *some* evidence of its practical efficacy (Morgan 1983; Health and Safety Executive 1985c; Pearce and Tombs 1990, 1997; Tombs 1995b). Moreover, recent years have seen regulators themselves explicitly recognising the significance of deterrence. And of further interest is the fact that some corporations have urged the operationalisation of this principle as central to their demands for the equalisation of the conditions of competition (see National Institute of Justice 1993: 10; Tombs 1995b). Thus, contrary to the claims of neo-liberals and advocates of deregulation, the opposition of corporate representatives to all kinds of regulation need not be based upon principle, but also on perceptions of practical effects. Corporations are neither moral nor immoral – they are *amoral* calculating bodies. What is important is the ability of regulators to enforce in a way that any company complying has some certainty that others not complying will face sanctions (Levi, Margaret 1987). This meets concerns of equity on the part of corporate representatives, but also ensures that they do not see compliance as implying a loss of competitive advantage (National Institute of Justice 1993: 7–10; see also Barnett 1994: 79).

Tombs argues not simply that deterrent *sanctions* represent a rational, just and effective response to corporate crime (see Chapter 9). Rather, the argument runs, effective forms of deterrence constitute a condition of existence for law-abiding behaviour on the part of organisations or corporations: that is, the existence of a likelihood of detection and credible sanctions following successful prosecution makes it possible for corporations to obey the law, and thus is central to effective *regulation*. This is consistent with our conceptualisation of corporations as amoral calculators. It is also consistent with the empirical evidence of the concerns of corporate capital over competitive advantage. Further, it is consistent with empirical work on the internal dynamics of corporate crime, which almost always identifies the existence of socially responsible individuals or groups within and around corporations, typically drawn from, compliance or safety officers, engineers, middle or lower-level managers, workers, and local publics (see, for example, Braithwaite 1984; Cullen *et al.* 1987; Jones 1988; Vandivier 1982; Vaughan 1996; Wells 1993). Deterrence can help to empower such individuals and groups, through creating conditions where their voices receive a hearing in the interests of the corporation as a whole. In a sense, then, deterrent law has the same characteristics that some now ascribe to law in general, namely that it is facilitative and productive rather than merely constraining and negative.

Does compliance-oriented enforcement *work*?

We return now to a question that we are in a much better position to answer. Much of the work of the compliance school focuses upon the limitations of that which it opposes, namely 'punitive' regulatory enforcement. Nevertheless, it must be said that what compliance theorists very rarely do is to detail the extent to which a compliance strategy *works* – their concern is more to highlight that 'alternatives', and most notably more punitive forms of enforcement, are unworkable. There are some generalisations that can be made about the practices and effects of regulatory enforcement agencies, usefully summarised recently by Snider (1993a). First, she notes that 'nonenforcement is the most salient, obvious, and frequently found characteristic of regulatory agencies' (1993a: 120); this is partly a function of 'a generally gentle and educative attitude toward those they are regulating, often to the point of identifying with the industry and its problems' (*ibid.*: 122; see, for example, Whyte and Tombs 1998; Whyte 1998). Second, enforcement activity tends to focus upon the smallest and weakest individuals and organisations; while the largest and most powerful corporations will 'enjoy the best relations with regulatory officials', they will also be 'the most likely to challenge legally any investigation or sanction' (Snider 1993a: 122). Third, sanctions following regulatory activity are light (*ibid.*: 124). We will deal with the latter issue in Chapter 9, but it is worth noting here that Snider's first observation points to the prevalence of compliance-oriented enforcement, while the second highlights the reality of corporate power to which this body of work points, but with which it deals inadequately.

Even in the terms that Snider sets out here, compliance-oriented enforcement, as the norm, hardly seems to be enormously successful. Indeed, as the norm by which corporations are regulated, then the litany of death, injury, impoverishment and environmental destruction to which we pointed in Chapters 3 and 4 are hardly a ringing endorsement for compliance-oriented enforcement. Snider notes that it is notoriously difficult to assess the effectiveness of particular regulatory strategy. Nevertheless, reviewing evidence which allows some consideration of the relative effects and effectiveness of 'compliance' and 'punitive' oriented enforcement strategies, she concludes that 'it is obvious that, if there is evidence that criminalisation does not work (which there is), there is equally compelling evidence that co-operation does not work either' (*ibid*.: 142). What needs emphasising, however, as Snider herself notes, is that we have far greater evidence of the consequences of compliance-oriented enforcement than we do relating to more punitive modes. We *know* that it is a failure; we cannot say that for certain about more punitive-oriented techniques, such as those based upon deterrence, or indeed the principles of interventionism and rehabilitation (see Pearce and Tombs 1998).

Notwithstanding the fact that any dichotomy between compliance-seeking and punitive regulation is both misleading and unhelpful, a more interesting question is raised by the failure of compliance-oriented enforcement, namely: why have regulatory techniques, which have so patently failed, assumed seemingly greater significance in recent years?

The answer perhaps lies in what has been termed elsewhere the discourses or the fetish of deregulation (Tombs 1996; Whyte and Tombs 1998). These phrases refer to a series of processes over the past two decades which have seen elevated to the status of an almost incontestable truth the claim that regulation is to be avoided if possible: it is ineffective and bureaucratic; it is a burden upon business; it distorts the workings of the free market which, however imperfect, should be left to operate as far as is possible in an unrestrained way; it adds to the costs of production to the point where greater regulation forces companies to relocate to less regulated contexts. These discourses entail practices such as cost-benefit analyses of all regulation, restrictions upon the powers of (some) regulators, cutbacks in regulatory resources, and even the removal of some bodies of law. The work of some academics has (either wittingly or unwittingly) supported the elevation of such claims to the status of truth. As Snider again has observed, in 'recent years ... with increasingly sophisticated studies of regulatory agencies, criminalisation models have come under heavy attack', charging that 'criminal law does not work against corporate offenders' and that 'criminalisation actually increases the amount of harm corporate crime does' (1993a: 134); on such views, criminalisation and effectiveness are incompatible, and criminal law is too slow and too expensive to regulate corporations (*ibid.*: 136). For Snider, and for ourselves, the reception accorded to such ideas 'must be understood in ideological terms' (*ibid.*: 140):

> Regulation is too expensive, while the overwhelming importance of business to the development of the capitalist economy, they would argue, warrants overlooking any minor 'mistakes' it might commit in its legitimate pursuit of profit. The congruence between this [New Right] movement, then, and the academic critiques of criminalisation explains much more about the popularity of co-operative models than any 'objective' examination of the evidence can provide ... In fact ... the emphasis these models place on co-operation is nothing new. Virtually every regulatory agency studied has attempted, in the first instance, to co-operate with the business sector it is regulating. When the regulatory target is large and powerful rather than small and isolated, co-operation is mandatory, however strict and unbending the directives of the enabling legislation. Indeed ... *every law requires those who would control to negotiate some minimal level of consent from their target group ... The limits of this negotiation, its starting and ending points, are the crucial factors.*
>
> (*ibid.*: 141, emphases added)

Thus the emergence of these discourses themselves need to be understood within the contexts of a re-emergence of neo-liberal agendas across the industrialised and industrialising economies, and an increase in the structural power of capital.

Conclusion

Clearly, then, any consideration of the effectiveness or otherwise of any form of regulation requires a consideration of a vast range of factors beyond modes of enforcement – these range from the detailed wording of regulation (Black 1997), to the type and aim of the law at issue (Hopkins 1994), to an understanding of levels and changes in staffing, resources, legal mandates, through to an analysis of local, national and international economic and political contexts. In particular, we need to be able to theorise – and empirically grasp – the relative power of capital, states, and those forces engaged in struggles for regulatory change towards greater protection. In assessing the limits of reform, we are also led to consider the issue of what particular forms of regulation at particular times in particular places are intended to do.

To frame this somewhat differently, we need to ask, what is a regulatory agency? In the context of a general text such as this on corporate crime, of which only one part is devoted to an explicit consideration of regulation, we can only highlight some of the issues involved here. Yet we must note that considering the nature of any regulatory agency also entails a consideration of the state form within which that agency is imbricated. We have already hinted at this in our previous comments on ways in which terms such as 'backlash' and 'regulatory unreasonableness' need to be understood. While this is not the place, then, to discuss state forms, or theories of regulation, in any detail, some cursory comments upon various ways of conceptualising these phenomena are in order.

According to Capture Theories of regulation, regulatory agencies do not represent any public interest; even if this is the rationale for their creation, an inevitable life-cycle of enthusiasm, the provocation of reaction from the regulated, and the demise of original agency zeal, ensures that the interests of some generalised public become subsumed to the demands of a regulated industry (Bernstein 1955). Thus regulatory bodies increase the state's vulnerability to corporate influence. They are captured by the regulated through: the activity of interest/lobbying groups; the two-way flow of personnel between regulator and regulated; the outcome of decision-making in favour of regulated. These factors undermine the state's attempts to constrain the influence of corporate capital, or are evidence that such an aim was never meant to be pursued. Somewhat differently, for instrumental Marxists, these factors combine to subordinate the regulatory agency to a state which is itself simply an instrument of capital/ruling class; thus regulatory agencies are largely symbolically created and maintained as a means of pre-empting class conflict over certain forms of corporate activities or inactions. The common feature of these (different) perspectives is the result that regulatory agencies are shown to operate in a 'biased' fashion, serving the interests of capital despite the conscious efforts of a state, or via a state which is itself an instrument of a ruling class. There is a determination regarding the nature and effect of regulation.

While for us it is problematic to view regulatory bodies in any deterministic sense, subject to a natural life-cycle, or the structural inevitability of failure, or as the simple instrument of a ruling class, and so on, there is still much to commend capture and instrumentalist theories of regulation. That is, we should view these not as explanatory theories, but as indicating those empirical features which can contribute to our understanding of the construction and activities of regulatory bodies, and thus their differing modi operandi and extent to which different agencies are more or less effective in enforcement. Thus it remains important for us to examine the outcomes of the regulatory process rather than become trapped in the minutiae of descriptions of this process itself; we need to account for external factors such as the changing mandates of regulatory bodies, changing levels of funding, changes in personnel within these bodies (particularly at senior levels) and shifts in political discourses on regulation and regulatory agencies. That all of these phenomena are of significance in understanding regulatory processes is illustrated perhaps most clearly classically in Barnett's sensitive analyses of the changing contours and dynamics of 'Superfund' enforcement in the US (Barnett 1994, 1995). Such elements of overt political activity are important for an adequate account of regulation – it is only in *remaining* at this level of analysis that one descends into any empiricism.

For us, a more adequate conception of a regulatory agency is that developed by Mahon, and we shall draw heavily upon this conception in these concluding pages. Mahon seeks to understand such agencies within the context of a theory of the state which itself draws upon the work Poulantzas and Gramsci. While there are important differences between the versions of Marxism developed and represented by these two theorists, for each the state itself is understood not as a thing, to be captured or used as an instrument, not an entity external to classes and class power, but as a relation. Indeed, it is through the state that the interests of various fractions and classes are combined and recombined: in the development of the unity of a historic bloc, in the constant struggle to secure hegemony, the formation of authority is a continuous process of incorporating the interests of various forces through the state. Thus the articulation of class struggle in the state produces the authority of the hegemonic class/fraction. Poulantzas argues that,

> The notion of the general interest of the people, an ideological notion, covering an institutional operation of the capitalist state, expresses a real fact: namely that this state, by its very structure, gives to the economic interests of certain dominated classes guarantees which may even be contrary to the short term interests of the dominant class but which are compatible with their political interest ... their real hegemonic domination.
>
> (Poulantzas, cited in Mahon 1979: 155)

The relative autonomy of the state allows this securing of hegemony; it also permits the state to function as 'political organiser of the various dominant fractions and to arrange the "corporate" compromises that provide the conditions for the expanded reproduction of capital and of the bourgeoisie as the dominant class' (Mahon 1979: 155). Thus the state 'expresses and organises the political relations of class domination. It is not captured by the dominant class' (Mahon 1979). Rather, inscribed in the state is '"an unequal structure of representation" historically produced by the class struggle ... through which the "unstable equilibrium of compromises" is arranged' (*ibid.*: 157–8).

Within such an analysis, a regulatory agency is most likely to have its origins in an issue that cannot be 'resolved' within existing structures of law. The creation of such a body provides 'a framework for facilitating an exceptional compromise in the face of a political challenge that can only be met by altering the juridical rights of capital' (*ibid.*: 160). Thus a regulatory agency must be 'independent ... apparently insulated from partisan politics and the regular administrative apparatus':

> ... because the kind of issue which gives rise to the establishment of a regulatory agency – giving it its status as 'special case' – is a potentially explosive one, the threat may resurface, possibly necessitating renegotiation of the agency's terms, powers, and relationships to other parts of the state apparatus. That the particular compromise is institutionally located at an

apparently greater distance than the rest of the apparatus from the overtly
political institutions (the assembly and the executive) indicates the
importance of neutralising/insulating the compromise. Yet it is precisely the
special political nature of the issue that may lead to a future rupture.

(*ibid.*: 160)

A theoretical understanding of a regulatory agency as a hegemonic
apparatus forces us to ask a rather different series of questions to those
raised by the versions of regulation considered thus far in this chapter:
what (issue) created the need for compromise; what is the hegemonic
fraction; what place does the regulated industry hold in the social
formation; what is the nature of the compromise; and what are the
conditions of existence of this compromise – crudely, how stable is this?
Of course, these questions must be treated through reference to the
empirical (Carson 1982: 12), although it is also clear that developing our
understanding of the nature and limits of regulation then requires a
further shift back to a more abstract, theoretical level, now interrogated
and refined through theoretically informed empirical analyses (*ibid.*:
233–4). The point is, however, that neither our questions nor our answers
are entirely foreclosed. Understanding regulatory agencies as hegemonic
apparatuses means that their effects are not pre-determined, that there is
always space for more (and, of course, less) effective regulatory strategies,
forms, modes of enforcement. The strength or weakness of regulation
therefore is interpreted dynamically, within the context of struggle
between members of classes and a range of social forces. What this calls
for is precisely that which is omitted by many descriptive/normative
treatments of regulation, namely a political economy of regulation and
regulatory enforcement.

Theorising the state and regulatory agencies in this way allows for very
different forms of analyses of regulatory activity. Research on enforcement is not now an effort to describe, though the understanding of the
participants, the process itself, and then (at best) to attempt to articulate
this within some vague notions of a legal and political context. To be sure,
these forms of analysis remain crucial – but they do not constitute
explanation, nor do they prescribe the limits of what is possible *vis-à-vis*
regulatory enforcement. Viewing regulatory agencies within a materialist
understanding of the state, an understanding which represents the
struggle or hegemony as one of material and ideological practices, and
one which is always more or less open, forces us to examine a wider range
of phenomena when speaking of, describing, assessing regulation. Moreover, such an approach forces those arguing for more punitive enforcement to address squarely the reality of corporate power, but this is not
simply acknowledged as a resource which in a simple and once-and-for-all
fashion constrains, but as a phenomenon which takes many forms, and
which is always ubiquitously and unevenly available.

There are some analyses which, even if they are not consciously
developed within this framework, can be usefully articulated within it.

The work of Carson, Woolfson and Whyte and colleagues, referred to previously in this chapter, on regulation and the UK oil industry is one set of instances; the work of Grunberg (1983, 1986), Nichols (1997) and Tombs (1990, 1995b, 1996), on the macro- and micro-dynamics of enforcement of safety legislation in the UK is another; important comparative insight is offered by Navarro (1983) and Tucker (1990, 1992, 1995). Pearce and Tombs (1998) have attempted to develop this theoretical schema, through an articulation of empirical material relating to the international chemical industry. Carson and Henenberg (1989) have ambitiously attempted to set out the range of factors that need to be taken into account in a full-blown political economy of regulation, while Snider has attempted to determine the differing political economies of four forms of regulatory process (1987, 1991, 1993).

Thus such an approach allows us to be more sensitive to the different forms in which different corporate activity is regulated. It points us towards the need to understand regulation from the point of view of states, economies, societies. The views of regulation outlined in the chapter do not provide the basis for this all-embracing perspective; an approach grounded in a Marxist political economy does precisely that.

Note

1. Many of the criticisms of the compliance school highlighted in this chapter are taken from two papers by Pearce and Tombs (1990, 1991). Each of these also generated responses from Hawkins (1990, 1991). This debate has been referred to frequently in subsequent commentaries.

Chapter 9

Punishing corporations?

Introduction

One distinctive problem in the area of corporate crime is the issue of how such non-human legal personalities should be punished if they are convicted of crimes. This is not a purely penological question. If the punishments that could be imposed upon organisational offenders are of questionable effectiveness (for example because fines are simply passed on to consumers), then it may seem pointless for prosecutions to be brought because no positive outcome can possibly flow from criminal proceedings against offenders.

In this chapter we examine the issues that touch on how companies and organisations can be punished, how they should be punished according to the arguments of various commentators, and what intellectual and practical predicaments are entailed by the prosecutorial policies being proposed.

Crimes against 'social regulation' and crimes against 'economic regulation'

There is one point we should emphasise at the outset of this exploration. As we have noted in Chapters 3 and 4, there is a significant difference between crimes which are against social regulation and crimes which are against economic regulation. Into the former category would come offences like those which result in people being killed and injured at work, or having their water poisoned. Into the latter category would come offences like those against the Inland Revenue, or those against Customs and Excise.

Snider argues:

> the state's willingness to crack down upon the corporate sector will vary with:
> the strength of the forces promoting and opposing regulation; the type of

corporate crime, especially its visibility; the perceived regulatory alternatives; the relation of corporate crime to key structural factors such as the needs of capital; its relation to dominant societal values; the past and present relationship of the particular state and its bureaucracies to the major classes.

(1991: 218)

For Snider, the regulation of corporate crime is an ever-changing dialectical process and, at any given period, some corporate crimes will be perceived, more than others, to be against the interests of capitalism. She argues that states are not even-handed in the way they enforce laws governing corporate behaviour, as those which concern offences against economic regulation are much better policed than other crimes.

Whilst punishments have often been notably weak and lenient in respect of companies convicted of 'social regulation' offences, they have often been quite strong in respect of 'economic regulation' offences. The socio-economic system of modern capitalism is much more allergic to financial chaos or subversion than it is to the sacrifice of consumers or workers in the pursuit of profit. This point is neatly summed up in the quotation from Jonathan Swift's *Gulliver's Travels*, cited by Weait:

> They look upon fraud as a greater crime than theft and therefore seldom fail to punish it with Death: for they allege that care and Vigilance, with a very common Understanding, may preserve a Man's Goods from Thieves; but Honesty hath no Fence against superior Cunning; And since it is necessary that there should be a perpetual Intercourse of buying and selling, and dealing upon Credit, where Fraud is permitted or connived at, or hath No Law to punish it, the honest Dealer is always undone, and the Knave gets the advantage.

(1995: 83)

Following various commercial frauds in the 1980s, the Serious Fraud Office was set up under the Criminal Justice Act 1987 to mount an effective and co-ordinated response to serious fraud. Its aim is to 'deter fraud and maintain confidence in the United Kingdom's financial systems'. It is an objective of the SFO (Weait 1995: 91) to 'pursue the appropriate and prompt investigation and prosecution of fraud'. Here, unlike, for example, violations against food hygiene or health and safety, there are no elaborate systems of warning, caution, and then, if all else fails, prosecution for minor regulatory offences. Prosecutions in this area are framed as indictments for Crown Court trial.

In *R* v. *Kazmi* (1985, 7 Cr App R (S) 115) it was held that in times of economic stress the court should mark offences of commercial fraud with severe penalties to deter others. In the leading case of *R* v. *Barrick* (1985, 7 Cr App R (S) 142), the Court of Appeal issued some general guidelines about sentencing in cases of theft and breaches of trust by employers and professional persons. In effect, the Court's view was that such cases were so serious that only a custodial sentence could usually be justified. That view has since been followed in most cases (Levi 1989; Henman 1995). The SFO handles around 60 cases of serious and complex fraud at any one time where the money at risk in each case is £1 million or more. In 1990–91 45 out of 72 defendants were convicted, and in 1991–2 38 out of 58 defendants were convicted.

The Metropolitan and City Police Company Fraud Department, formed in 1946, is responsible for the investigation of large and complicated frauds involving limited companies and banks, and also, more recently, offences of public sector corruption. Six hundred cases are under investigation at any one time by this Department and the total amount of money at risk in these cases is invariably several hundred million pounds. Additionally, many other bodies co-operate in the regulation of corporate misconduct. These include the Department of Trade and Industry, the Bank of England, and the Securities and Investments Board.

Relatively few crimes against economic regulation are detected and prosecuted to conviction (Levi 1987, 1993a). Nevertheless, the State is *seen* to be devoting considerable resources to these matters (*Guardian*, 7 November, 1997, p. 23), and sentencing, when it does occur, is fairly stringent (Levi and Pithouse forthcoming).

In the following pages we concentrate on the way the State has responded to corporate crimes against social regulation. After setting out the current sanctions available against corporate bodies under English law, we begin exploring the penological debate by looking at the issue of violent corporate crime to illustrate the theoretical and practical challenges.

The current sanctions available against corporations

(i) The criminal courts

There are two ways in which a company can be criminally liable.

Vicarious liability is a form of strict liability arising from the employer–employee relationship without reference to any fault of the employer. A corporation is responsible to exactly the same extent as an individual employer for the acts of its employees. (*National River Authority* v. *Alfred McAlpine Homes East Ltd, Independent*, 3 Feb., 1994, Lexis CO/11003/93 (Queens Bench Divisional Court).)

When it comes to crimes involving blameworthiness, the criminal liability of corporations extends to cover *direct liability* for acts performed by natural persons identified with it (see Chapter 2). English criminal law has developed the fiction of corporate personality – the idea that a company is a legal 'person' – which can sue and be sued in its own name. A corporation can only act through individual persons. If there is an individual who has committed the actual criminal conduct required for an offence (what lawyers term the *actus reus*) with the appropriate culpable frame of mind (which lawyers term the *mens rea*, and which can be, amongst other things, intention or recklessness) and who is sufficiently important in the corporate structure for his or her acts to be identified with the company itself, the company as well as the individual can be criminally liable (unless the statutory provision creating the offence precludes this). This is known as the identification doctrine and was explained by Lord Reid in *Tesco Supermarkets* v. *Nattrass* [1972] AC 153:

> A corporation . . . must act through living persons, though not always one or the same person. Then the person who acts is not speaking or acting for the company. He is acting as the company and his mind which directs his acts is the mind of the company. There is no question of the company being vicariously liable. He is not acting as a servant, representative, agent or delegate. He is an embodiment of the company or, one could say, he hears and speaks through the persona of the company, within his appropriate sphere, and his mind is the mind of the company. If it is a guilty mind then that guilt is the guilt of the company.

Under this principle a company can even be liable for a common law offence, such as conspiracy to defraud where the mental element is central to liability, as in *ICR Haulage Ltd* [1944] KB 551 where the agreement and intention of the managing director were regarded as those of the company.

The only criminal penalty that can be imposed on a company in English Law is a fine and/or compensation order. A company is a creature of the law with no physical existence. Accordingly, it cannot be tried for murder or treason as the only punishments available to the court on conviction are life imprisonment or death.

In principle there seems no reason why a company should not be capable of committing any criminal offence punishable by a fine, provided the identification principle has been satisfied. There are, however, certain offences which, by their very nature, cannot be committed by corporations such as rape, incest, bigamy and perjury. In these cases a corporation could only be liable as an accessory, although the law provides that, upon conviction, an accessory is liable to be punished up to the same maximum sentence as applies to the principal offender.

In *R* v. *P&O European Ferries (Dover) Ltd* (1990) 93 Cr App R 72 it was held a company could be liable for manslaughter.

All criminal offences fall into one of the following categories:

- summary offences, that is, those which must be tried in the Magistrates' Court;
- offences triable only on indictment, that is, those which must be tried in the Crown Court;
- offences which are triable either way.

The liability of a company for an offence is, as has already been mentioned, additional to the liability of the individual employee. In the

Magistrates' Court, the maximum penalty which can be imposed on a company for a summary offence is a fine of £5 000 but to £20 000 for breaches of ss 2–6 of the Health and Safety at Work Act 1974. For the individual the maximum penalty for a summary offence is six months imprisonment or a £5 000 fine or both.

Maximum penalties for most offences tried on indictment in the Crown Court are laid down by statute and may include a fine and/or imprisonment. Financial penalties have no limit for companies tried on indictment. For example, on 8 December, 1994, a company OLL Ltd was convicted of manslaughter and fined £60 000 at Winchester Crown Court following the deaths of four sixth-formers in the Lyme Bay canoe tragedy (*Blackstones Criminal Practice*, 1997: 76). The managing director was also convicted of manslaughter and sentenced to three years imprisonment (*R* v. *Kite* [1996] 2 Cr App R (S) 295).

(ii) The civil courts

In most cases, the plaintiff is seeking damages for personal injuries. Very few cases actually ever reach the courts, the vast majority being settled out of court (Harpwood 1993: 18.1). The term 'personal injuries' includes disease, impairment of physical or mental condition, and death.

Claims for damages in respect of personal injuries where the plaintiff does not reasonably expect to recover more than £50 000 must be commenced in a County Court (*High Court and County Court Jurisdiction Order 1991, art. 5*). Generally cases with a value below £25 000 are started in the County Court and those worth more than £50 000 are commenced in the High Court.

Quantification of damages involves a prediction of what would have happened to the plaintiff if the accident had not occurred. The great majority of claims are for less than £50 000 and is the sum of the plaintiffs claim for:

(a) special damages for actual financial losses incurred before trial or settlement;
(b) general damages for pain, suffering and loss of amenity relating to the injury itself; and
(c) future losses, such as future loss of earnings and the cost of future medical care.

Losses where damages under heads (a) and (b) exceed £50 000 are comparatively rare but where the injury results in the plaintiff being unable to work or only capable of low-paid work, the total award is likely to justify commencing proceedings in the High Court.

It is notoriously difficult to succeed in proceedings in personal injury claims against corporations. Corporations often have the resources to stretch proceedings, and the delays (many take five years to come to trial in the High Court), uncertainties and the possibility of having to pay the other side's costs, are frequently enough to persuade plaintiffs to settle out of court for a compensation sum much lower than they would get if they went through with the case and won it (Harris 1984).

General issues of corporate punishment

Companies are enormously powerful social actors. Virtually everything we eat, drink, wear, travel on, live and work in is designed, produced and maintained by people working for companies. Increasingly, therefore, when damage, loss or injury is suffered it can be traced back to corporate fault. When this fault is criminally culpable the question arises as to the most suitable sanction against a company.

The emerging criminology of corporate crime, and related questions of sentencing, may be faced with the same chronic problem as the long-established criminology of ordinary individual crime: that policies of legal framework, policing, prosecution and sentencing all appear to have significantly less influence on crime levels than do social and economic factors.

Historically, the legal framework governing corporations was built up in response to what corporations were actually doing or trying to do in commercial practice. This reflects what happens in most areas of law, and might be a truism, but it is too important a point to go unarticulated. Most of what appears, for example, in authoritative books on company law (e.g. Farrar *et al.* 1996; Pennington 1995) was not promulgated by Parliament after deliberations *in the abstract* about how companies should be run and governed – the law is based upon elemental principles of commercial practice. The law can, of course, modify the effect of these principles but it cannot repudiate them.

Once an enterprise is set up legally as a corporation it follows that certain definable duties are imposed on some of its personnel, and rights accrue to certain people (like shareholders) involved with the new body. The preponderance of these legal rules facilitate commercial operations.

Whether the criminal law and sentencing can now be successfully adapted to control endemic commercial delinquency is an important question to be addressed.

The principles of criminal law were evolved in the common law tradition to cater for individual responsibility. Now, however, corporate actors are a ubiquitous and extremely powerful element in social life yet the criminal law has not been properly adapted to meet this social development. In much of her pioneering work in this area, Celia Wells has argued for 'the development of liability which is better tailored to the organisational facts of corporate existence' (1993a, b). Wells urges a move away from corporate liability derivative from one specific individual. No sooner do we begin to unravel the appropriate ways for the criminal law to deal with corporations, particularly in respect of issues of *mens rea* and the doctrine of identification than we are faced with very challenging penological questions. If fining companies or putting them on probation are ineffective sanctions what about custodial sentences for individual directors? There are many problems here too. Individuals, for example, could thus be easily scapegoated for what is really an organisational fault.

There is no clearly established body of theory on how companies and company directors convicted of criminal offences in relation to their enterprise should be dealt with by the courts. Recent developments internationally and in Britain have intensified the debate around this issue. In 1993 Emmett Roe, owner of Imperial Foods chicken processing plant in North Carolina, USA received a 20-year custodial sentence for involuntary manslaughter after a factory fire killed 25 employees. In South Africa, Van de Vyer and William Smith, factory managers at Thor Chemicals, were arrested and charged with culpable homicide after two employees died of mercury poisoning. The plant reprocesses toxic waste from companies in Britain and the United States. Natal University safety expert Dr Mark Colvin remarked: 'For the first time management has been bust and I know of a lot of industries where management is suddenly very nervous' (Slapper 1994c: 126).

Corporate fines

There are many types of corporation and the reporting of sentencing in relation to most of these types is quite spasmodic and random. The reporting of sentences imposed on construction companies is, however, reasonably consistent. This might be because of the keen interest taken by the relevant trade unions and safety campaign groups, and the very poor safety record of this industry. Whatever the reasons, the data are sufficiently comprehensive for us to refer to them here in the course of discussing penological issues.

The record for the largest fine ever imposed on a construction company for a health and safety offence in Britain was broken in April 1993 when a London firm was fined a total of £160 000 and ordered to pay £28 000 costs at Knightsbridge Crown Court, following the electrocution of a worker on the London Water Ring Main Project. The record was broken again in November 1993 at Maidstone Crown Court when a fine of £200 000 was imposed on the Channel Tunnel consortium TML after it pleaded guilty to failing to ensure the safety of a worker crushed to death between two trains. The five UK construction companies in the Transmanche-Link consortium were each ordered to pay £40 000. Then, in

1997, the record was again broken when four companies were fined £1.7 million following the collapse of a walkway on the Kent coast (below).

Relatively large fines imposed on smaller companies and their directors have also been making the news. In 1993, the owner of an outdoor activity centre, and his company, were fined £15 000 each after admitting to breaches of the Health and Safety at Work etc. Act 1974 which led to the death of an 11-year-old girl on a school holiday. The company had employed an unqualified instructor who was supervising a group of 30 children on a night hike. The girl received fatal head injuries after falling down a steep bank when the instructor decided that the group should take a short-cut down a 55-degree slope, a move which was criticised by the court as 'stupid'. The girl was only attended to by a doctor 75 minutes after the accident owing to company safety procedures which were 'nothing short of lamentable' (*Health and Safety at Work*, December 1993).

Are heavy fines an appropriate way to deal with corporate wrong? It can be argued, for example, that the burden of such fines is inappropriately borne by shareholders or, if the fine affects the company very badly, by employees who are eventually made redundant, or by consumers in the form of higher prices. Fisse (1990) notes that fines are inappropriate in the context of offences committed by quasi-governmental authorities as they would simply result in 'some budgetary shuffling with money deducted from one arm of government passing back into general revenue' (cited in Clarkson and Keeting 1994: 243).

A cogent case for an improved system of fining companies has been put by David Bergman. He has noted that presently, when sentencing convicted companies, magistrates and judges do not have the same detailed information of the offender as they do for individuals awaiting sentence; in the case of the latter educational details, income, expenditure, and antecedents are known and often social inquiry reports will also be furnished with an assessment of the offender's likely response to probation. Whereas:

No such care is taken in relation to corporate offenders. No police officer or similar person gives evidence and there is no document available to the court similar to the social inquiry report. The court remains unaware of the most basic information on the company – its turnover, annual profits, history of relationship with the regulatory agency or its general health and safety record.
(1992: 1312)

Bergman, in arguing for higher fines, advocates the use of 'corporate enquiry' reports detailing essential financial and safety information. He cites as a model the system in the United States under which a federal probation officer is required to undertake a pre-sentencing investigation into each convicted company to help the court decide an appropriate level of fine.

Since its emergence and development during the later stages of Anglo-Saxon law, the fine has always been a problematic sanction. In recent history there is evidence that many offenders see the penalty as a risked 'add-on' cost to their criminal enterprise and, if the prospective gain from crime is sufficiently high, are undeterred. If they are caught, offenders will see paying the fine simply as a form of taxation on crime. Econometric criminologist Gary Becker has suggested in some detail just how such calculations are made by offenders (1968: 169–217).

One recent Home Office study (see *Guardian*, *The Times*, 22 April, 1998) conducted by the Institute of Criminology at Cambridge found that six out of ten suspects arrested by police were found to be drug users. *If* such a claim is accurate, then for corporate crime, the fine appears a far more suitable disposal because, unlike individuals whose offending is often committed whilst the person is affected by alcohol or drugs (and are thus not considering the current sentencing tariffs when they commit crimes), corporations generally behave rationally. They conduct business through decision-making processes that *are* susceptible to rationally predictable outcomes like profits and fines. Businesses use cost-benefit analysis as a routine procedure. The trouble is that such calculations are as much based on the likelihood of *being caught* as they are upon the level of fine if caught and convicted.

In the United Kingdom, Dunlop (the tyre manufacturer) faces having to pay more than £1 million to two families involved in a head-on car crash which left a child dead, a woman blinded and seven people injured after defective tyres were blamed for the accident. Lord Justice Judge sitting with Lord Justice Auld and Lord Justice Nourse at the Court of Appeal, said Dunlop had concealed defects in the 165 SR 13 SP4 radial tyre to protect their commercial viability. The evidence considered by the Court of Appeal showed that the company had become aware of a potentially lethal fault in the tyre but had failed to disclose this to the Department of Transport. One production report from the factory where the tyre had been produced was not made available by the company, and Lord Justice Judge observed that:

> The absence of this report may not be of huge significance. It was however symptomatic of a recurring fault in this litigation. It underlined that throughout the approach of Dunlop to discovery [the process of providing documents] was lamentable and was consistent with overwhelming evidence to suggest that Dunlop's reaction if and when a defect in the manufacture of their tyres emerged was that it should, for commercial reasons, be concealed.
> (*Carroll & Others* v. *Fearon & Others*, LawTel Transcripts, 20 January, 1998, draft judgment C8800018, p. 11)

The case evidence revealed that although several fatal accidents appeared to be caused by the defectively produced tyre, and the company was aware of this danger, it decided neither to alert government authorities (who could, for example, have ordered all such tyres to be condemned when presented at the annual tests required for all vehicles over three years old: so-called 'MOT' (Ministry of Transport) tests), nor to order a product recall (Slapper 1998).

Many companies decide to take the risk of unsafe systems as there is a very low chance of being inspected (in London, for example, there are about 20 Health and Safety inspectors for 200 000 sites). There are numerous documented case studies of such corporate malpractice. Often the money to be made from evading regulations is of a different order from anything the company is likely to be fined if caught.

Fines, which sometimes appear high compared to personal penalties, are still quite meagre when measured against the net income of the relevant companies. For example the HSE Annual Report 1987/88 boasts:

> The fine of £750,000 imposed in March on British Petroleum Ltd in the Scottish Courts for the failure of safety precautions at Grangemouth resulting in the loss of three lives represents a landmark in the application of safety law, and marks the seriousness with which the judiciary are prepared to regard serious breaches by firms with the heaviest responsibilities and where there is the potential for disaster.
>
> (HSE, 1988a: 30)

But this fine should be evaluated in its proper context. When we turn from the HSE's Annual Report for 1987 to that of BP for the same year, we see that the £750 000 fine should be judged against BP's profit (after taxation but before extraordinary items) which was £1 391 000 000 (British Petroleum 1987: 53). The fine therefore amounts to 0.05 per cent of the company's profit after taxation. This is the equivalent of a £7.50 fine for a person whose net earnings are £15 000, an unlikely disposal for someone whose culpable conduct has resulted in three deaths.

The court must inquire into the financial circumstances of the offender before fixing the amount of a fine (s. 18 Criminal Justice Act 1991, as amended). Equality in sentencing means equality of impact. It has been argued that if large corporations with vast profits were to be fined according to their means a new attitude to corporate violence and other crime might start emerging (Clarkson and Keating 1994: 242). Under European antitrust laws it is possible to impose a sanction equivalent to 10 per cent of the previous year's turnover (Wells 1993: 33–5).

What is the appropriate level of fine for a company? In Bergman's view, it is essential for the courts to get the level right because if the fine rises past 'a certain level' then managers and directors simply pass on the burden to consumers, shareholders or workers.

The real problem is that, according to the sentencing theory used in courts for most crimes (Thomas 1997), fines in general are meant to reflect the seriousness of the culprit's *error*, not necessarily the outcome of that error. Sometimes a small or low level or error has terrible consequences (a motorway car driver's split-second lapse in concentration leading to multiple deaths). Misunderstanding that point often leads to legally unwarranted journalistic outrage. Take, for example, a recent case from France. A man who killed a British skier when he hurtled into her in the French Alps was fined £300 by a French court. He had been convicted of manslaughter and given a three-month suspended sentence (*Independent*, 9 December, 1993). The sum of money here is clearly not calculated to reflect the value of the deceased's life but to represent the culpability of the mistake of the defendant who was himself badly hurt. Similarly, commenting on the £160 000 fine imposed on the company guilty of offences leading to the electrocution of a worker on the London Water Ring Main (above), Jeff Hinksman, Deputy Chief Inspector with the HSE said:

> This was a bad accident. The *level of fine against the company reflects a widespread corporate failure* and should serve as a warning to all firms in the construction industry to take their management responsibilities for health and safety seriously.
>   (Health and Safety Information Bulletin April 1993) [emphasis added]

So, as fines are legally calculated to betoken a level of error, it seems most improbable that putting artificial ceilings on them to ensure they do not 'rise above a certain level' could operate effectively and fairly equiparating (i.e. equalising the value of) the burden in different companies committing the same offence.

It may be that much more important than the juridical differences between personal and corporate liability is the certainty of prosecution following from commercial recklessness, coupled with a severe fine. Record fines against directors and companies have risen notably over the last ten years (Slapper, ed. 1995). A factor arguably conducive to companies acting with greater prudence in relation to their strategic safety policies is the high level of awards recently evidenced here and within the jurisdiction of the American courts.

Limits to 'general deterrence' theory in corporate crime

The trouble is, however, that the *general* deterrent effect of this sort of corporate punishment on large firms is unproven. (General deterrence being the effect upon corporations who observe one of their kind being punished.) There is some evidence that punishing one corporation with an appropriately serious sanction for an offence has a chastening effect upon others (Braithwaite and Geis 1982: 304; Yoder 1978; Clinard and Yeager 1980). However, an almost exactly similar case to Chrysler (above) involving the Ford Motor Company ten years previously – a case with major international high-profile coverage – failed subsequently both to ensure a good safety design policy at Chrysler, and then, when the fault became known to chasten the company into ordering a prompt recall. In

1987, in the case of the Pinto (Slapper 1993), the Ford Motor Company (the largest car manufacturer in America) allowed an unsafe car to go on to the roads, and failed to recall it with the result that many lives were lost in dreadful circumstances. A prosecution for corporate manslaughter failed but, in the light of very negative evidence about the company's attitude to safety which was elicited during the trial, many civil claims against the company were settled.

The corporate wrongs complained about in some legal actions actually occurred many years ago (even if, at the time of the wrong, the company still should have been aware of the injury or loss it was causing). In a landmark civil case in 1996, June Hancock successfully sued the giant Turner & Newall corporation for the cancer she had developed as a result of the company's cavalier attitude to asbestos. The gruesome and painful way in which mesothelioma sufferers die from the asbestos they have absorbed, and the fact that the lethal dangers of the substance have been known since the 1920s have probably influenced the seriousness with which asbestos-related offences are now seen. The Court of Appeal upheld an award of £65 000 and 20 other cases were pending against the company (*The Times*, 3 April, 1996). Expert evidence suggests that there may be up to 500 000 deaths in Britain during the next 30 years as a result of people coming into contact with asbestos (*Daily Telegraph*, 28 October, 1995; *Guardian*, 24 October, 1996).

Nonetheless, much contemporary corporate wrongdoing takes place in circumstances where the wrongdoer should be in no doubt about the injurious consequences of its conduct. Yet, despite rising fines against companies, there is evidence that some companies remained undeterred. In February 1997 four companies were fined a record £1.7 million over the collapse of a ferry walkway which killed six people and seriously injured another seven. Two Swedish companies who designed built and installed the walkway at the Port of Ramsgate in Kent were fined a total of £1 million, the Port £200 000 and Lloyd's Register of Shipping, which gave the device a safety certificate, £500 000. This was the first criminal conviction for the Register in its 237-year history (*New Civil Engineer*, 6 March, 1997).

In October 1997, Chrysler, the third largest car manufacturer in America, was ordered to pay a record $262.5 million (£162 million) damages to the parents of a six-year-old boy who was killed as the result of one of its mini-vans. A South Carolina jury awarded the parents of the boy, Sergio Jimenez, $12.5 million in actual damages and $250 million in punitive damages. A faulty latch allowed the boy to be thrown from the vehicle after it was involved in a collision. The jury said that Chrysler was negligent in the design and testing of the mini-van, that it had known about these faults but had tried to cover them up. One particularly damaging document revealed in court was an internal memo from the vice-chairman to the president and chairman of the company which said: 'If we want to use political pressure to try to squash a recall letter [i.e. a compulsory recall of all similar Chrysler vehicles on the road] we need to go now' (*Guardian*, 10 October, 1997).

The temptation for some directors to try anything to avoid a huge corporate cost (like large-scale vehicle or tyre recall) seems irresistible in the light of the gains to be made if such atrocious behaviour succeeds in its aim. In the Dunlop case (above) it came to light that prior to 1988, the company had been made aware of a number of accidents, similar to the fatal one it was considering which occurred on 9 July, 1988. The cases all involved a sudden and catastrophic stripping of the tread of the tyres by metal cords situated within the tyres. These accidents had been carefully logged by a senior official at the factory where the tyres were made. In relation to two similar earlier fatal incidents, the Vehicle Inspectorate had asked Dunlop to disclose the 'number of similar reports of which you are aware'. Although a great many were known to the company, no answer was given because, as the factory official acknowledged:

> an accurate answer would have led the Ministry to come down on Dunlop like
> 'a ton of bricks'. Senior management was informed of the problem by Mr
> Paine [the factory official] and he suggested that the decision not to answer
> the simple question directly was taken at a higher level. It was plainly hoped
> that the incomplete information would satisfy the Inspectorate and thus avoid
> the problems connected with a request for a recall of tyres.
> (Lord Justice Judge, *Carroll & Others* v. *Fearon & Others*, LawTel Transcripts,
> 20 January, 1998, draft judgment C8800018, p. 14)

How far practicable deterrent policy can be established by the regulatory and criminal justice systems has been considered in Chapter 8. It is important to consider the difficulties in arguing that heavy fining or personalising criminal liability offer significantly better ways forward. It may be that in the fight against corporate crime, the search for the silver bullet to deal with the threat is no more likely to succeed than the corresponding search by criminologists in the field of street crime.

Fines and neoclassical theory

Etzioni (1993) has written cogently against the use of fining as a way to end corporate crime. Neoclassical economists (like Becker 1985) have argued that fines need to be calculated on a cost-benefit basis. Thus, according to neoclassical theorists, 'if a corporation made a profit of $6 million from selling an unsafe product and the fine were, say, $7 million, it would refrain from committing this crime' (Etzioni 1993: 152). This formula, however, as Etzioni points out, completely fails to take into account the detection rate for the crime in question. As not all crimes are detected and punished, fines should be raised (in neoclassical theory) as detection ratios decrease. A corporation might otherwise rationally calculate that since it has, say, only a 1 in 10 chance of being caught, even if the fine is somewhat larger than the gain to be had from breaking the law, it is still more profitable to proceed and break the law because the corporation will only get hit with a fine once every ten times it commits the offence. Etzioni presents evidence (1993: 153–4) that only about 1 in 50 corporate crimes is detected. Fines would thus have to be multiplied by 50 to accommodate the neoclassical theory, and this would produce fines of 'astronomical figures' and effectively put many companies out of business which, apart from being a scheme lacking political feasibility, would, Etzioni concludes, be unfair.

Social and political context

The importance of the social and economic context of punishment has been graphically argued by Etzioni (1993). Looking at the US Sentencing Commission's work on corporate crime, he argues that its initial work and report (1989) had to be abandoned because in its deliberations about implementation it failed to take into account 'major social and political forces'. The first guidelines required the introduction of huge fines, up to one-third of $1 billion, for crimes that had previously resulted in fines of tens of thousands of dollars. The maximum fine provided for in the guidelines was $364 million. In contrast, four-fifths of all corporate convictions between 1975 and 1976 resulted in fines of $5 000 or less. Fines were low for even serious wrongs. For example Elm Lilly & Company, the pharmaceutical manufacturer, was fined $25 000 for a guilty plea to a misdemeanour charge for failing to inform the government of four deaths and six illnesses related to its arthritis drug Oraflex. The company was charged only with a misdemeanour, despite the fact that the drug had been linked to at least 26 deaths in the US and many more overseas (Etzioni 1993: 149).

Not surprisingly, the proposed new sentencing régime was greeted with fierce opposition from representatives of industry and the political Right. Etzioni quotes the response of the US National Association of Manufacturers, whose representative testified that 'The proposed guidelines . . . are extremely harsh, punitive, unwarranted, and will place many businesses on the threshold of insolvency' (1993: 149).

Eventually the Commission withdrew its recommendations, and later released a drastically scaled-back version of its earlier proposals. In some case the fines were reduced by as much as 97 per cent! For example, as we have noted, under the Commission's original guidelines, the maximum penalty proposed was $364 million. In the revised guidelines, that maximum penalty was reduced to $12.6 million. Business pressure groups continued to lobby against the proposals, and the final report of the Commission on sentencing corporations (1991) did enhance some of the proposed fines but also introduced a list of 'extenuating circumstances' that allowed offending corporations to reduce penalties to relatively small amounts. The mitigating factors included such things as:

- lack of knowledge of the offence on the part of high level management;
- prompt reporting of the offence to governmental authorities;
- clearly demonstrated recognition and acceptance of responsibility for criminal conduct; and
- full co-operation in any investigation.

When the fine is first set, the defendant is given a culpability score of 5. Corporations can then subtract various points for meeting the mitigating factors. For example, a corporation that met the last three criteria above could reduce the set penalty to only 5 per cent of the original fine.

Alternative sanctions to the fine

Noting that a small fine on a corporation may have no impact and a large one might simply be passed on to the shareholders or consumers, causing injustice, Punch (1996) records the alternatives used in the American system – probation, adverse publicity, equity fines, community service, making a company lend an executive to a charity for a year, direct compensatory orders and punitive injunctions. Notwithstanding the fact that a detriment borne by shareholders for the wrongs committed by their company can easily be regarded as a proper outcome, it is helpful to draw attention to the innovative American approach to corporate punishment.

The idea of community service for corporations is, for some, an intriguing one. Etzioni has stated that the penalty could be achieved by the corporation using its facilities and resources to arrange:

> ... soup kitchens for the homeless if it had previously sold adulterated food; sending its executives to do volunteer work in emergency rooms if they deliberately built cars that became fire bombs when hit from the rear; or requiring its board to work in Veterans Administration hospitals if the corporation profited from systematically falsifying test records on drugs, declaring them safe when they were not.
>
> (1993: 156)

Punch notes an unprecedented judgement from a judge in Virginia in which a company was 'jailed' for involvement in price-fixing (*The Economist*, 10 September, 1988):

> Judge Doumar made it clear that he did not actually expect to have the company incarcerated, but said that he could have all [the company's] facilities padlocked for the full three years of the sentence. He said that it was unfair for a company to make large illegal profits and then get away with a simple fine.
>
> (Punch 1996: 261)

In the event, Mr Doumar relented a little. He suspended the sentence (and $50 000 of the £1 million fine), placed the company on probation and ordered four of its senior executives to work full-time for the community for up to two years.

Corporate probation

Bergman (1992) has argued for a disposal known as 'corporate probation' which has been available nationally in the USA since 1987. Under such sanctions the judge can compel the senior management of a company to change how the company devises and implements safety procedures. The result of such a sanction is a highly interventionist form of regulation. Its use echoes escalation up Braithwaite's 'pyramid' of sanctions (see Chapter 8) It also allows an exploration of the potential of rehabilitation with respect to the corporation (Pearce and Tombs 1997, 1998). As with personal probation, conditions can be imposed by the court; for example insistence on certain safety procedures and the employment of certain safety staff. The first use of probation against a corporation in the USA was in 1971 in *US* v. *Atlantic Richfield Co.* (465 F.2d 58, cited in Lofquist 1993: 160). ARCO was placed on probation and ordered to develop an oil-spill response programme. The sentence was used rather haphazardly until the US Sentencing Reform Act 1984, and guidelines issued by the Sentencing Commission (May 1991) which clarified the proper use of such a disposal, and made probation mandatory in many instances, not just a way of ensuring that a company paid a fine.

The guidelines say that the court must order a term of probation in some circumstances, including the following:

- if necessary to ensure satisfaction of other sanctions;
- if an organisation of 50 or more employees lacks an effective programme to prevent and detect law violations;
- if the organisation or high-level personnel participating in the offence have been convicted of a similar offence in the past five years;
- if necessary to ensure that changes are made within the organisation to reduce the likelihood of future criminal conduct.

The guidelines say that there should be certain mandatory conditions of the probation, including those that say: no further crimes must be committed by the company, and that it must also pay a fine or restitution or performance of community service.

The commentary accompanying these provisions in the guidelines notes that regulatory agencies should be consulted in developing and monitoring probation conditions, which might include use of regulatory officials as probation officers.

For Lofquist (1993), the real significance of corporate probation is that as an 'organization-specific statutory sanction', it helps strengthen the legal foundation of corporate liability and avoids the conception of company crimes as crimes committed by individuals within companies. He utilises a theoretical distinction between 'market-based sanctions' and 'politics-based sanctions'. The former are founded upon the assumption that corporations are unitary, rational profit-maximising entities and that crime results from these characteristics. Thus, 'corporate crime control is best pursued through sanctions designed to increase the costs of crime above the potential benefits' (1993: 164). 'Politics-based sanctions', by contrast, are founded upon the assumption that corporations are complex, differentiated entities, simultaneously in pursuit of different and often conflicting goals. Corporate crime, on this assumption, is viewed as emanating from structural characteristics of the organisation. Thus, crime control is most effectively exercised by 'altering organizational structures and procedures in a manner designed to improve internal accountability and coordination of goals and activities' (*ibid.*: 165). However, as we have argued in Chapter 8, these views of the corporation are hardly exclusive.

It seems likely, however, that two of the main advantages of such a system do not transfer well from paper into practice. First, it has been argued that such orders can impose punitive burdens on management which are more difficult to transfer than the economic impact of fines. Ultimately, however, additional, court-imposed corporate responsibilities can, just like fines, be paid for by companies. Second, it is sometimes argued that by requiring conditions that lower the reputation of the company in a public manner, probation can impose greater punishment and deterrence than mere economic sanctions. There is no evidence, however, that companies which have been technically disgraced by a conviction and a huge fine for a very serious wrong *are* lowered in the estimation of the public. In 1987, for example, BP was fined £750000 after an incident in which three workers were killed. This was a major news item at the time yet there is no evidence of any consumer boycott of BP products as a result.

Some traditionally expected outcomes of sanctions

In the field of crime committed by individuals, the evidence suggests that despite a long history of punishments designed to effect individual and general deterrence, only a tiny fraction of offenders are convicted, and recorded rates of recidivism are high (Morgan 1994). Home Office evidence suggests that only two crimes from every 100 committed results in a conviction (Home Office 1995: 25) and approximately two-thirds of all young offenders and almost half of all adults are reconvicted at least once within two years of being released from a custodial sentence (Home Office 1990: chapter 9).

Sentencing policies which seek to reduce crime – reductive sentencing – have therefore suffered from a fading credibility and 'just deserts' models have enjoyed wider acceptance. According to the essence of this thinking, punishment is given simply because offenders deserve it.

A useful guidance to the legally accepted purpose of punishment was recently provided by the most senior criminal law judge, Lord Bingham, the Lord Chief Justice. In a very significant speech in July 1997, Lord Bingham gave an authoritative articulation of sentencing principles which were advanced as *general* guidelines and thus apply to corporations. He identified an unusual problem:

> We have the extraordinary paradox, that judges and magistrates have been roundly criticised for over-lenient sentencing during a period when they have been sending more defendants to prison for longer periods than at any time in the last 40 years. The increase in the prison population is not explained by any recent increase in sentencing powers, and I have no doubt that it is related to the pressure of public opinion.

Lord Bingham said this was not necessarily wrong because judges should be alive to the views of their fellow citizens. Nevertheless, he argued, it was only a few years ago since the judiciary was being criticised for being too severe in its sentencing so it should take care not to 'be blown hither and thither by every wind of political or penal fashion'. Going into more detail he said:

> . . . in determining the sentence in any given case, the judge should close his or her ears to public and media clamour concerning the case. It would, for example, be an abdication of the rule of law for a judge to take into account a newspaper campaign designed to encourage him to increase a particular sentence.

Lord Bingham noted that a trial judge is currently supposed to decide upon appropriate sentence in the following stages. This explanation is very helpful because, subtly, it incorporates various 'do's' and 'dont's' in the light of recent heated debates.

1. The judge should note the nature and circumstances of the crime, and the precise crime for which the defendant falls to be sentenced. It is the wrongness of the defendant's act or omission which is critical rather than how dire were the consequences of such behaviour. Sometimes a bad but not heinous mistake could lead to death (as in a traffic accident involving neither drunkenness nor excessive speed or recklessness) but it was not the judge's function to simply equate the loss of life with so many years or months in prison.
2. The judge should consider the personal circumstances of the

offender. Prompt guilty pleas and previous good character were relevant in mitigation of sentence. Nevertheless, the character of the offence always had to be kept in mind. In minor offences like shoplifting there would come a point at which a repeat offender's sentence should not be increased any more because it would then become disproportionate to the gravity of the offence.

3. The effect of the crime on the victim. Contrary to common misconception, it has always been the custom of prosecution counsel to tell the court of the effects of the crime on the victim, but it would be contrary to the interests of justice to accord the victim any significant say in determining the appropriate level of sentence: 'the passing of sentence must be governed by reason and guided by precedent, not coloured by emotion or by a desire for revenge'.

4. The sentencer must always have regard to the wider public interest in order to maintain public confidence. If informed public opinion perceived that sentences failed to match the gravity of crimes then the public may be tempted to take justice into its own hands and resort to private vengeance.

Lord Bingham stated that in addition to the three traditional purposes of sentencing (retribution, deterrence, and rehabilitation) there should now be recognised two others:

- incapacitation (putting it out of the power of the offender to commit further offences); and
- the maintenance of public confidence.

In an interesting interpretation of these principles, the Lord Chief Justice said that the different types of sentence served the various purposes of sentencing in different measure, and that a sentence of imprisonment was 'very largely retributive' and not usually passed with a view to rehabilitating the offender.

It costs the state over £30 000 to keep a person in prison for one year and empirical research has revealed that in many of today's custodial settings, rehabilitative treatment programmes have had little or no demonstrable effects upon reducing criminal behaviour (Genders and Player 1993).

Braithwaite and Geis (1982) suggest that even though rehabilitation has failed as a doctrine for the control of traditional crime, it can succeed with corporate crime. A large-scale survey by Lipton, Martinson and Wilks (1975) afforded much data to cast serious doubt on any rehabilitative function that correctional programmes in America could offer. A similar conclusion has been reached in the United Kingdom (Brody 1975). The Green Paper *Punishment, Custody and the Community* (HMSO 1988), and the subsequent White Paper of 1990 recognised the limitations of prisons as places for rehabilitating offenders and made it clear that judges should no longer use imprisonment as a sentence if they seek to bring about the rehabilitation of the offender. In this context the Lord Chief Justice's lack of enthusiasm for prison sentences for many types of crime is understandable. It is interesting to consider how far these principles are applicable to corporate defendants.

Braithwaite and Geis (1982) concede that there would be little purpose to be served by compelling individual criminals to undergo 'correctional' programmes. Certainly, confronting white-collar criminals with high-minded banking accountants, health and safety practitioners, or morally upright computer experts, would seem to be of questionable value as the offenders would usually be sufficiently expert to appreciate, for example, exactly what damage, loss or injury would follow from their wrongful conduct and why it is wrong.

Corporate rehabilitation

Corporate crimes frequently arise from defective control systems, insufficient checks and balances within the organisation, and poor communication systems (Braithwaite 1983). These failings are sometimes deliberate, and made by the corporation to facilitate the commission of offences or the avoidance of detection, and sometimes the failings are inadvertent. Either way, it is possible for legal orders to force corporations to correct criminogenic policies and practices. The idea is that:

> Rehabilitation is a more workable strategy with corporate crime than with traditional crime because criminogenic organizational structures are more malleable than are criminogenic human personalities. A new internal compliance group can be put in place much more readily than a new superego.
>
> (Braithwaite and Geis 1982: 310)

One example given by Braithwaite and Geis is that of a pharmaceutical company whose chief executive repeatedly ignores the fact that his quality control manager is being overruled by the production manager where the former is objecting to batches of medicines on grounds of impurity. Here, the company could be made to reform so that the person responsible for achieving production targets was no longer able to overrule quality control, and the only way that a quality control decision could be overruled was by the chief executive, in writing. Braithwaite and Geis cite evidence to suggest that most companies convicted of offences did take measures afterwards to reduce the chance of further offending. In examples like the one above, however, how far a recalcitrant company fired by an unbridled competitive spirit would be able to overcome the new restrictions by appointing 'the right sort of person' to head quality control is open to debate.

Etzioni has also argued in favour of 'corporate rehabilitation'. He advocates rehabilitation orders against companies even where no other penalty is exacted or even if they are able to pay their fine:

> Imagine, for instance, a corporation that is found to have systematically neglected the safety of its consumers. It seems socially productive to put it on a five year diet of closer inspections. If it is found to have truly mended its ways, the inspectors should report that the firm has been rehabilitated and fully restore it to membership among decent and law abiding corporations.
>
> (1993: 155)

Enforced adverse publicity as a sanction

Braithwaite and Geis have further argued that the doctrines of crime control through deterrence, public disgrace and incapacitation, although discredited in relation to individual crime, would operate much better in relation to corporate offenders. They argue that 'principles developed in relation to traditional crime should not be assumed to apply to corporate offenses' (1982: 294). Regarding the specific deterrence to individual convicts, incarceration in prison will not necessarily deter conventional offenders who, it is argued, learn better ways of committing crimes whilst in jail. The skills of jailed accountants, on the other hand, will just go stale and become outdated. Also, the stigmatising process associated with labelling theory, whereby convicts get pushed further and further into a criminal self-image, and thus into further criminality (Lemert 1951; Becker 1964; West and Farrington 1977) does not apply to corporate offenders as 'they are likely to regard themselves as unfairly maligned pillars of respectability, and no amount of stigmatization is apt to convince them otherwise' (Braithwaite and Geis 1982: 301). They say:

> Although the labelling hypothesis makes it unwise to use publicity as a tool to punish juvenile delinquents, it is sound deterrence to broadcast widely the names of corporate offenders. Corporations and their officers are genuinely afraid of bad publicity arising from their illegitimate activities.

Fisse (1971) has developed this in some detail. He first notes the relative deficiency of the fine as a corporate sanction, and the alternative approaches including pursuing individual directors, and programmes designed to rehabilitate corporations by making them carry out their operations with more organisational care. His own interest is in devising new 'entity sanctions' that is, punishments against the whole organisation. He contemplates:

> mass media advertisements setting out the details of a corporation's criminal conduct, compulsory notification to shareholders and others by means of the annual report, and even a temporary ban on advertising ...
>
> (1971: 108)

Several Bread Acts in force in England in the nineteenth century contained provisions which authorised magistrates to order the publication of convictions of people responsible for adulterating bread. The Bread Act 1822, section 10, for example states:

> It shall be lawful for the Magistrate ... before whom any such Offender or Offenders shall be convicted, to cause the Offender's Name, Place of Abode and Offence, to be published in some Newspaper which shall be printed or published in or near the City of London ... and to defray the Expense of publishing the same out of the Money to be forfeited.
>
> (quoted in Fisse 1971: 110)

The intention of the legislature was to warn prospective buyers but the collateral effects of punishment and deterrence must have been considered. There are several similar provisions today in food and medicine laws in Australia and New Zealand.

Fisse (1971) argues that publicity sanctions which are directed at lowering prestige or inducing governmental intervention (like formal inquiries or the appointment of auditors) rather than inflicting a monetary loss have end effects which are not shared by conviction and fine alone. He contends that publicity sanctions of this nature do not require widespread public reaction but rather depend on the reactions of business executives, official persons and 'opinion leaders', so, he argues, the conventional pessimism surrounding their use is unwarranted. He denies a need to persuade the general public that D's products should not be purchased, saying such an approach would be undesirable given that the fine is a much more certain and ready method of inflicting a monetary loss. A 'Do Not Buy' instruction would only be fitting where it was considered necessary to warn consumers of defects. The notices, he suggests, should also indicate whether D has taken, or plans to take, remedial measures.

There are several possible objections to the use of publicity as a corporate sanction. First, Fisse is not clear about the purpose of the sanction. He notes (1971: 117–18) that the case for using publicity as a deterrent measure is weak if infliction of monetary loss is the only effect desired: 'why not simply increase fines to such a level that the same monetary loss can be inflicted?' He suggests that a much stronger case can be made out if it is sought to achieve deterrence 'by inducing loss of prestige or respect, provided that "prestige" and "respect" are not merely qualities which reflect financial standing'.

Fisse says 'even the wealthy may wilt from social disapproval'. Perhaps they might, although some might argue that where business tycoons or captains of industry make clinical business decisions to improve their company's 'performance' or 'economic leanness' by 'downsizing' the workforce or relocating to another continent, they appear to be oblivious to any disapproval from the general public. More significantly, Fisse has tacitly shifted the focus of his punishment from the company itself, 'entity sanctions' in his phrase, to the individuals who would be shamed by adverse publicity. It is difficult to see how a non-human entity, the corporation, can experience shame.

Secondly, although there is very limited experience of formal, court-imposed adverse publicity following convictions, there has been a great deal of informal adverse publicity by the media taking their own initiative in the form of news reports, commentaries and documentaries.

The Ford Motor Company was not convicted of manslaughter in the infamous Pinto case but it suffered very badly from the undisputed revelation that it had used a cost-benefit analysis in deciding to leave on the road thousands of vehicles whose safety was in question. The cost of paying for a possible 180 deaths and serious injuries was balanced against the cost of a recall of all the Pintos on the road. The car was not recalled. Also revealed in court was the haste with which the car was raced through design and production, with some exhortations for better safety being ignored, in order to win a significant slice of a highly competitive market (Dowie 1977; Cullen *et al.* 1987).

The case received very widespread, comprehensive, detailed and dramatic news coverage by the media (Swigert and Farrell 1981), yet the Ford Motor Company is still the world's leading motor manufacturer. There has been no apparent loss of prestige or financial standing; and, as to the power of such negative publicity to produce a general end, the Chrysler case, mentioned above, is evidence that motor companies were not chastened into better behaviour by the Ford case. In fact, despite new technologies, based on robotology and total quality management, General Motors produced a truck with an almost identical defect to that of the Ford Pinto and was heavily sued for negligence (*Wall Street Journal*, 5 February, 1993; cited in Punch 1996: 248).

A third objection to the 'publicity as sanction' schemes is that the sheer might of corporations like The Ford Motor Company, and the culture of these gigantic corporations, cannot be meaningfully tackled by a few *ad hoc* publicity campaigns.

One notable example is the tardiness of Britain's top insurance companies in compensating for their pensions mis-selling scandal (see *Independent*, 13 May, 1997; *Financial Times*, 20 November, 1997; *Financial Times*, *The Times*, 10 December, 1997). The Personal Investment Authority (PIA) estimates that a total of up to 1.5 million investors may have been wrongly advised by corporate agents during the late 1980s and early 1990s to buy personal pensions, moving out of occupational schemes that would have given them a better return.

Since 1994, the PIA tried to get the insurance companies concerned to pay compensation, yet several thousands of victims of the pensions mis-selling scandal were still waiting to have their cases resolved in 1998. The situation was particularly dramatic because nearly 560 000 people were deemed to be 'priority cases' for compensation as they had retired or were close to doing so. Some policyholders (an estimated 18 000) died before the companies offered any compensation. Just over 12 650 people were paid a total of £100 million compared with the final estimated bill which is expected to cost the industry between £4 billion and £11 billion.

Helen Liddell, economic secretary at the Treasury, said statistics alone could not capture the full drama of the situation which was 'a story about anxiety, frustration and in some cases downright despair' (*Financial Times*, 8 October, 1997).

The government looked at 'naming and shaming' individual directors for mis-selling but could not overcome the practical and legal obstacles. It was too difficult to establish a paper-trail tying a director directly to mis-selling, and many individuals who were directors of pension companies in the late 1980s and early 1990s – when the mis-selling occurred – left before the issue became public. The government then began a policy to 'name and shame' individual directors and managers for *slow progress* in clearing up the scandal. In late 1997, the government concentrated on 'naming and shaming' companies while regulators fined and reprimanded them for mis-selling and slow progress. The PIA said, although it had considered naming individual companies, it had received legal advice that this could be seen as a form of discipline without due process (*Financial Times*, 15 May, 1997).

In spite of the government taking a hard line with the pension companies, there is still concern that too many victims still had to suffer inordinate delay, and that as well as many falling through the compensation net, others will not receive a fair amount, and that a new end of 1998 deadline set by the PIA and the Securities and Investment Board (SIB) will, as previous deadlines, be missed by a wide mark (*Financial Times*, 17 May, 1997).

Jean Eaglesham further argues (*ibid.*), that the companies have a clear financial interest in not trying too hard to track down missing policyholders – why chase someone simply to hand them money? – although they claim they are doing what they can to find people.

A leading financial recruitment consultancy also warned that skill shortages were likely to hamper efforts to tackle the scandal: 'It is self-evident that the pensions companies desperately need to employ large numbers of people to deal with the logjam ... This makes it impossible to resolve the problem by the end of 1998 as the government is insisting' (*Financial Times*, 15 May, 1997).

Fisse (1971: 124) notes the Bureau of Corporations which was set up in 1903 by Theodore Roosevelt with the purpose of marshalling public opinion against various malpractices of some corporations. It was to investigate companies and also to maintain inquiry on an industry-wide level. The Bureau was disbanded after a very short time because of the need to obtain election funds from the large corporations! In the light of recent revelations about the extent to which companies fund political parties in Britain (*The Times*, 12, 13 November, 1997), similar difficulties would presumably exist in this jurisdiction.

Part of the theoretical assumption of those who advocate publicity sanctions is the ability of corporations to be deterred by punishment. Chambliss (1967) has argued that white-collar offenders are among the most deterable types of offenders because they satisfy two conditions: they do not have a commitment to crime as a way of life; and their offences are instrumental rather than expressive. The crimes are not spontaneous or emotional but calculated risks taken by rational actors. Braithwaite (1989) argues that corporations are 'future oriented' (worried about the effect of punishment on their future plans), concerned about their reputations and 'quintessentially rational' because although most individuals do not possess the information necessary to calculate rationally the probability of detection and punishment, corporations do have sophisticated informa-tion-gathering systems, lawyers and accountants at their service.

It has been argued, however, that the concept of deterrence (used in a sweeping sense to refer to any decisions to refrain from criminal activity whatever its source) unduly confuses the role of formal and informal sanctioning systems (Moore 1987: 381). Moore maintains that social stigma and other informal sanctions such as adverse publicity are con-ceptually and substantively different from formal legal sanctions such as the fine or loss of liberty. Informal sanctions cannot be *mandated* by the state and are by definition forms of *social* sanction that fall beyond the law's coercive powers and may be 'imposed' often with greater effective-ness through the media, consumer boycotts or by other means. For this reason, he maintains, it is preferable to limit the concept of deterrence to any omission of an act that results from the fear or risk of *legal* sanction.

Individual directors

Will putting business-people behind bars act as a deterrent to the commission of corporate manslaughter? Professor Celia Wells (1997) has conjectured that much of the concern to enable companies to be prosecuted for manslaughter might be at variance with the popular 'cultural expectation' that *individual directors* should be made liable for fatal commercial disasters. Asking why the prosecution failed in the P&O case, Professor Wells states that, amongst other factors, there might have been a 'confusion in the target of blame'. She says:

> Perhaps it is the directors, those who take the money for making decisions which have far-reaching implications for thousands of employees and even more consumers, to whom the blame is being attached.

This might well be so. Certainly, following the Southall train crash (19 September, 1997) there were many renewed calls from lawyers, academics and some campaign groups for tougher action against reckless directors (see *Guardian*, letters, 4 October, 1997).

Charles Woolfson has written:

> Whatever the legal complexities of a new law of corporate killing, and they
> cannot be exaggerated, there is a fundamental human axiom the efficacy of
> which is to be commended, particularly with respect to the jailing of
> individual company directors – when one goes down, all sit up.
>
> (*Guardian*, letters, 4 October, 1997)

Nevertheless, if there is to be a refocusing of attention on reckless directors, the effectiveness of such a policy should be fully explored. One of the central themes of those who argue for directors to be imprisoned for manslaughter (e.g. Bergman 1994; *Safety and Health Practitioner* December 1997) is that it will discourage other directors from steering their companies into criminally wrongful conduct. The argument is founded upon an assumption that potentially criminal directors will be chastened by the public reporting of imprisoned directors. However, during the last three years, accompanied by some high profile news coverage, five company directors have been jailed for manslaughter and serious safety offences yet the rate of deaths and major injuries at work has not changed significantly. It could be argued that the public reporting of the imprisonments *did* discourage directors from being reckless or intentionally criminal, and that the rate of deaths at work, for example, would have been even higher had the imprisonments not been made. The precise effect of the imprisonments with reference to general deterrence is perhaps a matter of speculation.

Business people convicted of crimes relating to property like fraud, embezzlement, tax evasion and theft have often been imprisoned (Punch 1996; Levi 1987, 1989). These crimes involve attacks on the smooth running of capitalism and (as we describe in Chapter 1) have been treated with greater solemnity by the state. Crimes involving offences against 'social regulation' (see Chapter 4) have been largely treated with less seriousness. The recent cases involving imprisonments for crimes against safety therefore provide some illustration of the type of case now being prosecuted in this way.

Thus British legal history was made at Bristol Crown court in 1995 when Roy Edwin Hill, a demolition company director, became the first person to be given an immediate jail sentence for violating health and safety legislation.

Until this case, no one had ever been imprisoned for offending against health and safety legislation – legislation which has been on the statute books since 1802. Latterly, under the 1974 Health and Safety at Work Act, there had been a couple of custodial sentences but both were suspended. Mr Hill was sentenced to three months and ordered to pay £4 000 costs.

Mr Hill had been responsible for the demolition of the former Lucas Building in Brislington near Bristol in December 1994. The factory was demolished with an excavator without any precautions being taken to prevent the spread of asbestos contained in the roofing and in pipework lagging.

Peter Kite, the director of OLL Ltd, was jailed in 1994 after being convicted of manslaughter following the death of four young people in the Lyme Bay canoe incident (NLJ [1994] 1714 and see above). He was the first director to be jailed for the common law offence of manslaughter, and this jailing was given major coverage by the print and broadcast media.

There is some evidence that the courts are taking a sterner view of those who, in the course of commercial activity, expose members of the public or employees to danger. This is especially so in cases that involve potentially lethal dangers like the asbestos in Mr Hill's case.

In April 1996, two company directors were jailed following a trial at Bradford Crown Court in which the Health and Safety Executive (HSE) prosecuted Calder Felts Limited of Sowery Bridge, under ss. 2 and 33(1)(g) of the Health and Safety at Work etc. Act 1974, and the directors under s. 37(1) of the Act (*Yorkshire Post*, 24 April, 1996).

The prosecutions followed an incident on a textile garneting machine in which a 19-year-old employee, Michael Pollard, lost his arm after becoming trapped between spiked rollers on the machine which produces fibre for the manufacture of carpet felt. His arm was torn off at the shoulder and shredded by high speed rollers when he was in a part of the large machine to clean it. Mr Pollard was employed as a heavy goods vehicle mechanic and was not supposed to be asked to do the work he was doing when the accident occurred. Additionally, a safety gate was not working so he was able to be in the machine while it was operating. It became apparent that a Prohibition Notice that had been served by the HSE on the company after the terrible incident to prevent it using the dangerous machinery until it was made safe had been flatly ignored by the company.

The HSE discovered the machines being used by the company within months of the incident in exactly the same unsafe way as they were when Mr Pollard's arm was shredded. Section 37 of the 1974 Act allows the court to impose a custodial sentence of up to six months on directors where a Prohibition Notice has been defied or ignored by their company with their consent or connivance.

In November 1996, Alan Jackson, director of Jackson Transport (Ossett) Ltd was fined £1 500 and imprisoned for 12 months on a charge of manslaughter. His company was also convicted of manslaughter and statutory offences and fined £22 000 (£15 000 of which was in respect of the manslaughter charge). The trial at Bradford Crown Court followed the death of James Hodgson, a 21-year-old employee, who was killed after being sprayed in the face with a toxic chemical while cleaning chemical residues from a road tanker. The case centred on the gross negligence that the company had shown in regard to the supervision, training and supply of protective equipment for someone being asked to perform hazardous work (*The Safety and Health Practitioner*, December 1996, p. 3).

The Company Disqualification Act 1986 provides for the court to make a disqualification order against a person convicted of an indictable offence connected with the promotion, formation, management or liquidation of a company. It was perhaps thought, in some quarters, that the conduct at which the legislation was aimed, defined in s. 2, was financial in nature. It is now clear, however, that the act will also apply in respect of health and safety matters (*Hansard*, H.C., 22 November, 1991, col. 1429–30). Speaking in the House of Lords in 1991, Viscount Ullswater said:

> In our view section 2 of the Directors Disqualification Act 1991 is capable of applying to health and safety matters ... We believe that the potential scope of section 2(1) of that Act is very broad and that 'management' includes the management of health and safety.

The foregoing interpretation of the Act has facilitated proceedings to be taken against the director of a company who, with his consent, connivance or due to his negligence, has committed an offence (Slapper 1997: 225). Accordingly in such cases, criminal proceedings are inescapably appropriate.

In many instances, however, the prosecution of individuals may be inappropriate as it ignores the corporate pressures that might have been placed upon them by the corporate structure. If the corporation is, for example, intent on cutting corners on environmental emissions, it can easily replace one irresponsible environmental director with another. Company directors may be censured and removed, but the company remains – 'as do the criminogenic forces that led to unlawful behaviour in the first place' (Moore 1987: 395). Thus even though legal sanctions (or the threat thereof) may prove effective in deterring company officials, there is no guarantee that this will translate into a decline of unlawful behaviour on the part of the company itself.

The public inquiry into the *Herald of Free Enterprise* disaster, chaired by Mr Justice Sheen, reported that '... a full investigation leads inexorably to the conclusion that the cardinal faults lay higher up on the company' (Burles 1991: 609). Whereas in this case, the wrongdoing is the result of a systems failure, prosecution of individuals seems pointless and unfair. The responsibility for the deaths lay with the company for failing to implement safety procedures. But argues Burles,

> Is it right that a company which has caused avoidable death and injury because of gross negligence spread throughout its organisation should be considered innocent just because no senior employee is guilty of the crime in his own right?

> (1991: 611)

Foerschler (1990: 1303) proposes that for the purposes of criminal liability, the subjects of inquiry should be the corporation's internal structure and decision-making processes. A corporation, she argues, can exhibit its own *mens rea* through its corporate policy. Corporate policies and acts should be attributed to the corporate structure as a whole and considered as conceptually independent from the intents of the individuals within the corporation. That is not to say, that corporate policies or acts are never reducible to the intents of individuals, but rather that they are not *necessarily* reducible. The focus ought to be on the responsibility of the company itself. Corporate liability should no longer be dependent on the finding of individual guilt.

When the true fault lies with the company, it is important to develop strategies which have an immediate and material impact on corporate criminality.

Braithwaite and Geis (1982: 307) have argued for incapacitation as a highly successful strategy in the control of corporate crime – 'capital punishment for the corporation'. This would entail the company being nationalised or put into the hands of a receiver. Alternatively, they argue for sentences which would limit the charter of a company by preventing it from continuing those aspects of its operations where it had seriously failed to respect the law.

Following Braithwaite and Geis, for the purposes of 'incapacitating' or 'rehabilitating' the corporate offender Moore (1987: 395–6) suggests for the former that a corporation may be limited in the type of economic activity or regions in which it could legitimately operate. Or a more drastic approach might entail the imposition of a 'death penalty' which could be accomplished through absolute revocation of a corporation's charter or through nationalisation. Moreover, to preserve jobs as well as the goods and services provided by the firm, the assets of the offending company could be sold or otherwise transferred to a new parent company or companies with an established record of compliance with the law.

Moore argues that his alternative strategy of 'rehabilitation' could be achieved by putting the offending corporation on supervised probation with the stipulation that it must implement stated reforms. Failure to comply could warrant other, more severe sanctions (e.g. incapacitation) to be applied. The object of internal reform, he concludes, is the same as that which *might* be accomplished by adverse publicity (Fisse and Braithwaite 1983) and is a preferable alternative to a deterrence strategy based on increased sanctions to control corporate wrongdoing through punitive means.

Fisse and Braithwaite (1988) argue strongly in favour of *corporate* criminal liability but are also conscious of the need in many cases to punish or discipline *individuals* within the corporation. As many company structures are impenetrable to outsiders they propose that companies 'activate and monitor [their own] private justice systems of corporate defendants' (cited in Clarkson and Keating 1994: 244). If an offence is proven to have been committed by, or on behalf of, a corporation, the court, if equipped with a suitable statutory injunctive power, could require the company to take internal disciplinary measures. Failure to comply with the orders of the court would result in criminal proceedings against the company and its top managers.

A shift towards greater official recognition of corporate, as opposed to individual, responsibility is marked by the contents of the Law Commission's report *Legislating the Criminal Code: Involuntary Manslaughter* (Law Com. No. 237 (1996)) in which it is recommended that there should be a specific offence of 'corporate killing' broadly comparable to 'killing by gross negligence' on the part of an individual.

If the proposals are implemented, a company would become liable for prosecution if a 'management failure' by the corporation results in death, and that failure constitutes conduct falling 'far below what can reasonably be expected of the corporation in the circumstances'. Thus, rather than use the ancient principle *actus non facit reum nisi mens sit rea* (an act cannot be criminal unless it is accompanied by a guilty mind), and require a search for at least one person with a culpable mind, the new law would judge the corporation by the results of its collective efforts.

Interestingly, the report suggests that where a company is convicted of corporate killing the judge should have the power both to fine the company an unlimited sum, and order it to remedy the cause of death. It also suggests that the offence should apply to foreign corporations operating in this country (Slapper 1997: 224).

It was reported in October 1997 (*Independent*, 2 October) that in the wake of yet another major disaster (a train accident in which seven people were killed and scores injured) the government is committed to introduce legislation along the lines of the Law Commission's proposals, to facilitate charges of manslaughter being brought against companies. It was announced in December 1998 that Great Western Trains Company Limited is to be prosecuted for manslaughter as a result of investigations into the Southall rail crash mentioned above.

Conclusion

The penological issues arising in the field of corporate crime are very important because, in simple terms, how society resolves to punish particular behaviour has many key consequences. The gravity of the punishment is supposed to reflect a real or judicially-desired level of social appropriation. Punishment levels, for that reason, can act as indicators of seriousness relevant to those responsible for policing and prosecuting. The more often, for example, that corporations have imposed on them serious sentences for recklessness resulting in loss of life or severe damage to the environment, the more that these offences will be likely to enter the public consciousness as serious crimes.

We noted at the outset that there is a significant difference between penological policy in relation to crimes against 'social regulation' as contrasted with crimes against 'economic regulation'.

For Snider, the regulation of corporate crime is a changing dialectical process and some corporate crimes have been perceived, more than others, to be against the interests of capitalism. Whilst punishments have often been notably weak and lenient in respect of companies convicted of 'social regulation' offences, they have often been quite strong in respect of 'economic regulation' offences.

Are heavy fines an appropriate way to deal with corporate wrong? We noted that, as businesses behave rationally and use cost-benefit analyses to govern their conduct, fines would be a good general deterrent if companies were certain or almost certain to be caught and fined every time they offended. The trouble is that for most types of crime committed by companies, there is only a very small chance that offenders will be prosecuted. It is very important to recognise the social and economic context of punishment.

Additionally, it has been argued that the burden of such fines may be inappropriately borne by shareholders or, if the fine affects the company very badly, by employees who are eventually made redundant, or by consumers.

Apart from the fine, several other forms of corporate punishment have been tried and proposed. Corporate probation, which has been used in the USA since 1987, has the merit that it is an 'organization-specific' sanction, and helps strengthen the legal foundation of corporate liability, and avoids the conception of company crimes as crimes committed by individuals within companies.

Another option is to imprison the particular company directors whose decisions lead to the commission of crime by a corporation. The obvious virtue of this policy is that 'when one goes down, the rest sit up' but it is perhaps equally arguable that such a penological approach will not really make an impact upon corporate crime levels because companies will always be able to find someone willing, in exchange for the right sort of remuneration, to take very high-risk decisions.

Corporate rehabilitation is seen by some as an eminently workable policy because criminogenic organisational structures are more malleable than are criminogenic human personalities. A new internal compliance group can be put in place much more readily than a new superego. One problem here though is the potentially enormous resource requirements in order to effectively monitor such work for hundreds of corporate convicts.

Enforced adverse publicity is another possible sanction but the evidence is not yet substantial that firms do actually suffer as a result of limited bad publicity. Also, there is perhaps not yet a compelling case to show how such a punishment chastens the company without causing all sorts of undesired secondary and collateral economic damage.

One final, unavoidable problem in the debate about how to punish corporations is that where they are faced with very efficiently policed and regulated work places, and where punishment for violators is seen to be almost inevitable, swiftly enforced, and heavy, some may decide to move their operations to another country, usually a developing country, with the result that it is foreign workers who get killed, foreign rivers that get polluted, and foreign consumers who get injured and defrauded (Punch 1996; Jones 1988; Slapper 1998). While it may be the case that, all things being equal, companies prefer less rather than more regulation, it is also certain that industry consistently exaggerates the threat of relocation, as a means of pre-empting tougher regulation and sanctions (Whyte and Tombs 1998).

Chapter 10

Conclusion

We began this text with a critical examination of a classic debate between Sutherland and Tappan regarding the proper definition of corporate crime, and its legitimate place within criminology. As we saw there, for Tappan, such a concept had no special place within the discipline; for Sutherland, a call for its incorporation was a call for the redrawing of the boundaries of that discipline. In many respects, this call has been largely unheeded. While we have been able to point to considerable academic work on corporate crime much of this has taken place beyond criminology; relatively little of this has been based in the UK; and this work has been relatively unsuccessful in raising many forms of corporate crime to mainstream political agendas, if indeed this was an aim. In popular and political terms, corporate crime, despite our argument that such phenomena represent a key crime, law and order problem, but perhaps because of our claim that this is in many respects a class phenomenon, remains relatively invisible. This invisibility is sustained by the lack of attempts within criminological theory to account for its incidence; and this in turn allows inadequate conceptions (and indeed practices) of appropriate and feasible modes of regulation and sanction to remain relatively unchallenged.

There remains a curiousness about the absence of academic attention to this phenomenon. Certainly in the face of lacunae in knowledge, one group to whom we might look are academics: they possesses the economic, social and technical capacities/resources to bring to the empirical and analytical fore hitherto neglected social problems. As we have indicated throughout the text, the record of academics in terms of corporate crime is not particularly impressive.

Punch has noted that there are two places within academic institutions where one might expect to find corporate crime representing an object of study, namely those places where businesses are studied and those where crime is studied (Punch 1996: 41). Neither is actually the site of much energy being devoted to corporate crime.

Punch argues that business schools tend to have strong links with business that may readily inhibit such research 'for practical and ideological reasons' (*ibid.*: 41–2). The importance of the practical is obvious. It is believed that one of the reasons behind Sutherland's decision to remove the names of offending companies and one chapter of case histories from the original version of *White-Collar Crime* was pressure from administrators at his university for fear 'of alienating some of its wealthy business contributors' (Geis and Goff 1983: x). As the era of mass higher education has reached a funding crisis, business schools increasingly employ staff sponsored by local business; they compete for tenders to train staff of such businesses, and also to attract their employees as part-time students to undergraduate, postgraduate and professional courses; they seek research and consultancy funding from such sources. This does not necessarily mean that they will not engage in or support critical research, but it does render it somewhat less likely.

Such practical issues dovetail with the effects of the ideology of business and management schools. We referred in Chapter 5 to the significance of the ideologies of business as contributing to the relative invisibility of corporate crime. It was argued that such ideologies pervade society and that particular versions of these ideologies have become dominant in the UK in the past 20 years. It is hardly unsurprising, then, to find such ideologies dominant across business schools. Yet equally significant, and slightly different, is the pervasiveness, or perhaps more accurately the conscious transmission, of ideologies *in* business. By such ideologies we mean the understanding that business is the survival of the fittest, that within business anything goes, that business is an amoral occupation where success requires at best a moral flexibility and at worst an immorality, and so on (for classic statements of this general position, see Carr 1985, and Friedman 1970). Thus values of individualism and competition are predominant. Certainly when the law is encountered within business curricula it is as something to be known, of course, but also to be negotiated or controlled; in terms expertly summarised by Box (1983), the law is classically part of the 'external environment' which provides a possible source of interference with business activities, the end and only goal of which must be to maximise profitability (Pearce and Tombs 1997). The ideologies *in* business meet, and of course cohere with, the ideologies *of* business.

Within such a value system, one which most students and academics embrace, addressing issues of corporate crime is hardly likely to be welcome or taken seriously. Certainly, as Punch has noted, there are now emerging within business school curricula small enclaves which address ethics and social responsibility, though these areas are more significant in North America and some parts of Western Europe than in Britain. Yet as he rightly goes on to argue, these are frequently seen as soft areas of, and indeed are marginal within, the overall curriculum. Such areas of concern stand in marked contrast to the real areas of business teaching (and research), namely those of finance, marketing, strategy. In these areas, business schools teach the how to do of business, and do so in a way which is characterised by theoretical poverty and an 'unreflective empiricism' (Punch 1996: 42). Any considerations of criminality or ethics are overwhelmed by the main agendas within business schools.

For these reasons, then, the 'social organisation of management studies does not usually lend itself to critical, penetrating, cross-disciplinary studies of business practice' (*ibid.*: 43).

If we turn to the work of socio-legal scholars and criminologists, we also find aspects of the economic, political and social organisation of academic study which have militated against a focus upon corporate crimes.

First, Lacey has written recently of the dominance of the common-sense category of crime is reproduced in, and under-analysed by, those working within the discipline of law (1995). Now, while criminology and sociologies of crime and criminology may provide some critique of the phenomenon of crime, there is no little irony in the fact that what is subject to critique is that which is offered by dominant construction of crime and criminality. Thus the work of academic criminologists remains partly trapped by popular definitions of the crime problem (see Garland 1994: 28–31). Levi provides an illustration of this which is of particular relevance given the focus of this text:

> The conceptual issue of what acts count as violence does not cause too many difficulties for criminologists because they usually ignore it. Almost all of the literature on explaining violent crime focuses exclusively on violence as conventionally defined.
>
> (1994: 322)

One explanation for this conceptual conservatism may be found in Garland's account of the development of criminology. Historically, he charts how this discipline, in a struggle to assert both its legitimacy and its scientificity, has sought rather eagerly to be perceived as seeking to be respectable and at the same time responsive to the powerful. This was certainly one of the issues at stake in the Sutherland–Tappan dispute; it is clearly raised sharply in the study of a phenomenon which often challenges key economic and political interests, while at times explicitly abandoning the illusions of value-neutrality (Kramer 1989).

Both a consequence of, and a further basis for, this conceptual conservatism is the fact that within criminology as a discipline, there are relatively few publication outlets for work on corporate crime. For example, Levi notes, journals 'tend to mirror the divisions in the legal process as defined by the state' (1987: xxiii). Somewhat differently, standard criminological references tend to make either little or no reference to corporate crime. *The Oxford Handbook of Criminology*, now in its second edition, and set to become a standard reference point of students in criminology and related disciplinary areas, encapsulates the degree of conceptual myopia at issue here. Certainly the text contains one essay which discusses corporate crime – though there is no little irony that a contribution organised around the discussion of 'Seven Types Of Ambiguity' should take as its highly ambiguous title *White-Collar Crime* (Nelken 1994, 1997). Yet within the other 1 200 pages and 32 essays, corporate crime barely rates a mention (with minor exceptions in the contributions by Levi 1997, Reiner 1997, Maguire 1997, Sanders 1997a and Taylor 1997). This absence extends, even more curiously, to critical criminology (Tombs and Whyte 1997). Whatever the actual explanation for this relative lack of focus amongst criminologists on corporate crime, it remains the case that criminologists *still* tend to focus relatively little on corporate crime (Punch 1996: 41).

Second, it remains the case that the majority of academic work on corporate crime remains American. This is not problematic in the sense that some of this work raises empirical, conceptual, methodological and theoretical issues of more general, that is cross-national, relevance. But it also has to be said that much of this work is context specific, with its reference points being systems of law and enforcement which are specific to US-state and federal levels; indeed, some have remarked upon its insularity (Levi 1987: xx).

Third, within existent work on corporate crime there remains a tendency to focus upon economic crimes, rather than upon, for example, safety and health crimes, or crimes against the environment. Kramer notes that 'Most of the literature on white-collar and corporate crime – and the public perception of these crimes – tends to focus on the economic effects of these acts' (1989: 149); thus he argues for the need to include physical harms (*ibid.*).

In their brief review of 'scholarship on white-collar crime', Geis, Meier and Salinger note how this history 'shows rather clearly how academic work can parallel political and social climates' (1995: 13). It is therefore unsurprising that there has hardly been any upsurge in corporate crime research either in Britain or the United States during years which have seen a reassertion of neo-liberal hegemony. Reviewing recent scholarship on corporate crime, Snider has lamented the fact that recent decades have seen the elimination of 'large chunks of the field of corporate crime' (1997: 6), partly through the removal of laws designed to regulate corporate activity, and partly through the use of funding mechanisms. Thus,

> The literature has become increasingly conservative in recent decades, the big empirical surveys and largest grants from major government and private agencies have gone to studies of occupational rather than organisational (corporate) crime.
>
> (*ibid.*)

Certainly in Britain, almost two decades of Conservative Government have seen the terrain of acceptable academic discourse shift to the Right (Hillyard and Sim 1997). One of the consequences of this shift has been to place upon even critical work a greater burden of suggesting immediate and feasible reform rather than concluding in fundamental and societal critique: immediate and feasible social reform tends not to be the consequence of corporate crime research. Furthermore, the UK has been the site of considerable reordering of relationships between academic research and sources of funding. These have largely tended to render any form of critical, partisan social science in general, and criminology in particular, less rather than more likely. Changes in the funding and the organisation of research have resulted in a greater emphasis upon utility rather than critique, towards research which is 'more focused and market driven' (Partington 1997: 23), and towards more rather than less monitoring from 'stakeholders' (Hillyard and Sim 1997). Government-funded research has become more proactive, with the greater scarcity of funding being just one of the factors that allows for a much closer specification of terms and conditions of contract research (ibid.: 56–7). The definitions of both feasible reform and utility are increasingly open to influence by those who provide funding for research. Indeed, the availability of funding affects not simply the use of the outcomes of research but the types of research that does (and does not) get done, with changing commitments of the ESRC in general, and the nature and aims of its *Governance and Regulation* theme in particular, being paradigmatic (ibid.: 54–6). In this context, the distinction between official and critical research becomes more significant (Harvey 1990).

In his attempt to 'sum up the shortcomings of British criminal justice research' in general, Sanders actually provides a concise statement of some of the more contemporary factors militating against corporate crime research in Britain:

> First, topics of short-term significance to administrators are given priority over matters of more fundamental significance. Second, and more important, the *approaches* adopted are those which are geared to the short-term interests of administrators. Research is, in 90s jargon, consumer-led. The 'consumer' is usually defined as the administrator. But even when it is the victim or suspect, as in exposé research, the problem – failure to stand outside categories defined *for* the intellectual rather than *by* the intellectual – is fundamentally the same. Finally, there is a widespread failure to subject the law to scrutiny: to see the law as both part of the phenomenon requiring explanation and as part of the explanation for the problem under examination.
>
> (1997b: 187)

One further aspect of a general socio-political shift to the Right in both Britain and North America, and which will also inhibit corporate crime research, has been a concerted effort by corporations to respond to the emergence of social activism and criticism in the late 1960s and through the 1970s. Ironically, much of this has involved invoking the law. In some respect these corporate initiatives have entailed the use of new techniques, whilst in others it has simply meant long-standing techniques becoming more evident. We have already noted Kramer's remark, to the effect that researching corporate crime means researching – and confronting – 'powerful political and economic interests' (1989: 152). Certainly corporate crime researchers and activists have always faced the real or putative power of corporations. The potential use of libel laws in the USA was, after all, one reason behind Sutherland's decision to remove the names of offending companies and one chapter of case histories, from the original version of *White-Collar Crime* (Geis and Goff 1983: x–xi). For obvious reasons, we are not able to say how much corporate crime research does not get begun or published due to perceived or actual concerns regarding libel; however, we have anecdotal evidence that such considerations are far from rare, and certainly not unique to Sutherland's self-censorship. This might particularly be the case where, as with Sutherland, corporate crime research focuses upon the world's largest (now, transnational) corporations, for these have access to enormous legal resources: as one senior manager, a publisher, put it to one of us recently, suggesting that we wish might to reconsider text regarding illegal activity by a particular group of corporations, 'you need to be careful ... there are some very large and powerful corporate interests out there'.

Indeed, if we shift beyond the relatively conservative confines of the academy, we find that when faced with charges of criminality, corporations are hardly averse to flexing their not inconsiderable muscle. Perhaps most famously, Hoffman-la-Roche confronted the whistle-blower Stanley Adams with legal action and, despite the company being found guilty of the price-fixing to which he had drawn public attention, Adams was imprisoned for industrial espionage, bankrupted and lost his wife to suicide (Adams 1984). BA's campaign of dirty tricks – a euphemism for criminal attacks and espionage – against Virgin employees is well-documented (Gregory 1994). Even more recently, there has been an upsurge in the use of Strategic Lawsuits Against Public Participation (Beder 1997; Monbiot 1997; Rowell 1996), which have been developed partly as a means of pre-empting even having to resort to libel laws, which as McDonald's found in the celebrated 'McLibel' case can be highly costly and, some would argue, ultimately counter-productive (Vidal 1997).

Each of the phenomena highlighted above is likely to make it less rather than more likely that a critical social science, let alone criminology, of corporate crime will be developed within Britain. This emerging political economy of research will influence what work is done, where it is done, how it is done, who funds it, by whom it is done, for what it is done and what ends up being done with it. This new political economy does not bode well for a critical academic assault upon corporate crime. Yet, as we have documented throughout this text, such an assault is crucial.

As authors of this text, we understand that we are engaged in a critical, indeed partisan, enterprise – a partisan scholarship. There is no need here to re-enter arguments regarding the nature of social scientific enterprise and its relationships to 'objectivity' and partisanship. Our own position – one common to many forms of Marxism and feminism – is that there is no necessary contradiction (though there may be contingent tensions) between adherence to criteria of good scholarship, or methodological rigour on the one hand, and political engagement on the other. Indeed, given the politicised nature of enquiries into corporate crime, it is far preferable that academic interventions into this sphere are openly represented also as political interventions. Certainly many of those who enter the academic study of corporate crime do so precisely from some radical perspective (Nelken 1994a) and are often open about their partisanship. Thus, for example, Ronald Kramer has famously urged criminologists to play a leading role within a social movement against corporate crime (Kramer 1989). This entails a particular conception of what being an academic means, a conception which is explicitly counter-hegemonic:

> We will have to engage in … 'sociological interventionism'; that is, we must serve as advisers to social movement groups and attempt to make visible to activists and the public the social relations that are masked and distorted by the power and ideology of the corporate system.
>
> (*ibid.*: 162–3)

Similarly an old advocate of praxis, now seemingly of little interest to most criminologists or social scientists, once remarked that 'The philosophers have only *interpreted* the world, in various ways; the point, however, is to *change* it' (Marx 1845/1968: 30).

We hope that we have stimulated, provoked, surprised and encouraged. We hope that in doing so, we have raised issues which demand further consideration throughout curricula, journals, other texts. We remain uncertain about the extent to which these issues can or will be addressed within criminology; but they are surely appropriate objects of inquiry for a critical social science. That they *are* addressed seems to us to be crucial, and one contribution that critical academics can make in the struggle for a more equitable social order.

Suggestions for further reading

Below, under the chapter headings of this book, we present some suggestions for further reading.

Chapter 1: Introduction

Cressey, D. (1989) 'The Poverty of Theory in Corporate Crime Research', in Adler, F. and Laufer, W.S., eds, *Advances in Criminological Theory*, New Brunswick, NJ: Translation, 31–55.

Friedrichs, D.O. (1992) 'White-Collar Crime and the Definitional Quagmire: a provisional solution', *Journal of Human Justice*, 3(2), 5–21.

Kramer, R.C. (1984) 'Corporate Criminality: The Development of an Idea', in Hochstedler, E., ed., *Corporations as Criminals*, Beverly Hills: Sage Publications.

Shapiro, S.P. (1983) 'The New Moral Entrepreneurs: corporate crime crusaders', *Contemporary Sociology*, 12, 304–7.

Sutherland, E. (1945) 'Is "White-Collar Crime" Crime?', *American Sociological Review*, 10, 132–9.

Tappan, P. (1947) 'Who Is the Criminal?', *American Sociological Review*, 12, 96–102.

Chapter 2: The emergence of corporate crime

Hadden, T. (1977) *Company Law and Capitalism*, London: Weidenfeld and Nicolson.

Hannah, L. (1979) *The Rise of the Corporate Economy*, London: University Paperbacks, Methuen.

Holdsworth, W. *A History of English Law*, Vol. II. London: Methuen & Co./Sweet and Maxwell.

Ireland, P., Grigg-Spall, I. and Kelly, D. (1987) 'The Conceptual Foundations of Modern Company Law', *Journal of Law and Society*, Vol. 14, No. 1, p. 149.

Leigh, L.H. (1969) *The Criminal Liability of Corporations in English Law*, London: Weidenfeld and Nicolson.

Plucknett, T.F.T. (1956) *A Concise History of the Common Law*, London: Butterworths.

Welsh, R.S. (1946) 'The Criminal Liability of Corporations', *Law Quarterly Review*, 62, 345.

Chapter 3: Mapping and measuring the extent of corporate crime

Braithwaite, J. (1984) *Corporate Crime in the Pharmaceutical Industry*, London: Routledge and Kegan Paul.

Clinard, M. and Yeager, P. (1980) *Corporate Crime*, New York: The Free Press.
Pearce, F. and Snider, L., eds (1995) *Corporate Crime: contemporary debates*, Toronto: University of Toronto Press.
Pearce, F. and Tombs, S. (1998) *Toxic Capitalism: corporate crime and the chemical industry*, Aldershot: Ashgate.
Sutherland, F. (1983) *White Collar Crime. The Uncut Version*, New Haven: Yale University Press.

Chapter 4: Counting and costing corporate crime

Box, S. (1983) *Power, Crime and Mystification*, London: Tavistock.
Cook, D. (1997) *Poverty, Crime and Punishment*, London: Child Poverty Action Group.
Health and Safety Executive (1993) *The Costs of Accidents at Work*, London: HSE Books.
Levi, M. (1993) 'White-Collar Crime: the British Scene', in Geis, G. and Jesilow, P., eds, *White Collar Crime*, Newbury Park, Ca.: Sage, 71–82.
Pontell H.N. and Calavita, K. (1993) 'White-Collar Crime in the Savings and Loan Scandal' in Geis, G. and Jesilow, P. (eds), *White Collar Crime*, Newbury Park, Ca.: Sage, 31–45.
Reiman, J. (1995) *The Rich Get Richer and the Poor Get Prison. Third Edition*, Boston: Allyn & Bacon.
Szockyi, E. and Fox, J.G., eds (1996) *Corporate Victimisation of Women*, Boston, Mass.: Northeastern University Press.
Tombs, S. (forthcoming) 'Official Statistics and Hidden Crimes: researching health and safety crimes', in Jupp, V., Davies, P. and Francis, P., eds, *Criminology in the Field: the practice of criminological research*, London: Macmillan.

Chapter 5: Crime, law and order agendas: the (in)visibility of corporate crime

Box, S. (1983) *Power, Crime and Mystification*, London: Tavistock.
Pearce, F. (1976) *Crimes of the Powerful*, London: Pluto.
Pearce, F. and Tombs, S. (1998) *Toxic Capitalism: corporate crime and the chemical industry*, Aldershot: Ashgate.
Reiman, J. (1995) *The Rich Get Richer and the Poor Get Prison. Third Edition*, Boston: Allyn & Bacon.
Slapper, G. (1993) 'Corporate Manslaughter: an examination of the determinants of prosecutorial policy', *Social & Legal Studies*, 2, 423–43.
Wells, C. (1993) *Corporations and Criminal Responsibility*, Oxford: Clarendon Press.

Chapter 6: Accounting for corporate crime: corporations and pathology

Clinard, M. and Yeager, P. (1981) *Corporate Crime*, New York: The Free Press.
Fisse, B. and Braithwaite, J. (1988) *The Allocation of Responsibility for Corporate Crime: Individualsim, Collectivism and Accountability*, 11 Sydney L. Rev. 468 at 479–508 and 511–12.
Gioia, D.A. (1992) 'Why I didn't recognise Pinto fire hazards: How organizational scripts channel managers' thoughts and actions' in M.D. Ermann and R. Lundman (1995) (eds), *Corporate and Governmental Deviance: Problems of Organizational Behaviour in Contemporary Society*, Oxford: Oxford University Press.
Hirschi, T. and Gottfredson, M. (1987) 'Causes of White-Collar Crime', *Criminology*, 25, 949–74.
Needleman, M.L. and Needleman, C. (1979) 'Organisational Crime: two models of criminogenesis', *Sociological Quarterly*, 20, Autumn, 517–28.

Passas, N. (1990) 'Anomie and Corporate Deviance', *Contemporary Crises*, 14, 157–78.

Punch, M. (1996) *Dirty Business. Explaining Corporate Misconduct*, London: Sage.

Tonry, M. and Reiss, A.J. (1993) *Beyond The Law: Crime in Complex Organizations*, London: University of Chicago Press.

Chapter 7: Accounting for corporate crime: corporations and political economy

Braithwaite, J. (1979) *Inequality, Crime and Public Policy*, London: Routledge.

Cain, M. and Hunt, A. (1979) *Marx and Engels on Law*, London: Academic Press.

Carson, W.G. (1979) 'The Conventionalization of Early Factory Crime', *International Journal of the Sociology of Law* 7, 37–60.

Carson, W.G. (1982) *The Other Price of Britain's Oil*, Oxford: Martin Robertson.

Coleman, J. (1987) 'Toward an Integrated Theory of White-Collar Crime', *American Journal of Sociology*, 93, 406–39.

Dowie, M. (1977) 'Pinto Madness' in Stuart Journal Hills, S.L. (ed.) (1987) *Corporate Violence: Injury and Death for Profit*, New Jersey: Rowman and Littlefield.

Fisse, B. and Braithwaite, J. (1993) *Corporations, Crime and Accountability*, Cambridge: Cambridge University Press.

Jones, T. (1988) *Corporate Killing: Bhopals Will Happen*, London: Free Association Books.

Pearce, F. (1976) *Crimes of the Powerful*, London: Pluto.

Vaughan, D. (1992) 'The Macro-Micro Connection in White-Collar Crime Theory', in Schlegel, K. and Weisburd, D., eds (1992) *White-Collar Crime Reconsidered*, Boston, Mass.: Northeastern University Press, 124–45.

Chapter 8: Regulating corporations?

Ayres, I. and Braithwaite, J. (1992) *Responsive Regulation. Transcending the deregulation debate*, Oxford: Oxford University Press.

Carson, W.G. (1982) *The Other Price of Britain's Oil*, Oxford: Martin Robertson.

Fisse, B. and Braithwaite, B. (1993) *Corporations, Crime and Accountability*, Cambridge: Cambridge University Press.

Haines, F. (1997) *Corporate Regulation. Beyond punish or persuade*, Oxford: Clarendon Press.

Hawkins, K. and Thomas, J. eds (1984) *Enforcing Regulation*, Boston: Kluwer-Hijhoff.

Hopkins, A. (1994) 'Compliance with What? The fundamental regulatory question', *British Journal of Criminology*, 34(4), Autumn, 431–43.

Mahon, R. (1979) 'Regulatory Agencies: captive agents or hegemonic apparatuses?', *Studies in Political Economy*, 1(1), Spring: 154–68.

Michalowski, R.J. and Kramer, R.C. (1987) 'The Space Between the Laws: the problem of corporate crime in a transnational context', *Social Problems*, 34, 34–53.

Pearce, F. and Tombs, S. (1997) 'Hazards, Law and Class: contextualising the regulation of corporate crime', *Social & Legal Studies*, 6(1), 79–107.

Snider, L. (1991) 'The Regulatory Dance: understanding reform processes in corporate crime', *International Journal of the Sociology of Law*, 19, 209–36.

Chapter 9: Punishing corporations?

Braithwaite, J. and Geis, G. (1982) 'On Theory and Action for Corporate Crime Control', *Crime and Delinquency*, April, 292–314.

Etzioni, A. (1993) 'The US Sentencing Commission on Corporate Crime: a critique', in Geis, G. and Jesilow, P. (eds), *White-Collar Crime*, Newbury Park, Ca.: Sage, 147–56.

Fisse, B. (1971) 'The Use of Publicity as a Criminal Sanction Against Business Corporations', *Melbourne University Law Review*, Vol. 8, 107–50.

Fisse, B. and Braithwaite, J. (1983) *The Impact of Publicity on Corporate Offenders*, Albany: State University of New York Press.

Geis, G. and Dimento, J. (1995) 'Should We Prosecute Corporations and/or Individuals?', in Pearce, F. and Snider, L. (eds) *Corporate Crime: Contemporary Debates*, 72–86.

Moore, C.A. (1987) 'Taming the Giant Corporation? Some Cautionary Remarks on the Deterrability of Corporate Crime', *Crime & Delinquency*, Vol. 33, No.2: 379–402.

Snider, L. (1991) 'The Regulatory Dance: Understanding Reform Processes in Corporate Crime', *International Journal of the Sociology of Law*, 19: 209–36.

Chapter 10: Conclusion

Garland, D. (1994) 'Of Crimes and Criminals: the development of criminology in Britain', in Maguire, M., Morgan, R. and Reiner, R., eds, *The Oxford Handbook of Criminology*, Oxford: Clarendon, 17–68.

Hillyard, P. and Sim, J. (1997) 'The Political Economy of Socio-Legal Research', in Thomas, P., ed., *Socio-Legal Studies*, Aldershot: Dartmouth, 45–75.

Kramer, R.C. (1989) 'Criminologists and the Social Movement Against Corporate Crime', *Social Justice*, 16(2), 145–64.

Lacey, N. (1995) 'Contingency and Criminalisation', in Loveland, I., ed., *Frontiers of Criminality*, London: Sweet and Maxwell, 1–27.

Bibliography

Aaronovitch, S. and Sawyer, M. (1975) *Big Business: Theoretical and Empirical Aspects of Concentration and Merger in the United Kingdom*, London: Macmillan Press.

Abercrombie, M.L.J. (1969) *The Anatomy of Judgement*, London: Penguin.

Abraham, J. (1995) *Science, Politics and the Pharmaceutical Industry. Controversy and bias in drug regulation*, London: UCL Press.

Adams, S. (1984) *Roche versus Adams*, London: Jonathan Cape.

Adler, F. (1996) 'Offender-Specific vs. Offence-Specific Approaches to the Study of Environmental Crime', in Edwards, S.M., Edwards, T.D. and Fields, C.B. (eds), *Environmental Crime and Criminality*, New York: Garland, 35–54.

Althusser, L. (1984) *Essays on Ideology*, London: Verso.

Andrews, J. (1973) 'Reform in the Law of Corporate Liability', *Criminal Law Review*, [1973] 91–7.

Arthurs, H.W. (1985) *Without the Law: Administrative Justice and Legal Pluralism in 19th Century England*, Toronto: University of Toronto Press.

Ashworth, A. (1991) *Principles of Criminal Law*, Oxford: Clarendon Press.

Atiyah, P.S. (1997) *The Damages Lottery*, Oxford: Hart.

Aubert, V. (1952) 'White Collar Crime and Social Structure', *American Journal of Sociology*, 58: 263–71

Auletta, K. (1986) *Greed and Glory on Wall Street. The fall of the house of Lehman*, New York: Warner.

Ayres, I. and Braithwaite, J. (1992) *Responsive Regulation. Transcending the deregulation debate*, Oxford: Oxford University Press.

Bagdakian, B.H. (1997) *The Media Monopoly, fifth edition*, New York: Beacon.

Baker, J.H. (1971) *An Introduction to English Legal History*, London: Butterworths.

Bandura, A. (1977) *Social Learning Theory*, New Jersey: Prentice-Hall Inc.

Bardach, E. and Kagan, R. (1982) *Going by the Book: the problem of regulatory unreasonableness*, Philadelphia: Temple University Press.

Barkan, S.E. (1997) *Criminology – a sociological understanding*, Upper Saddle River, NJ: Prentice Hall.

Barnett, H.C. (1982) 'The Production of Corporate Crime in Corporate Capitalism', in P. Wickham and T. Dailey, eds, *White Collar and Economic Crime*, Lexington: Lexington Books, 157–70.

Barnett, H.C. (1992) 'Hazardous Waste, Distributional Conflict and a Trilogy of Failures', *Journal of Human Justice*, 3(2), 93–110.

Barnett, H.C. (1993) 'Crimes Against the Environment: Superfund enforcement at last', in Geis, G. and Jesilow, P., *White-Collar Crime. The Annals of the American Academy of Political and Social Science*, Vol. 525, January, 119–33.

Barnett, H.C. (1994) *Toxic Debts and the Superfund Dilemma*, Chapel Hill: The University of North Carolina Press.

Barnett, H.C. (1995) 'Can Confrontation, Negotiation, or Socialisation Solve the Superfund Enforcement Dilemma?', in Pearce, F. and Snider, L. (eds), *Corporate Crime. Contemporary Debates*, Toronto: University of Toronto Press, 322–38.

Bartlett, F.C. (1932) *Remembering*, Cambridge: Cambridge University Press.

Bartrip, P. and Fenn, P.T. (1980) 'The Conventionalization of Factory Crime – A Re-assessment', *International Journal of the Sociology of Law*, 8, 175–86.

Beck, U. (1992) *Risk Society: Towards a New Modernity*, London: Sage.

Beck, U., Giddens, A. and Lash, S. (1994) *Reflexive Modernisation. Politics, Tradition and Aesthetics in the Modern Social Order*, Cambridge: Polity.

Becker, G. (1968) 'Crime and Punishment an Economic Approach', *Journal of Political Economy*, 76(2): 169–217.

Becker, G. (1985) 'The Economic Approach to Fighting Crime', *Business Week*, 28 October, 1985, p. 20.

Becker, H.S. (1963) *Outsiders*, New York: The Free Press.

Becker, H.S. (1967) 'Whose Side Are We On?', *Social Problems*, 14(3), 239–47.

Beder, S. (1997) *Global Spin. The corporate assault on environmentalism*, Totnes: Green Books.

Bergman, D. (1990a) 'Manslaughter in the Tunnel', *New Law Journal*, 3 August, 1108.

Bergman, D. (1990b) 'Recklessness in the Boardroom', *New Law Journal*, 26 October, 1496–7.

Bergman, D. (1991) *Deaths at Work. Accidents or Corporate Crime*, London: Workers' Educational Association.

Bergman, D. (1992) 'Corporate sanctions and corporate probation', *New Law Journal*, Vol. 144: 1312.

Bergman, D. (1993) *Disasters. Where the Law Fails. A new agenda for dealing with corporate violence*, London: Herald Families Association.

Bergman, D. (1994) *The Perfect Crime? How companies can get away with manslaughter in the workplace*, Birmingham: West Midlands Health and Safety Advice Centre.

Berman, D.M. (1978) *Death on the Job*, New York: Monthly Review Press.

Bernstein, B.H. (1955) *Regulating Business by Independent Commission*, Princeton, NJ: Princeton University Press.

Bibbings, R. (1996) *Managing Occupational Road Risk. Discussion Paper*, Birmingham: RoSPA

Bilimoria, D. (1995) 'Corporate Control, Crime and Compensation: an empirical examination of large corporations', *Human Relations*, 48(8), August, 891–908.

Black, J. (1997) *Rules and Regulators*, Oxford: Clarendon Press.

Black, W.K., Calavita, K. and Pontell, H.N. (1995) 'The Savings and Loan Debacle of the 1980s: white-collar crime or risky business?', *Law & Policy*, 17(1), January, 23–55.

Blackstone, W. (1769/1979) *Commentaries on the Laws of England*, facsimilie of first edition, Chicago: University of Chicago Press.

Blackstones Criminal Practice (1997), London: Blackstone Press.

Block, A. (1993) 'Defending the Mountaintop: a campaign against environmental crime', in Pearce, F. and Woodiwiss, M. (eds), *Global Crime Connections*, London: Macmillan, 91–140.

Block, A. and Scarpitti, F. (1985) *Poisoning for Profit*, New York: William Morrow.

Boisjoly, R., Curtis, E. and Mellican, E. (1989) 'Ethical Dimensions of the Challenger Disaster', in Ermann, M. and Lundman, R. (eds) *Corporate and Governmental Deviance: Problems of Organizational Behaviour in Contemporary Society* (1995), Oxford: Oxford University Press, 111–13.

Bonger, W. (1905 and 1969) *Criminality and Economic Conditions*, Bloomington: Indiana University Press.

Boris, E. and Pruegl, E. (eds) (1996*) Homeworkers in Global Perspective. Invisible no more*, London: Routledge.

Bork, R. (1978) *The Antitrust Paradox*, New York: Basic Books.

Bottomley, A.K. (1973) *Decisions in the Penal Process*, London: Martin Robertson.

Bottomley, A.K. and Pease, K. (1986) *Crime and Punishment: Interpreting the Data*, Milton Keynes: Open University Press.

Bower, T. (1995) *Maxwell. The final verdict*, London: HarperCollins.

Bowles, M.L. (1991) 'The Organization Shadow', *Organization Studies*, 12(3), 387–404.

Box, S. (1983) *Power, Crime and Mystification*, London: Tavistock.

Box, S. (1987) *Recession, Crime and Punishment*, London: Macmillan.

Box, S. and Hale, C. (1982) 'Economic Crisis and the Rising Prisoner Population in England and Wales', *Crime and Social Justice*, 17, 20–35.

Braithwaite, J. (1979) *Inequality, Crime and Public Policy*, London: Routledge.

Braithwaite, J. (1982) 'Challenging Just Deserts: punishing white-collar criminals', *Journal of Criminal Law and Criminology*, 73, 723–63.

Braithwaite, J. (1984) *Corporate Crime in the Pharmaceutical Industry*, London: Routledge and Kegan Paul.

Braithwaite, J. (1985) *To Punish or Persuade: enforcement of coal-mine safety*, Albany: State University of New York Press.

Braithwaite, J. (1989) 'Criminological Theory and Organisational Crime', *Justice Quarterly*, 6, 333–58.

Braithwaite, J. (1993) 'Transnational Regulation of the Pharmaceutical Industry', in Geis, G. and Jesilow, P. (eds), *White-Collar Crime*, 12–30.

Braithwaite, J. (1995) 'White-Collar Crime', in Geis, G. *et al.*, eds, *White-Collar Crime. Classic and Contemporary Views. Third Edition*, New York: The Free Press, 116–42.

Braithwaite, J. and Fisse, B. (1985) 'Varieties of Responsibility and Organisational Crime', *Law and Policy*, 7, 315–43.

Braithwaite, J. and Fisse, B. (1987) 'Self-Regulation and the Control of Corporate Crime', in Shearing, C.D. and Stenning, P.C. (eds), *Private Policing*, Beverly Hills: Sage, 221–46.

Braithwaite, J. and Geis, G. (1982) 'On Theory and Action for Corporate Crime Control', *Crime and Delinquency*, April, 292–314.

Braithwaite, J. and Makkai, T. (1991) 'Testing an Expected Utility Model of Corporate Deterrence', *Law and Society Review*, 25: 7–41.

Braithwaite, J. and Makkai, T. (1994) 'The Dialectics of Corporate Deterrence', paper presented at the Annual Meeting of the Academy of Criminal Justice Sciences, 8–12 March, Chicago.

Braithwaite, J., Makkai, T., Braithwaite, V. and Gibson, D. (1993) *Raising the Standard: resident centred nursing home regulation in Australia*, Canberra: Australian Government Publishing Service.

Brake, M. and Hale, C. (1992) *Public Order and Private Lives: The Politics of Law and Order*, London: Routledge.

Brazier, M. (1988) *Street on Torts*, London: Butterworths.

Brickman, R., Jasanoff, S. and Ilgen, T. (1985) *Controlling Chemicals. the politics of regulation in Europe and the United States*, Ithaca: Cornell University Press.

Bright, J. (1997) *Turning the Tide*, London: Demos.

British Petroleum PLC (1987) *Annual Report*, London: BP.

Brittan, Y. (1984) *The Impact of Water Pollution Control On Industry: A case study of 50 dischargers*, Oxford: Centre for Socio-Legal Studies.

Brodeur, P. (1985) *Outrageous Misconduct: The Asbestos Industry on Trial*, New York: Pantheon.

Brodrick Report (1971) *Report of the Committee on Death Certification and Coroners*, Cmnd. 4810 (Chairman Mr, later Judge, Norman Brodrick QC).

Brody, S.R. (1975) *The Effectiveness of Sentencing*, Home Office Research Study no. 35, London: HMSO.

Brownlee, I. (1998) 'New Labour – New Penology? Punitive Rhetoric and the Limits of Managerialism in Criminal Justice Policy', *Journal of Law and Society*, 25(3), September.

Bryant, B. and Mohai, P. (eds) (1992) *Race and the Incidence of Environmental Hazards*, Boulder, Co: Westview Press.

Bryman, A. (1988a) *Quality and Quantity in Social Research*, London: Unwin Hyman.

Bryman, A., ed. (1988b) *Doing Research in Organisations*, London: Routledge.

Buchanan, D.R. and Mason, J.K. (1995) 'The Coroner's Office Revisited', *Medical Law Review*, 3, Summer, 142–60.

Buckle, M. and Thompson, J. (1995) *The UK Financial System. Second Edition*, Manchester: Manchester University Press.

Bullard, R. (1990) *Dumping in Dixie. Race, Class and Environmental Quality*, Boulder: Westview Press.

Burke, K. (1967) *Language as Symbolic Action*, London: University of California Press.

Burles, D. (1991) 'The Criminal Liability of Corporations', *New Law Journal*, May 3, 609–11.

Burton, J.D.K., Chambers, D.R. and Gill, P.S. (1985) *Coroner's Inquiries: a guide to Law and Practice*, Coroner's Society of England and Wales: Kluwer Law.

Cain, M. (1973) *Society and the Policeman's Role*, London: Routledge and Kegan Paul.

Cain M. and Hunt, A. (1979) *Marx and Engels on Law*, London: Academic Press.

Cahill, S. (1997) 'Killing for Company', *Company Secretary*, March, 24–6.

Calavita, K. (1983) 'The Demise of the Occupational Safety and Health Administration: A Case Study in Symbolic Action', *Social Problems*, 30, 4, 437–8.

Calavita, K. and Pontell, H.N. (1995) 'Saving the Savings and Loans? US Government Response to Financial Crime', in Pearce, F. and Snider, L. (eds), *Corporate Crime: Contemporary Debates*, 199–213.

Calhoun, C. and Hiller, H. (1986) 'Insidious Injuries: Johns-Manville and Asbestos Exposure', in Ermann, M. and Lundman, R. (eds) *Corporate and Governmental Deviance: Problems of Organizational Behaviour in Contemporary Society*, Oxford: Oxford University Press.

Campbell, M. (1981) *Capitalism in the UK*, London: Croom Helm.

Carlen, P. (1992) 'Criminal Women and Criminal Justice: the limits to, and potential of, feminist and left realist perspectives', in Matthews, R. and Young, J. (eds), *Issues in Realist Criminology*, London: Sage, 51–69.

Carlen, P. and Collison, M. (eds) (1980) *Radical Issues in Criminology*, Oxford: Martin Robinson.

Carr, A. (1985) 'Is Business Bluffing Ethical?', in desJardins, J. and McCall, J., *Contemporary Issues in Business Ethics*, Belmont, Ca: Wadsworth Publishing, 3–10.

Carr, E.H. (1961) *What is History?*, London: Macmillan.

Carson, W.G. (1970a) 'White-Collar Crime and the Enforcement of Factory Legislation', *British Journal of Criminology*, 10, 383–98.

Carson, W.G. (1970b) 'Some Sociological Aspects of Strict Liability and the Enforcement of Factory Legislation', *Modern Law Review*, 33, July, 396–412.

Carson, W.G. (1974) 'Symbolic and Instrumental Dimensions of Early Factory Legislation: a case study in the social origins of criminal law', in Hood, R. (ed.), *Crime, Criminology and Public Policy*, London: Heinemann, 107–38.

Carson, W.G. (1979) 'The Conventionalization of Early Factory Crime', *International Journal of the Sociology of Law*, 7, 37–60.

Carson, W.G. (1980a) 'The Other Price of Britain's Oil: regulating safety on offshore oil installations in the British sector of the North Sea', *Contemporary Crises*, 4, 239–66.

Carson, W.G. (1980b) 'Early Factory Inspectors and the Viable Class Society – A Rejoinder', *International Journal of the Sociology of Law*, 8, 187–91.

Carson, W.G. (1982) *The Other Price of Britain's Oil*, Oxford: Martin Robertson.

Carson, W.G. and Henenberg, C. (1989) 'Social Justice at the Workplace: the political economy of health and safety laws', *Social Justice*, 16, 3.

Carter, T.S. (1997) 'The Failure of Environmental Regulation in New York', *Crime, Law and Social Change*, 26, 27–52.

Cass, V.J. (1996) 'Toxic Tragedy: illegal hazardous waste dumping in Mexico', in Edwards *et al.* (eds), *Environmental Crime and Criminality. Theoretical and Practical Issues*, 99–119.

Cassels, J. (1993) *The Uncertain Promise of Law*, Toronto: University of Toronto Press.

Castleman, B. (1979) 'The Export of Hazard to Developing Countries', *International Journal of Health Services*, 9, 4, 569–606.

Castleman, B. (1985) 'The Double Standard in Industrial Hazards' in Ives, J. (ed.), *The Export of Hazard*, 60–89.

Castellano, T. and Sampson, R.J., (1981) 'Annotations and References of the Literature on the Relationship between Economic Conditions and Criminality' in K. Danser and J. Laub, *Juvenile Criminal Behaviour and its Relation to Economic Conditions*, Albany: Criminal Justice Research Centre, 1981.

Chambliss, W. (1967) 'Types of Deviance and the Effectiveness of Legal Sanctions', *Wisconsin Law Review*, Summer 1967, 703–19.

Chambliss, W.J. and Seidman, B. (1971) *Law, Order and Power*, London: Addison-Wesley.

Chambliss, W.J. (1988) *Exploring Criminology*, New York: Macmillan.

Chartered Institute of Public Finance and Accountability (1994) *The Investigation of Fraud in the Public Sector*, London: CIPFA.

Chibnall, S. (1977) *Law-and-Order News. An analysis of crime reporting in the British press*, London: Tavistock.

Cicourel, A. V. (1968) *The Social Organisation of Juvenile Justice*, New York: Wiley.

Clark, R.D., Lab, S. and Stoddard, L. (1995) 'Environmental Equity: a critique of the literature', *Social Pathology*, 3(1), 252–68.

Clarke, M. (1981) *Fallen Idols*, London: Junction Books.

Clarke, M. (1986) *Regulating the City*, Milton Keynes: Open University Press.

Clarke, M. (1990) *Business Crime. Its nature and control*, Cambridge: Polity

Clarke, M. (1993) 'EEC Fraud: a suitable case for treatment', in Pearce, F. and Woodiwiss, M. (eds), *Global Crime Connections*, 162–86.

Clarke, M. (1996) 'The Regulation of Retail Financial Services in Britain: an analysis of a crisis', paper presented at the conference Regulation and Organisational Control, Liverpool, 20 November.

Clarkson, C.M.V. and Keating, H.M. (1994) 3rd ed. *Criminal Law: Text and Materials*, London: Sweet & Maxwell.

Clegg, S. (1989) *Frameworks of Power*, London: Sage.

Clinard, M. and Yeager, P. (1980) *Corporate Crime*, New York: The Free Press.

Clinard, M.B., Yeager, P.C., Brisselte, J., Petroshek, D. and Harries E. (1979) *Illegal Corporate Behaviour*, Washington, DC: US Department of Justice.

Cloward, R. and Ohlin, L. (1960) *Delinquency and Opportunity: a theory of delinquent gangs*, Glencoe ILL: The Free Press.

Cohen, S. (ed.) (1971) *Images of Deviance*, Harmondsworth: Penguin.

Cohen, S. (1985) *Visions of Social Control: Crime, Punishment and Classification*, Oxford: Polity Press.

Cohen, S. (1988) *Against Criminology*, Oxford: Transaction Books.

Coleman, J. (1982a) 'Power and the Structure of Society', in Ermann, M. and Lundman, R. (eds) *Corporate and Governmental Deviance: Problems of Organizational Behaviour in Contemporary Society*, Oxford: Oxford University Press.

Coleman, J. (1982b) *The Asymmetric Society*, Syracuse: University Press.

Coleman, J. (1985) 'Law and Power: the Sherman Anti-Trust Act and its enforcement in the petroleum industry', *Social Problems*, 32, 264–74.

Coleman, J. (1987) 'Toward an Integrated Theory of White-Collar Crime', *American Journal of Sociology*, 93, 406–39.

Coleman, J. (1989) *The Criminal Elite*, New York: St. Martin's Press.

Coleman, J. (1990) *Foundations of Social Theory*, Cambridge Ma: Harvard University Press.

Coleman, J. (1992) 'The Theory of White-Collar Crime: from Sutherland to the 1990s', in Schlegel, K. and Weisburd, D. (eds) *White-Collar Crime Reconsidered*, Boston: 53–77.

Conklin, J.E. (1977) *Illegal But Not Criminal*, Englewood Cliffs, NJ: Prentice Hall.

Conklin, J.E. (1981) *Criminology*, New York: Macmillan.

Cook, D. (1989) *Rich Law, Poor Law*, Milton Keynes: Open University Press.

Cook, D. (1997) *Poverty, Crime and Punishment*, London: Child Poverty Action Group.

Cooper, D. (1972) *The Death of the Family*, Harmondsworth: Penguin.

Cornish, D.B. and Clarke, R.V. (eds) (1986) *The Reasoning Criminal: Rational Choice Perspectives on Offending*, New York: Springer-Verlag.

Cosin, B.R. (ed.) (1972) *Education: Structure and Society*, Harmondsworth: Penguin.

Cotterell, R. (1984) *The Sociology of Law: An Introduction*, London: Butterworths.

Craig, M. (1981) *Office Workers' Survival Handbook. A guide to fighting health hazards in the office*, London: The Women's Press.

Cranston, R. (1979) *Regulating Business: Law and Consumer Agencies*, London: Macmillan.

Cranston, R. (1985) *Consumers and the Law*, London: Butterworths.

Cressey, D.R. (1953) *Other People's Money: a study of the social psychology of embezzlement*, Glenco Ill: The Free Press.

Cressey, D.R. (1989) 'The Poverty of Theory in Corporate Crime Research', in Adler, F. and Laufer, W.S., eds, *Advances in Criminological Theory*, New Brunswick, NJ: Translation, 31–55.

Croall, H. (1988) 'Mistakes, Accidents and Someone Else's Fault: The Trading Offender in Court', *Journal of Law and Society*, 15(3), 293–315.

Croall, H. (1989) 'Who Is the White-Collar Criminal?', *British Journal of Criminology*, 29(2), 157–75.

Croall, H. (1992) *White Collar Crime*, Buckingham: Open University Press.

Cross R. and Harris J.W. (1991) *Precedent in English Law*, Oxford: Clarendon Press.

Crump, J. (1987) 'The Thin Red Line: Non-Market Socialism in the Twentieth Century' in Rubel, M., and Crump, J. (1987) *Non Market Socialism in the Nineteenth and Twentieth Centuries*, London: Macmillan Press.

Cullen F.T. Link, B.G. and Polanzi, C.W. (1982) 'The seriousness of crime revisited', *Criminology*, 20: 83–102.

Cullen, F.T., Maakestad, W.J. and Cavender, G. (1987) *Corporate Crime Under Attack*, Cincinnati: Anderson.

Cullinan, P., Acquilla, S. and Ramana Dahra, V. (1997) 'Respiratory Morbidity Ten Years after the Union Carbide Gas Leak at Bhopal', *British Medical Journal*, v314, 1 February, 338–43.

Curran, J. and Seaton, J. (1988) *Power Without Responsibility. The Press and Broadcasting in Britain*, London: Routledge.

Cutler, T. and James, P. (1996) 'Does Safety Pay? A critical account of the Health and Safety Executive Document: "The Costs of Accidents"', *Work, Employment & Society*, 10(4), 755–65.

Daly, K. (1986) 'Gender and White Collar Crime', paper presented at Annual Meeting of American Society of Criminology, Atlanta, Georgia.

Davies, M., Croall, H. and Tyrer, J. (1995) *Criminal Justice. An introduction to the criminal justice system in England and Wales*, London: Longman.

Davies, N.V. and Teasdale, P. (1994) *The Costs to the British Economy of Work Accidents and Work-Related Ill-Health*, London: HSE Books.

Dawson, S., Willman, P., Bamford, M. and Clinton, A. (1988) *Safety at Work: the limits of self-regulation*, Cambridge: Cambridge University Press.

Deakin, S. and Hughes, A. (eds) (1997) 'Enterprise and Community: new directions in corporate governance', *Journal of Law and Society. Special Issue*, 24(1).

Dember, W. (1969) *The Psychology of Perception*, London: Holt, Reinhart & Winston.

Dentan, R. (1968) *The Semai: A Nonviolent People of Malaya*, New York: Holt, Reinhart & Winston.

Denzin, N.K. (1977) 'Notes on the Criminogenic Hypothesis: a case study of the American liquor industry', *American Sociology Review*, 42 (Dec.) 905–20.

Denzin, N.K. (1990) 'Reading "Wall Street": postmodern contradictions in the American social structure', in Turner, B.S. (ed.) *Theories of Modernity and Postmodernity*, London: Sage, 31–44.

Devlin, P. (1965) *The Enforcement of Morals*, Oxford: Oxford University Press.

Diamond, S. (1971) 'The Rule of Law Versus the Order of Custom', in Reasons, C.E., *Sociology of Law: a conflict perspective*, (1978) London: Butterworths.

DiMento, J.F. (1986) *Environmental Law and American Business: dilemmas of compliance*, New York: Plenum.

Dizard Jr., W. (1997) *Old Media, New Media: mass communication in the information age*, Longman: New York.

Doran, N. (1996) 'From Embodied "Health" to Official "Accidents": class, codification, and British factory legislation, 1831–1844', *Social & Legal Studies*, 5(4), December, 523–46.

Douglas, J.D. and Johnson, J.M. (1978) *Crime at the Top. Deviance in Business and the Professions*, Philadelphia: J.B. Lippincott.

Douglas, J.D. and Johnson, J.M. (1981) *Official Deviance. Readings in Malfeasance, Misfeasance and Other Forms of Corruption*, Philadelphia: J.B. Lippincott.

Dover Port Committee (1988) *Heroes Then Sacked Now. Why the sacked P&O seafarers must win*, Dover: Dover Port Committee of the National Union of Seamen.

Dowie, M. (1977) 'Pinto Madness' in Hills, S.J. (ed.) (1987) *Corporate Violence: Injury and Death for Profit*, Totowa, NJ: Rowman and Littlefield.

Dowie, M. (1979) 'Pinto Madness', in Skolnick, J. and Currie, E. (eds) *Crisis in American Institutions*, 4th edn., Boston: Little Brown, 4–29.

Doyal, L., Green, K., Irwin, A., Russell, D., Steward, F., Williams, R., Gee, D. and Epstein, S.S. (1983) *Cancer in Britain: The Politics of Prevention*, London: Pluto Press.

Drewry, G. (1975) *Law, Justice and Politics*, London: Longman.

Du Cann, R. (1980) *The Art of the Advocate*, Harmondsworth: Penguin.

Duff, A. (1990) *Intention, Agency and Criminal Liability*, Oxford: Basil Blackwell.

Durkheim, E. (1897/1979) *Suicide. A study in sociology*, London: Routledge and Kegan Paul.

Durkheim, E. (1893/1984) *The Division of Labour in Society*, London: Macmillan.

Dyer, C. (1997) 'Justice on the Never-Never', *Guardian*, October 17: 19.

Easton, J. (1984) 'The Climbing Boys', *New Society*, 20.12, 450–2.

Edelhertz, H. (1970) *The Nature, Impact and Prosecution of White-Collar Crime*, National Institute for Law Enforcement and Criminal Justice, Department of Justice: Washington DC.

Edwards, S.M, Edwards, T.D. and Fields, C.B. (eds) (1996) *Environmental Crime and Criminality. Theoretical and Practical Issues*, New York and London: Garland Publishing.

Eiser, J.R. and Stroebe, W. (1972) *Categorization and Social Judgement*, London: Academic Press.

Ekblom, P. (1986) *The Prevention of Shop Theft: An Approach Through Crime Analysis*, Home Office Crime Prevention Paper No. 5, London: Home Office.

Ekblom, P. (1987) *Preventing Robbery at Sub-Post Offices*, Home Office Crime Prevention Paper No. 9, London: Home Office.

Ellis, D. (1988) *The Wrong Stuff*, Toronto: Macmillan.

Engels, F. (1845/1969) *The Condition of the Working Class in England*, London: Panther.

Engels, F. (1886/1973) *Ludwig Feuerbach and the end of Classical German Philosophy*, Moscow: Progress Publishers.

Epstein, R.A. (1980) 'Is Pinto a Criminal?' 4 Regulation 15.

Ermann, M.D. and Lundman, R.J. (eds) (1982) *Corporate and Governmental Deviance: Problems of organisational behaviour in contemporary society*, New York: Oxford.

Ermann, M.D. and Lundman, R.J. (eds) (1992) *Corporate and Governmental Deviance: Problems of Organizational Behaviour in Contemporary Society*, Oxford: Oxford University Press.

Ermann, M.D. and Lundman, R.J. (eds) (1995) *Corporate and Governmental Deviance: Problems of Organizational Behaviour in Contemporary Society*, New York: Oxford University Press.

Etzioni, A. (1993) 'The US Sentencing Commission on Corporate Crime: a critique', in Geis, G. and Jesilow, P. (eds), *White-Collar Crime*, 147–56.

Ewing, K. (ed.) (1996) *Working Life. A new perspective on labour law*, London: Lawrence and Wishart.

Farberman, H.A. (1975) 'A Criminogenic Market Structure in the Automobile Industry', *Sociological Quarterly*, 16, (Autumn), 438–57.

Fagan, T. (1997) 'Risk and Social Science – why risk? Why now?', *Open D-bate*, 19, May, 13–16.

Farrar, J., Furey, N., Hannigan, B. and Wylie, P. (1996) *Company Law*, London: Butterworths.

Field, Simon (1990) *Trends in Crime and Their Interpretation*, Home Office Research Study No. 119.

Field, Stewart (1990) 'Without the law? Professor Arthurs and the Early Factory Inspectorate', *Journal of Law and Society*, 17: 445.

Field, S. and Jörg, N. (1991) 'Corporate Liability and Manslaughter: should we be going Dutch?', *Criminal Law Review* [1991] 156–71.

Fine, B., Kinsey, R., Lea, J., Picciotto, S. and Young, J. (eds) (1979) *Capitalism and the Rule of Law: from deviancy theory to Marxism*, London: Hutchinson.

Finlay, L.M. (1996) 'The Pharmaceutical Industry and Women's Reproductive Health', in Szockyi, E. and Fox, J.G. (eds), *Corporate Victimisation of Women*, Boston: Northeastern University Press, 59–110.

Fisse, B. (1971) 'The Use of Publicity as a Criminal Sanction Against Business Corporations', *Melbourne University Law Review*, Vol. 8, 107–50.

Fisse, B. (1990) 'Recent Developments in Corporate Criminal Law and Corporate Liability to Monetary Penalties', 13 UNSWLJ 1 at 1–19 (cited in C.M.V. Clarkson and H.M. Keating (1994) *Criminal Law: Text and Materials*, London: Sweet & Maxwell, 241).

Fisse, B. and Braithwaite, J. (1983) *The Impact of Publicity on Corporate Offenders*, Albany: State University of New York Press.

Fisse, B. and Braithwaite, J. (1988a) *The Allocation of Responsibility for Corporate Crime: Individualism, Collectivism and Accountability*, 11 Sydney L.Rev. 468 at 479–508 and 511–12, in C.M.V. Clarkson and H.M. Keating (1994) *Criminal Law: Text and Materials*, London: Sweet & Maxwell, 239).

Fisse, B. and Braithwaite, J. (1993) *Corporations, Crime and Accountability*, Cambridge: Cambridge University Press.

Fleming, J.G. (1983) *The Law of Torts*, Sydney: Law Book Co. of Australia.

Foerschler, A. (1990) 'Corporate Criminal Intent: Toward a Better Understanding of Corporate Misconduct', *California Law Review* Vol. 78: 1286–311.

Foley, C. (1990) *Slaughter on Britain's Building Sites*, London: Connolly Publications.

Foucault, M. (1977) *Discipline and Punish*, London: Allen Lane.

Frank, N. (1987) 'Murder in the Workplace' in Hills, S. (ed.) *Corporate Violence: Injury and Death for Profit*, Totowa, NJ: Rowman & Littlefield.

Frederick, W.C., Post, J.E. and Davis, K. (1992) *Business and Society. Corporate strategy, public policy, ethics*, New York: McGraw-Hill.

Freyer, P.A. (1992) *Regulating Big Business: antitrust in Great Britain and America, 1880–1990*, New York: Cambridge University Press.

Friedman, M. (1970) 'The Social Responsibility of Business is to Make Profits', *New York Times Magazine*, 13 September, 32–3, 122–6.

Friedrichs, D.O. (1992) 'White-Collar Crime and the Definitional Quagmire: a provisional solution', *Journal of Human Justice*, 3(2), 5–21.

Fry, M. (ed.) (1992) *Adam Smith's Legacy*, London: Routledge.

Garland, D. (1990) *Punishment and Modern Society*, Oxford: Clarendon Press.

Garland, D. (1994) 'Of Crimes and Criminals: the development of criminology in Britain', in Maguire, M., Morgan, R. and Reiner, R. (eds) *The Oxford Handbook of Criminology*, Oxford: Clarendon, 17–68.

Gautschi, F.H. and Jones, T.M. (1987) 'Illegal Corporate Behaviour and Corporate Board Structure', *Corporate Social Performance and Policy*, 9, 93–106.

Geis, G. (1967) 'The Heavy Electrical Equipment Antitrust Cases of 1961', in

Ermann, M. and Lundman, R. (eds) *Corporate and Governmental Deviance: Problems of Organizational Behaviour in Contemporary Society* (1992) Oxford: Oxford University Press, 75–95.

Geis, G. (1968) *White Collar Criminal: The Offender in Business and the Professions*, New York: Atherton Press.

Geis, G. (1975) 'Victimization Patterns in White Collar Crime', in Drapkin, I. and Viano, E. (eds) *Victimology: a New Focus. Volume V*, Lexington: Lexington Books, 89–105.

Geis, G. (1990) 'Foreword' in Green, G., *Occupational Crime*, Chicago: Nelson Hall, xiii–xv.

Geis, G. (1992) 'White-Collar Crime: what is it?', in Schlegel, K. and Weisburd, D. (eds), *White-Collar Crime Reconsidered*, 31–52.

Geis, G. (1996) 'A Base on Balls for White-Collar Criminals', in Shichor, D. and Sechrest, D.K. (eds), *Three Strikes and You're Out. Vengeance as Public Policy*, Thousand Oaks, Ca: Sage, 244–64.

Geis, G. and Dimento, J. (1995) 'Should We Prosecute Corporations and/or Individuals?', in Pearce and Snider (eds), *Corporate Crime: Contemporary Debates*, 72–86.

Geis, G. and Goff, C. (1983) 'Introduction', in Sutherland, E., *White Collar Crime. The Uncut Version*, New Haven: Yale University Press, ix–xxxiii.

Geis, G. and Jesilow, P. (eds) (1993) *White-Collar Crime. Special Issue of the Annals of the American Academy of Political and Social Science*, 525, January, Newbury Park, Ca: Sage.

Geis, G. and Meier, R.F. (eds) (1977) *White-Collar Crime: offenses in business, politics and the professions*, New York: The Free Press.

Geis, G. and Stotland, E. (eds) (1980) *White-Collar Crime: theory and research*, Beverly Hills: Sage.

Geis, G., Meier, R.F. and Salinger, L.M. (eds) (1995) *White-Collar Crime. Classic and Contemporary Views*, New York: The Free Press.

Genders, E. and Player, E. (1993) 'Rehabilitation in Prisons: A Study of Grendon Underwood', in Freeman, M.D.A. and Heddle, B.A. (eds) *Current Legal Problems*, Vol. 46, Oxford University Press.

Genn, H. (1987) 'Great Expectations: The Robens Legacy and Employer Self-Regulation', unpublished paper presented to the Health and Safety Executive.

Genn, H. (1988) 'Multiple Victimization', in Maguire, M. and Ponting, J. (eds) *Victims of Crime: A New Deal?*, Milton Keynes: Open University Press, 90–100.

Gill, S. and Law, D. (1988) *The Global Political Economy*, Baltimore: Johns Hopkins University Press.

Giordano P., Kerbel, S. and Dudley, S. (1981) 'The Economics of Female Criminality: an analysis of police blotters 1890–1976', in Lee Bowker (ed.) *Women and Crime in America*, New York: Macmillan.

Gioia, D.A. (1992) 'Why I didn't recognise Pinto fire hazards: How organizational scripts channel managers' thoughts and actions', in Ermann, M.D. and Lundman, R. (eds) (1995) *Corporate and Governmental Deviance: Problems of Organizational Behaviour in Contemporary Society*, Oxford: Oxford University Press, 139–57.

Glasbeek, H. (1988) 'The Social Responsibility Movement: the latest in Maginot Lines to save capitalism', *Dalhousie Law Journal*, 11, 363–402.

Glasbeek, H.J. (1989) 'Why Corporate Deviance is not Treated as Crime', in Caputo, T.C., Kennedy, M., Reasons, C.E., and Brannigan, A. (eds) *Law and Society. a critical perspective*, Toronto: Harcourt Brace Jovanovich, 126–45.

Glaser, D. (1978) *Crime in our Changing Society*, New York: Holt, Reinhart & Winston.

Glasgow University Media Group (1976) *Bad News*, London: Routledge and Kegan Paul.

Glasgow University Media Group (1982) *Really Bad News*, London: Writers and Readers.

GMB (General and Municipal Boilermakers and Allied Trades Union) (1987) *Hazards of Work*, London: GMB Health and Safety Publication.

Gobert, J. (1994a) 'Corporate Criminality: four models of fault', *Legal Studies*, (14) 393–410.

Gobert, J. (1994b) 'Corporate Criminality: New Crimes for the Times', *Criminal Law Review*, [1994] 722–34.

Goff, C. and Reasons, C. (1978) *Corporate Crime in Canada: a critical analysis of anti-combines legislation*, Scarborough, Ont.: Prentice-Hall.

Goldman, L. (1994) 'Accident and Absolute Liability in Anthropology', in Gibbons, J. (ed.) *Language and the Law*, London: Longman, 51–99.

Gordon, D. and Pantazis, C. (1997) 'Beyond Victimisation: towards a theory of social harm', paper presented at XXV Conference of the European Group for the Study of Deviance and Social Control, 11–14 September, Kazimierz n. Wisla, Poland.

Gottfredson, M. and Hirschi, T. (1990) *A General Theory of Crime*, Stanford University Press: Stanford.

Gould, J. (1986) *Quality of Life in American Neighbourhoods*, Boulder, Co: Westview Press.

Gower, L.C.B. (1992) *Principles of Modern Company Law*, London: Sweet and Maxwell.

Grabosky, P. (ed.) (1992) *Complex Commercial Fraud*, Canberra: Australian Institute of Criminology.

Graef, R. (1989) *Talking Blues*, London: Fontana.

Green, G.S. (1990) *Occupational Crime*, Chicago: Nelson Hall.

Gregory, M. (1994) *Dirty Tricks*, Boston: Little Brown.

Gross, E. (1978) 'Organizational Crime: A Theoretical Perspective', in Denzin, N. (ed.) *Studies in Symbolic Interaction*, Vol. 1 Greenwich CT: JA pp. 55–85.

Grunberg, L. (1983) 'The Effects of the Social Relations of Production on Productivity and Workers' safety: an ignored set of relationships', *International Journal of Health Services*, 13(4), 621–34.

Grunberg, L. (1986) 'Workplace Relations in the Economic Crisis: a comparison of a British and a French automobile plant', *Sociology*, 20(4), 503–29.

Gunningham, N. (1995) 'Environment, Self-Regulation and the Chemical Industry: assessing Responsible Care', *Law & Policy*, 17(1), January, 57–109.

Habermas, J. (1976) *Legitimation Crisis*, London: Heinemann.

Hadden, T. (1977) *Company Law and Capitalism*, London: Weidenfeld and Nicolson.

Hagan, J. (1994) *Crime and Disrepute*, Thousand Oaks, Ca: Pine Forge Press.

Haines, F. (1992) *Deaths in the Workplace and the Dynamics of Response*, unpublished.

Haines, F. (1993) 'The Show Must Go On: The Response to Fatalities in Multiple Employer Workplaces', *Social Problems*, Vol. 40, No. 4 November 1993, 547–63.

Haines, F. (1997) *Corporate Regulation. Beyond punish or persuade*, Oxford: Clarendon Press.

Haines, F. and Polk, K. (1989) *Work Death in Victoria: An Exploratory Analysis*, paper presented at the annual Australian Law and Society Conference, December, La Trobe University.

Haines, F. and Sutton, A. (1992) *Workplace Deaths, Contracts and Ambiguity: Corporate Rationalizations on Economic Reality*, paper presented at the 8th Annual Australian and New Zealand Society of Criminology Conference, 30 September, St. Hilda's College, University of Melbourne.

Hall, J. (1952) *Theft, Law and Society*, New York: Bobbs Merrill.

Hall, S. (1983) 'The Great Moving Right Show', in Hall, S. and Jacques, M. (eds) *The Politics of Thatcherism*, London: Lawrence and Wishart, 19–39.

Hannah, L. (1979) *The Rise of the Corporate Economy*, London: University Paperbacks, Methuen.

Harding, A. (1966) *A Social History of England*, Harmondsworth: Penguin.

Harpwood, V. (1993) *Law of Tort*, London: Cavendish Publishing.

Harris, D. (1984) 'Claims for Damages' in D. Harris (ed.) *Compensation and Support for Illness and Injury*, Oxford: Clarendon Press.

Harrison, K. (1992) 'Manslaughter by Breach of Employment Contract', *Industrial Law Journal*, 21, 1, 31–43.

Hart, H.L.A. (1961) *The Concept of Law*, Oxford: Clarendon Press.

Harvard Law Review (Editorial), (1987) 'Getting Away with Murder: Federal Occupational Safety and Health Administration Pre-emption of State Criminal Prosecutions for Industrial Accidents', 101: 535–54.

Harvey, L. (1990) *Critical Social Research*, London: Unwin Hyman.

Hawkins, K. (1984) *Environment and Enforcement: regulation and social definition of pollution*, Oxford: Clarendon Press.

Hawkins, K. (1990) 'Compliance Strategy, Prosecution Policy and Aunt Sally: a comment on Pearce and Tombs', *British Journal of Criminology*, 30, 4, 444–66.

Hawkins, K. (1991) 'Enforcing Regulation: More of the Same from Pearce and Tombs', *British Journal of Criminology*, 31, 4, Autumn 1991, 427–30.

Hawkins, K., and Thomas, J. (eds) (1984) *Enforcing Regulation*, Boston: Kluwer-Hijhoff.

Hay, D. (1977) 'Property, Authority and the Criminal Law', in D. Hay, P. Linebaugh, J. Rule, E. Thompson and C. Winslow (eds) *Albion's Fatal Tree*, Harmondsworth: Peregrine.

Health and Safety Commission (1996a) *Annual Report 1995/96*, Sudbury: HSE Books.

Health and Safety Commission (1996b) *Health and Safety Statistics, 1995/96*, Sudbury: HSE Books.

Health and Safety Commission (1997) *HSC Plan of Work for 1997/98*, London: HSE.

Health and Safety Commission (1998) *Health and Safety Statistics, 1997/98*, Sudbury: HSE Books.

Health and Safety Executive (1983) *Annual Report of the Chief Inspector of Factories, 1982,* London: HMSO.

Health and Safety Executive (1985a) *Deadly Maintenance. Plant and Machinery. A Study of Fatal Accidents at Work,* London: HMSO.

Health and Safety Executive (1985b) *A Guide to the Control of Industrial Major Accident Hazards Regulations 1984. HS(R) 21,* London: HMSO.

Health and Safety Executive (1985c) *Measuring the Effectiveness of HSE Field Activities. HSE Occasional Paper 11,* London: HMSO.

Health and Safety Executive (1986) *Agricultural Blackspot,* London: HMSO.

Health and Safety Executive (1987) *Dangerous Maintenance: a Study of Maintenance Accidents in the Chemical Industry and How to Prevent Them,* London: HMSO.

Health and Safety Executive (1987a) *Safety in Roofwork,* London: HMSO.

Health and Safety Executive (1988) *Blackspot Construction,* London: HMSO.

Health and Safety Executive (1988a) 1987/88, *Annual Report,* London: HMSO.

Health and Safety Executive (1989) 1988/89, *Annual Report,* London: HMSO.

Health and Safety Executive (1990) 1989/90, *Annual Report,* London: HMSO.

Health and Safety Executive (1991) *Successful Health and Safety Management,* London: HSE Books.

Health and Safety Executive (1992) 1991/92, *Annual Report,* London: HMSO.

Health and Safety Executive (1993a) 1992/93, *Annual Report,* London: HMSO.

Health and Safety Executive (1993b) *The Costs of Accidents at Work,* London: HSE Books.

Health and Safety Executive (1994a) 1993/94, *Annual Report,* London: HMSO.

Health and Safety Executive (1994b), *The Costs to the British economy of work accidents and work-related ill-health,* Sudbury: HSE Books.

Health and Safety Executive (1996) *The Costs of Accidents at Work,* London: HMSO.

Helmkamp, J.C., Townsend, K.J. and Sundra, J.A. (1997) 'How Much Does White-Collar Crime Cost?', paper presented to the American Society of Criminology 49th Annual Meeting, 19–22 November, San Diego.

Henham, R. (1995) 'Criminal Justice and the Trial and Sentencing of White-Collar Offenders', *Journal of Criminal Law,* Vol. 59, Part I, Feb 1995, 83–96.

Hidden, A. (1989) *Investigation into the Clapham Junction Railway Accident,* Cm 820, London: HMSO.

Hills, S. (1987) *Corporate Violence. Injury and Death for Profit,* Totowa, NJ: Rowman and Littlefield.

Hillyard P. and Sim, J. (1997) 'The Political Economy of Socio-Legal Research', in Thomas, P. (ed.) *Socio-Legal Studies,* Aldershot: Dartmouth, 45–75.

Hirschi, T. (1969) *Causes of Delinquency,* Berkeley Ca: University of California Press.

Hirschi, T. (1984) 'A brief commentary on Akers' "Delinquent Behaviour, Drugs, and Alcohol" what is the relationship?', *Today's Delinquent,* 3, 49–52.

Hirschi, T. and Gottfredson, M. (1987) 'Causes of White-Collar Crime', *Criminology,* 25, 949–74.

Hirst, P.Q. (1972) 'Marx and Engels on Law, Crime and Morality', *Economy and Society,* Vol. 1., 1, (February).

Hobsbawn, E. (1968) *Industry and Empire*, London: Weidenfeld and Nicolson.

Hofrichter, R. (ed.) (1993) *Toxic Struggles. The Theory and Practice of Environmental Justice*, Philadelphia, Pa: New Society Publishers.

Hoggart, R. (1957) *The Uses of Literacy: Aspects of Working Class Life With Special Reference to Publications and Entertainments*, London: Chatto and Windus.

Holdsworth, W. (1924) *A History of English Law*, Vol. II. London: Methuen & Co/ Sweet and Maxwell.

Holgate, G. (1993) 'Corporate Liability', *Solicitors Journal*, [1993] 826 (20 August).

Holroyd, J. (1993) 'Convicting Criminal Directors', *Solicitors Journal*, [1993] 1218 (3 December).

Home Office (1990) *HM Prison Brixton*, London: Home Office.

Home Office (1995) *Digest 3: Information on the Criminal Justice System England and Wales*, London: HMSO.

Home Office (1997) *Preventing Offending Children: A Consultation Document*, London: Home Office.

Hood Phillips, O. and Jackson, P. (1987) *Constitutional and Administrative Law*, London: Sweet and Maxwell.

Hopkins, A. (1994) 'Compliance with What? The fundamental regulatory question', *British Journal of Criminology*, 34(4), Autumn, 431–43.

Hopkins, A. and Parnell, N. (1984) 'Why Coal-Mine Safety Regulations in Australia are not Enforced', *International Journal of the Sociology of Law*, 12, 179–94.

Howarth, W. (1991) 'Crimes Against the Aquatic Environment', *Journal of Law and Society*, 18(1), 95–109.

Hutter, B. (1986) 'An Inspector Calls', *British Journal of Criminology*, 26, 2 (April), 114–28.

Hutter, B. (1988) *The Reasonable Arm of the Law? The Law Enforcement Procedures of Environmental Health Officers*, Oxford: Clarendon Press.

Hutter, B. (1993) 'Regulating Employers and Employees: health and safety in the workplace', *Journal of Law and Society*, 20(4), Winter, 452–70.

Hutter, B. (1997) *Compliance: regulation and the environment*, Oxford: Clarendon Press.

Hyatt, W.D. and Trexler, T.L. (1996) 'Environmental Crime and Organised Crime: what will the future hold?', in Edwards, S.M., Edwards, T.D. and Fields, C.B. (eds) *Environmental Crime and Criminality*, New York: Garland, 245–62.

Iacocca, L., with Novak, W. (1986) *Iacocca. An autobiography*, New York: Bantam Books.

International Transport Workers Federation (1987) *Relationship between Road Transport Working Conditions, Fatigue Health and Traffic Safety*, London: ITF, 133–5 Great Suffolk Street, London SE1.

Ireland, P. (1992) *Capitalist Development and Industrial Organisation*, unpublished paper.

Ireland, P., Grigg-Spall, I. and Kelly, D. (1987) 'The Conceptual Foundations of Modern Company Law', *Journal of Law and Society*, Vol. 14, No. 1, p. 149.

Ives, J. (ed.) (1985) *The Export of Hazard. Transnational corporations and environmental control issues*, Boston: Routledge and Kegan Paul.

James, P. (1992) 'Reforming British Health and Safety Law: a framework for discussion', *Industrial Law Journal*, Vol. 21, No. 2, June 1992, 83–105.

Jamieson, K.M. (1994) *The Organization of Corporate Crime*, Thousand Oaks: Sage.

Jamieson, M. (1985) *Persuasion or Punishment – The Enforcement of Health and Safety at Work Legislation by the British Factory Inspectorate*, Oxford: unpublished M.Phil. thesis.

Jervis, J. (1993) *On the Office and Duties of Coroners*, see under Matthews, P. and Foreman, J., authors of the 11th edition.

Jessop, B., Bonnett, K., Bromley, S. and Ling, T. (1988) *Thatcherism. A tale of two nations*, Cambridge: Polity.

Johnston, L. (1992) *The Rebirth of Private Policing*, London: Routledge.

Jones, K. (1982) *Law and Economy: The Legal Regulation of Corporate Capital*, London: Academic Press.

Jones, K. (1984) 'Everywhere Abroad but Nowhere at Home: the global corporation and the international state', *International Journal of the Sociology of Law*, 12, 85–103.

Jones, T. (1988) *Corporate Killing: Bhopals Will Happen*, London: Free Association Books.

Joyce, D. (1989) 'Why Do Police Officers Laugh at Death', *The Psychologist*, Vol. 12, No. 9, September.

Kagan, R. (1984) 'On Regulatory Inspectorates and Police', in Hawkins, K. and Thomas, J. (eds) *Enforcing Regulation*, Boston: Kluwer-Hijhoff, 38–64.

Kagan, R. and Scholz, J. (1984) 'The Criminology of the Corporation and Regulatory Enforcement Strategies', in Hawkins, K. and Thomas, J. (eds) *Enforcing Regulation*, 67–95.

Katz, J. (1980) 'The Social Movement Against White-Collar Crime', in Bittner, E. and Messenger, S. (eds) *Criminology Review Yearbook, Vol. 2*, Beverly Hills: Sage, 161–84.

Keane, A. (1994) *The Modern Law of Evidence*, London: Butterworths.

Keane, C. (1995) 'Loosely Coupled Systems and Unlawful Behaviour: organisation theory and corporate crime', in Pearce, F. and Snider, L. (eds) *Corporate Crime: Contemporary Debates*, 168–77.

Kelman, H.C. and Hamilton, V.L. (1989) 'Crimes of Obedience', in Ermann, M.D. and Lundman, R.J. (eds) (1992) *Corporate and Governmental Deviance: Problems of Organisational Behaviour*, Oxford: Oxford University Press.

Kelman, S. (1981) *Regulating America, Regulating Sweden*, Cambridge: MIT Press.

Kharbanda, O.P and Stallworthy, E.A. (1991) 'Industrial Disasters – Will Self-Regulation Work?', *Long Range Planning*, 24, 3, 84–9.

Kinney, J.A., Weiss, K., Sufalko, K., Gleason, A. and Maakestad, W. (1990) *Criminal Job Safety Prosecutions*, Kansas City: National Safe Workplace Institute.

Kinsey, R., Lea, J. and Young, J. (1986) *Losing the Fight against Crime*, Oxford: Blackwell.

Kiralfy, A. (1958) *Outline of English Legal History*, London: Sweet & Maxwell.

Kituse, J.I. and Cicourel, A.V. (1963) 'A Note on the Official Uses of Statistics', *Social Problems*, 12, 131–9.

Knapp Commission (1973) *The Knapp Commission Report on Police Corruption*, New York: G. Braziller.

Knightley, P., Evans, H., Potter, E. and Wallace, M. (1980) *Suffer the Children: the story of Thalidomide*, London: Futura.

Kogan, M. (1978) *The Politics of Educational Change*, London: Fontana.

Kramer, R.C. (1983) 'A Prolegomenon to the Study of Corporate Violence', *Humanity and Society*, 7, 149–78.

Kramer, R.C. (1984) 'Corporate Criminality: The Development of an Idea', in Hochstedler, E. (ed.) *Corporations as Criminals*, Beverly Hills: Sage Publications.

Kramer, R.C. (1989) 'Criminologists and the Social Movement Against Corporate Crime', *Social Justice*, 16(2), 145–64.

Kramer, R.C. (1992) 'The Space Shuttle *Challenger* Explosion: a case study of state-corporate crime', in Schlegel, K. and Weisburd, D. (eds) *White-Collar Crime Reconsidered*, 214–43.

Kreisberg, S.M. (1976) 'Decision-Making Models and the Control of Corporate Crime', *Yale Law Journal*, 85, 1091–129.

Kuczynski, J. (1973) *Labour Conditions Under Industrial Capitalism*, Vol. 2. The United States of America, London: Muller.

Labour Research (1990) 'Workplace Death – Who to blame?', *Labour Research*, Vol. 79, No. 9, p. 13.

Labour Research Department (1996) *Women's Health and Safety*, London: Labour Research Department.

Lacey, N. (1988) *State Punishment, Political Principles and Community Values*, London: Routledge.

Lacey, N. (1995) 'Contingency and Criminalisation', in Loveland, I. (ed.) *Frontiers of Criminality*, 1–27.

Lacey, N., Wells, C. and Meure, D. (1990) *Reconstructing Criminal Law*, London: Weidenfeld and Nicolson.

Lashmar, P. (1994) 'Death by Deregulation', *New Statesman*, 6 May, 16–19.

Lavalette, M. and Wright, C. (1991) 'The Cullen Report – making the North Sea Safe?', *Critical Social Policy*, July, 60–9.

Law Commission (1989), Law Com. No. 177, *Criminal Law: A Criminal Code for England and Wales*, Vol. I, Report and Draft Criminal Code Bill. London: HMSO.

Law Commission (1994a) *Involuntary Manslaughter*, Consultation Paper No. 135. London: HMSO.

Law Commission (1994b) *The Year and a Day Rule in Homicide*, Consultation Paper No. 136. London: HMSO.

Law Commission (1996) *Legislating the Criminal Code: involuntary manslaughter*, London: HMSO.

Layard, R. (ed.) (1974) *Cost-Benefit Analysis*, Harmondsworth: Penguin.

Lee, J.A. (1981) 'Some Structural Aspects of Police Deviance in Relations with Minority Groups', in Shearing, C. (ed.), *Organisational Police Deviance*, 49–82. Toronto: Butterworths.

Lee, J. and Wrench, J. (1980) 'Accident-Prone Immigrants: an assumption challenged', *Sociology*, 14(4), 551–66.

Lee, R.B. (1979) *The !King Sun: Men, Women and Work in a Foraging Society*, Cambridge: Cambridge University Press.

Leigh, L.H. (1969) *The Criminal Liability of Corporations in English Law*, London: Weidenfeld and Nicolson.

Leigh, L.H. (1977) 'The Criminal Liability of Corporations and other Groups', 9 *Ottawa Law Review* 247.

Leigh, L.H. (1985) *Police Powers in England and Wales*, London: Butterworths.

Lemert, E. (1951) *Social Pathology*, New York: McGraw-Hill.

Lemert, E. (1967) *Human Deviance, Social Problems, and Social Control*, New Jersey: Prentice-Hall.

Leonard, W.N. and Weber, M.G. (1970) 'Automakers and Dealers: a study of criminogenic market forces', *Law and Society Review*, 4 (Feb) 407–24.

Lever, L. (1992) *The Barlow Clowes Affair*, London: Macmillan.

Levi, M. (1981) *The Phantom Capitalists: the organisation and control of long-firm fraud*, Aldershot: Gower.

Levi, M. (1987) *Regulating Fraud: white collar crime and the criminal process*, London: Tavistock.

Levi, M. (1989) 'Suite Justice: Sentencing for Fraud', *Criminal Law Review* [1989] 420–34.

Levi, M. (1992) 'White-Collar Crime Victimisation', in Schlegel, K. and Weisburd, D. (eds) *White-Collar Crime Reconsidered*, Boston, Mass.: Northeastern University Press, 169–92.

Levi, M. (1993) 'White-Collar Crime: the British Scene', in Geis, G. and Jesilow, P. (eds) *White Collar Crime*, 71–82.

Levi, M. (1993a) *The Investigation, Prosecution and Trial of Serious Fraud. The Royal Commission on Criminal Justice, Research Study No. 14*, London: HMSO.

Levi, M. (1994) 'Violent Crime', in Maguire, M., *et al.* (eds) *The Oxford Handbook of Criminology*, 295–353.

Levi, M. (1995) 'Serious Fraud in Britain: Criminal Justice versus Regulation' in Pearce, F. and Snider, L. (eds) *Corporate Crime: Contemporary Debates*, 181–98.

Levi, M. (1997) 'Violent Crime', in Maguire, M., Morgan, R. and Reiner, R. (eds), *The Oxford Handbook of Criminology, Second Edition*, Oxford: Clarendon Press, 891–924.

Levi, M. and Pithouse, A. (1992) 'The Victims of Fraud', in Downes, D. (ed.) *Unravelling Criminal Justice*, London: Macmillan, 229–46.

Levi, M. and Pithouse, A. (forthcoming) *Victims of White-Collar Crime. The social and media construction of business fraud*, Oxford: Oxford University Press.

Levi, Margaret (1987) *Of Rule and Revenue*, Berkeley: University of California Press.

Lewes, G.H. (1879) *Problems of Life and Mind*, London: Trübner.

Lipton, D., Martinson, R. and Wilks, J. (1975) *The Effectiveness of Correctional Treatment: A Survey of Treatment Evaluation Studies*, New York: Praeger.

Lofquist, W.S. (1993) 'Organisational Probation and the US Sentencing Commision', in Geis, G. and Jesilow, P. (eds) *White Collar Crime*, 157–69.

London Hazards Centre (1991) *Corporate Manslaughter, Inquests and Deaths at Work*, London: London Hazards Centre.

Lorimer, R. (1994) *Mass Communications: a comparative approach*, Manchester: Manchester University Press.

Loveland, I. (ed.) (1995) *Frontiers of Criminality*, London: Sweet and Maxwell.

Luhmann, N. (1988) 'The Unity of the Legal System', in Teubner, G. (ed.) *Autopoietic Law: A New Approach to Law and Society*, Berlin: De Gruyer, 12–35.

Maguire, M. (1997) 'Crime Statistics, Patterns, and Trends: changing perceptions and their implications', in Maguire, M. *et al.* (eds) *The Oxford Handbook of Criminology, Second Edition*, Oxford: Clarendon Press, 135–88.

Maguire, M. and Ponting, J. (1988) *Victims of Crime: A New Deal?*, Milton Keynes: Open University Press.

Mahon, R. (1977) 'Canadian Public Policy: the unequal structure of representation', in Panitch, L. (ed.) *The Canadian State: Political Economy and Political Power*, Toronto: University of Toronto Press.

Mahon, R. (1979) 'Regulatory Agencies: captive agents or hegemonic apparatuses?', *Studies in Political Economy*, 1(1), Spring: 154–68.

Mann, K. (1985) *Defending White-Collar Crime*, New Haven: Yale University Press.

Mannheim, K. (1936) *Ideology and Utopia*, London: Routledge & Kegan Paul.

Marx, K. (1898/1978) *Wages, Price and Profit*, Moscow: Progress.

Marx, K. (1845/1968) 'Theses on Feuerbach', in Marx, K. and Engels, F., *Selected Works in One Volume*, London: Lawrence & Wishart, 28–30.

Marx, K. (1847/1955) *The Poverty of Philosophy*, London: Lawrence & Wishart.

Marx, K. (1859/1970) *Contribution to a Critique of Political Economy*, New York: International Publishers.

Marx, K. (1878/1949) *Wage, Labour and Capital*, Moscow: Progress.

Marx, K. (1887/1954) *Capital: A Critique of Political Economy*, Volume I. London: Lawrence & Wishart.

Marx, K. (1976) *Collected Works*, Vol. 5. London: Lawrence & Wishart.

Marx, K. and Engels, F. (1845/1985) *The German Ideology. Edited by C.J. Arthur*, London: Lawrence & Wishart.

Marx, K. and Engels, F. (1848/1977) *Manifesto of the Communist Party*, Moscow: Progress.

Marx, K. and Engels, F. (1959) *Selected Works*, Vol. 2. London: Lawrence & Wishart.

Maryon, S. (1993) 'Company cars', *Safety and Health Practitioner*, May, 4.

Mathews, P. and Foreman, J. (1994) *Jervis on the Office and Duties of Coroners*, London: Sweet & Maxwell.

Mathiesen, T. (1990) *Prison on Trial*, London: Sage.

Mathiesen, T. (1997) 'The Viewer Society: Michel Foucault's "Panopticon" Revisited', *Theoretical Criminology*, 1(2), May, 215–34.

Matza, D. (1964) *Delinquency and Drift*, New York: Wiley.

Matza, D. and Sykes, G.M. (1957) 'Techniques of Neutralization: a theory of delinquency', *American Sociological Review*, 22, Dec., 667–70.

Mawby, R. and Walklate, S. (1994) *Critical Victimology*, London: Sage.

Maxwell Atkinson, J. (1971) 'Societal Reactions to Suicide: The Role of Coroners' Definitions', in Cohen, S. (ed.) *Images of Deviance* (1971), Harmondsworth: Penguin.

McBarnet, D. (1981) *Conviction: Law, the State, and the Construction of Justice*, London: Macmillan.

McBarnet, D. (1991) 'Whiter than White-Collar Crime: tax, fraud insurance, and the management of stigma', *British Journal of Sociology*, 42, 323–44.

McBarnet, D. (1992a) 'Tax Evasion, Tax Avoidance, and the Boundaries of Legality', *Journal of Human Justice*, 3(2), 56–74.

McBarnet, D. (1992b) 'It's Not What You Do But the Way that You Do It: tax evasion, tax avoidance, and the boundaries of deviance', in Downes, D. (ed.) *Unravelling Criminal Justice*, London: Macmillan, 247–67.

McCabe, S. and Sutcliffe, F. (1978) *Defining Crime*, Oxford: Blackwell.

McChesney, R.W. (1997) *Corporate Media and the Threat to Democracy*, New York: Seven Stories Press.

McColgan, A. (1994) 'The Law Commission Consultation Document on Involuntary Manslaughter – Heralding Corporate Liability?', *Criminal Law Review* [1994] 547–57.

Meier, R.F. and Short, J.F. Jnr. (1995) 'The Consequences of White-Collar Crime', in Geis, G. *et al.* (eds) *White-Collar Crime. Classic and Contemporary Views. Third Edition*, New York: The Free Press, 80–104.

Mendeloff, J. (1979) *An Economic and Political Analysis of Occupational Safety and Health Policy*, Cambridge, Mass.: MIT Press.

Merton, R.K. (1957) *Social Theory and Social Structure*, Glencoe: The Free Press.

Michalowski, R. (1985) *Order, Law and Crime – an introduction to criminology*, New York: Random House.

Michalowski, R. (1990) 'Crime and Justice in Socialist Cuba: What can left realists learn?', a paper presented at a conference on Left Realist Criminology, 24–25 May, Vancouver, British Columbia.

Michalowski, R.J. and Kramer, R.C. (1987) 'The Space Between the Laws: the problem of corporate crime in a transnational context', *Social Problems*, 34, 34–53.

Miller, T.R., Cohen, M.A. and Wiersema, B. (1996) *Victim Cost and Consequences: a New Look. National Institute of Justice Research Report (NCJ 155282)*, Washington DC.

Mills, B. (1994) 'The Code for Crown Prosecutors', *New Law Journal*, Vol. 144, No. 6654, 899.

Mills, C.W. (1956) *The Power Elite*, Oxford: Oxford University Press.

Milsom, S.F.C. (1981) *Historical Foundations of the Common Law*, London: Butterworths.

Mintz, M. (1985) *At Any Cost: Corporate Greed, Women and the Dalkon Shield*, New York: Pantheon Books.

Mintzberg, H. (1996) 'Who Should Control the Corporation?', in Mintzberg, H. and Quinn, J.B., *The Strategy Process. Concepts, contexts, cases*, Upper Saddle River, NJ: Prentice-Hall, 391–405.

Mirrlees-Black, C. and Ross, A. (1995) *Crime Against Retail and Manufacturing Premises: findings from the 1994 commercial victimisation survey. Home Office Research Study 146*, London: Home Office Research and Statistics Directorate.

Mirrlees-Black, C., Mayhew, P. and Percy, A. (1996) *The 1996 British Crime Survey, England and Wales. Home Office Statistical Bulletin 19/96*, London: Home Office Research and Statistics Directorate.

Molotch, H. (1973) 'Oil in Santa Barbara and Power in America', in Chambliss, W.J. (ed.) *Sociological Readings in the Conflict Perspective*, Reading, Mass.: Addison-Wesley, 297–323.

Monbiot, G. (1997) 'Law and the Profits of PR', *Guardian*, 21 August.

Moore, C.A. (1987) 'Taming the Giant Corporation? Some Cautionary Remarks on the Deterrability of Corporate Crime', *Crime & Delinquency*, Vol. 33 No. 2: 379–402.

Moore, R. (1991) *The Price of Safety: the market, workers' rights and the law*, London: The Institute of Employment Rights.

Moran, L.J. (1992) 'Corporate Criminal Capacity: nostalgia for representation', *Social & Legal Studies*, 1(3), 371–91.

Morgan, P. (1983) 'The Costs and Benefits of the Power Presses Regulations', *British Journal of Industrial Relations*, (2), 181–96.

Morgan, P. (1994) 'Imprisonment' in Maguire, M., Morgan, R. and Reiner, R. (eds) *The Oxford Handbook of Criminology*.

Morris, W. (1947, 1877) *On Art and Socialism: Essays and Lectures*, London: Lohn Lehmann.

Morrison, A. and McIntyre, D. (1971) *Schools and Socialization*, Harmondsworth: Penguin.

Mueller, G. (1996) 'An Essay on Environmental Criminality', in Edwards, S.M., Edwards, T.D. and Fields, C.B. (eds) *Environmental Crime and Criminality*, 3–33.

Nader, R. (1965) *Unsafe at Any Speed. The designed-in dangers of the American automobile*, New York: Grossman.

Nagel, W.G. (1977) 'A Statement on Behalf of a Moratorium on Prison Construction', *Crime and Delinquency*, 23(2), April: 154–72.

Napier, M. (1990) 'Zeebrugge: the Way Forward', *The Law Society's Gazette*, No. 40, 7 November, p. 2.

National Institute of Justice (1993) *Local Prosecution of Environmental Crime*, Washington, DC: US Department of Justice.

Navarro, V. (1993) 'The Determinants of Social Policy. A Case-study: regulating health and safety at the workplace in Sweden', *International Journal of Health Services*, 13(4), 517–61.

Needleman, M.L. and Needleman, C. (1979) 'Organisational Crime: two models of criminogenesis', *Sociology Quarterly*, 20, Autumn, 517–28.

Nelken, D. (1982) 'Is there a Crisis in Law and Legal Ideology?', *Journal of Law and Society*, Vol. 9, No. 2, Winter, 177–89.

Nelken, D. (1983) *The Limits of the Legal Process: A study of Landlords, Law and Crime*, London: Academic Press.

Nelken, D. (1987a) 'Book Review – Without the Law: Administrative Justice and Legal Pluralism in Nineteenth Century England', *Public Law* (1987) 293–5.

Nelken, D. (1987b) 'Critical Criminal Law', *Journal of Law and Society*, Vol. 14, No. 1, Spring, p. 105.

Nelken, D. (1990) 'Why Punish?', *Modern Law Review*, 53, 829–34.

Nelken, D. (1994a) 'White Collar Crime', in Maguire, M., Morgan, R., Reiner, R. (eds) *The Oxford Handbook of Criminology*, Oxford: Clarendon Press.

Nelken, D. (ed.) (1994b) *White-Collar Crime*, Aldershot: Dartmouth.

Nelken, D. (1997) 'White-Collar Crime', in Maguire, M., Morgan, R. and Reiner, R. (eds) *The Oxford Handbook of Criminology, Second Edition*, Oxford: Clarendon Press, 891–924.

Nichols, L.T. (1997) 'Social Problems as Landmark Narratives: Bank of Boston, mass media and "money laundering"', *Social Problems*, 44(3), August, 324–41.

Nichols, T. (1984) *The British Worker Question: A New Look at Workers and Productivity in Manufacturing*, London: Routledge and Kegan Paul.

Nichols, T. (1986) 'Industrial Injuries in British Manufacturing in the 1980s: a commentary on Wright's article', *Sociological Review*, 34(2), 290–306.

Nichols, T. (1991) 'Industrial Injuries in British Manufacturing Industry and Cyclical Effects: continuities and discontinuities in industrial injury research', *Sociological Review*, 39(1), 131–9.

Nichols, T. (1997) *The Sociology of Industrial Injury*, London: Mansell.

Norrie, A. (1993) *Crime, Reason and History*, London: Weidenfeld and Nicolson.

Office of Population and Surveys (1987) *Occupational Mortality, Decennial Supplement parts 1 and 2, 1979–80, 1982–3*, London: HMSO.

Ogus, A. (1994) *Regulation, Law and Economic Theory*, Oxford: Clarendon.

O'Malley, P. (1987) 'In Place of Criminology: a Marxist Reformulation', paper presented to the Annual Meeting of the Canadian Sociology and Anthropology Association, 2–5 June, Hamilton, Ontario.

Organisation for Economic Co-operation and Development (1980) *Occupational Accidents in OECD Countries*, July, Paris: Employment Outlook.

Organisation for Economic Co-operation and Development (1989) *Occupational Accidents in OECD Countries*, July, Paris: OECD.

Paehlke, R. (1995) 'Environmental Harm and Corporate Crime', in Pearce, F. and Snider, L. (eds) *Corporate Crime: Contemporary Debates*, 87–108.

Palast, G. (1998) 'How a Few Little Piggies Tried to Rig the Market', *Observer*, 25 October.

Palmer, J. (1976) 'Evils Merely Prohibited', *British Journal of Law and Society*, 3(1), 1–16.

Parsons, T. and Bales, R.F. (1956) *Family: Socialization and Interaction Process*, London: Routledge and Kegan Paul.

Partington, M. (1997) 'Socio-Legal Research in Britain: shaping the funding environment', in Thomas, P. (ed.) *Socio-Legal Studies*, Aldershot: Dartmouth, 23–44.

Pashukanis, E.B. (1924/1983) *Law and Marxism – A General Theory*, London: Pluto Press.

Passas, N. (1990) 'Anomie and Corporate Deviance', *Contemporary Crises*, 14, 157–78.

Passas, N. (1996) 'The Genesis of the BCCI Scandal', in Levi, M. and Nelken, D. (eds) *The Corruption of Politics and the Politics of Corruption*, Oxford: Basil Blackwell, 57–72.

Passas, N. and Nelken, D. (1993) 'The Thin Line Between Legitimate and Criminal Enterprise: subsidy frauds in the European Community', *Crime, Law and Social Change*, 19, 223–43.

Paulus, I. (1974) *The Search for Pure Food: a Sociology of Legislation in Britain*, London: Martin Robertson.

Peacock, A. (ed.) (1984) *The Regulation Game: how British and West German companies bargain with Government*, Oxford: Basil Blackwell.

Pearce, F. (1976) *Crimes of the Powerful*, London: Pluto.

Pearce, F. (1989) *The Radical Durkheim*, London: Unwin Hyman.

Pearce, F. (1990a) 'Responsible Corporations and Regulatory Agencies', *Political Quarterly*, 61(4).

Pearce, F. (1990b) *Second Islington Crime Survey. Commercial and conventional crime in Islington*, Middlesex: Centre for Criminology, Middlesex Polytechnic and Queens University Ontario.

Pearce, F. and Snider, L. (1995) 'Regulating Capitalism', in Pearce, F. and Snider, L. (eds) *Corporate Crime. Contemporary Debates*, Toronto: University of Toronto Press, 19–47.

Pearce, F. and Snider, L. (eds) (1995) *Corporate Crime: Contemporary Debates*, Toronto: University of Toronto Press.

Pearce, F. and Tombs, S. (1989) 'Bhopal, Union Carbide and the Hubris of a Capitalist Technocracy', *Social Justice*, 16, June, 116–45.

Pearce, F. and Tombs, S. (1990) 'Ideology, Hegemony and Empiricism: Compliance Theories of Regulation', *British Journal of Criminology*, 30(4), 423–43.

Pearce, F. and Tombs, S. (1991) 'Policing Corporate "Skid Rows". A reply to Keith Hawkins', *British Journal of Criminology*, 31(4), 415–26.

Pearce, F. and Tombs, S. (1992) 'Realism and Corporate Crime', in Matthews, R. and Young, J. (eds) *Issues in Realist Criminology*, London: Sage.

Pearce, F. and Tombs, S. (1993) 'US Capital versus the Third World: Union Carbide and Bhopal', in Pearce, F. and Woodiwiss, M. (eds) *Global Crime Connections*, London: Macmillan.

Pearce, F. and Tombs, S. (1994) 'Class, Law, and Hazards', paper submitted to *The Permanent Peoples' Tribunal (Industrial Hazards and Human Rights)* 28 November–2 December, London.

Pearce, F. and Tombs, S. (1997) 'Hazards, Law and Class: contextualising the regulation of corporate crime', *Social & Legal Studies*, 6(1), 79–107.

Pearce, F. and Tombs, S. (1998) *Toxic Capitalism: corporate crime and the chemical industry*, Aldershot: Ashgate.

Pearce, F. and Woodiwiss, M. (eds) (1993) *Global Crime Connections*, London: Macmillan.

Pennington, R. (1995) *Company Law*, London: Butterworths.

Peppin, P. (1995) 'Science, Law and the Pharmaceutical Industry', in Pearce, F. and Snider, L. (eds) *Corporate Crime: Contemporary Debates*, 87–108.

Perry, S. and Dawson, J. (1985) *Nightmare: women and the Dalkon Shield*, New York: Macmillan.

Plucknett, T.F.T. (1956) *A Concise History of the Common Law*, London: Butterworths.

Pontell, H.N. and Calavita, K. (1993) 'White-Collar Crime in the Savings and Loan Scandal', in Geis, G. and Jesilow, P. (eds) *White Collar Crime*, Newbury Park, Ca: Sage.

Posner, R.A. (1972) *Economic Analysis of Law*, Boston: Little, Brown & Company.

Powis, D. (1977) *The Signs of Crime: A Field Manual For Police*, London: McGraw-Hill.

Prosser, T. (1997) *Law and the Regulators*, Oxford: Clarendon.

Proudhon, P.-J. (1840 and 1966) *Qu'est-ce que la propriété/ou recherches sur le principe du droit et du gouvernement, premier mêmoire*, Paris: Garnier-Flammarion.

Punch, M. (1996) *Dirty Business. Explaining Corporate Misconduct*, London: Sage.

Quinney, R. (1970) *The Social Reality of Crime*, Boston: Little, Brown.

Radzinowicz, L. (1948) *A History of English Criminal Law*, Vol. 1. London: Stevens.

Randall, D. (1995) 'The Portayal of Business Malfeasance in the Elite and General Media', in Geis, G., *et al.* (eds) *White-Collar Crime*, 105–15.

Reasons, C., Ross, L., and Paterson, C. (1981) *Assault on the Worker: occupational health and safety in Canada*, Toronto: Butterworths.

Reed, M. (1989) *The Sociology of Management*, New York: Harvester Wheatsheaf.

Reed, M. (1992) *The Sociology of Organisations*, Hemel Hempstead: Harvester Wheatsheaf.

Reichman, N. (1993) 'Insider Trading', in Tonry, M. and Reiss, A. (eds) *Beyond the Law: Crime in Complex Organisations*, Chicago: University of Chicago Press.

Reiman, J.H. (1979) *The Rich Get Richer and the Poor Get Prison. Ideology, class, and criminal justice*, New York: John Wiley & Sons.

Reiman, J. (1995) *The Rich Get Richer and the Poor Get Prison. Third Edition*, Boston: Allyn & Bacon.

Reiner, R. (1978) *The Blue-Coated Worker*, Cambridge: Cambridge University Press.

Reiner, R. (1985) *The Politics of the Police*, Brighton: Wheatsheaf.

Reiner, R. (1988) 'British Criminology and the State', *British Journal of Criminology* Vol. 28, No. 2, 138–59.

Reiner, R. (1991) *Chief Constables*, Oxford: Oxford University Press.

Reiner, R. (1994) 'Policing and the Police', in Maguire, M., Morgan, R., Reiner, R. *The Oxford Handbook of Criminology*, Oxford: Clarendon Press.

Reiner, R. (1996) 'The Case of the Missing Crimes', in Levitas, R. and Guy, W. (eds) *Interpreting Official Statistics*, London: Routledge, 185–205.

Reiner, R. (1997) 'Media Made Criminality: the representation of crime in the mass media', in Maguire, M., *et al.* (eds) *The Oxford Handbook of Criminology, Second Edition*, 189–231.

Reiss, A. Jnr. and Biderman, A. (1980) *Data Sources on White-Collar Law-Breaking*, Washington, DC: US Department of Justice.

Reuter, P. (1993) 'The Cartage Industry in New York', in Tonry, M. and Reiss, A. (eds) *Beyond the Law: Crime in Complex Organisations*, Chicago: University of Chicago Press.

Reville, N. (1989) 'Corporate Manslaughter', *Law Society's Gazette*, 19 October.

Richardson, G. and Ogus, A. (1979) 'The Regulatory Approach to Environmental Control', *Urban Law and Policy*, 2, 337–57.

Richardson, G. with Ogus, A. and Burrows, P. (1983) *Policing Pollution*, Oxford: Clarendon.

Ridgway, J. (1980) *Who Owns the Earth*, London: Collier Macmillan.

Robens (Lord) (1972) *Safety and Health at Work*. Report of the Committee (1970–72), Cmnd. 5034. London: HMSO.

Rodino, P.W. Jnr. (1978) *Testimony*. Subcommittee on Crime, White-Collar Crime. Hearings, 21 June, 12 July, 1 December, 1978. US House of Representatives, Committees of the Judiciary, Washington DC.

Roshier, B. and Teff, H. (1980) *Law and Society in England*, London: Tavistock Publications.

Ross, D. (1996) 'A Review of EPA Criminal, Civil, and Administrative Enforcement Data: are the efforts measurable deterrents to environmental criminals?', in Edwards *et al.* (eds) *Environmental Crime and Criminality. Theoretical and Practical Issues*, 55–76.

Ross, E.A. (1907) 'The Criminaloid', *Atlantic Monthly*, 99 January, 44–50, reprinted in Geis, G. and Meier, R.F. (eds) *White-Collar Crime: Offenses in Business, Politics, and the Professions*, New York: The Free Press.

Ross, I. (1980) 'How Lawless are Big Corporations?', *Fortune*, December, 55–61.

Roth, I. and Frisby, J. (1989) *Perception and Representation: A Cognitive Approach*, Milton Keynes: Open University Press.

Rowan-Robinson, J., Watchman, P. and Barker, C.R. (1990) *Crime and Regulation: A Study of the Enforcement of Regulatory Codes*, Edinburgh: T & T Clark.

Rowell, A. (1996) *Green Backlash. Corporate Subversion of the Environment Movement*, London: Routledge.

Royal Commission on Environmental Pollution (1995) *Eighteenth Report. Transport and the Environment*, Oxford: Oxford University Press.

Royal Institute of Naval Architects (1986) *The Technical Investigation of the Sinking of the Ro-Ro Ferry European Gateway*, London: RINA.

Royal Society for the Prevention of Accidents (1997a) *Managing Occupational Road Risk. Campaign Update 12th March*, Birmingham: RoSPA.

Royal Society for the Prevention of Accidents (1997b) *Managing Occupational Road Risk. Campaign Update 12th April*, Birmingham: RoSPA.

Royal Society for the Prevention of Accidents (1998) *Managing Occupational Road Risk*, Birmingham: RoSPA.

Ruggiero, V. (1993) 'The *Camorra*: "clean" capital and organised crime', in Pearce, F. and Woodiwiss, M. (eds) *Global Crime Connections*, London: Macmillan, 141–61.

Ruggiero, V. (1996) *Organised and Corporate Crime in Europe. Offers that can't be refused*, Aldershot: Dartmouth.

Ruggiero, V. (1998) 'Review. Maurice Punch, Dirty Business', *Theoretical Criminology*, 2(1), February, 123–5.

Rutherford, A. (1993) *Criminal Justice and the Pursuit of Decency*, Oxford: Oxford University Press.

Sanders, A. (1985) 'Class Bias in Prosecutions', *Howard Journal*, 24, 3, August, 176–99.

Sanders, A. (1994) 'Judicial Statistics', *New Law Journal*, Vol. 144. No. 6655, p. 946.

Sanders, A. (1997a) 'From Suspect to Trial', in Maguire, M., *et al.* (eds) *The Oxford Handbook of Criminology, Second Edition*, 1051–93.

Sanders, A. (1997b) 'Criminal Justice: the development of criminal justice research in Britain', in Thomas, P. (ed.) *Socio-Legal Studies*, Aldershot: Dartmouth, 185–205.

Scheppele, K.L. (1991) 'Law Without Accidents', in Bordieu, P. and Coleman, J.S. (eds) *Social Theory for a Changing Society*, Boulder: Westview, 267–93.

Schlegel, K. and Weisburd, D. (eds) (1992) *White-Collar Crime Reconsidered*, Boston, Mass.: Northeastern University Press.

Schlesinger, P. and Tumber, H. (1994) *Reporting Crime. The Media Politics of Criminal Justice*, Oxford: Clarendon.

Schmalleger, F. (1996) *Criminology Today*, Englewood Cliffs, NJ: Prentice-Hall.

Schrager, L.S. and Short, J.F. (1977) 'Towards a Sociology of Organisational Crime', *Social Problems*, 25, 407–19.

Scott, C. (1995) 'Criminalising the Trader to Protect the Consumer: the fragmentation and consolidation of trading standards regulation', in Loveland, I. (ed.) *Frontiers of Criminality*, 149–72.

Scottish Office Statistical Bulletin (1995) *Homicide in Scotland, 1984–1994*, Edinburgh: Scottish Office Central Statistics Office.

Scraton, P. (1984) 'The Coroner's Tale', in Scraton, P. and Gordon, P. (eds) *Causes for Concern*, Harmondsworth: Penguin.

Seib, G.F. (1978) 'Dallas Ordinance against Car Repair Frauds', in Johnson, J.M. and Douglas, J.D. (eds) 1978, *Crime at the Top*, Philadelphia: J.B. Lippincott Company, 319–22.

Seigart, P. (1980) *Breaking the Rules*, London: Justice.

Serious Fraud Office (1989) *First Annual Report From 6 April 1988 to 4 April 1989*, London: HMSO.

Serious Fraud Office (1990) *Annual Report From 5 April 1989 to 4 April 1990*, London: HMSO.

Serious Fraud Office (1991) *Annual Report From 5 April 1990 to 4 April 1991*, London: HMSO.

Serious Fraud Office (1992) *Annual Report 91–92*, London: HMSO.

Serious Fraud Office (1995) *Annual Report 94–95*, London: HMSO.

Serious Fraud Office (1996) *Annual Report 95–96*, London: HMSO.

Serious Fraud Office (1997) *Annual Report 96–97*, London: HMSO.

Shapiro, S.P. (1983) 'The New Moral Entrepreneurs: corporate crime crusaders', *Contemporary Sociology*, 12, 304–7.

Shapiro, S.P. (1984) *Wayward Capitalists. Target of the Securities and Exchange Commission*, New Haven: Yale University Press.

Shapiro, S. (1985) 'The Road Not Taken: the elusive path to criminal prosecution for white-collar offenders', *Law and Society Review*, 19, 179–217.

Shapiro, S. (1987) 'The Social Control of Impersonal Trust', *American Journal of Sociology*, 93, 623–58.

Shapiro, S.P. (1990) 'Collaring the Crime, Not the Criminal: reconsidering the concept of white-collar crime', *American Sociological Review*, 55, 346–65.

Sheehy, P. (1993) *Inquiry into Police Responsibilities and Rewards*, Vols 1 and 2. Cm 2280.I, London: HMSO.

Sherman, L. (1982) 'Deviant Organizations', in Ermann, D. and Lundman, R. (eds) *Corporate and Governmental Deviance*, New York: Oxford University Press.

Simon, D.R. and Eitzen, D.S. (1986) *Elite Deviance*, Toronto: Allyn and Bacon.

Simpson, S. (1987) 'Cycles of Illegality: antitrust violations in corporate America', *Social Forces*, 65, 943–63.

Sinden, P. (1980) 'Perception of Crime in Capitalist America: the question of consciousness manipulation', *Sociological Focus*, 13, 75–85.

Slapper, G. (1992a) 'Corporate Manslaughter: the difficulties posed by current law', in *Criminal Lawyer*, No. 26, 5.

Slapper, G. (1992b) Glogg v. South Coast Shipping Co. Ltd. and others (February) Casenote, *Solicitors Journal*, Vol. 136, No. 7, 156.

Slapper, G. (1992c) 'The Marchioness case: Judicial Review', *Solicitors Journal* 136, No. 25, p. 161.

Slapper, G. (1992d) 'A Safe Place to Work', *Law Society Gazette*, No. 38, 23–5.

Slapper, G. (1992e) 'Where the Buck Stops', *New Law Journal*, Vol. 144, 1037–8.

Slapper, G. (1993a) 'Manslaughter and Civil Negligence', *Professional Negligence*. Vol. 4. No. 9, 52.

Slapper, G. (1993b) 'Corporate Manslaughter: An Examination of the Determinants of Prosecutorial Policy', *Social and Legal Studies*, Vol. 2, 423–43.

Slapper, G. (1994a) 'Manslaughter, Mens Rea and Medicine', *New Law Journal*, Vol. 144, No. 6655, 941.

Slapper, G. (1994b) 'Corporate Punishment', *New Law Journal*, Vol. 144, 29.

Slapper, G. (1994c) 'Companies, Crime and Punishment', *Business Law Review*, 126, May.

Slapper, G. (1994d) 'Fault lines in Kingston', *New Law Journal*, Vol. 144, 1232, 16 September.

Slapper, G. (1994e) 'A Year and a Day', *New Law Journal*, Vol. 144, 748.

Slapper, G. (1994f) 'A Corporate Killing', *New Law Journal*, Vol. 144, No. 6676, 1714.

Slapper, G. (1995) *Companies in the 1990s*, London: Cavendish Publishing.

Slapper, G. (1996) 'Murder: however long it takes', *The Times* (Law) 20 August 1996, p. 36.

Slapper, G. (1997) 'Litigation and Corporate Crime', *Journal of Personal Injury Litigation*, Issue 4/97, 220–33.

Slapper, G. (1998) 'Dangerous Product Litigation', *New Law Journal* [1998], 345–7.

Slapper, G. (1999) *Blood in the Bank*, Aldershot: Ashgate.

Smart, C. (1995) *Law, Crime and Sexuality. Essays in Feminism*, London: Sage.

Smith, A. (1776/1976) *An Inquiry into the Nature and Causes of the Wealth of Nations*, Vol. 1. The Glasgow Edition ed. R.H. Campbell and A.S. Skinner. Indianapolis: Liberty Press.

Smith, D. and Gray, J. (1985) *Police and People in London*, Aldershot: Gower.

Smith, D. and Tombs, S. (1995) 'Beyond Self-Regulation: towards a critique of self regulation as a control strategy for hazardous activities', *Journal of Management Studies*, 32(5) 619–36.

Smith, J. C. and Hogan, B. (1996) *Criminal Law*, London: Butterworths.

Smith, N. Craig (1990) *Morality and the Market*, London: Routledge.

Smith, R. (1994) 'Judicial Statistics', *New Law Journal*, Vol. 144, No. 6659, 1088.

Snider, L. (1987) 'Towards a Political Economy of Reform, Regulation and Corporate Crime', *Law & Policy*, 9(1), 37–68.

Snider, L. (1990) 'Co-operative Models and Corporate Crime: panacea or cop-out?', *Crime and Delinquency*, 36, 373–91.

Snider, L. (1991) 'The Regulatory Dance: understanding reform processes in corporate crime', *International Journal of the Sociology of Law*, 19, 209–36.

Snider, L. (1992) 'Commercial Crime', in Sacco, V. (ed.) *Deviance, Conformity and Control in Canadian Society*, Toronto: Prentice Hall.

Snider, L. (1993a) *Bad Business. Corporate Crime in Canada*, Toronto: University of Toronto Press.

Snider, L. (1993b) 'The Politics of Corporate Crime Control', in Pearce, F. and Woodiwiss, M. (eds) *Global Crime Connections*, London: Macmillan, 212–39.

Snider, L. (1997) 'Downsizing, Deregulation and Corporate Crime', paper presented to the Annual Meeting of the American Society of Criminology, 19–22 November, San Diego.

Social Justice. Varieties of State and Corporate Crime, 16, 2, Summer 1989.

South, N. (1998) 'Corporate and State Crimes Against the Environment: foundations for a Green perspective in European criminology', in Ruggiero, V., South, N. and Taylor, I. (eds) *European Criminology: crime and social order in Europe*, London: Routledge.

Sparks, R. (1978) *Testimony*. Subcommittee on Crime, White-Collar Crime. Hearings, 21 June, 12 July, 1 December, 1978. US House of Representatives, Committee of the Judiciary, Washington DC.

Start, R.D., Delargy-Aziz, Y., Dorries, C.P., Silcocks, P.B. and Cotton, D.W.K. (1993) 'Clinicians and the Coronial System: Ability of Clinicians to Recognise Reportable Deaths', *British Journal of Medicine*, Vol. 306, 1038.

Start, R.D., Usherwood, T.P., Carter, N., Dorries, C.P. and Cotton, D.W.K. (1995) 'General Practitioner's knowledge of when to refer deaths to a coroner', *British Journal of General Practice*, 45, 191–3.

Steffensmeier, D. (1987) 'Update on Male-Female Arrest Patterns', Paper presented to the Annual Meeting of the American Society of Criminology, Montreal.

Steffensmeier, D. (1989) 'On the Causes of "White-Collar" Crime: an analysis of Hirschi and Gottfredson's Claims', *Criminology*, 27, 345–58.

Stephen, J.F. (1883) *A History of the Criminal Law of England*, London: Macmillan.

Stephenson-Burton, A. (1995) 'Through the Looking Glass: public images of white-collar crime', in Kidd-Hewitt, D. and Osborne, R. (eds) *Crime and the Media*, London: Pluto, 131–63.

Stessens, G. (1994) 'Corporate Criminal Liability: A Comparative Perspective', *International and Comparative Law Quarterly*, Vol. 43, 493–520.

Stevens, G. (1992) 'Workplace Injury: a view from HSE's trailer to the 1990 Labour Force Survey', *Employment Gazette*, December, 621–38.

Stinchcombe, A. (1963) 'Institutions of Privacy in the Determination of Police Administrative Practice', *American Journal of Sociology*, 69/2: 150–60.

Stockdale, E. and Casale, S. (1992) *Criminal Justice Under Stress*, London: Blackstone.

Stone, D.G. (1991) *April Fools. An insider's account of the rise and collapse of Drexel Burnham*, New York: Warner.

Strange, K.H. (1982) *The Climbing Boys 1773–1875*, London: Alison Busby.

Stretesky, P. and Lynch, M. (1997) 'Class Structure and Predictions of Distance to Accidental Chemical Releases: spatial geography, urban justice and chaotic strange attractors', paper presented at the Annual Meeting of the American Society of Criminology, 19–22 November, San Diego.

Sullivan, R.F. (1973) 'The Economics of Crime: An Introduction to the Literature', *Crime and Delinquency*, 19(2) 138–49.

Sumner, C. (1994) *The Sociology of Deviance. An Obituary*, Buckingham: Open University Press.

Sutherland E. (1940), White-collar criminality, *American Sociological Review*, 5: 1–12.

Sutherland, E. (1945) 'Is "White-Collar Crime" Crime?', *American Sociological Review*, 10, 132–9.

Sutherland, E. (1947) *Criminology*, Philadelphia: Lippincott.

Sutherland, E. (1949) *White-Collar Crime*, New York: Holt, Reinhart & Winston.

Sutherland, E. (1983) *White Collar Crime. The Uncut Version*, New Haven: Yale University Press.

Sutherland, E. and Cressey, D. (1966) *Principles of Criminology*, Philadelphia: Lippincott.

Sutton, A. and Wild, R. (1985) 'Small Businesses: white-collar villains or victims?', *International Journal of the Sociology of Law*, 13, 3, 247–59.

Swigert, V.L. and Farrell, R.A. (1980–81) 'Corporate Homicide: definitional processes in the creation of deviance', *Law & Society Review*, 15(1), 161–82.

Szasz, A. (1984) 'Industrial Resistance to Occupational Safety and Health Legislation 1971–1981', *Social Problems*, 32(2), 103–16.

Szasz, A. (1986a) 'The Reversal of Federal Policy Toward Worker Safety and Health: a critical examination of alternative explanations', *Science and Society*, 50, 25–51.

Szasz, A. (1986b) 'The Process and Significance of Political Scandals: A Comparison of Watergate and the "Sewergate" Episode at the Environmental Protection Agency', *Social Problems*, 33(3), 202–17.

Szasz, A. (1986c) 'Corporations, Organized Crime and the Disposal of Hazardous Waste: The Making of a Criminogenic Regulatory Structure', *Criminology*, 24(1), 103–61.

Szasz, A. (1994) *Ecopopulism. Toxic waste and the movement for environmental justice*, Minneapolis: University of Minnesota Press.

Szockyi, E. (1993) *The Law and Insider Trading: in search of a level playing field*, Buffalo, NY: Hein.

Szockyi, E. and Fox, J.G. (eds) (1996) *Corporate Victimisation of Women*, Boston, Mass.: Northeastern University Press.

Szockyi, E. and Frank, N. (1996) 'Introduction', in Szockyi, E. and Fox, J.G. (eds) *Corporate Victimisation of Women*, 3–32.

T&G (1997) *Rogue Haulage*, Leeds: T&G North and North East Region.

Taft, D. (1966) 'Influence of the General Culture on Crime', *Federal Probation*, 30, Sept. 16–24.

Tappan, P. (1947) 'Who Is the Criminal?', *American Sociological Review*, 12, 96–102.

Taylor, I. (1981) *Law and Order: Arguments for Socialism*, London: Macmillan.

Taylor, I. (1997) 'The Political Economy of Crime', in Maguire, M. *et al.* (eds) *The Oxford Handbook of Criminology, Second Edition*, Oxford: Clarendon, 265–303.

Taylor, I., Walton, P. and Young, J. (eds) (1975), *Critical Criminology*, London: Routledge & Kegan Paul.

The Journal of Human Justice. Crimes of the Powerful (1992), 3, 2 Spring.

Thomas, D.A. (1979) *Principles of Sentencing*, London: Heinemann.

Thomas, D.A. (1997) *Current Sentencing Practice*, London: Sweet & Maxwell.

Thomas, M.W. (1948) *The Early Factory Legislation*, London: Thames Bank.

Thomas, P. (1991) 'Safety in Smaller Manufacturing Establishments', *Department of Employment Gazette*, January 1991.

Thomas, P. (ed.) (1997) *Socio-Legal Studies*, Aldershot: Dartmouth.

Thompson, A. (1981) 'Law and the Social Sciences: the Demise of Legal Autonomy', paper delivered at University of Kent, March 1981.

Thompson, E.P. (1967) 'Time, Work Discipline and Industrial Capitalism', *Past and Present*, No. 38, 56–97.

Thompson, E.P. (1975) *Whigs and Hunters: the origin of the Black Act*, Harmondsworth: Peregrine.

Thurston, G. (1976) *Coronership*, Chichester: Barry Rose Publishers.

Tigar, M.E. (1990) 'It does the Crime But Not the Time: Corporate Criminal Liability in Federal Law', *American Journal of Criminal Law* 17: 211, 211–34.

Tillman, R., Calavita, K. and Pontell, H. (1997) 'Criminalizing White-Collar Misconduct: determinants of prosecution in savings and loan fraud cases', *Crime, Law and Social Change*, 26, 53–76.

Timmer, D.A. and Eitzen, D.S. (1991) *Crime in the Streets and Crime in the Suites*, Toronto: Allyn & Bacon.

Todd, E. (1985) *The Explanation of Ideology: Family Structures and Social Systems*, Oxford: Basil Blackwell.

Tombs, S. (1989) 'Deviant Workplaces and Dumb Managements? Understanding and Preventing Accidents in the Chemical Industry', *Industrial Crisis Quarterly*, 3, Autumn, 191–211.

Tombs, S. (1990) 'Industrial Injuries in British Manufacturing Industry', *Sociological Review*, 38(2), 324–43.

Tombs, S. (1991) 'Injury and Ill-Health in the Chemical Industry: de-centring the accident-prone victim', *Industrial Crisis Quarterly*, 5, January, 59–75.

Tombs, S. (1992a) 'Safety, Statistics and Business Cycles: a response to Nichols', *Sociological Review*, 40(1), 132–45.

Tombs, S. (1992b) 'Stemming the Flow of Blood: the illusion of self-regulation', *Journal of Human Justice*, III, 2, 75–92.

Tombs, S. (1993) 'Crime, Technology and Major Hazards', *Technology Analysis and Strategic Management*, 5(4), 331–44.

Tombs, S. (1995a) 'Corporate Crime and New Organisational Forms', in Pearce, F. and Snider, L. (eds) *Corporate Crime: Contemporary Debates*, 132–46.

Tombs, S. (1995b) 'Law, Resistance and Reform: "regulating" safety crimes in the UK', *Social & Legal Studies*, 4(3), 343–66.

Tombs, S. (1996) 'Injury, Death and the Deregulation Fetish: the politics of occupational safety regulation in UK Manufacturing', *International Journal of Health Services*, 26(2), 327–47.

Tombs, S. (1997) 'Review of Diane Vaughan, The Challenger Launch Decision', *Sociology*, 31(3), August, 633–5.

Tombs, S. (1998) 'Health and Safety Crimes and the Problems of Knowing', in Davies, P., Francis, P. and Jupp, V. (eds) *Invisible Crimes, Invisible Victims*, London: Macmillan.

Tombs, S. and Whyte, D. (1997) 'Rounding up the Usual Suspects: law and order at work', paper presented to the XXV Annual Conference of the European Group for the Study of Deviance and Social Control, Kazmierez Dolny, Poland, 11–14 September.

Tombs, S. (forthcoming) 'Official Statistics and Hidden Crimes: researching health and safety crimes', in Jupp, V., Davies, P. and Francis, P. (eds) *Criminology in the Field: the practice of criminological research*, London: Macmillan.

Tonry, M. and Reiss, A.J. (1993) *Beyond The Law: Crime in Complex Organizations*. London: University of Chicago Press.

Transport and General Workers Union, (1994) *Fatigue: the hidden killer on our roads*, London: TGWU.

Treitel, G.H. (1991) *The Law of Contract*, London: Sweet and Maxwell.

Tucker, E. (1990) *Administering Danger in the Workplace*, Toronto: Toronto University Press.

Tucker, E. (1992) 'Worker Participation in Health and Safety Regulation: lessons from Sweden', *Studies in Political Economy*, 37, Spring, 95–127.

Tucker, E. (1995) 'And Defeat Goes On: an assessment of third wave health and safety regulation', in Pearce, F. and Snider, L. (eds) *Corporate Crime: Contemporary Debates*, 245–67.

Tugendhat, C. (1973) *The Multinationals*, Harmondsworth: Penguin.

Tumber, H. (1993) 'Selling Scandal: business and the media', *Media, Culture and Society*, 15, 345–61.

Turner, J.W.C. (1966) *Kenny's Outlines of Criminal Law*, Cambridge: Cambridge University Press.

Twining W. and Meirs, D. (1976) *How To Do Things With Rules*, London: Weidenfeld and Nicolson.

Tye, J. (1989) 'Safety Sacrificed at the Altar of Profit', *Independent*, London, 7 October 1989, p. 14.

United States General Accounting Office (1983) *Siting of Hazardous Waste Landfills and their Correlation with Racial and Economic Status to Surrounding Communities*, Washington, DC: US Environmental Protection Agency.

Vandivier, K. (1982) 'Why Should My Conscience Bother Me?', in Ermann, M.D. and Lundman, R.J. (eds) *Corporate and Governmental Deviance: Problems of organisational behaviour in contemporary society*, New York: Oxford University Press, 102–22.

Vaughan, D. (1982) 'Transaction Systems and Unlawful Organisational Behaviour', *Social Problems*, 29(4), April, 374–9.

Vaughan, D. (1983) *Controlling Unlawful Organisational Behaviour. Social Structure and Corporate Misconduct*, Chicago: University of Chicago Press.

Vaughan, D. (1992) 'The Macro-Micro Connection in White-Collar Crime Theory', in Schlegel, K. and Weisburd, D. (eds) *White-Collar Crime Reconsidered*, 124–45.

Vaughan, D. (1996) *The Challenger Launch Decision. Risky technology, culture, and deviance at NASA*, Chicago: Chicago University Press.

Vernon, M.D. (1952) *A Further Study of Perception*, Cambridge: Cambridge University Press.

Vernon, M.D. (1955) 'The Functions of Schemata in Perceiving', *Psychological Review*, 62, 180.

Vidal, J. (1997) *McLibel. Burger culture on trial*, London: Pan.

Vogel, D. (1986) *National Styles of Regulation: Environmental Policy in Great Britain and the United States*, Ithaca: Cornell University Press.

Vold, G. and Bernard, T. (1986) *Theoretical Criminology*, Oxford: Oxford University Press.

Walker, M.J. (1994) *Dirty Medicine. Science, big business and the assault on natural health care*, London: Slingshot.

Ward, J.T. (1962) *The Factory Movement 1830–1855*, London: Macmillan.

Warrington, R. (1977) 'Law – Its Image or its Reality', *City of London Law Review*, [1977] 29.

Warrington, R. (1983) 'Pashukanis and the Commodity Form Theory', in Sugarman, D. (ed.) *Legality, Ideology and the State*, London: Academic Press.

Waters, R. (1995) 'Saved – for the time being', *Financial Times*, 27 March.

Weait, M. (1989) 'The Letter of the Law: An enquiry into reasoning and formal enforcement in the industrial air pollution inspectorate', *British Journal of Criminology*, Vol. 29, 57–70.

Weait, M. (1992) 'Swans Reflecting Elephants: Imagery and the Law', *Law and Critique*, (III), 1, 51–67.

Weait, M. (1995) 'The Serious Fraud Office: nightmares (and pipe dreams) on Elm Street', in Loveland, I. (ed.) *Frontiers of Criminality*, 83–107.

Wells, C. (1988) 'The Decline and Rise of English Murder: Corporate Crime and Individual Responsibility', *Criminal Law Review* [1988] 788.

Wells, C. (1989) 'Manslaughter and Corporate Crime', *New Law Journal*, 7 July, p. 931.

Wells, C. (1991) 'Inquests, Inquiries and Indictments: The Official Reception of Death by Disaster', *Legal Studies*, 11: 71.

Wells, C. (1993a) *Corporations and Criminal Responsibility*. Oxford:. Clarendon Press.

Wells, C. (1993b) 'Corporations: Culture, Risk and Criminal Liability', *Criminal Law Review* [1994] 551–66.

Wells, C. (1995a) 'Cry in the Dark: corporate manslaughter and cultural meaning', in Loveland, I. (ed.) *Frontiers of Criminality*, 109–25.

Wells, C. (1995b) *Negotiating Tragedy: law and disasters*, London: Sweet and Maxwell.

Wells, C. (1997) 'Corporate Killing', *New Law Journal*, 1467, 10 October.

Welsh, I. (1996) 'Risk, Race and Global Environmental Regulation', paper presented at the British Sociological Association Annual Conference, 1–4 April, University of Reading.

Welsh, R.S. (1946) 'The Criminal Liability of Corporations', *Law Quarterly Review*, 62, 345.

West, D.J. and Farrington, D. (1977) *The Delinquent Way of Life*, New York: Crane Russak.

Westley, W.A. (1953) 'Violence and the Police', *American Journal of Sociology* 59, July, 34–41.

Wheeler, S. and Rothman, M.L. (1982) 'The Organisation as Weapon in White-Collar Crime', *Michigan Law Review*, 80, June, 1403–26.

Whitaker, B. (1964) *The Police*, Harmondsworth: Penguin.

Whitfield, M. (1992) 'Cost pressures keep safety on the sidelines', *Independent*, 9 December.

Whyte, D. (1998) 'Overcoming the Fear Factor: workforce involvement and health and safety offshore', *Public Money and Management*, October–December, 33–40.

Whyte, D., Smith, D. and Tombs, S. (1996) 'Offshore Safety Management after Cullen', in *Major Hazards Onshore and Offshore II. IChemE Symposium Series No 139*, Rugby: IChemE, 35–53.

Whyte, D. and Tombs, S. (1998) 'Capital Fights Back: risk, regulation and profit in the UK offshore oil industry', *Studies in Political Economy*, 57, 73–101.

Wikely, N. (1997) 'Turner & Newall: early organisational responses to litigation risk', *Journal of Law and Society*, 24(2), June, 252–75.

Wiles, P. (1971) 'Criminal Statistics and Sociological Explanations of Crime', in Carson, P. and Wiles, P., *Sociology of Crime and Delinquency in Britain*, Vol. 1, London: Martin Robertson, 198–219.

Williams, C. (ed.) (1996) *Social Justice. Special Issue: Environmental Victims*, 23(4), Winter.

Williams, G. (1983) *Textbook of Criminal Law*, London: Stephens.

Williams, G. (1985) 'Letting off the guilty and prosecuting the innocent', *Criminal Law Review* [1985] 115–22.

Williams, K.S. (1994) *Textbook on Criminology*, 2nd edition, London: Blackstone Press Ltd.

Williams, R. (1961) *The Long Revolution*, London: Chatto & Windus.

Wilson, L.C. (1979) 'The Doctrine of Wilful Blindness', *University of New Brunswick Law Journal*, 28, 175–94.

Winfield and Jolowicz on *Tort*, (1994) W.V.H. Rogers. London: Sweet and Maxwell.

Wolfgang, M.E. and Ferracuti, F. (1958) *The Subculture of Violence*, Beverly Hills, Ca: Sage.

Wolfgang, M.E. and Ferracuti, F. (1967) *The Subculture of Violence*, Beverly Hills, Ca: Sage.

Woodiwiss, A. (1990) *Rights v. Conspiracy: A Sociological Essay on the History of Labour Law in the United States*, Berg: New York.

Woolf, Lord (1996) *Access to Justice*, London: HMSO.

Woolfson, C. and Beck, M. (1997) *From Self-Regulation to Deregulation: the politics of health and safety in Britain*, Mimeo: Universities of Glasgow and St. Andrews.

Woolfson, C., Foster, J. and Beck, M. (1996) *Paying for the Piper? Capital and labour in the offshore oil industry*, Aldershot: Mansell.

Wrench, J. (1996) 'Hazardous Work: ethnicity, gender and resistance', paper presented at the British Sociological Association Annual Conference, 1–4 April, University of Reading.

Wrench, J. and Lee, J. (1982) 'Piecework and Industrial Accidents: two contemporary case studies', *Sociology*, 16(4), 512–25.

Wright, R.A. and Friedrichs, D.O. (1997) 'The Most Cited Scholars and Works in Critical Criminology', paper presented to the Annual Meeting of the American Society of Criminology, 19–22 November, San Diego.

Yeager, P. (1991) *The Limits of the Law: The Public Regulation of Private Pollution*, Cambridge: Cambridge University Press.

Yochelson, S. and Samenow, E. (1976) *The Criminal Personality*, New York: Jason Aronson.

Yoder, A. (1978) 'Criminal Sanctions for Corporate Illegality', *Journal of Criminal Law and Criminology*, Spring, 40–58.

Young, J. (1971) 'The Role of the Police as Amplifiers of Deviancy', in S. Cohen (ed.) *Images of Deviance*, Harmondsworth: Penguin.

Young, J. (1981) 'Thinking Seriously About Crime: some models of criminology', in Fitzgerald, M, McLennan, G. and Pawson, J. (eds) *Crime and Society. Readings in history and theory*, London: Routledge/Open University Press, 248–309.

Young, J. (1994) 'Incessant Chatter: Recent Paradigms in Criminology', in Maguire, M., Morgan, R. and Reiner, R. (1994) *The Oxford Handbook of Criminology*, Oxford: Clarendon Press.

Young, M. (1991) *An Inside Job: Policing and Police Culture*, Oxford: Clarendon Press.

Young, P. (1992) *Crime and Criminal Justice in Scotland*, Edinburgh: The Stationery Office.

Young, T.R. (1981) 'Corporate Crime: a Critique of the Clinard Report', *Contemporary Crises*, 5, 323–36.

Zedner, L. (1997) 'Victims', in Maguire, M., *et al.* (eds) *The Oxford Handbook of Criminology*, 577–612.

Index

Ollscoil na hÉireann, Gaillimh

3 1111 40077 3121